PIERO SAN GIORGIO

$URVIVE

THE ECONOMIC COLLAPSE

A PRACTICAL GUIDE

ARKTOS
LONDON 2021

ISBN	978-1-914208-62-1 (Paperback)
	978-1-914208-64-5 (Hardback)
	978-1-914208-63-8 (Ebook)

| EDITING | Constantin von Hoffmeister |

| COVER & LAYOUT | Tor Westman |

⊕ Arktos.com   𝟋 fb.com/Arktos   ✈ @arktosmedia   ⊙ arktosmedia

SURVIVE THE
ECONOMIC COLLAPSE

CONTENTS

1. Risks and Impacts

2. The Collapse

3. Survival

4. Preparing Oneself

5. Appendices

For My Family

Foreword

BY JAMES HOWARD KUNSTLER

"NOTHING IS FUNNIER THAN UNHAPPINESS," Samuel Beckett once quipped, a reminder that, when all else seems to be lost, there is still comedy. Hence, I was prone to take a cheeky attitude about the awful and tremendous dislocations now underway in the so-called "developed" world when I wrote my own recent books about it. As we march toward a reckoning with the mandates of reality, delusional thinking increases in direct proportion to the general anxiety level; the net effect appears to be an aggregate loss of intelligence, especially among people who ought to know better. What is more comically sublime than smart people acting stupidly?

Political leadership especially appears mystified by the changes underway in the world. The most conspicuous feature in this period of history is the incapacity of the educated and ruling classes to construct a coherent narrative about what is happening to us and to form an intelligent consensus concerning what to do about it. This is tragic, of course, but watching it unfold has been a pretty riveting show, and the action is only beginning. Piero San Giorgio is arguably less prankish than I am in this very clear and useful guidebook to the present and future, but we share an appreciation for the comic gravity and strangeness of our time.

The three horsemen bearing down on industrial-technocratic humanity are well-known now: 1) peak oil (at least peak *affordable* oil); 2) the impairments of capital formation due to peak debt accumulation; and 3) the very tangible effects of climate change (or, at least, disorders of the weather). In the galloping charge of these horsemen, certain consequences seem predictable. For instance, we can see presently the relationship between fossil fuels and money. There is a direct link between the availability and quantity of cheap oil *inputs* to advanced economies and the expansion of cheap credit, which, when activated, is converted into debt. So, at the moment of peak oil, you also arrive at peak debt. And in passing the peak of each, we begin to witness the epochal unwinding of that debt as claims on things of value exceed the existing collateral. The unwinding presents itself as the disappearance of money and, more to the point, of aggregate wealth possessed by a society. That translates into falling standards of living.

For, perhaps, an even more direct example, we can see the tangible effects of climate change (or weird weather) express itself in crop failure, food shortages, and higher prices; or in the destruction of seaboard city neighborhoods and infrastructure when great storms strike; or the desertification of drought-stricken regions driving people from their homes. In all these cases, people suffer terrible losses of health, property, or economic standing.

So the salient point that an interested observer would make of the situation is that the terms of existence are certain to become harsher for just about everybody, as we compete for scarcer resources amid crumbling infrastructures for daily life and ecological breakdown. There are peculiar and pernicious side effects, of course, such as the tendency for the remaining wealth of nations to become concentrated in fewer hands, the notorious "one percent." But that, too, leads to other effects, for instance, political upheaval, in which the "one percent" (or the aristocracy or the elite or ruling class) is subject to overthrow and physical assault — as in heads rolling. This, in turn, often leads to more widespread civil disorder in which a very general suffering prevails, while economies crumble and new elites attempt to establish rule.

The threat of that disorder, widespread among civilized people, has never been so ominous, though as of early 2013, the people in these societies remain deluded, confused, and apathetic (as in the U.S.) or only verging on manifest discontent (as in Europe). This excellent book provides a roadmap for understanding the journey through socioeconomic upheaval, and what to do at the destination.

I concur with Piero San Giorgio that there is much we can do besides hand-wringing, prayer, and needless political conflict to facilitate the transition into the next era of human history. I think we also agree on the nature of that journey's destination: a "reset," shall we say, to far less complex living arrangements in a world that has grown wider, with fewer people, smaller sovereign units of governance, and reconstructed local economies. The "to do" list of crucial tasks for civilized people can be stated succinctly: we have to grow our food differently as industrial farming goes obsolete; we have to inhabit the landscape in ways other than suburbia and colossal metroplex cities; we have to move people and things in ways other than airplanes and automobiles; and we have to rebuild the fine-grained, local networks of economic interdependence that will constitute commerce as we leave the economic dinosaurs of Walmart (and things like it) behind.

In this agenda, there is no room for crybabies, scapegoating, or pettifogging. Piero San Giorgio lays all this out here with a most refreshing clarity of purpose, which I commend to you as a valuable cram course in how to survive the rest of your life.

James Howard Kunstler is best known as the author of The Long Emergency *and* The Geography of Nowhere. *He is also the author of many novels, including his tale of the post-oil American future,* World Made by Hand. *His shorter work has appeared in* The New York Times, The Washington Post, The Atlantic Monthly, Metropolis, Rolling Stone, Playboy, *and many other periodicals.*

Foreword to the French Edition

BY MICHEL DRAC

THE CRISIS THAT BEGAN IN 2008 with the bursting of the subprime mortgage bubble is no ordinary downturn. All observers understood this intuitively. Something has gone wrong with our world, something lying at the very foundation of our way of living, producing, and consuming — and even of our way of thinking.

This something that has just been broken is our faith in the millenarian mechanism of Progress.

For three centuries, Western man has had the idea that he does not need God, since he is his own savior. Humanity is the messiah of humanity: thus proclaimed the new religion. A religion that entered into Catholicism on tiptoes with Descartes. A religion, also, that ended up substituting itself everywhere in the place of the ancient faith.

People sometimes laugh at *Juche*, that ridiculous North Korean ideology, whose only article states that man can transform nature indefinitely. Wrongly. In more sophisticated forms, all contemporary systems rest upon the postulate of human omnipotence. China has razed the house of Confucius and frenetically converted to the religion of growth. Eternal India — yes, even India — has set itself to conceiving the future as a rising curve.

All mankind has gradually entered into the naïve communion of the new religion, much less rational than it seems: technology to perform miracles, banks to serve as temples of the monetary idol.

Monetarist neoliberalism — the last ideology, standing victorious upon the corpses of Jacobinism, classical liberalism, social democracy, communism, and fascism — would lead man to the millennium, the long-lost terrestrial paradise soon to be regained.

It was a false promise and a trap. We ought to have been suspicious. For the past few decades, the facade of the progressivist temple has begun to crack...

Since the 1970s, various Cassandras have been warning us: a project of indefinite growth cannot be carried out in a finite world. Their arguments have been swept under the rug as "not taking account of scientific perspectives."

In the 1980s, the collapse of the USSR following the Chernobyl catastrophe provided food for thought for anyone willing to think: "so, an extremely large, over-integrated system *can* collapse suddenly, once a certain threshold of fragility is reached?" Here again, we have refused to draw the lessons from the event, preferring to blame the collapse on communist ideology without posing the question of over-concentration and over-integration *as such*.

During the 1990s, the West was giddy with triumph. Those were the mad years of the internet bubble. "Who cares that the material world is finite: capitalism will invade virtual worlds of its own construction!" But the dream ended abruptly when the model of the new economy revealed its real nature — it was a mirage, an illusion. If there was a dizzying fall at the turn of the millennium, it was not that of the Twin Towers, but the collapse of hopes placed in virtual reality, the escape hatch through which were pushed the ever more insurmountable internal contradictions of a capitalist system driven mad by the permanent confusion between the monetary map and the economic landscape.

Once again, people decided to see nothing, to learn nothing. In order to maintain at all costs the illusion that the millenarian utopia could construct the meaning of history, the financial oligarchy put the economic system on life support, giving the American economy fix after fix of debt. It was an absurd effort that, besides, pointed out the absurdity of neoliberal monetarist semantics.

This absurdity could only endure for so long. In the fall of 2008, its time was up.

A great shiver ran down the spine of the hundred-thousand-headed beast — the ruling class. Amidst the crash, still more dollars were injected into the system, like so many symbols that concealed nothing, but which once more, for a few years, perhaps, allowed the neoliberal propaganda machine to keep grinding away at all costs.

These were just the last, dilatory maneuvers that will not change anything in the end: it is all an illusion. It hardly matters that financial indices are artificially maintained by lowering interest rates to zero. Breaking the thermometer never cured a fever.

Economic rationality alone is not able to provide the meaning of history. Technology cannot accomplish everything. A project of infinite development cannot be conducted on a finite planet. Man cannot have everything he wants; he must want what he is able to get.

We are faced with a return to *limits*.

Mankind will not be its own messiah — the humanist religion is a failure.

The beast with a 100,000 heads is, indeed, behaving like a beast — in particular, it is as dangerous as a wounded animal that feels its hour has struck. Back from the failure of the credit system that served as an ideological shelter for their power, the elites and their trustees are now struggling to save their power, to preserve the messianic fiction, while gradually restricting it to themselves. On the one hand, a superior humanity that wants to be a messiah for itself and itself alone; on the other, an inferior humanity sent back into the symbolic shadows of thought's absence, the non-existence of meaning — in fact, into the negation of its status as an autonomous subject, where it is forbidden to define a mental space free of the constraints placed upon it. A humanity skinned of its spirit.

Such is the generative schema of the next decades. The future is menacing. We might as well understand this. The humanist religion is going to transform itself into an anti-human ideology.

This turnabout, the creating of a monster by those who sought to make an angel, has been underway since the 1970s. But the 2010s will mark a perceptible acceleration in this process. And life, in consequence, will soon be very difficult for many of us.

In this context, the stakes of the game, for true men, will soon be to *survive*. That's all — to survive.

Going back to the ranks of the powerful madmen is not an option. You might obtain the intoxicating illusion of superiority, and certainly easier living conditions, but only at the price of your soul. Resigning yourself to vegetating among the mass of the ruled is hardly less depressing. (And amidst that oppressed and impoverished body, violence will be the norm.) Our contemporaries have too deeply assimilated the perverse logic of the consumer society to convert suddenly to the voluntary simplicity that might save them.

Survival will almost certainly play itself out away from today's bustle, in refuges we must know how to create and defend. Physical survival, yes; but also psychological and spiritual survival.

Of course, this is no exalted ideal. But at this stage, resisting the inhuman machine will often mean passing by it unnoticed, and above all, being able to do without it.

A modest struggle, but hardly a contemptible one.

For one day, when that machine has exhausted all the possibilities of its original *élan*, it will totter and fall. Then, for us, it will be enough to be numerous, to maintain solidarity, so as collectively to regain control of our Earth after we have fiercely defended our few areas of retreat. It is in order to be there, at that decisive moment, that we must survive now. So do not be ashamed: let us build our refuges! Remember that a rebel wins if he can hold out one hour longer than his adversary. Let us organize ourselves to do so.

So, my friend ... wipe away that sad, drawn smile. Raise up those eyes you have kept lowered for so long. Look straight ahead at the horizon. Hold your chin up. Your life has meaning — to survive one hour longer than the machine.

Pass the word on: *comrade, our children are counting on you.*

Michel Drac is a writer, political commentator, and economist. For fif-teen years, he worked as a controller. He is the author of numerous books and the founder of the publishing house Le Retour aux Sources. He is also a member of the national association Equality & Reconciliation.

Welcome to a better world__

in 1944, in order to furnish an emergency source of nourishment for american soldiers operating in the extreme north pacific, twenty-nine reindeer were introduced onto st. matthew's island in the bering sea by the u.s. coast guard.

with no predators and abundant sources of food, the reindeer population exploded, reaching 1,350 in 1957, then 6,000 in the summer of 1963, the equivalent of a thirty percent growth per year.

six months later, the entire population was dead of hunger, except forty-two females; the vegetation had been gravely and lastingly damaged.

a study showed that this sudden collapse was due to the drop in food-stuffs available caused by the overpopulation of reindeer, as well as by the unusually harsh winter of 1963–4.

by 1980, no reindeer survived.

<<first gas became rare and expensive, and now there is no more. the automobile age has ended. electricity, too. no computer is working. the big corporations no longer exist. paper money is no longer worth any-thing. cities have been destroyed. epidemics have decimated the popu-lation. there is no more government. there still seems to be a president … but that may only be a rumor.

james howard kunstler

_the witch of hebron

/2011/

<<truth is to be sought among facts.

mao zedong

politician

//1893–1976//

Introduction

THIS BOOK COULD SAVE YOUR LIFE. The problems the world must face in the next 10 years are considerable: overpopulation, lack of oil and raw materials, climate change, lowered food production, the drying up of sources of potable water, unbridled globalization, colossal debt…

The convergence of all these problems will probably involve an economic collapse that will not leave anyone — rich or poor — unscathed. How can you prepare yourself? How can you survive these next years of great changes — sudden, rapid, and violent?

Are you ready for this? Will you have access to potable water if nothing comes out of your tap? What if the supermarkets are empty? How will you defend your family or your famished neighborhood from the local gang of riffraff, or from a government that's become a kind of totalitarian mafia? How will you protect your fortune in a world without financial institutions?

If you do not think these questions are absurd, in this volume, you will find plans, tools, and solutions to survive and prepare yourself gradually for the crises ahead. These solutions are based upon practical examples and the experience of those who have already attempted the adventure. This book may be the best investment you ever made.

Save your life? Really? The world is going to get that bad?

I began writing these pages on a marvelous spring day in 2011. The weather was fine, and the view of Lake Geneva was splendid. I have a wonderful life and enjoy the comforts of a king: warm water for my shower and shave each morning, thirty-second tea from my kettle, toast, fresh fruits from the fridge. In a few hours by car, I can go to work or pass a weekend on the Côte d'Azur or the Italian Riviera … crisscross the Piedmont, Burgundy, Savoy … go hiking in the Swiss Alps, the Jura, the Black Forest… When I travel by airplane, in a few hours, I can be in London, Paris, Amsterdam, Brussels, Madrid, Berlin, Copenhagen, Prague, Frankfurt, Munich, Zurich, Vienna, Budapest, Rome, Lisbon, Stockholm, New York, Boston, Montreal, Moscow, Dubai… A king, I was saying? This is the comfort level of an Olympian god!

For two generations, at least in the West, we have lived in an unprecedented period of peace and technological progress: for fully half the world, hunger and physical suffering have disappeared, access to knowledge and civic rights is universal, potable water and electricity are taken for granted.

This progress is a dangerous trap. Peace, justice, democracy, and affluence for all are not the norm — not in our world, not in history.

It is enough to travel in order to discover immense, swarming masses living in extreme poverty, violence, or under the heel of a dictatorship. Gradually, we are going to behold a similar spectacle in the West.

Before entering the heart of our subject, I would like to take a few lines of this introduction to describe the path that led me to write this book, which may seem alarmist, I admit, but which, in fact, is more relevant than ever.

Let me introduce myself: Swiss, forty-two years old, married with children, culturally Italian by my parents, French by schooling, Swiss by my surroundings, and American by my work. I grew up in the 1970s playing Lego and watching Japanese anime — *Grendizer*, *Harlock*, *Star Blazers* — which embodied a very Japanese vision of the world, including patriotism, self-sacrifice, and teamwork to save Planet Earth from all sorts of problems and invasions.

From childhood, I have been interested in history, thanks especially to the *Once Upon a Time ... Man* series by Albert Barillé. History struck me then as almost nothing but the study of wars and migrations: often violent, cruel, inhuman ... fascinating.

Two historical periods especially left their mark on me. First, the Roman era, whose principal tales were recounted to me by my father. Especially intriguing to me was Rome's fall. Following a convergence of several factors — debt, inflation, loss of confidence in institutions and elites, ever-greater migratory pressure and, finally, destructive invasions — it collapsed, carrying with it a civilization that benefited from advanced technologies and a comfort comparable to what we enjoyed in the 19th century. For the Roman citizen who lived under the *Pax Romana*, the rapid crumbling of the Western Empire, involving the disappearance of infrastructure such as aqueducts, sewers, hospitals, baths, and roads, must have caused a great trauma. Rome went from a metropolis of more than one million inhabitants in 280 AD to a village of less than 30,000 souls in 600 AD.

Then it was the period 1914–1945 that fascinated me. Following the economic crisis of 1907, all the groundwork had been laid for nationalism, spoiling for a fight, to collide with imperial ambition. The latter, aided by the world of finance, set off the first round (1914–1918) of what must be considered the beginning of Europe's decline, indeed, her suicide. And, to the surprise and horror of all, it turned into a true mass slaughter. With the victors' ambitions unsatisfied and the unjust peace treaty igniting the desire for vengeance among the defeated, the second round was inevitable. Again, the catalyst was a financial crisis. The stock market crash of 1929 and the Great Depression that followed would pave the way for the next war.

That Second World War, even more murderous than the first, left almost no one on the surface of the Earth untouched. The destruction and suffering was immense, and, for the first time, the world saw the death of civilians on an industrial scale in the ghettos and camps of Poland, the forests of Russia, the terror bombings of Germany and

Japan. They were neither the first nor the last mass crimes in history; but nothing prepared the inhabitants of Europe or Asia in the 1930s and '40s for such a degree of violence.

As a child, I saw the documentaries: images of deported civilians on the roads, in trains, all at the mercy of the whims of war. I told myself that I would never let my family become refugees, never accept being subjugated to powers and events that I could not affect or change.

So naturally, as a good little boy of the West growing up amid the Cold War, soaked in NATO propaganda, I first became an anti-Communist. Then, when the danger of the bloody, baby-eating Soviets had passed, I melted into the only remaining ideology — liberalism — with its only slogan: make money and consume.

Welcome to a Better World

I spent the 1990s between studying marketing and advancing professionally. The work was interesting and well-paid: I was working for American software companies, first in charge of marketing in Switzerland, then Africa, and finally in the emerging markets.

Stock options and day trading with friends and colleagues, investing in tech stocks and internet startups: Cisco, Netscape, CommerceOne… easy dough, big cars, a big apartment suite, chicks, trips to Africa and the Middle East… I was living the perfect yuppie dream. Like so many of my young contemporaries in advertising, finance, or technology, I recognized myself in Octave, the character in Frédéric Beigbeder's novel 99 Francs. It seemed obvious to me that technology was going to change the world ever more rapidly — and normal that companies with barely any revenue and making no profit should be worth billions on the stock market! In 2000, I founded my own startup. I arrogantly believed that I would become rich and famous by what was about to reveal itself as a bubble! It was a frenzy soon shattered by the stock-market crash and the consequences of the September 11 attacks. My whole fortune, ginned up with financial leveraging — *poof!* Up in smoke. I awoke to find myself nearly shirt-less in my BMW convertible.

For me, a period of realization had begun.

With the slowdown, reducing the personnel of my little company from sixteen to four, I discovered that work could be difficult, success not as obvious as it had always been, and that the boss, who must pay everybody's salary out of his own pocket, is all alone.

Depression

Being broke and depressed forced me not to go out, to limit my social life, but also gave me time for reflection. This is when I was struck by the flagrant dishonesty of the second Bush administration in justify-ing its policy of war against Saddam Hussein. It was simply too obvi-ous. I got interested in the details of what went on behind the scenes: the neoconservatives, the military-industrial-oil complex and the financial world. Something smelled fishy: Colin Powell and his bogus vial at the UN, Dick Cheney as a corrupting Dark Sith Lord, Dubya's "plain ole' Cowboy" routine...

If they lie to us about something as important as a war, what else are they lying to us about? I went back to my history books and gathered information on the web. By digging, even without going very deep, you find the Spanish-American War of 1898, the Tonkin incident, the attack on the USS Liberty, the Kennedy assassination, the Bologna massacre, Operation Ajax, Operation Northwoods, the invasion of Panama, the Gulf War, September 11... I swallowed the red pill. Thanks to my experience with the financial milieus of New York, where I worked with some of my clients, my realizations have continued. I began to perceive the manipulation of the markets by ar-rogant and unscrupulous bankers and traders. I discovered analysts, authors, and commentators denouncing the financial system: Niall Ferguson, Nassim N. Talib, Marc Faber, Gerald Celente, Max Keiser, Pierre Jovanivic, Pierre Leconte, Myret Zaki, Alex Jones, and many more who look behind the headlines and talking points. "So *that's* how it works!" It was frightening.

I quickly understood that all the media babble, the political debates, the economists' blind dogmatism, the staggering incompetence
and powerlessness of the political class, entirely occupied with defending its own privileges ... all this only serves to distract the public.
As the French writer Alain Soral emphasizes, "[T]he higher your level
of consciousness, the less you try to get!" In 2005, I benefited from the
sale of my business, which had developed into something profitable,
and put my entire fortune — quite small now — in gold. It remains
the best investment I have ever made. The British and American
subprime housing crisis, the Ponzi schemes of Bernhard Madoff and
others, the burst bubble of credit default swaps no longer affect me.
They are merely the symptoms of an incipient collapse — and one that
will soon accelerate.

During this time, my personal life settled down. Marriage, the first
baby. I took advantage of this by resuming salaried work in a solid
internet company; thanks to several trips around the world, to my
experience, and a little luck, I find myself in a position that allows me
a lot of free time for reading and reflection.

During a business trip to the U.S., I had another realization, this
time economic and ecological: a monstrous traffic jam on the edge of
a metropolis, hundreds of thousands of commuters bumper to bumper, each one with the air conditioner cranked up to the max; a congested airport with jam-packed airplanes taking off at a rate of one per
minute; a night flight over an illuminated city, millions of houses and
apartments with the lights on and the air conditioner or heater turned
up all the way; millions of people guzzling energy from one shopping
center to another, swarming, using billions of kilowatt-hours, gulp-
ing millions of barrels of oil every day, all of this multiplied by all the
cities of all the countries in the world. An immense complexity. An
immense consumption of energy. To paraphrase a famous expression
by Emile Henry Gauvreay: we are consuming the planet's resources to
buy crappy items we don't need, with money we don't have, in order to

impress people we don't like; and all to end up depressed, unsatisfied, and unhappy.

Malaise

Contrary to the first cosmonauts, who felt small compared to planet Earth, I began to feel that the latter was too small in relation to man. I was reminded of Godfrey Reggio's *Koyaanisqatsi: Life Out of Balance* (1982), with the music of Phillip Glass. I discovered authors like Jared Diamond, David Holmgren, Richard Heinberg, James Howard Kunstler, Dmitri Orlov, Graeme Taylor, and many others who analyze the problems connected with diminishing resources, overpopulation, climate change, and ecological change, which are likely to impact human activities in the coming years. Among them, Chris Martenson deserves special mention; his book *The Crash Course* is an impressive work of economic popularization, which shows clearly the connection between the economy, energy from natural resources, and the environment. (These are the subjects I will be covering in the first two parts of this book.)

However, whereas these authors do a good job of describing the problems, the solutions they propose amount essentially to "encouraging awareness" and "changing our way of life." Yes, but what if that change does not happen?

The stakes being so high, full of good will and naïve hope, I joined a little think-tank that wished to influence local politics. A big failure. The differences between individual members, the inertia of the political world, the relative futility of contributing to a blog, constant slander and manipulation of the political and media establishment are barriers that require a lifetime of efforts and militancy to be overcome. Well, if I couldn't change the world, at least I could change myself, and maybe save my own skin. And, with the second baby arriving, that of my family as well.

Continuing my research and reflections, in 2007, I discovered the American world of survivalism and prepping with its rule of the three Gs: Gold, Guns, and a Getaway. My attention was directed especially to the works of James Wesley Rawles. His Survivalblog.com and his books *How to Survive the End of the World as We Know It* and *Patriots* were revelations. To this American survivalist icon, I owe the idea of rolling up my sleeves and getting a project started, which is the source of this book and which I will relate in the third and fourth parts.

So, I actively began preparing myself in 2007 for the possibility that we would go through some very difficult years in the near future. When our third baby girl arrived, I bought and equipped a farm, trained myself for survival and interviewed others who were doing similar things. By documenting these processes, I gradually acquired know-how, experiences, and ideas that have led me to try to convince those around me. To my surprise, the reception I got was not as hostile as I had expected. On the contrary, my friends and colleagues also felt that *something was rotten in the state of Denmark*, and that all their tomorrows were not going to be as rosy as they might have thought after the fall of the Berlin Wall.

In my free time, I began offering counseling services to help friends get their projects started. By word of mouth, ever more people began contacting me to verify the quality of their survival strategy, to check whether there was any solution to their concerns, to identify an ideal spot of refuge, or to be put in touch with more specialized instructors in specific areas. The time I spent with them added to my experience, and I learned about some interesting examples of preparation that I will share with you.

As you can see, this book is my very Eurocentric, and even Swisscentric, vision of how to survive the economic and social collapse that may occur in the coming decade. To develop this vision, I depended heavily on a synthesis of works by numerous authors who are cited either in the book itself or in the bibliographical section.

This book is not, however, a do-it-all manual. First of all, nothing can be guaranteed 100 percent, least of all survival. Furthermore, the number of fields relevant to the subject is colossal. I do hope this book will be a point of departure in your quest for knowledge and know-how, while giving you an essential basis for survival in whatever future scenarios. Finally, I have compiled large bibliographies for each chapter, which offer you a wide choice of good books to consult.

To close this introduction, I must emphasize that I do not wish for an economic collapse and the end of the world. Not being an adept of the Mayan calendar, taking seriously neither the *Book of Revelations* nor the prophecies of Malachy nor the revelations of Fátima—although the coincidences are troubling—I am not trying to indulge in gloom and doom. If you want to do so yourself, go see a disaster movie. I do not think The End of the World is coming. I think that it will be the end of *a* world, of *our* world.

Read this book, do your own research, develop your own views, and take note of Henri Poincaré's saying: "Doubting everything, like believing everything, is a solution which dispenses us from thinking." Then, roll up your sleeves and get to work!

I must also advise the reader that some of the advice contained in this book is only applicable if and when a chaotic situation without the rule of law arrives. I encourage you to inform yourself about all laws in force in your country and to respect them scrupulously, especially concerning firearms, the practice of medicine, agriculture, and urbanism. If you end up in jail, none of this will help you! I cannot accept responsibility for your actions or harm caused to yourself or third parties by the application of advice or principles read in this book. The author and publisher are not responsible for any action taken by a reader. Do not hesitate to consult a specialist or doctor if you have doubts.

At the end of each chapter, you will find a little work of fiction, set off in a different font, which is designed to illustrate, imaginatively, some of the points treated in the chapter. Obviously, these texts are fictional and represent neither the advice nor the wishes of the author.

"Grandfather, is it true that men went to the moon?"

"Yes, it's true. It was a few years before my grandfather was born. The Americans did it with a rocket as high as that mountain over there. It made a noise louder than a thousand thunderbolts!"

"Ooooh!" the children exclaimed in unison, seated in a circle around the big fire that warmed them. They looked at the old man with rapt and admiring attention.

"What is a rocket, grandfather?" one of them asked.

"Shhh!" said one of the bigger children.

"It's a big tube of metal with a pointy end that flies through the sky and among the stars, like a giant rifle bullet…"

"Are there still Americans?" asked one of the older children. "Of course," said another, "they aren't all dead."

"No, in fact," continued the old man, his wrinkles visible in the light of the den, "there must be quite a few of them in their mountains, which are larger than ours. Who knows what our mountains are called?"

"The Alps!" responded the children in unison.

"Very good, children. Yes, in my father's time, long before there was a hurricane season, there were many marvelous things! I remember when I was a child playing with images that moved on a screen. And then, there were so many people in the world, and you could travel anywhere easily on machines that flew through the air. People bought things with little plastic cards. They knew how to treat almost any disease. They threw away everything—even unspoiled food!"

"Grandfather, why aren't things like that anymore?"

"Oh, that, children, that's a story I'll tell you tomorrow. Alright, everybody to bed! You've got to gather your strength for tomorrow, because tomorrow you go to school… You are lucky to go to school! Beyond the big river, in the plain, there is no school, and the children live in the ruins of the big cities where there are horrible monsters. Alright, up you go to bed!"

When the children had left, a young woman came to help the old man get up.

"Oh, thank you, dear. My leg has never recovered from that old fracture…"

"Thank you for taking care of the little ones this evening, grandfather. But you know, you should not exaggerate like that with your stories. Machines flying like birds — really now!"

PART I

RISKS AND IMPACTS

<<the human race's greatest fault is that it cannot understand exponential equations.

albert bartlett

physicist

/1998/

<<the end of our foundation is the knowledge of causes and the secret motion of things; and the enlarging of the bounds of human empire, to the effecting of all things possible.

francis bacon

_new atlantis

/1627/

<<in times of universal deceit, speaking the truth becomes a revolutionary act.

george orwell

[attributed]

Overpopulation

PLANET EARTH IS SEVERAL BILLION years old. In the course of this very long period, many species have appeared, developed, and evolved. The overwhelming majority has disappeared, sometimes due to sudden mass extinctions, but more often through their inability to adapt to changes in their biological niche, their habitat.

Man — *Homo sapiens* — appeared only a few hundred thousand years ago, which represents a minuscule fraction of time in geological terms. In a short period, he has had such an influence on the terrestrial system that certain scientists have proposed establishing a new geological period beginning in 1784, the year of James Watt's steam engine. They call this new period the *Anthropocene*, or Age of Man, and it would succeed the Holocene which began 10,000 years ago. The idea is not senseless, even if it may seem arrogant, especially when we see man's inability to foresee and protect himself from natural catastrophes like hurricanes, tsunamis, earthquakes... In any case, we must note that no other known species has ever, for better or for worse, left such a mark on its environment. This would not be so if humans were not so numerous.

Before going further, we must establish a mathematical concept without which it is difficult to appreciate the significance of events we shall face in the 21st century. Few people enjoy math, I know. But it is the language of the universe, and it is better to know the basic notions than to suffer the Law with a capital "L" — the Law of Physics, which is expressed in mathematical form. It is a law one cannot compromise or negotiate with. The Law is cold and pitiless, present always and everywhere. You can respect or ignore a human law; for example, you can run a red light; but you cannot choose to ignore a hundred-mph car crash that occurs as a result. Woe unto those who do not know the Law!

In terms of collapse, the mathematical concept you must understand is exponential growth. It is one of the hardest mathematical concepts for the human brain, because we have a tendency to think in lines, according to linear progressions, while an exponential progression is a curve. But you will see that it is an easy concept to understand if only time is taken to explain it.

In the case of *linear* or *arithmetic growth*: you add the same new quantity each time. For example: 1, 2, 3, 4, 5, 6, 7, etc. — that is a linear or arithmetic sequence. Each time the same number — in this case, 1 — is added to the previous number; growth is constant. On the other hand, as a percentage, growth diminishes: one hundred percent, fifty percent, thirty-three percent, etc.

Slightly more difficult now — in the case of *exponential or geometrical growth*: the quantity added each time grows. For example, the sequence 1, 2, 4, 8, 16, 32, 64, etc. follows the rule that each number is the double of the preceding value; you multiply by two each time. The quantity you add depends upon the preceding number. It gets larger while the percentage added remains constant, in this case one hundred percent. But you can have geometrical growth with any other percentage — fifty percent, twenty percent, ten percent, one percent, 0.25 percent — the principle is the same.

To make sure we understand what exponential growth is, let's take, for example, the growth of a population at ten percent per year. This means that the population multiplies by 1.1 each year. Thus, for an initial population of 1,000 individuals:

> in one year, it grows to 1,100 individuals (1,000 x 1.1);

> at the end of two years, it grows to 1,210 (1,000 x 1.1 x 1.1 or 1,000 x 1.1^2);

> at the end of seven years, it has nearly doubled to reach 1,948.7 (1,000 x 1.1^7);

> at the end of one hundred years, it has been multiplied by 13,780 and reaches 13,780,000 (1,000 x 1.1^{100}).

The general formula is $p(n) = p(o)$ x $growth^n$, where $p(o)$ is the starting population, $p(n)$ is the population after n years, and growth is the given annual percentage growth.

Ok, are you following so far?

Let's return to the first two number sequences. The linear sequence grows by "1" each time: 1, 2, 3, 4, etc. Let's compare it with the exponential series that grows by doubling: 1, 2, 4, 8, etc. We will extend each series out thirteen times. Here are the results:

ITERATION	LINEAR SERIES	EXPONENTIAL SERIES
1	1	1
2	2	2
3	3	4
4	4	8
5	5	16
6	6	32
7	7	64
8	8	128
9	9	256
10	10	512
11	11	1,024
12	12	2,048
13	13	4,096

A graphic illustration of the first ten iterations gives the following curves:

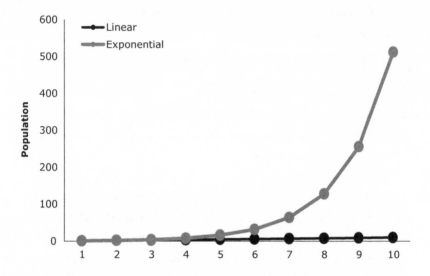

You see that after a certain time, the exponential progression clearly detaches itself from the linear one. If we prolong the iterations to thirteen, we get a graph with the following curves:

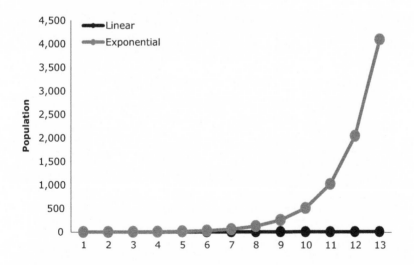

We see that the exponential progression quickly yields a very different curve from its linear counterpart. At first, the difference is not so great, then it becomes perceptible to the eye, and then, because of its mathematical properties, it seems to explode, and the difference gets ever more immense. Math is cool, isn't it?

Let's take a very theoretical but striking example from Chris Matheson's book *The Crash Course*. If an investor had put one cent — i.e., one one-hundredth of a dollar — in a bank 2,000 years ago, and this cent earned him two-percent interest during these 2,000 years … well, the difference in the account during the first year would be two hundredths of a cent — 0.02 percent x 1 cent. But 2,000 years later, that account would be worth more than 1.5 quadrillion dollars, and that's twenty times the amount of money in the world today! Math is powerful, isn't it? If only some Roman, Gallic, Berber, or Germanic ancestor of ours had thought to put a couple *Sesterces* into a Swiss bank account for us!

So we have demonstrated that the exponential growth of a population quickly advances towards infinity. This is called an exponential *explosion*. This theoretical evolution is always defeated by reality: no population can grow indefinitely, since its growth is limited by the environment in which it lives. Viruses, for example, reproduce in a population until their hosts die, or develop an immunity, or until the conditions of infection and multiplication are no longer both met. At that moment, the virus dies. Exponential growth is always self- limiting. Nothing grows to infinity — nothing. Not even the reindeer which were left on St. Matthew's Island.

The first man to point out this problem was the cleric Thomas Malthus (1766–1834). He calculated that if a population grows in an exponential or geometrical fashion, while the resources available undergo linear (or, in any case, *limited*) growth, the result is that the population outgrows the carrying capacity of its environment. A demographic catastrophe becomes inevitable. For millennia, populations remained more or less stable, or only grew slowly. Then, suddenly, the children who would have died of natural causes started surviving; they grew up and had a bunch of children … who themselves survived and, during the last century, contributed to the massive increase of the population. The exponential growth of population, therefore, is a reality that is not only limited by agricultural production, but also by complex phenomena connected to the growing wealth of society and the individual choices this seems to inspire: people tend to have fewer children or prefer not having any at all. In any case, Malthus stated that exponential growth would, sooner or later, outrun the environment's capacities. That this has not yet happened does not mean that his thesis was illogical or false. His analysis remains structurally valid over the long term. Poor Malthus has been denounced and pilloried because his prediction did not come true. His pessimistic prognostication was soon delayed, since the world just happened to experience a great increase in resources and agricultural yields.

Let us return to our *Homo sapiens*, running naked in the savannahs and gradually discovering that a sedentary agricultural way of life allows his little tribe to grow more efficiently. It required nearly the whole of human history — slightly over 100,000 years — before world population reached 5 million (around 10,000 BC). Then it took nearly 12,000 years to reach, around the year 1800, one billion. In the following one hundred years — only one century — this population doubled to 2 billion. One more century, and we are over 7 billion in 2013. Each year there are 90 million more people.

According to the most optimistic predictions — which take account of lowered birth rates in many countries — we will be 9 billion in 2050. Why did it require 100,000 years to get to 5 million, and why does it now only require forty years to add another 3 billion? It is because population growth follows an exponential progression.

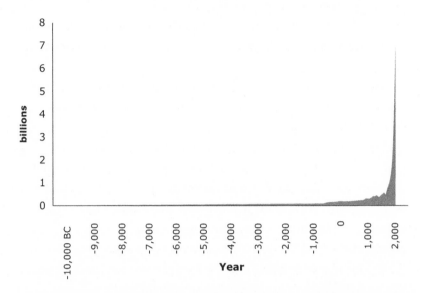

You will gather that the hockey-stick curve is the result of the mathematical function that represents the exponential growth of the human population. The important thing is to define clearly the graph's two axes. If you only examine one part of the graph, you could almost make the mistake of thinking it is a linear curve. For example, if you only consider human growth in the period 1800–1900, you would see that it took an entire century for the population to double. You wouldn't notice that it took only five hundred years for it to grow from half a billion to a billion, nor that, starting in 1900, the population quintupled in just one century. The key lies in understanding the proper scale. If the planet has enough resources for 100 billion people, going from one billion to seven or even 17 billion is not really a serious matter. But what if the limit is, to take a number at random, 1.5 billion? In fact, it is the rapidity of growth that is impressive. A billion people are being added to the total ever more quickly. If a population of one billion has an average growth rate of one percent annually, it will reach 2 billion in seventy years. If growth continues at that same rate, it will take just forty-one more years to reach 3 billion people, just twenty-nine years to reach 4 billion, just twenty-two years to reach five billion, eighteen years to reach 6 billion, and no more than twelve years to reach 7 billion. In the world of exponential growth, things move ever faster. Especially toward the end. Are you still following me?

This also means that in the world of exponential growth, awareness of problems only comes very late, and the time for action is short. Often, it comes *too late*.

The exponential law applies to growth of any kind, including economic growth and the energy consumption that results from it. Between 2000 and 2009, China reported eight percent annual economic growth. This means that between 2000 and 2009, the Chinese economy doubled, and with it the consumption of energy, minerals, etc. At this rate, it will double again between 2009 and 2018 — nine years. This means that if China has fourteen nuclear power plants, it will probably need twice as many (twenty-eight are being constructed as of 2011, in fact), that if China consumes 10 million barrels of oil each day, it will be consuming 20 million in 2018, or twenty percent of current world production. If a country has a more modest growth rate of five percent per annum, its economy will double in fourteen years. The same formula works for everything: if crime increases seven percent per annum, it will double in ten years, etc.

We will conclude our little math course here, but you must admit that it is an important concept for understanding the problems we will be facing in the coming years. We will soon run into exponential growth again. For now, let us go back to our population of 7 billion people.

Can we agree on the following propositions?

1   The greater a population, the greater the need for food, drinking water, etc.

2   The greater a population, the greater the need of each individual composing it for education, medical care, housing, transportation, employment, consumer goods and services… Thus, the greater the need for economic growth.

In order to support current global population growth, which is 2.8 percent per annum, the world economy must double (i.e., grow by 100 percent) between 2010 and 2035. Then it must double again between 2035 and 2060 (i.e., our current economy must quadruple), and then it must double yet again between 2060 and 2085, and finally double again between 2085 and 2110. At the very least, then, this means expanding the economy by a factor of sixteen in a hundred years!

Is this possible?

If the population of the world were living amidst affluence today, it might be possible to imagine that, yes, we still have room to grow. But, as urban theorist Mike Davis shows in his book *Planet of Slums*, more than half the world's population today lives in shantytowns and *favelas*, amid filth and squalor, crime, violence, and corruption. Is this because of unfair sharing of wealth, exodus from the countryside, economic exploitation, geographical or political factors, even plain bad luck? Sure. But all things being equal, the greater the population, the more problems to solve. It's as simple as that.

Due to female literacy, birth rates are beginning to slow in almost all countries; but despite this fact, exponential growth will remain with us through sheer inertia at least until 2050. Phew! So we'll *just* have to quadruple the world economy! We are entering an unprecedented historical period. People have never been so numerous. Things are going to get extremely difficult.

The difference between ourselves and the reindeer introduced in 1944 to St. Matthew's Island in the Bering Strait is that we are able to understand the limits of growth, to change our way of life, to reconstruct damaged ecosystems and create a durable economy.

Or are we?

Are we able to see these problems? Can we change our habits in time? A new Anthropocene geological era, you say? It may not last long. Let us examine why.

Maurice has run out of luck.

His car broke down, and his wife left with the children for a few days at her parents'. He will have to take public transportation. It has been twenty years since he took the bus or subway in his city. From his suburb, Maurice must get to his workplace. He is employed in a multinational firm. Instead of the forty-five minutes it usually takes by car, he discovers that it is much longer today. It's the waiting for buses (always running late), missed connections, trips in jam-packed rush-hour trains... If he finds walking rather refreshing in comparison to sitting in his car stuck in a traffic jam reading his emails on an iPhone, he also really hates being stuffed like a sardine and shaken by that swarming mass of people.

He is dripping with sweat, and the physical contact with so many people leaves him uneasy. He is suddenly afraid of catching something. He didn't remember there being so many people when he was a student and often took the subway. The makeup of the crowd has greatly changed, too. Whereas in his day, nearly all the people were ... how to say it ... "like him" ethnically, now things are different: he is the one in the minority. He has nothing against foreigners, but he suddenly finds that his own city greatly resembles that of countries where he sometimes goes on business. And how many of them! The escalators: full! The buses: full! The subway: full! Finally, he gets to his office, feeling liberated from that strange world. He heaves a sigh of relief

... but then notices that his wallet has been stolen.

<<what's going to happen is, very soon, we're going to run out of petroleum, and everything depends on petroleum... this is the end of the world.

kurt vonnegut

/2006/

<<it's a perfect storm headed our way—a steady rise in global demand for oil crashing up against an increasingly limited supply.

william l. chambers

researcher

/2010/

<<we cannot afford to bet our long-term prosperity and security on a resource that will eventually run out.

barack obama

politician

/2011/

The End of Oil

OUR CIVILIZATION IS SUSTAINED BY FOSSIL FUELS. These are products of the immense power of the Sun, which have accumulated for hundreds of thousands of years. The Sun has gradually transformed biological debris into fossil energy that we now use on a massive scale.

Among these fuels, petroleum (commonly referred to as "oil") is a substance with extraordinary properties: liquid at room temperature, easy to transport and handle (by tanker, truck, train, or pipeline, etc.), it contains a great amount of energy in relation to its size, and is easily transformable into various useful by-products, such as gasoline, diesel fuel, kerosene, etc., which efficiently power our vehicles, generate electricity, or heat our buildings. Petroleum is not only useful for transportation; it plays a role in the manufacturing of a host of products we use every day: plastics, polymers, pharmaceutical and chemical products, pesticides, computers, glues, paints, road surfacing, car seats, nylon stockings… The list is practically endless. Nothing compares with petroleum in terms of its combination of energy, versatility, transportability, and ease of storage.

Look around you: everything you see, everything you are wearing, all that you eat, our whole civilization is based on petroleum. What's more, it is so inexpensive and easily available that even people at the bottom of the social ladder benefit from it. Inexpensive, yes, but of great intrinsic value. To prove it, imagine you filled your car tank with a gallon of gas, then drove a few miles before running out, and that you then had to walk back to your starting point or push the car the entire distance you drove with that gallon. How much would you pay for having an extra gallon available to avoid that effort and lost time? A gallon of gas represents hours of manual labor. Now, since it is traded in dollars, and the prices are kept artificially low, petroleum is one of the cheapest liquids in the world, hardly more expensive than bottled water!

Is this going to last much longer?

If the answer is yes, *whoopee!* We can continue with our current way of life and let it spread to the rest of the planet.

But what if it isn't?

The International Energy Agency estimates that current deposits are declining at a rate of 6.7 percent per annum. This means that in ten years, existing deposits will give us only half the petroleum they give us now. So it will be necessary not only to find new deposits to replace that annual loss, but also to satisfy the new demand. Of course, one might try to pump more quickly from the known deposits in order to compensate for the diminution, but this would be like pressing harder on a toothpaste tube to make the paste come out more quickly: it does not change the total amount.

Roughly speaking, if these predictions are correct — and numerous studies seem to corroborate them — between 2011 and 2016, we are going to lose the equivalent of 18 million barrels per day. Now, some recently discovered deposits give us, at the moment, a bonus of 7.6 million barrels per day. But that still leaves a gap of 10.4 million barrels per day. And this is only the case if the economy remains stationary — zero growth. If, on the other hand, we can expect three percent growth, that makes 13 million barrels per day that we shall lose. If growth is four percent, that makes 14 million barrels; if five percent, fifteen million. And if we boost the economy in the Chinese fashion, reaching ten percent growth, we shall be losing 20 million barrels a day.

Before going further, we must see if these data and predictions are correct. This is all the more relevant since the concept of lowered production is not new: it is something called *peak oil*.

Peak oil is the highest point of the production curve of an oil well or oil field. It is the moment when production flattens out before beginning to decline due to the exhaustion of the usable oil deposits.

The life cycle of an oil deposit is quite variable. It always extends for several decades from the time of the first discovery. The tapping of a new deposit generally occurs between a few years and a few decades after the discovery of the oil. The oil production from a deposit generally extends over several decades as well: the first North Sea wells began production in 1970, and the last drop of oil will probably be extracted by 2050.

As you can see from the graph below, the volume of oil produced over time can be represented by a bell-shaped curve. Between the beginning and the end, production passes through a maximum, which corresponds roughly to the moment when half the oil has been extracted. The declining phase is much longer than the time passed between the start of production and its peak.

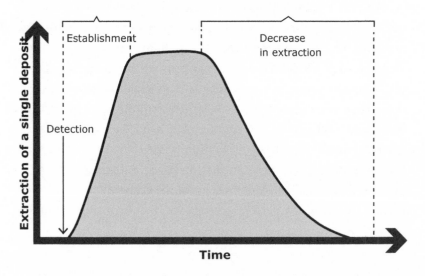

When production starts, the oil spontaneously shoots out of the well from natural pressure. In the second phase, the oil must be forced out by the introduction of air or gas, which requires an increasing expenditure of energy. Finally, even more costly techniques must be used, such as injecting steam to increase the fluidity of the oil. Production stops when the energy needed to extract a gallon is greater than the energy contained in the gallon of oil itself (also accounting for other costs such as maintenance, transportation, and labor). During the declining phase, production decreases at a pace that depends on the geology of the deposit and the methods of extraction employed: the average is four percent per annum, or twenty-five years to exhaust a reserve after it peaks.

The expression "peak oil" as we will employ it refers to the peak of global production. The methods for estimating this peak are derived from the work of the geologist Martin King Hubbard, who in the 1950s successfully predicted the peak of American oil production. The following graph shows the evolution of all accumulated deposits:

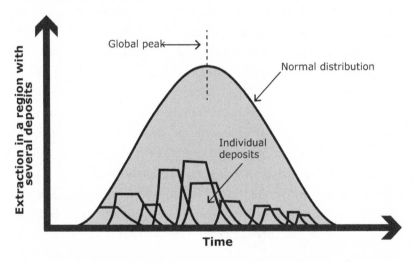

To know whether total oil production in the last few years corresponds to a curve like the one we have just described, we must compile all the data on all the oil deposits of these past few decades. This is what the

Association for the Study of Peak Oil (ASPO) has done. The results are in the graph below, which show world oil production by region and in millions of barrels per day:

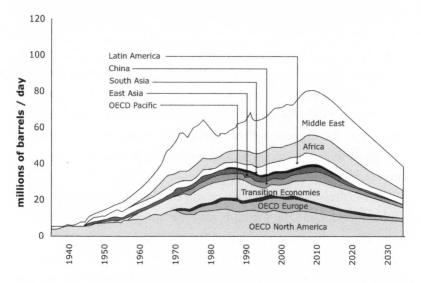

Between 2008 and 2010, global oil production began to wane, mostly due to the industrial consequences of the financial crisis (lowered demand, relatively lower transportation costs, etc.). Data since then has revealed that production worldwide has returned to its steady secular increase of the past quarter century. The United States has experienced a sharp rise in production in the years since the crisis, and a reversal of a downward trend of some two decades. This was the result of the development of new technologies, such as horizontal drilling and hydraulic fracturing, as well as the exploitation of North Dakota's Bakken formation. We will have to wait for official production data in subsequent years to know if these phenomena amount to the last gasp of the oil era, or whether the peak in production is still many years away. Determining this is a little like looking in the rear-view mirror to foresee how much traffic we can expect up ahead. It is not possible to know in advance if we have reached the peak. We can only measure the lowering of production by looking at last year's figures.

Another index of whether we are close to peak oil is the condition of existing deposits. Here, the figures are very difficult to determine, since each country declares only its *official* deposits. Do these figures correspond to reality? In fact, it is well known that the more significant the announced deposits, the more the country is considered strategically important, with all the commercial advantages (and corruption) that entails. It is also well known that OPEC, the Organization of Petroleum Exporting Countries, bases the production rights assigned to each member on these deposits, encouraging these states to declare as much of their respective deposits as possible in order to boost production and thus revenue. Numerous CIA reports show that OPEC has been warning American authorities of this danger since 1980.

It remains for us to see if the discovery of new oil deposits will compensate for lost production. After all, if these new deposits are huge, it could set peak production back a long way. However, according to the ASPO, the discovery of new deposits, measured in billions of barrels, has been sinking since 1964, as the graph below shows.

This means that new deposits are getting gradually smaller, which makes sense, since we have been exploring every corner of the world for a century now. Geologists know very well where deposits are likely to be found. We began by tapping the easiest and least costly deposits.

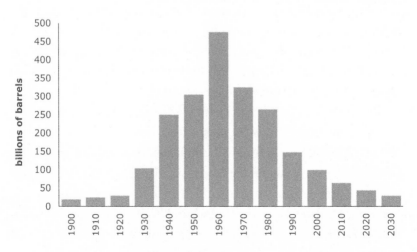

In fact, oil is divided into a very small number of enormous deposits and a large number of small ones. This gap is illustrated by the fact that sixty percent of the world's oil comes from only one percent of active deposits. When a very large deposit starts to become exhausted, perhaps hundreds of little deposits must be tapped to make up for the loss in production. This decrease in the economies of scale will have repercussions on costs. The oil industry has invested heavily in new technologies, including better exploration and production techniques, but these have not succeeded in uncovering major new deposits.

Since 1980, we have been consuming four barrels of oil for every new one we have discovered. Annual oil consumption surpassed the world's annual gross product in 2002. Put simply, we are facing a radical divergence between supply and demand.

Are there other oil sources available?

There is also the question of abiotic and unconventional oil. The abiotic theory is based on the notion of a chemical, non-biological (thus *a*-biotic) origin of oil in the deepest strata of the Earth. This theory holds that oil is formed from deep carbon deposits dating back perhaps to the very formation of the Earth. Supporters of this hypothesis suggest that great quantities of oil may still remain to be discovered, migrating upward from the Earth's mantle via carbon-carrying fluids. However, this theory has never generated real interest among geologists and is generally considered scientifically invalid. Besides, the theory does not involve commercially significant or accessible quantities. The question is not quite closed, but until proven otherwise, abiotic oil will not solve our problem.

Oil can also be produced or extracted using techniques other than the usual method of oil wells; these often involve additional costs or technologies because of the greater difficulty or risk. Such unconventional production includes the tapping of oil shale, bituminous sands, heavy oil, deep offshore drilling, and drilling in polar conditions.

As for oil shale, bituminous sand, and heavy oil, the idea is that as the price of oil rises, it will become economical to tap these difficult or remote deposits. In terms of oil shale, whereas the last few years showed some increase in production, the exploitation is extremely capital-intensive, and available reserves seem to be much lower than originally publicized, not to mention the potentially dangerous and expensive ecological impact of techniques such as hydraulic fracking. In the case of deep offshore oil (i.e., drilling in very deep water), research projects have had to be revised downward due to costs and the technical and ecological problems involved, as the *Deepwater Horizon* fiasco of 2010 demonstrated. The cost of foraging under polar conditions—a hostile environment for man, to say the least—is equally prohibitive.

Before reserves are totally exhausted, the rising price of oil may weigh drastically upon operations. Before oil, carbon, or bituminous sand can be extracted, energy is necessary to get the trucks rolling, the drills working, the pipelines laid, etc. All that requires more oil. In other words, it could happen that extraction no longer makes economic sense, whatever the market price. If it costs a barrel of oil to extract a barrel, it will no longer be done—even if the price of a barrel climbs to a million dollars! Neoliberal economists never seem to understand this.

It is clear that, whatever the available reserves of oil, they represent a finite quantity, and one day they shall all be consumed.

If oil specialists and economists are debating peak oil, the general public has practically never heard of it. The oil crises of 1973 and 1979 were perceived as temporary difficulties, which were overcome by discoveries in Alaska and the North Sea. The illogical conclusion drawn is that all future problems can be overcome in the same way. Besides, since the end of the 1960s, there have been so many prophets crying wolf—without any wolf showing up under our noses—that the public has stopped becoming alarmed. At elementary school in the 1970s, I remember a teacher who told us that oil would soon disappear. How could such a thing be taken seriously when oil and gas have been so cheap since 1980? Even among informed people, it is thought that peak oil is no more than another false alarm, like the Y2K bug which was supposed to bring about the end of the world. The September 11 attacks were also said to have "changed everything." Well, we are still here; everything's going fairly well; we still drive big cars, take low-cost flights, and we're all just hoping not to lose our jobs during the next wave of outsourcing.

It is quite understandable that, for many Europeans and Americans who have never known life without petroleum, it is simply impossible to imagine a different way of life. I have to think of the stories my grandmother told me about country life in northern Italy in the 1920s and '30s to imagine existence without oil. Several families lived together on great farms where you worked as an agricultural laborer, and each infrequent trip to the nearest town was an adventure that left an impression in your memory.

The oil lobby, or simply the industries with an interest in the status quo, go into denial, give out misinformation, or conceal facts such as the following:

> Oil consumption is rising steeply, especially because of the arrival of new industrial powers such as China, India, and Brazil. At the rate of 24 billion barrels of oil consumed in 2004, the one trillion barrels of known oil reserves will only last thirty-seven years. (And there is good reason to believe that world reserves are actually not one trillion at all, but only 200 or 300 billion barrels.)

> The U.S. has only three percent of world reserves, but consumes twenty-five percent of production. It imports seventy percent of what it consumes. Shale gas and oil seem to be a bubble that will only last a few years — not the long-term economic bonanza as portrayed by many in the media.

> The barrels-of-oil-equivalent energy required to pump a barrel of oil has gone from one for twenty-eight in 1916 to one for three in 2004 and continues to worsen. This is the most worrisome fact, because it means that soon it will no longer be economical to extract oil.

In summary, the optimists think that with first-rate technologies, new deposits will be discovered, and the cost of extracting from them will go down; the pessimists think that we are headed for irreversible decline. The latter put forward the following arguments:

> Oil in existing deposits is decreasing by 6.7 percent per annum.

> The discovery of new deposits reached its maximum in the 1960s, and for the last few years, few discoveries have been made, even in deep water.

> Even though more oil can be extracted from the deposits in Saudi Arabia, Iraq, and Iran, the point of maximum extraction has been passed in most of the deposits currently being tapped.

> It is quite possible that oil-producing countries have exaggerated the size of their reserves for political and financial reasons.

> Although enormous quantities of oil exist in the form of bituminous sand, the cost and, above all, the energy necessary for extracting them will soon be prohibitive—not to mention the environmental costs.

Is this the end of oil?

No. Oil will continue to exist; perhaps there's more left than all that has been consumed up to now. However, that which remains is getting ever more difficult to extract, and thus ever more expensive.

It's the end of *cheap* oil.

The rising prices will lead us to concentrate our use of oil on the most valuable applications, such as transportation and chemistry. The aeronautics industry will be hit first, full force, along with every other activity which depends on a long logistical chain. There will be no more fish caught off the coast of Chile or Iceland, cleaned in Morocco, and consumed in Japan. No more South African raisins in the springtime, Kenyan green beans, California dates. The effects on personal transportation will be considerable, enough to put in question the whole urbanization model of the Western world. Many off-shored factories will be repatriated. Distribution chains dependent on road transportation will be entirely rethought.

Nothing will be as it was.

Max spends another afternoon baking in his car as he waits in the gas line.

He doesn't understand why gas is so expensive. And not only expensive, but rationed. He's limited to twenty gallons per week, but at $20 a gallon, he can't afford that much anyway

... There are no taxis or chauffeurs, no special exemptions for gasoline. And he has had his fill of lining up for two hours every week! Fortunately, a friend of his, Dylan, with whom he makes evening supermarket runs, and who has tuned up cars with him, has a good plan: at night they break into the gas tanks of cars in the road and siphon gas into a jerry can. The taste is disgusting, but it works. Every night they get twenty or thirty liters.

<<few people are capable of expressing with equanimity opinions which differ from the prejudices of their social environment. Most people are even incapable of forming such opinions.

albert einstein

scientist

/1953/

<<the economic process being of an entropic nature, the shrinking of productive activity is inevitable in physical terms.

nicholas georgescu-roegen

economist

//1906–1994//

<<i think it's not going to be possible. not possible. not possible.

zebda

_essence ordinaire

/1998/

The End of All Resources

THERE ARE TWO KINDS OF RESOURCES: renewable and nonrenewable. Resources are considered renewable when their stock is practically infinite (the sun, the wind, the tides, etc.), or if they renew themselves over time (assuming, of course, that they are not exploited beyond their capacity to renew themselves). Nonrenewable resources are those whose stocks are not renewed, at least on a human timescale — it takes millions of years to create coal or oil, for example — or those whose quantities are finite (minerals, etc.).

In the previous chapter, we found that human civilization consumes all resources with an unprecedented rapacity that is constantly growing, which is what is leading us toward peak oil. Even as world commerce declined thirty percent in the aftermath of the 2008 crisis, oil consumption only went down 1.5 percent. Even though this was one of the biggest economic slowdowns ever recorded, it shows that demand for oil is the example *par excellence* of an inelastic demand. It is easy to eat somewhat less, go less often to restaurants or to the movies, postpone the purchase of a house or new clothes, but it is quite difficult to reduce the number of miles between our home and workplace, between school and the supermarket, etc. With our current way of life, it is impossible to do without cheap oil. And in the current state of knowledge, no possible combination of renewable resources is capable of preserving that way of life for us. None of these forms of energy could sustain even a small fraction of the systems that provide for our present needs. Moreover, petroleum has a great number of uses that cannot be supplied by electricity, which is difficult to store anyway. Ninety-five percent of energy used in transportation comes from petroleum. It's hard to imagine a billion vehicles (cars, trucks, freighters, planes) working on electricity.

In 2009, 30.8 billion barrels of oil were produced. Converted into energy, this corresponds to over 6,800 nuclear power stations (for comparison, about 440 of these are operating today), or 7 million giant wind turbines, or 30,000 square kilometers of solar panels. And this is just for the year 2009! Imagine how it will be in the future, with the prospect of exponential population growth. Needless to say, realizing that number of nuclear power stations (not very fashionable since Chernobyl and Fukushima, either), wind turbines, and solar panels is likely to take time and cost a lot ... And there is no indication that enough uranium or rare-earth metals even exist to make them in any case.

On the table below, we see the growth in demand for energy expressed in its petroleum equivalent (in millions of barrels per day) between 2004 and 2030. The rate of growth remains very high everywhere in the world.

	2004	2030	RATE OF GROWTH
North America	55	69	25%
Latin America	13	24	85%
Europe	39	46	18%
Africa	12	19	58%
Middle East	11	18	64%
Russia and Central Asia	20	28	40%
Japan	11	12	9%
India	11	29	164%
China	26	52	100%
Other Asian Countries	22	38	78%

Can we find a replacement for oil?

To answer this question, we must first define a concept fundamental to understanding how energy behaves — *entropy*. Entropy is an irreversible process: the energy we use is converted principally into heat; this caloric energy, once dissipated, can never become mechanical energy again. This principle applies to all energy resources on earth, which by definition constitute a limited and nonrenewable capital.

Classical liberal economics does not know the law of entropy, i.e., the irreversibility of transformations of material into energy. This system of economics does not distinguish between stock and flow, the environmental equivalents of capital and revenue.

> The first law of thermodynamics states that energy cannot be created or destroyed; it can only change form.

> The second law of thermodynamics states that, in a closed system, the change of state of any quantity of energy goes only in one direction: from concentration to dispersal, from order to disorder. This is why a cup of tea cools off to match the ambient temperature — and not the other way around. No cup of tea warms up spontaneously. No pile of ashes reconstitutes itself into a log. No rusty piece of iron returns spontaneously to its pristine state. No perpetual motion can exist. You can only go from low entropy to high entropy.

Each time energy changes its state, a little energy is lost — sometimes a lot — in the form of heat, which is dispersed. This dispersal of heat can be useful: to heat us in the winter, run a steam engine, make an explosion, or turn a turbine; but energy is always lost in the transformation. In Switzerland, for example, hydroelectric plants generate electricity by using the weight of water that, coming down from the reservoirs, turns turbines. This electricity sells for a lot, since it can respond to the hours of day with the highest electrical demand. During the night, while nuclear electricity especially is abundantly available and cheap (electricity must be used as it is produced, or it is lost), the water is pumped back up into the reservoirs. This procedure requires much more energy than is generated by the same quantity of water. A caloric absurdity can be an economic advantage.

Many optimists predict that new technologies can help us do things more efficiently than in the past, increase production, do more with less. Technology can entertain us and help us communicate in an extraordinary way. Technology can also help us transform and use energy with innovative applications, it is true. But technology can never *create* energy.

In many situations, new technologies are only marginally useful. Take the example of extracting minerals. Imagine a copper mine. When I was doing business in Africa in the 1990s, I was fortunate enough to visit the copper mines of Konkola, Nchanga, and Chingola in northern Zambia. These mines are four hundred meters deep. Huge excavators tear enough earth to construct a villa from the mountain with each shovelful. Gigantic trucks as tall as three-story apartment buildings transport thousands of cubic meters of soil, which is then treated to extract the mineral. A considerable quantity of diesel fuel must be used every day to keep those machines running. And the mineral content of the soil extracted is 0.3 percent; i.e., to get three kilos of copper, you have to process a ton of earth.

Once oil gets expensive, it will no longer be economical to work this way, and even materials that are not yet scarce will become very expensive. One can easily imagine extraction stopping altogether. Here, too, we are dealing with a curve rather than a straight line. The more difficult extracting raw materials becomes, the more energy it requires (fuel for trucks, cranes, drills; electricity for the chemical processing; etc.). As the richness of a vein goes down, the costs rise in proportion — both exponentially. Humans, like other animals, first seek out resources that are easier to obtain: those closest to the surface and closest to the markets. The best ores get worked first, the biggest trees cut down first, the high-yield mines exploited first. Over time, encouraged by the rarity of materials, the more difficult sources are worked, less pure and more costly. This is less economical; the energy needed to get the same result becomes ever greater.

Coal follows the same logic, and, despite the disinformation spread concerning its future availability, it, too, is becoming rarer. The best coal, anthracite, has already almost totally disappeared. On the other hand, there remains a lot of lesser quality coal, such as forge coal and gas coal, which will be available for another forty or fifty years. We should also mention lignite, less attractive but still useful, which will probably be available for fifty years, and perhaps one hundred, if the economy settles a bit, and oil is not systematically replaced by coal.

The phenomenon we have described for oil, copper, and coal also occurs for any nonrenewable resource: natural gas, zinc, nickel, lithium, etc. In the following graph, we can see the number of years which remains for these minerals based on known reserves and estimated population growth and rates of extraction:

MINERAL	YEARS REMAINING
Silver	12
Gold	15
Zinc	15
Lead	20
Tungsten	23
Copper	23
Manganese	29
Nickel	30
Iron	40

This situation is starting to have concrete effects: between foreseeable shortages, growing extraction costs, and financial speculation, prices have fluctuated violently in the past few years, mainly going up.

We can already see that massive theft will take place in Western cities similar to what I witnessed in African countries: theft of aluminum seats in Toronto, of cast iron sewer plates in Scotland (resold in China where the local underworld stole 24,000 sewer plates in 2006

in Shanghai alone!), theft of copper telephone cable in Spain and
Hungary, theft of 136 aluminum pylons in Baltimore, Maryland. In
India, eight unlucky people have died in 2010 by falling into sewer
holes whose covers had been stolen. In California, gangs specialize in
stealing platinum catalytic converters from automobiles in less than
ninety seconds. Such bits of trivia may raise a smile, but they are
revealing.

We are facing not merely peak oil, but *peak everything.*

Some relatively good news is that, thanks to rising costs, recycling
is increasing (the U.S. exports 61 billion dollars worth of metals for
recycling each year to China), product design is getting more economical with resources, people repair things instead of throwing
them away, etc. Unfortunately, even if we succeed in recycling one
hundred percent of the materials we use — metals, plastics and everything else — since economic growth is accelerating, we will need
even more raw materials for making new cars, televisions, telephones,
etc., which the economy bids us produce. We are quickly and surely
headed toward the exhaustion of all resources.

Next, we must look at the impact of the rarity of irreplaceable metals. There are materials that, once mixed, are impossible to separate
again at any reasonable cost in energy. Cobalt, for example, which is
mixed with steel to make stainless steel, is lost forever. The phosphates
in fertilizer, once spread on a field, end up being dissolved in water
and finally running into the sea where they are impossible to recuper-
ate. Finally, there are materials lost by dispersion, such as when iron
rusts: the oxidized atoms are lost, too widely dispersed to be reused.
We are using more resources than we can renew or discover, and demand continues to grow.

Economists often make the mistake of imagining that the economy
exists in a void, without external parameters as vulgar as resources or
waste. Alas, the actual economy is not a neat theoretical model; it is a
subset of the natural environment. The complexity of a modern global
economy — able to make, transport, track, use, and dispose of billions

upon billions of objects — is enormous. Obviously, this complex system can only exist through a continual injection of energy.

A number of economists consider the argument that the world is about to run out of resources to be both old and discredited. In 1980, a good number of them foresaw a scarcity of raw materials and higher prices. In fact, prices continued to decline during the 1980s and '90s. This is because those who foresaw the inevitable in the 1960s and '70s had not understood the time factor. But they were correct; they were just a little early.

Conventional economists think growth is a good thing. They argue against the idea that physical resources are limited by maintaining that if a resource becomes rare, its price will rise, thereby providing an incentive for discovering other resources or developing or inventing less expensive substitutes. According to them, market forces (the "invisible hand") and human ingenuity will always be able to find a solution to the increasing demand for resources. This will happen thanks to the exploration of virgin territories, more efficient manufacturing processes, or replacing oil with another form of energy. For them, there can be no theoretical limit to growth. The facts have supported them for the past two hundred years, and since 1989, most see no reason for the lowered acceleration of economic expansion. According to liberal doctrine, all means for encouraging economic activity are good, and more is always better. From this point of view, energy has the same value as any other raw material, when in fact, it is the necessary condition for obtaining other resources.

In fact, peak oil and peak resources will not have the most violent impact: that will be the moment demand becomes permanently greater than supply. Consider a country which produces 3 million barrels of oil a day, uses one itself, and exports the other two. If in ten years production goes down to 2 million barrels per day, while domestic consumption increases by 0.5 million barrels per day, the country can then only export 0.5 million barrels a day, seventy-five percent less than ten years before. Very soon thereafter it will not be able to export any. In this scenario, the price per barrel will increase sharply, and net importers of oil will quickly be left high and dry *whatever the price of oil.* Producing countries will quickly put an embargo on exports, considering domestic demand a higher priority, in order to guarantee economic and social stability and create a small strategic reserve.

The same phenomenon occurs with all other resources. One may debate over the exact moment when oil or this or that mineral reaches peak production, but the key moment will occur *before* that, when an ever growing number of countries becomes unwilling or unable to export. At that point, the economy will slow, the price of goods will rise sharply, and there will be outbreaks of panic.

Unfortunately, Western public opinion no longer takes seriously the view so often put forward that resources are going to be exhausted. When it happens, it will come as a shock — economically and, especially, psychologically. The optimists tell us it is useless to think about it; progress is natural and self-correcting. "Malthus was wrong," they say; "he didn't foresee chemical fertilizer and intensive agriculture! With technological progress, we shall end up finding a way to develop new resources to replace those becoming exhausted!" We are in the situation of a drug addict who keeps on looking for his drug at whatever price, since he cannot replace it with anything else. The problem is that in the case of the drug oil, the addicts — ourselves — are in the majority. Those who still have access to their daily dose have no intention of giving it up, and those who don't, dream of acquiring it as quickly as possible.

The risk of social problems and revolts following an economic downturn will increasingly motivate politicians to take a gamble on war, so as to, at least, guarantee the provision of resources. On many fronts, the war has already begun. It is hard to predict future conflicts, especially when so many "false flag" or "special" operations prevent our knowing who is responsible for what and who is fighting whom. The wars will be dressed up in the language of "human rights": "*We must bomb them to bring them democracy, kill them for their own good, occupy their countries to liberate them from their dictators."* (The hypocrisy is revealed when one notices that military interventions never occur where there are no resources.) Who knows? Maybe some day, the mask of newspeak will fall, and we will march off to war with the courage to declare our true purpose — *theft.*

These wars will become ever more futile, for not only do they themselves consume resources, but they also risk destroying the means of production. Just as a drug addict smashes a pharmacy window and grabs everything he can get his hands on, these wars will increasingly resemble acts of desperation. The risk of conflagration and of such conflicts spreading is great, especially when countries which pursue neo-imperialist policies, like the U.S., collide with the strategic interests of new powers like China and Russia. Such conflicts may become not the Third World War, but the Last World War.

In fact, wars over resources are a form of denial: *"If our efforts produce no result, if we don't want to change our way of life, at least we can still wage war! Oh, if only we can win this war, the oil will start gushing out of the ground again, and we can go on driving our cars! If only we could have a few more resources for just a little longer, we could continue our way of life for a time and hope for the technological miracle which will save us!"*

In the past, there was always a new continent, new territories to explore in which new resources could be found or looted. There was always a new oil or gas well to be dug, or existing deposits to be tapped more efficiently. All that is over. We are living beyond our means. It is as if we were spending all our revenue and all our capital as well. At the end — bankruptcy. And at the global scale, there is no providential State to save us.

The notion of an *ecological footprint* refers to the area of productive ground necessary for producing the energy, resources, food, etc., consumed by one inhabitant. If we measure this footprint in available hectares per inhabitant of the planet, this figure amounts to 1.8 hectares in 2003. As population and consumption per person rise, the footprint increases. The average footprint is over 1.9 in developing countries, such as China, and 6.4 hectares in wealthy ones. The United States, a country at once rich and wasteful, has an ecological footprint of 9.6 hectares per inhabitant. If the entire world wanted to live as the United States now does, it would require the equivalent of five times the existing surface of the Earth, or five additional planets of comparable size.

This is not going to be possible.

Michael runs a small firm with forty employees.

He makes high-quality machinery. Although the competition is fierce (especially from those cheap Chinese machines) and he must pay employer contributions and increasingly scandalous taxes, he is hanging in there. But this week, there is a problem: almost all of his suppliers are out of stock. No more electronic components or parts for some things, no more lubrication or metal for others. What is going on? He is trying to find replacement sources, but the cost is prohibitive—five times the normal prices! His customers call up, panicky. If he doesn't find a solution soon, he will have to take radical measures and let some of his employees go. At this point, he is not paying himself a salary every month. He can't risk losing his company because of a passing crisis. It is just a passing crisis … isn't it?

<<this we know: the earth does not belong to man; man belongs to the earth.

chief seattle

[attributed]

//1754–1866//

<<every day the planet becomes uglier, poorer, more uniform. it is turning into a vast garbage dump with unbreathable air.

alain de benoist

/2007/

"it is quite possible to run out of oil and pollute the planet to destruction simultaneously.

david strathan

writer

/2007/

Ecological Collapse

THERE WAS A TIME WHEN every peasant was an expert in sustainable ecology. Public authorities were as well: Louis XIV's minister of finances, Jean-Baptiste Colbert, regulated the lumber industry to ensure forests would grow back; he ordered the planting of oaks that would furnish masts for ships three hundred years in the future. Ancient and traditional societies understood that no social life was possible without taking into account the natural milieu in which it takes place. For my grandmother's generation, and those which came before, waste was the sin *par excellence*, since it meant gambling with our stock of the means of survival. Even among the old bourgeoisie, frugality was still among the cardinal virtues, since it was supposed to allow the accumulation of capital.

A profound change in the meaning of waste occurred in the era of fossil fuels. For two centuries, roughly, our civilization has not ceased to act as though natural reserves could be multiplied to infinity, including the capacity of nature and the ecosystem to absorb all sorts of rubbish.

We must consume! It has become a kind of duty. We consume and throw away. Products quickly become obsolete, out of fashion, broken, intended to be replaced rather than repaired. Into the trash with them! Packaging everywhere and for everything: into the trash!

In Europe, the amount of trash produced by each person on average in 2009 amounted to 1,150 pounds. In the U.S., the amount is double. Municipalities dealing with waste management expect to have to double their capacity between now and 2020. In Naples, Italy, in 2008, we got a spectacular lesson in what happens when trash is not collected: the city was literally submerged within a few weeks! This ought to be compared to the USSR, where there was no need to organize trash collection: the lack of consumer goods saw to that. Practically nothing got thrown out, because the least bit of trash was useful and got reused.

Each year, space must be found for storing or, in the best cases, sifting and recycling these millions of tons of waste. In the worst cases, waste is incinerated, producing a little heat and a lot of pollution. Often, waste is shipped off on cargo ships to poor countries, where it is warehoused in a slipshod manner or recycled under horrible working conditions, especially when garbage contains electronic devices or scrap-iron. In these poor countries, waste is allowed to accumulate in the very streets, or piled up on the edge of cities, untreated. This creates toxic and unhealthy zones, which become the residential quarters for the poorest of the poor.

Sometimes, these countries even serve as illegal dumping grounds for the worst toxic waste of industries the world over. This traffic, conducted by crime syndicates, amounts to slow-motion ecological bombs, since no one knows exactly where the toxic matter gets dumped. No one knows what the effect of such pollution will be. A striking example is the Somali coast, where during the '90s and 2000s, the Neapolitan mafia (the Camorra), which specializes in the treatment of highly toxic products (acids, ammonia, etc.), profited from the local anarchy and absence of government by dumping whole shiploads of the stuff into the sea. It is hardly surprising that the local fishermen, soon finding themselves with a sea empty of fish, had to adapt by taking up piracy!

This is not an exception. It is an example of deferred consequences. We have been massively polluting our ecosystem for a long time: mineral extraction has devastating effects, chemical pollution is terrible for our land, especially agricultural land. The worst poisons are petroleum derivatives (pesticides, plastics, harmful chemical products) or substances resulting from petroleum or carbon combustion (nitrogen oxides, etc.). We forget that this has consequences; and when someone near us gets cancer, we blame fate or regret the inability of medical science to treat it. We consider normal a way of life that is sick, highly aberrant, and cannot last. We will pay dearly for this.

The World Health Organization has examined mortality tied to the presence of chemical substances in the environment. The results were that in 2004 chemical pollution caused 4.9 million deaths (8.3 percent of the total mortality). By comparison, the impact of chemical substances is greater than that of cancer, which represents 5.1 percent of that year's total loss of life. Fifty-four percent of the damage done by chemical substance has affected children under fifteen. Seventy percent of illnesses are due to the association of multiple atmospheric pollutants. This study is limited to "the known impact of a limited number of chemical substances; the unknown effects may be considerable."

The following graph shows the strong recent growth (measured in ppm — parts per million in the atmosphere) of emissions of certain greenhouse gases such as carbon dioxide (CO_2), nitrous oxide (N_2O) and methane gas (CH_4). Note that these curves all happen to be exponential and correspond perfectly to the population growth we saw above.

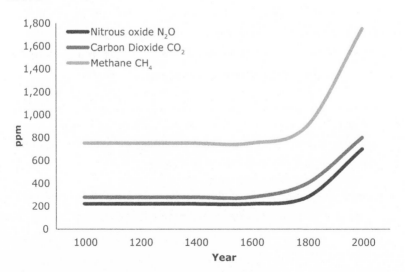

The pollution and the emission of these gases caused by our way of life are often cited as the cause of *global warming*. If there is near-unanimity among scientists concerning the measurable and undeniable fact that we are going through a period of climate change rather than a true warming, the causes are still up for debate. Whether due to human activity (emission of greenhouse gases, methane, carbon dioxide, etc.) or to long cycles of solar activity, or to other still unknown causes (cosmic radiation, etc.), the changes *are* taking place. They are increasingly measurable, perceptible, and strong. We have no idea what is going to happen climatically in ten, twenty, or fifty years. All the specialists agree that temperature and climate disturbances will have violent and unexpected effects that are difficult to predict. Since this will coincide with the period of falling oil production, we risk being greatly at a disadvantage in facing this series of crises.

Beyond impressive momentary events like a bad hurricane season, drought, or flash flooding, the long-term changes are above all to be feared. The Intergovernmental Panel on Climate Change predicts a significant rise in sea levels in the course of the coming century.

What effects will these changes have on the economy?

Above all, the effect on agricultural production must be feared. Farmers are only able to adjust to slow climate changes, by adapting the seeds and techniques they employ. But if the changes occur in a sudden and unforeseeable manner, it will be difficult to adapt from year to year, from one harvest to the next. Steven Solomon, author of the book *Water: The Epic Struggle for Wealth, Power and Civilization*, describes the dramatic example of Pakistan:

> Consider what will happen in water-distressed, nuclear-armed, terrorist-besieged, overpopulated, heavily irrigation-dependent and already politically unstable Pakistan when its single water lifeline, the Indus river, loses a third of its flow from the disappearance of its glacial water source.

A further warming, whose effects can be seen already, is going to allow parasites and insects to expand to new latitudes, which will also increase the number of persons exposed to diseases born by tropical mosquitoes (dengue, malaria). This will have major effects on harvests and probably cause sanitation crises. If sea levels rise due to melting ice, it will cause serious problems for the fifteen percent of the world's population which lives along the coasts at less than one meter above current sea level. Mass migrations and climatic refugees could have a large destabilizing effect, especially in Bangladesh, India, Egypt, and other countries with densely populated coastal regions.

The most important economic effect will be felt on port infra-structure that cannot be protected by dams or moved. There is a risk that the loss of ports will strike a terrible blow against world trade. They will either have to be moved or new ones constructed. The cost will be enormous. We risk losing some of our most productive assets in the middle of a major crisis. Rising sea levels may also contami-nate aquifers close to the coast with salt, rendering them useless for agriculture. This will accentuate the fresh-water shortage. Finally, and most terrifying, if global temperatures rise more than six degrees Celsius, this could set off a chain reaction, releasing methane, now imprisoned by the arctic permafrost, into the atmosphere. If this hap-pens, the massive increase in this greenhouse gas will cause colossal climate changes. It is imaginable that changes in the North Atlantic currents will lead to a strong cooling, even the beginning of a new ice age. We cannot know. But when we know that four of the five known mass extinction events were caused or intensified by sudden changes of climate, we can surely say that it is neither intelligent nor prudent to play sorcerer's apprentice.

Even without climate change, modern agriculture seems already to be at a breaking point.

Let's start with water: 97.5 percent of the water in the world is seawater, i.e. saltwater, and therefore unsuited to either consumption or agriculture. Out of the remaining 2.5 percent of water remain-ing (freshwater), 68.9 percent is in the form of ice, 30.8 percent in subterranean aquifers, and only 0.3 percent is found in rainwater, lakes, and rivers.

A normal human being consumes four liters of water per day in one form or another, in beverages or food. Now, to produce our food, 2,000 liters per person, five hundred times as much, are necessary! This explains why seventy percent of fresh water is used for irrigation, twenty percent for industry, and only ten percent for personal consumption (drinking, cleaning, and hygiene).

The demand for water is increasing exponentially since it follows the progress of population. The more people, the more food they need, and the more water this requires. All signs indicate that we have already reached the limit: irrigation is so intensive that more and more rivers are no longer flowing all the way to their mouths. This is the case with the Colorado River in the U.S. and the Yellow River in China.

The water in subterranean aquifers, "fossil water," which takes centuries to form and become purified, is lost as soon as it has been used. These aquifers are being pumped well beyond their capacity to renew themselves; they soon will no longer be able to bring water to the populations dependent upon them. Water is a limited resource and is not divided equitably. While abundant in certain parts of the world, one third of the population lives in areas with a water shortage. This is going to get worse. Most of the 21 million wells in India are on the point of running dry; in Pakistan, Saudi Arabia, the Southwestern United States, Spain, North Africa, and the Sahara, the aquifers have already dried up. Ever more water must be pumped from ever deeper down until it disappears entirely, and it is no longer possible to continue the cultivation of these regions. This will have an impact on food production. It is estimated that fifteen to thirty-five percent of world agriculture is already on the edge of a chronic shortage of fresh water for irrigation. What will these millions of peasants do? What will the millions of people without food do? Will they wait patiently for the aid agencies, revolt, or emigrate?

Of course, seawater can be desalinated, if you invest a lot of energy (i.e., petroleum) and if you can pay for the technical installation. One hopeful note is the relative success of initiatives for bringing drinking water to the Third World by developing better hygienic conditions that do not pollute water sources. But to continue down that path, 100 billion dollars must be found every year, while the annual budget of existing programs is only 4.5 billion. The poor peasant carries no weight in comparison to Wall Street!

Water will be a limiting factor for demographic and economic growth in the next few years. The programmed exhaustion of fossil energy has already led to oil wars. We can expect water wars, especially between India, Bangladesh, China, and Pakistan; between China, Vietnam, Laos, and Myanmar; between Turkey, Iraq, and Syria; between Egypt, Sudan, Ethiopia, and Uganda; between Israel, Lebanon, Jordan, and Palestine; between Guinea, Mali, Niger, Benin, and Nigeria, etc.

Expert opinion agrees with that of the FAO (Food and Agriculture Organization of the United Nations), which writes in one of its recent reports:

> [J]ust satisfying the expected food and feed demand will require a substantial increase of global food production of 70 percent by 2050, involving an additional quantity of nearly 1 billion tons of cereals and 200 million tons of meat…. Much of the natural resource base already in use worldwide shows worrying signs of degradation. According to the Millennium Ecosystem Assessment, 15 out of 24 ecosystem services examined are already being degraded or used unsustainably. These include capture fisheries and water supply.

The last decades have witnessed dramatic improvements in productivity on the world's mega-farms: irrigation, fertilizers, mechanization, economies of scale, and genetically designed seeds have all increased yields. But how can agricultural output be increased *another* seventy percent, when practically all cultivable land is already under cultivation, when productivity is running up against the law of diminishing returns, and we are at risk of no longer having the cheap oil needed for fertilizers, irrigation, pesticides, and mechanization? Logically, there must be a limit to the amount of productive land on the earth's surface, the remainder being too hot, too cold, or too dry. It will require energy and considerable effort to make land usable when it is naturally ill-adapted to agriculture.

Over the course of this last century, the number of persons devoted to agriculture has fallen significantly, and agriculture itself has been reorganized on an unprecedented scale. We have gone from an age when the farmer knew all the tools and the smallest details of his business to a world in which the farmer is a manager, an engineer, a trader. The sophistication and technology are impressive. From that point of view, the system of industrial agriculture in the U.S. is a success story: a mechanization and industrialization of food production that is able to produce cereals, vegetables, and animals, all more or less genetically modified, in order to furnish the population with massive amounts of food with a high fat and protein content, massive quantities of salt, sugar, and mysterious chemical products — not to speak of aberrations such as giving cattle flour made from animal carcasses... This industry, these food factories, are only possible thanks to oil (mainly in the form of diesel for agricultural machines and transportation) and natural gas (for producing fertilizer).

Modern industrial agriculture can nourish more people than any other previous system, and it can do so with a tiny number of farmers. Output per acre is much higher than at any point in history. Unfortunately, these gains in productivity also have a hidden cost. Soil is getting poorer, and its nutritive components are disappearing. A handful of healthy soil contains billions of bacteria, mushrooms, protozoa, nematodes, as well as earthworms, arthropods, and many other useful little animals. Intensive agriculture eliminates all that and rapidly makes the soil sterile.

Culture appears in the word "agriculture" for a good reason. This culture, or cultivation of the earth — I would even say, this *love* of the earth—is made up of knowledge, competence, tricks, secrets, work methods acquired over centuries and transmitted with care—and, indeed, *love*—to the next generation, from father to son, from mother to daughter.

In less than a century, blinded by the ease fossil energy has brought us, we have thrown all that knowledge away. We have transformed farms into automated factories. Agriculture has gone from family and community management to an industrial and global enterprise.

In this industry, we need sixteen calories to produce a calorie's worth of cereals, seventy calories to produce a calorie's worth of meat. Roughly two pounds of cereal are needed to produce a pound of fish or poultry; four pounds of cereal, for a pound of pork; seven, for a pound of beef. This costs a lot in terms of agricultural surface area. Not to speak of the horrible conditions, in most cases, of production and slaughter in what must be called meat factories—factories in which one can observe behavior which would have been inconceivable in the time of our grandparents. Animals are treated with unheard-of cruelty—and done so on a massive scale: in the United States alone, more than 9 billion animals are killed every year. Besides the ethical question, there is that of the quality of the food thus produced—not to mention the hundreds of millions of gallons of excrement (saturated with growth hormones, antibiotics, and chemical products) we don't know what to do with, and which ends up seeping into underground aquifers and waterways. The expression "eat shit" is becoming a reality.

This kind of industrial agriculture—for which it would be better to be a trained manager from a business school than a farmer—is at the moment highly productive. In one century, through what has been called the *Green Revolution*, yield per acre has gone up 250 percent! This magnificent increase has been due to several factors: above all to oil and the mechanization of agriculture, which allow vast surfaces to be cultivated efficiently with few work hands. Oil is also necessary for pumping water and the regular massive irrigation of the fields; and in the chemical industry, it helps in the creation of pesticides, herbicides, fungicides, etc. Other factors that come into play include the selection and use of more productive seeds, hybrids among them, and the massive use of fertilizer, which has gone from 14 million tons in 1950 to 141 million tons in 2000.

It's worth understanding how fertilizers are made. The three key elements for plant growth are nitrogen, phosphorus, and potassium. Artificial nitrogen found in fertilizer is produced with natural gas, which supplies the energy for converting atmospheric nitrogen into ammonia, a form of nitrogen that plants can absorb. This conversion is energy-intensive: to make a pound of ammonia, the equivalent of a pound of oil (in the form of natural gas) is necessary. The price of artificial nitrogen, and thus fertilizer, is going up. As for phosphorus, which is found in nature mainly in the form of phosphates, the situation is more alarming: mines are yielding ever less; reserves will be exhausted in thirty or forty years. Potassium is abundant, but obtained by the electrolysis of potassium hydroxide, a process which requires electricity, i.e., energy. These fertilizers are used to compensate for the impoverishment and sterility of soils, worn out by intensive monoculture. In fact, five centimeters of topsoil require hundreds of years to reach an optimal level of nutrients, but can be destroyed in a few years of intensive agriculture. Erosion is especially intense in monoculture, where the soil can no longer be described as healthy ground (i.e., a mixture of vegetable matter and interlocking roots that can retain their structure in the face of heavy rain). These fertilizers are going to pass, by the effect of rain and the elimination of agricultural waste, into our waterways and finally into the oceans. Too strong a concentration of nitrogen and phosphates in the ocean will create dead zones, nearly devoid of marine life due to the rapid growth and deadly expansion of algae which feed upon these elements.

Since 1985, world agricultural production per inhabitant has only gone down. If industrial agriculture is extremely efficient, it has also become extremely *fragile*. Worse, since we are no longer aware of it, the products of industrial agriculture have also lost their nutritive value: between 1938 and 1990, the protein content of wheat and barley has sunk thirty to fifty percent, and twenty-two to thirty-nine percent of the mineral content has been lost. Between 1920 and 2001, the concentration of protein, oils, and amino acids in maize has diminished by twenty-five percent.

Desertification is another process that has accelerated because of human activity. Often it is a matter of overgrazing on land with few plants. When the wind blows over these stripped lands, the thin layer of productive soil is carried off, and only arid soil remains, unable to hold rainfall, which makes the situation ever worse. Desert extends over these lands very quickly, making them sterile. Desertification is a problem for China, where the Gobi desert is now no more than 150 miles from Beijing. The problem is enormous on the African continent. In Nigeria, more than 1,350 square miles of land are lost in this way every year.

If a billion people are already suffering from malnutrition and chronic under-nourishment today, what would it be like tomorrow with a few billion more inhabitants? We are facing a predicament in which considerable efforts must be made to feed the world's population — and yet these efforts will further imperil an already fragile situation. The more time passes, the worse things get, and we risk seeing *on a global scale* phenomena that have hitherto been isolated to single countries. In Haiti, citizens can't feed themselves due to the exhaustion of their soil through decades of mismanagement; Rwanda experienced mass slaughters, which were motivated in part by the shortage of agricultural land in relation to the burgeoning population.

It is worth noting that China and Russia have implemented a policy of massive food reserves. These countries have not forgotten that the revolutions that caused so much death and destruction in the course of their history were catalyzed by food crises. So the governments of these countries have long-term views and stockpile rice and cereals to prevent such blows as sudden price rises or the collapse of production. And since agricultural products are considered of strategic importance, export limits have also been put in place.

No, Malthus was not wrong; he simply did not foresee oil and the Green Revolution.

However, we could produce more if we switched to a diet lower in animal proteins. In India, only five percent of cereal production goes to nourish animals, while the same proportion is sixty percent in the USA. The tendency in the world is toward a diet rich in animal proteins, following the example of Western nations. Additional agricultural land not being available to support this demand, the price of cereals is going to go up, and the poorest people will no longer be able to feed themselves. Bio-fuel production is not going to help the problem, since using a part of maize production for vehicles subtracts that amount from consumption as food. Finally, great quantities of food (estimated at one third) are wasted or thrown away, while in poor countries, ten to fifteen percent of food stocks are destroyed by rodents and insects.

The result of all this is that food prices are going up by ever greater and more frequent leaps. In 2007, between a heavy increase in demand, floods, droughts, higher fertilizer prices, and speculation, food prices increased by forty percent on average.

What are we going to do? Africa, a historically fertile and thinly populated continent, will reach a population of one billion by 2025. It will only be possible to nourish twenty-five percent of that population with the agricultural land there. So there will be 750 million Africans suffering from chronic famine who must be saved or who will emigrate, without which they will suffer a drastic decrease in their numbers — a polite euphemism for saying that *hundreds of millions* of them will drop dead on the spot. Such problems will not get taken care of without considerable trouble.

Many have put forward the argument that GMOs — genetically modified organisms — already in use for cotton, soybeans, and maize, will be the *miracle solution*. The first years of use seem to show that their productivity quickly wanes, not to speak of the risk of contaminating normal crops, nor of health effects still difficult to measure. Private management of GMOs takes from farmers the means of reproducing their own seeds, and tomorrow, of their own livestock. Yet there is a solution that, in spite of being simple, has been proven to work. In countries which still practice traditional agriculture, also known as permaculture or organic subsistence agriculture, there is no famine, water is not overused, and there is no need for fertilizer. Associated with low-birthrate policies, these techniques offer inspiration. But apart from initiatives by small groups of farmers, public authorities prefer to subsidize industrial agriculture. This is destructive, inefficient over the long term, and gobbles up water, energy, and polluting fertilizers; but, it has the support of well- organized lobbies.... .

While we are on the subject of lobbies, think of the fierce struggle of different countries to maintain or augment their fishing quotas. The number of fish has declined by ninety percent in one century. In 1950, 19 million tons of seafood were harvested from the sea; in 1997, this became ninety-three tons. Since then, it has been going down continuously. There are parts of the ocean where not a single fish can be found — genuine dead zones. By 2010, over seventy-five percent of marine ecosystems were considered exhausted.

My in-laws have vacationed on the Île d'Oléron, on the Atlantic coast of France, since the 1950s, and the stories they tell are anecdotal but edifying: for decades you could just wade in with a fishing net and catch a great number of fish and crustaceans. Today, hardly any fish can be caught apart from certain exotic specimens, which have apparently migrated there because of increased water temperatures.

When you add to this that veritable islands of plastic waste several times larger than France or Texas have formed by accumulation in the Atlantic and Pacific Oceans, you begin to recognize the harmful effects of an industry so careless about marine ecosystems that it is turning them into the world's ultimate garbage cans. Worse, the amount of plankton, the micro-organism that serves as the primordial food in the marine food chain, has diminished sharply: forty percent since the 1950s from pollution and changes in acidity (which also affects coral, another indirect victim of human activity). Rivers are also strongly affected by pollution, which causes the fish to disappear — as, for example, in China, where eighty percent of rivers no longer contain any fish. All this is accelerating. At this pace, there will be no more fishing industry by 2050 due to a lack of fish. This is a tragedy for fishing communities, which have only piracy as an alternative.

Just as devastating as the lack of food is the fact that since the last mass extinction event 65 million years ago, animal and vegetable species have never disappeared so rapidly. This disappearance represents twenty-five percent of mammals, fifteen percent of birds, fifty percent of reptiles, fifty percent of insects, thirty-three percent of conifers, seventy-five percent of flowering plants, etc. It is simply colossal. A species disappears every ten minutes. In reality, the exact figures are unknown, since we do not know how many species exist on earth. Estimates vary between 1.5 million and 100 million. What's certain is that such extinctions — due to deforestation, the disappearance of habitats, over-fishing, desertification, pollution from herbicides and insecticides, monoculture and what not — is making ecosystems even more fragile and leading them to collapse.

Everyone knows pollutants are dangerous, but the danger is generally underestimated. Besides killing the animals who interfere with them, pollutants cause deformities, changing the animals' social and reproductive behavior, and becoming more concentrated the farther you go up the food chain, ending up in the body of the ultimate predator — man. Cancers have never been more common. Fifteen percent of American women have enough mercury in their bodies to render pregnancies risky.

Natural balances are what made life possible. As soon as they are undermined, the risk of illnesses and poisoning rises. We are destroying useful species, as the worrisome mass death of bees demonstrates.

Humanity needs the multitude of blessings that plants, insects, and microbes bring. To destroy biodiversity is to commit suicide.

This fall in biological and alimentary diversity is reflected in the disappearance of a number of varieties of cultivated grains. In the U.S., the National Center for the Preservation of Genetic Resources compared the number of varieties sold in 1903 with those sold in 1983. The results speak for themselves:

VARIETY	1903	1983
Beets	288	17
Cabbages	544	28
Corns	307	12
Lettuces	497	36
Melons	338	27
Peas	408	25
Radishes	463	27
Squash	341	40
Tomatoes	408	79
Cucumbers	285	16

This diminution follows the same proportions for cereals, rice, and animals destined for breeding. This erosion of the genetic base leaves us fragile in the face of diseases or parasites tied to one of the species we depend on.

Is it possible to get people to manage the whole of nature better through economic principles? This is the question Alain de Benoist tries to answer in his book *Demain, la décroissance! Penser l'écologie jusqu'au bout* ("Tomorrow, Decline: Thinking Ecology through to the End"). The problem is that up to now, no measures have been able to prevent a global deterioration of the situation. Prohibitions have rarely been binding, and even more rarely respected. Taxes and fines are often laughable compared to the damage caused. Ecological practices, however fine, are insufficient to reverse general tendencies. The "polluter pays principle," which states that pollution ought to be taxed in proportion to the damage caused, has been applied here and there, but results have not been conclusive. Worse, studies have even shown that tricks have enabled certain enterprises to enrich themselves on the backs of taxpayers. "Pollution permits" could only be priced according to a made-up schedule based on guesswork, for it is impossible to determine the total price of an act of pollution — we do not know the long-range consequences. As for the "precautionary principle," how are risks to be evaluated? Who shall determine what measures will be taken? Political decision-makers? They are bound to a short-term electoral logic. Experts? They are often named by commissions answerable to political power. Scientists? They will be under suspicion of lobbying. Industrialists? They are blind to long- term and even medium-term fallout. And public opinion is far from being more enlightened; indeed, it is manipulated by media belonging to large industrial corporations.

All these problems are connected. If a water shortage begins, we will need oil to run the drills to dig new wells and run the pumps. If the price of oil rises, the result will be a steep rise in the price of foodstuffs. If we burn more oil and coal, there will be more pollution and greenhouse gases will keep building up. If deforestation increases in order to obtain more land for agriculture, we lose biodiversity and destroy ecosystems important for our survival. There is a good chance that whatever we do, we shall set in motion destructive cycles difficult to stop.

The ecosystem of which man is a part, and on which he depends, is fragile. It is on the road to collapse.

What can we do? Instead of preserving ecosystems, soils, species, and our environment in general, industrial activity destroys them. Yet these are the true and indispensable — and the only — foundations for all wealth on earth. Without nature, no food. Without food ... I think you get my drift.

Mike yells into the telephone:

"I don't give a damn about the phosphate crisis! What am I going to do about my thousand acres of maize? I need that damned fertilizer, especially since I can't afford diesel for my machines. I'm warning you, if I don't get the fertilizer I paid for, I'm going to miss the English soda market, and then I'll send my lawyers after your ass!"

Mike is in a tough situation. Although he's fifty-eight, he has ten more years of bank payments—bringing the new harvester-threshers up to European standards has cost him dearly ... and then he has already sold the futures on his harvest ... and this is not the time for a fertilizer shortage. He knows that his yields have been going down. It seems the soil is not like it was before. Too weak, the expert said two years ago. And the dryness doesn't help. Not a drop of rain in three months. Incredible. In forty-five years of work, he has never seen that. At least he has been able to water thoroughly—not like the farm next door, where there is no water for the pigs. So much the better, thinking about the mountains of shit produced by the pig factor! Pew!

<<what's good for wall street is bad for america.

paul krugman

economist

/2011/

<<the american federal reserve is neither american, nor federal, nor a reserve.

eustace c. mullins

researcher

//1923–2010//

<<it is well enough that the people of the nation do not understand our banking and monetary system, for if they did, I believe there would be a revolution before tomorrow morning.

henry ford

industrialist

//1864–1947//

<<the current monetary system, with the central role of the dollar in commercial exchanges and as a reserve currency, is a product of the past.

hu jintao

president of the people's republic of china

/2011/

<<inflation is like toothpaste. once it is out of the tube, it is impossible to get back in.

karl otto pöhl

economist

/1995/

The End of the Financial System

WE HAVE SEEN THAT WE LIVE in a world with ever more people, ever less oil and resources, and which is in danger of suffering nutritional and ecological crises. In such a world, economic growth is nothing less than a *necessity*.

The idea of economic growth seems natural to us today, but is, in fact, a new idea. It was unknown during the greater part of human history, when men sought merely to survive and reproduce their social structures, while marginally improving the conditions of their existence. Growth is the principal characteristic of the industrial economy. What's more, in the past century, growth has become an obsession, to such a point that recessions are called periods of "negative growth." You see this in all discourse and commentary: growth is good, the opposite is bad. We want more growth, more trade, more prosperity, more, more, always more. This economic growth has been made possible by the use of fossil energy; thus, what most people call "wealth" — digits in bank accounts — is really the product of more primary resources.

In any case, we must recognize that in the meteoric economic growth of the past two centuries, certain activities remain close to the main source of wealth. The activities that really contribute to prosperity are those connected to the production of energy and industrial goods, agriculture, research and technological progress, medical care, etc. But we see that for several years, the West has no longer been dominant in these areas. It is losing power. If we take the first economic power, the United States, as our benchmark, we see that it is in a phase of steep decline.

UNITED STATES IN 1950	UNITED STATES IN 2010
Greatest producer and exporter of oil worldwide	Greatest importer of oil worldwide
Greatest producer and exporter of industrial and consumer products	Greatest importer of industrial and consumer products
Creator of jobs and wealth	Destroyer of industrial jobs through outsourcing
Practically self-sufficient in all resources	Greatest worldwide importer of natural resources
Greatest worldwide creditor	Greatest worldwide debtor
Destination for skilled immigrant labor	Destination for the masses of unskilled labor
40 workers for every retiree	3.3 workers for every retiree

More than fifty percent of manufactured products bought by Americans and Europeans are imported. For the first time in two centuries, the West is not master of the game anymore. Three words can explain this failure: blindness, greed, and arrogance. Political and economic leaders bear a crushing responsibility. For years, we have watched the rise of Asia in fascination, only to discover, too late, that it was due to our aid and financing. By exporting our work and know-how, we have created the conditions for new dependence.

Everywhere in the West, the social elevator seems definitively blocked. Americans themselves are feeling dubious about the "American Dream." In Europe and in the U.S., by exporting jobs through off-shoring and outsourcing, business leaders and politicians have implicitly betrayed the confidence of their employees and constituents and trampled upon the social contract that cements a nation. In order for our current economic system to function at its peak—and to maximize the present to the detriment of the future and the profits of a tiny number of privileged persons to the detriment of the rest of humanity—all logistical, political, moral and cultural barriers had to be blown up. It became a *fait accompli* with the end of the Soviet Union. This is when the Indian and Chinese way of thinking changed, opening a source of cheap labor to the West. A process was quickly established for transferring Western jobs and industries to emerging countries. This globalization accelerated the dismantling of the industrial infrastructure that had enabled Europe and then the U.S. to dominate the world.

This process isn't "liberalism" (or "hyper-liberalism" as it's sometimes called in Europe): it's socialism for the rich, disguised with the tinsel of the "market" and "liberalism." Globalization is an ideal way to privatize the profits of big companies (by off-shoring production), socialize the losses (obtaining subsidies for the social costs of unemployment caused by local companies), then — the height of brazenness — obtaining state aid, i.e., taxpayer funding, for themselves whenever they are losing money. Never has an investment in lobbying been so profitable!

Globalization has also permitted large-scale distributors to massacre small businesses and artisans with cut-rate prices, made possible by economies of scale and production carried out in low-cost lands that are less particular about working conditions. These small businesses and artisans, however, were the heart of the social fabric, not only thanks to their work, useful in itself, but because their activity strengthened the communal bonds of their neighborhoods, towns, or regions. In Western Europe, for example, we first outsourced to Eastern Europe for five-euro-a-day wages, then to Asia for ninety-nine-cents-a-day wages. We have destroyed the economic topsoil of our nations in exchange for cheap products.

Alas, the multinationals are bound to no country. Nomadic and fatherless, nearly all of them are installed in financial Elysium. They pay very little in taxes, thanks to opaque accounting games, costs and income cleverly spread between subsidiaries of their complex organisms. Often, these large groups benefit from generous subsidies, where their local contribution is insignificant. In heavily off-shored areas, there is desolation: the closure of a factory that was often the only local source of employment can ruin a whole town after causing the professional and social death of its inhabitants. The Detroits and Coventrys of the world are more and more numerous.

Economic liberalism was originally just a synonym for free competition and free enterprise, both of which I am fond of; it meant access to capital, the right to do business without bureaucratic barriers, and transparency. The "liberalism" that predominates in today's global economy is something altogether different. (Edward Luttwak has termed it "turbo-capitalism.") There are no examples in world history of such a procedure: business leaders begin by killing off employment in their own neighborhoods in order to transfer it to countries whose low salaries and lack of social rights they like. Then, faced with the growing demands of the host country (whose role is getting stronger on the world stage), they agree to kill off innovation by letting it be seized. This is what the French journalist Eric Laurent describes in his book *The Scandal of Off-Shoring*: "The Rise of China and India is Built Upon the Future Cadaver of the West."

The human cost of these tribulations is as great in China and India as in the West. The real violence done to the workers of emerging countries, as well as that inflicted on Western workers whose jobs have been off-shored, is terrible. Workers who have not yet been off-shored no longer feel certain of loyal and predictable employers and are ever more subject to a Darwinian competition amongst themselves. Suppliers are forced to struggle fiercely against one another to survive. All of this is, theoretically, for the benefit of the consumer, who, soon to be out of work or in a precarious situation, will no longer have the means of consuming anyway! In order to obtain a short-term benefit, Western businesses have ruined the citizens and workers in their own countries and furnished future adversaries with the means to dominate them. Only one in three employees who has lost his job in Europe and the United States will find a new one, and always with lower pay. The fall in income and purchasing power of Western households and employees is accelerating. This is especially true for the middle class, which is becoming a class of the working poor, obliged to make increasing use of their credit cards to maintain their lifestyle.

Working longer, for less

Globalization has been a real maelstrom for wealthy countries, dragging them down, causing and accelerating de-industrialization, unemployment, precariousness, the emigration of capital, off- shoring, and slower productivity. American economist and Nobel Prize winner Joseph Stiglitz says outright:

> Playing ostrich by burying our heads in the sand and pretending that everybody will benefit from globalization is madness. The problem with globalization today comes precisely from the fact that few in the West will benefit, while the majority will suffer from it.

All this is decided by strangely-behaved elites. They hold the political, economic, and financial power. They are self-satisfied and devoted to self-worship, endowed with a lack of empathy toward those they place in difficulty. They like to evoke the supposed benefits of globalization, while these accelerate the decline of their own countries. Homogenous, nomadic, cosmopolitan, and working in networks, these elites disdain the human reality of their fellow-citizens and have little care for fates of the nations that host them.

It's starting to show.

At the beginning of the 1910s, the American banker J. P. Morgan estimated that the capitalist system could not function if the difference between the salaries of the directors and the workers went beyond a factor of thirty or forty. It is presently above one thousand! The twenty percent best-off Americans contribute half of consumer spending. The remaining eighty percent are quickly becoming impoverished, falling into spiraling debt that has entirely removed them from the cycle of investment and savings. Europe will approach the same statistics within a few years. In the world, the richest 1 percent possess twenty-three percent of the total wealth.

It's starting to show more and more.

What we're also starting to see is rising debt levels in Western countries. All are accumulating debt rapidly, and for some, it is dangerously high (Japan, the United States, Italy, France, Germany, the UK, Spain, Belgium, etc.). Take the U.S., for example: we see in the following graph that the growth of its national debt is impressive — seventeen trillion in 2013. You will notice that the curve looks familiar — it's exponential!

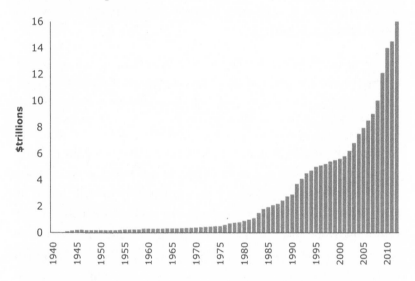

To understand how much a trillion is — a thousand billion — you must picture it in concrete terms. New hundred dollar bills are roughly one millimeter when stacked. One hundred thousand bills would be necessary to make a one meter high stack, and 100 million to reach a kilometer. A trillion is a million millions; it would represent a stack of hundred dollar bills one hundred kilometers high.

The graph below shows the public debt of the United States added to household debt, financial debt, corporate debt, etc. The figure is even more impressive: more than fifty trillion dollars!

According to certain economists, debt ought to include banks' contingent liabilities. With that addition, the true debt of the United

States would be two hundred or three hundred trillion dollars! These are dizzying numbers, and, in the end, mean just one thing: *bankruptcy*.

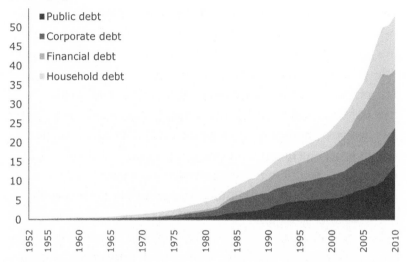

This is not only the fate of the United States. It is a situation that stretches all across the West. Indeed, if total debt (federal + financial + household, etc.) is measured as a percentage of GDP, then Japan and some European countries are revealed to have dizzying levels of indebtedness.

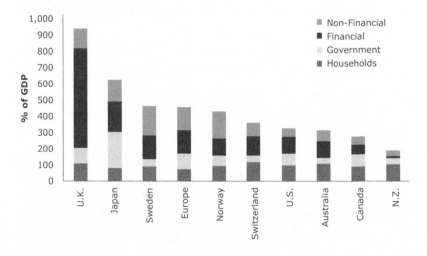

Why this explosion of debt?

Since the 1980s, Western economies, especially those of the U.S. and U.K., have become excessively financialized and excessively service-oriented, no longer producing as much real wealth (raw materials, industrial, or agricultural products). By not remaining competitive on an international scale, they have become, above all, gigantic debt-generators. The fractional-reserve system has allowed public and private banks to over-leverage their creation of credit (which means, for you and me, *debt*). The monetary system today is no longer founded on a standard commodity such as gold or silver, but, numerated in paper and digits, could potentially be expanded infinitely. The American Federal Reserve has generated money and credit at a rate never before attained in its history. This growth in the money supply does not correspond to any real new wealth. Worse, for sixty years, politicians have not stopped creating spending programs to finance their electoral promises: more welfare and entitlement programs, more subsidies to appease various pressure groups, more allocations and "pork" of all sorts for interest groups, more foreign-policy adventures... It doesn't matter that the real economy cannot generate enough reasonable tax revenue to finance them all. Debt is there to make up for the loss. The abundant offer of all sorts of easy credit is what allows the citizens to accumulate so much private debt. Gone are the days when you had to save first in order to spend. In the age of "everything right now," it's easy to get credit to buy real estate, to meet current consumption or even to play the stock market; when the resulting speculative bubbles pop, new ones are created.

This shocking belief—that the important thing economically is to get people to spend more—could be presented to the world as a new social philosophy. British economist John Maynard Keynes (1883–1946) and his disciples blame what they consider unsatisfactory about the economic situation on the insufficient tendency of people to spend. To make people prosperous, it's not an increase in production that's necessary, but an increase in spending. The idea of "propensity to consume" allows Keynes to consider savings as a remaining balance, a residue, what's left after consumption, a passive act.

This way of thinking is so universally accepted that our usual way of measuring a country's Gross National Product does not take the effect of debt into account. It completely ignores it. If, for example, it was necessary to borrow six dollars to invest in a venture, and thus create one additional dollar of profit, which would and should be added to the GNP, bizarrely, only that one dollar is counted and not the debt required to obtain it. For any individual or company, the debt must be listed as a liability on pain of fraud. But not when governments do it!

GNP also takes no account of the impoverishment resulting from the exhaustion of natural resources. That impoverishment should be deducted from the amount to obtain the real wealth. In any case, you can see that growth is zero or even negative, since all raw materials and all natural forms of energy being consumed today are essentially lost to future generations. Much like a compulsive gambler in a casino, debt begins in an *ad hoc* and seemingly acceptable manner. One must invest in productive assets like new roads, bridges, and other infrastructure. Then, social programs must be put in place (retirement funds, unemployment benefits, etc.) or public interest programs (primary education, universities, hospitals, etc.). Sometimes a war must be financed. Then one goes further into debt to finance a *permanent* national defense system. Then preventive wars must be fought, since strategic industries (or those supposed to be strategic) must be subsidized. Finally, a complex bureaucracy is needed to manage all these programs and activities. The political and economic decision-makers are so caught up in this mechanism that no one has a personal stake in changing the system. There are careers at stake, habits and, above all, the fear of disturbing something that seems to be working so well. Every time, experts comfort us in our daily habits and explain that this time, it'll be different. "Have confidence in us!"

This process is not peculiar to our modern societies. The citizens of Imperial Rome got free bread every day. It was a pledge of social stability, but for the Roman state it involved colossal purchases of Egyptian grain. Soon, to protect the grain, it was necessary to mobilize great navies and armies. It became impossible to resist the temptation of using these forces to conquer, occupy, and secure for themselves the source of supply.

In history, every time a nation has tried to live beyond its means through debt creation, it was unable to control it — which caused the collapse of its economy. When you inject ever more colossal sums into an economy at an ever accelerating rate, you get an artificial boom effect, which ends as soon as further fiduciary resources are no longer available on the loan market. The flight to the remaining real resources (gold, silver, land, productive assets) accelerates. Then the entire system may collapse, as happened in Weimar Germany, in Uruguay, in Argentina, and recently in Zimbabwe. The Austrian economist Ludwig von Mises (1881–1973), Keynes's adversary, thought that "debt [was] everywhere and always the antechamber of bankruptcy."

Let's now look at how this debt functions, and what its impact on the economy really is.

First, let's define "inflation": inflation occurs when monetary growth is greater than the production of goods and services. Higher prices are, ultimately, a consequence of inflation (even if these don't show up immediately).

Now let us agree on a simple and down-to-earth definition of "debt": a debt is a claim on future *wealth*. Now, all wealth is the fruit of human labor. A debt, therefore, is *a claim on future human labor*.

Debt operates on the principle of the future repayment of principle and interest. Since a creditor can reinvest his interest payments (i.e., turn them into more debt), he can, in essence, earn interest on interest. Debt expansion thus follows a non-linear function, which, as we have seen before, is … *Anyone? Anyone?* … yes, *exponential*. (Those in the back of the class, please pay attention!).

So, if debt is not paid or cannot be paid, it's necessary to work forever and, in this case, *debt is slavery*.

With every increase in debt, the creditor presumed that in order to be able to pay the debt and the interest, the future is going to be bigger than the present. And not just a little bigger, but exponentially bigger. More cars bought and sold, more houses constructed, more salaries paid, more taxes and duties collected, more oil consumed, exponentially more. Always MORE!

Well, if more and ever more is needed, and we are certain that nothing can grow forever, how do you think this is going to end?

The plain and inevitable result will be that a vast amount of what is considered wealth is going to *disappear*, go up in smoke, because there is too much debt upon a future whose potential for growth is too limited.

So how does one get out of debt? There are three ways:

1. **Pay it off.** For this, more productivity and growth are needed, which will be difficult in a world with finite resources. Alternatively, state revenues can be raised by raising taxes, which is rarely popular, especially if it is used to pay the interest on the debt rather than for an investment that will directly benefit the electorate. Another way is to reduce state expenditures by implementing an austerity program, a measure which will also not be very popular. Russia, for instance, did pay off its debt after ten years of painful sacrifices.

2. **Do not pay it off (default on it).** Defaulting is easy: you simply no longer pay your debts. It is extremely effective. Let's take an example: a pension fund owns 10 billion in claims upon the debt of a company such as Nestlé, L'Oréal, Coca-Cola, or Siemens. If these companies go bankrupt, they default on their debts and, once the productive assets have been liquidated, the claims are no longer worth anything. In that case, the retirees have 10 billion less to divide among themselves. *Presto!* Their incomes and standards of living sink. Sometimes it is necessary for companies and individuals to go bankrupt and renege on their obligations. But this is a very difficult policy for any *country* to follow: the process entails sacrifice, which politicians and populations want to avoid.

With a default, there can be no more refinancing of public debt, and thus there will be no more liquidity; the country will come to a stop (at least temporarily). In the beginning, the nation will become a pariah and others will fear lending it any more money. No other choice will remain but to reestablish the currency (or establish a new one) at a very low exchange rate. Politically, default is often a non-starter, since it risks creating unemployment and enormous poverty; governments also likely fear that it paves the way for extremist politics.

That said, default is an honest option and, in many cases, can establish a new basis for a productive economy after the initial pain subsides. Argentina defaulted in the early 2000s and eventually recovered. Iceland, too, defaulted after the 2008 subprime financial crisis and recovered quite quickly (thanks to the help of some significant investments and bailouts from Russia.)

3.   Print Money. This is the easiest short-term solution. It also involves the worst *long-term* consequences. Because the destructive effects of this policy are deferred until they become someone else's problem, this is what the great majority of nations saddled with a large debt have done, and will always do, all the while claiming that *this time it will be different!* But since the laws of economics, like the laws of physics, are the same wherever you are, whether in Washington or Zimbabwe, things do not turn out differently. Massive money printing always causes a wave of inflation (eventually). This is what happens when artificially created liquidity is diffused through the economy, when states are forced to monetize their debts because no one wants to finance them any longer. Interestingly, the money and credit created by the Federal Reserve in its ongoing "Quantitative Easing," as well as in similar programs by Japanese and European central banks, is also used to buy equities — and thus inflate the stock markets. This has created a synthetic and uneasy sense of euphoria among those with investments, without any change in the real economy to justify these levels. At the time this book was being prepared for publication in mid-2013, America's Dow Jones Industrial Index was at an all-time high … just waiting to have the rug pulled out from underneath it. The first dire effect of money printing is, paradoxically, a *fall* in the price of certain assets (or "deflation"). This is caused by the harsh competition between producers and distributors to stay afloat. Assets are sold off: cars, equipment, stock, etc. There are year-round sales. At the start, the effects on purchasing power are positive (with prices falling, each dollar can buy more), but soon, as the money supply continues to grow, you get galloping inflation. The cost of staple products in particular rises quickly. As happened in Germany between 1921 and 1923, people traded their cars for food. There is usually a risk that this will coincide with a phase of "stagflation," during which the economy experiences weak or negative growth, while monetarily-induced inflation is raging. In the final phase, you get the big plunge into hyperinflation — a paroxysm of inflation — characterized by money losing all its value and ceasing to act as a medium of exchange; people don't just want to spend money as soon as they get it — they refuse to use it for their transactions or to save it. In this situation, truck and barter, as well as the "black market," are substituted for monetary exchange as the economy collapses. Analyst Pierre Leconte, president of the Monetary Forum of Geneva, commented on this subject, 20 December 2010:

> Over these last few decades, central bankers have been the greatest counterfeiters in history; governments no longer have any way of avoiding hyperinflation, depression, and the collapse of all forms of paper money, one after the other. This will precede, coincide with, or follow the collapse of paper assets (stocks and bonds) founded on a pyramid of unsecured debt. This process is just now beginning in the West. Keynesian measures cannot stop it, but only postpone it for a time — all the while worsening the final outcome.

The result of credit expansion is always general impoverishment. The therapeutic treatment for hyperinflation is that the state takes over the economy by nationalizing it. This therapy often fails because of the nature of bureaucracy and the state's lack of experience in managing enterprises. Meanwhile, the population forgoes its savings and investment to simply stay alive. Ludwig von Mises offers a good image of the situation: "Having recourse to inflation to overcome passing difficulties is like burning one's furniture to warm one's house."

In the following graph, you can see that the price of goods in the U.S., expressed in constant 2005 dollars, remained about the same for most of the country's history, in spite of short periods of inflation in connection with wars (the War of Independence and of 1812, the Civil War, and the First and Second World Wars). Then in 1945, and especially since 1971, prices have soared. Inflation is underway.

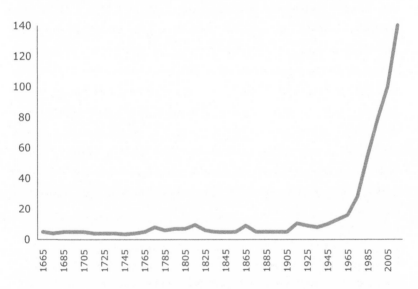

Given the level of their debt, the situation of the U.S. is quite worrisome, but we must remember that it is still the world's largest economy and, above all, the greatest military power. The American dollar is still the world's reserve currency, and the currency in which oil prices are negotiated. Since 1945, the world has gotten so used to the economic dominance of the United States, that its collapse is, for most, simply unimaginable. But the United States is no longer an industrial power. At the beginning of 2011, China replaced it as the biggest manufacturing nation. Between 2000 and 2008, American industries eliminated twenty-five percent of their jobs. According to some estimates, there are no longer more than 8 million industrial jobs in the United States, a country with more than 300 million people. Manufacturing's share of the economy has gone from twenty-eight percent in 1953 to eleven percent in 2009. By way of comparison, German industry has always been around twenty-five percent. By mid-2013, the national debt of the United States stood at some sixteen trillion, more or less one hundred percent of GDP. According to Congress's conservative estimate, it will reach twenty trillion by 2015, or 102 percent of GNP. Servicing the interest on this debt costs between twenty-four percent and thirty percent of total government receipts. But this is an optimistic estimate, since it supposes a growth rate of between 2.6 percent and 4.6 percent per year between 2010 and 2019, which is very high. Congress even foresees a debt of 180 percent of GNP for 2035!

Today, the United States is technically bankrupt. No growth will allow the repayment of what is owed, contrary to what the public is made to believe. The situation is certainly more serious than financial analysts dare say: they function on the assumption that U.S. debt is "as good as gold." (Until the summer of 2011, U.S. Treasuries were rated AAA, the highest possible score, by Standard & Poor's.) Is U.S. debt really of better quality than China's, which possesses a three-trillion-dollar currency reserve and whose government has practically no debt?

Swiss journalist Myret Zaki expounds the thesis of the collapse of the American economic model in her book *The End of the Dollar*. First of all, she shows that the American figures are a vast deception: GNP is disconnected from reality by methodological changes and constant *redefinition*, which go almost unnoticed by the general public. Real GNP is far lower than what is published — a thesis maintained as far back as 2002 by French historian Emmanuel Todd in his book *After the Empire*.

Inflation is greatly underestimated. The American stock market hides inflation in its profits. Productivity gains are real in certain sectors, but so much of the population has been turned into a nation of bartenders, nurses, and federal employees. The unemployment rate is twice the official figures. The Federal Reserve's balance sheets are faked. According to *Shadow Government Statistics* (www.ShadowStats.com), the real unemployment rate is not the official figure of 9.8 percent but 22.4 percent for December 2010, and twenty-three percent in early 2013—quite close to the twenty-five percent of the Great Depression. Likewise, according to this research site, GDP growth in 2012 wasn't two percent but *negative* two percent.

It is also estimated that more than half the products that make up the Consumer Price Index, the typical American "household shopping basket," are picked so as to underestimate inflation. For example, if the price of steak rises, it is replaced with a less expensive "equivalent" such as hamburger. Inflation is already on the march and accelerating: on average, worldwide basic food prices rose forty-eight percent between October 2009 and October 2010. Savers and consumers no longer have reliable information concerning their purchasing power, their investments, or their savings, and are on their way to pauperization. This group of fictional indicators is self-sustaining and self-promoting. The process of "creative accounting" that allows the figures to be prettied up makes the Greek and Irish politicians look like amateurs at the game: American statistics have become an exercise in public relations aimed at making the United States look good in international comparisons conducted by the International Monetary Fund, the World Bank, and the Organization for Economic Cooperation and Development. The mechanical retouching of official information given out by economic authorities resembles an exercise in disinformation and marketing.

Finally, one might ask what value an economy has where everything the Americans possess is owned by somebody else. Every dollar is borrowed, everything is mortgaged, there are no more real funds:

cars belong to leasing companies, houses to banks; retirement capital and health payments require financing that will diminish because of demography and the economic crisis; the state is taking in less and less revenue and, by losing its AAA rating, the debt will get ever more expensive.

The United States can no longer be the locomotive of global growth and continue to export its inflation to the world, which has already had enough of absorbing the effects of U.S. financial bubbles and toxic debt products. According to Nouriel Roubini, Marc Faber, Max Keiser and other analysts, a dollar crash is in the making. It will be inevitable. The principle global risk at the moment is an American debt crisis. The world's largest economy is nothing more than a gigantic illusion. What can you say about an economy that borrows fifty trillion dollars, paying four trillion a year interest on it, in order to produce fourteen trillion dollars of GNP? If the U.S. were a corporation, it would immediately be liquidated.

It is only a matter of time before we witness the bursting of the giant debt and dollar bubbles. The dollar has already lost 97 percent of its value since 1913, the year the Federal Reserve was created. The 17th-century French philosopher (and businessman) Voltaire said that "a paper currency founded only on confidence in the government that created it, always ends by returning to its intrinsic price — zero." Similarly, Pierre Leconte quipped to me in an interview, "If hyper-inflation were a way of creating wealth, Zimbabwe would be a rich country." In other words, the ultimate fate of the dollar is certain; it is only the timing that is in question. The mountain of dollars printed in these last years by the Federal Reserve is nothing but the biggest speculative bubble in history, and it is going to end in tears. The only remaining question is how much further harm is going to be inflicted upon the world economy.

What *is* different this time is that the dollar is not just a national currency (like the Weimar mark that blew up in 1924); the greenback is the linchpin of the global economy and postwar financial system.

This means that the dollar could have much longer staying power than national fiat currencies; it means that it could ostensibly be strengthened by a global panic; but it ultimately means that the consequences of the dollar's demise will be all the more catastrophic.

In the face of so much risk, who is going to purchase American debt? Japan and China have done so up to now, but each has been replaced as the greatest subscriber to American bonds by the Federal Reserve Bank, which is thus buying back the debt it is itself issuing! The Swiss analyst Marc Faber "guarantees 100 percent that the U.S. is going to experience a hyperinflation like that of Zimbabwe." Nouriel Roubini concludes that "the American financial system is insolvent."

This isn't all. American debt is only the tip of the iceberg. One must add unfunded liabilities for future income programs such as Social Security, Medicare, and pensions for 80 million baby boomers. Beginning in 2011, these latter will have to withdraw parts of their retirement funds in order to support their standard of living: this will unleash a long-term stock market sell-off like we have never seen. As far as industry is concerned, even if the value of the dollar falls by fifty percent, America will still not be competitive with China, a country in which the average salary is five to ten dollars a day (as opposed to 120 dollars a day in the U.S.) It is not surprising that to postpone their inevitable fall, their only escape route is a headlong rush forward!

There is one other option that should not be discounted — war. However immoral or unstable, war can be a means to overcome the effects of an economic depression. For governments, it's tempting. There are many advantages to waging war: it mobilizes patriotic sentiment, gets industry rolling, turns unemployed workers into cannon fodder, and, if you win, you can seize the resources of the vanquished or impose your domination on them! And there are plenty of enemies to be made. The only problem is that whereas it is known how wars begin, there is no way to predict how they will develop and end. I'll admit, it's a simplistic view, but the U.S. ought to have learned its lesson following the Korean and Vietnam Wars, and the disastrous and costly adventures (three trillion dollars at least) of Iraq and Afghanistan. So what to do? Another war against words ("terror," "drugs" ... why not "dandruff"?) or against a small-time power (Yemen, Syria, etc.)? A "humanitarian" war, in which the goal is (of course) to bring "democracy" and "human rights" to middle-sized countries (Iran, Venezuela, Syria, North Korea, Burma, Nigeria, etc.), would seem to fit the bill, but it would involve an expensive and dangerous occupation, unless others can be coerced or convinced to do it (as in Libya or Mali). All that remains then is thermonuclear war against Russia or China, which would be much more impressive and could actually provide a long-term solution to the problems of over-population, economic competition, and the exhaustion of resources. *Kaboom!* In 20 minutes, everything would be solved. Except that here, too, nothing is certain, and the nuclear blowback from the "Commie scum" could make this option unrealistic. I sure hope no one in power today is so insane as to go down the path that was satirized in Stanley Kubrick's movie *Doctor Strangelove!*

More realistically (hopefully!), the United States will not go out with a bang, but will instead complete a transition, in less than a century, from a real, sustainable economy to a terminally sick one. America will be mixed — with pockets of astounding wealth, innovation, and productivity and, sadly, great swaths that will resemble the Third World. The series of state bankruptcies like California's and Illinois' are harbingers of what's to come. All these transformations represent a tragic loss of potential. Some day, historians will laugh at the silliness of our contemporaries, who have raised to the status of official truth the fairy tale that infinite growth is possible by printing paper without practicing austerity, as if consuming on credit were the same as producing wealth. "If throwing money out of a helicopter were a viable monetary policy, it would have been discovered a long time ago, and we would all be living in a world of infinite prosperity today," writes Richard Duncan, financial analyst and author of *The Dollar Crisis*. The very professional American Armed Forces are not deceived; as Admiral Mike Mullen, Chairman of the Joint Chiefs of Staff, declared recently: "The national debt is the greatest threat to national security." In the end, it is not the "Clash of Civilizations" that we must fear, but the collapse of the social and political system following the implosion of our financial, economic, and monetary mechanisms.

Have measures been taken? In April, 2011, after long, stormy debates, Congress passed a law to reduce its expenses by $35 billion, including a $1.6-billion reduction in the defense budget. This represents one percent of the 2011 budget, or two weeks of expenses. This is a joke! Between 2008 and 2011, the American government increased spending by thirty percent — and then tries, painfully, to reduce it again by one percent. The process is out of control.

So… what? Death to America? Yankee go home? No, because the European countries are also on the edge of the financial abyss. The debt is such that the PIIGS (Portugal, Ireland, Italy, Greece, and Spain) of the Eurozone are going to have to declare bankruptcy sooner or later and return to their old national currencies, which they must then devalue (it is their only hope of reestablishing their competitiveness over the long term). Germany and a few other Northern European states, being better managed and undergoing austerity measures themselves, are not going to ruin themselves to allow others to live eternally beyond their means. All the more so as the European Central Bank has neither the financial capacity nor the will to buy back this bad debt from Southern and Eastern Europe; neither are the larger private banks of the eurozone, many of them in bad shape themselves. So the euro is also destined to disappear or split up, and we are going to see the economic crisis of the Southern European countries get worse. One should not count on anything but dogmatism from the EU bureaucracy, whose true nature was revealed in 2005 when France and Ireland voted against the European Constitution. The French government ratified it regardless of the people's vote, and Ireland was asked to vote again with a heavy hint that they'd have to vote again and again until the "right" outcome would be chosen. So much for democracy!

The EU then simply imposed the Lisbon Treaty on its member states, which made a former Italian minister exclaim: "Perfect! We don't even need the people and referenda any more!" Welcome to the E-USSR-K: *The European Union of Soviet Socialist Republics and Kingdoms!*

The inevitable bursting of the Treasury-bond bubble and European debt are going to have an impact on the most vulnerable investors, like retirees, who traditionally considered treasury bonds the safe investment *par excellence.* The shock wave will inevitably expand, bringing with it a strong rise in interest rates. These, being added to an already serious economic crisis, will bring about the inability of households to consume or to repay their debts. The only solution the eurocrats will think of will be the consolidation of public finances through heavy taxation on capital, and through bailouts of the largest banks. Finally, private creditors will probably be "invited" to offer extensions and renegotiate lower interest rates, or lose all their investments. In March 2013, the EU and IMF attempted an incredible "hold-up" of Cyprus bank-account holders, trying to, brazenly, *take* part of the money from savers and businesses to pay part of the country's debt. Robbery, pure and simple. Though that attempt was botched, due to incompetence, risk of social unrest, and pressure by Russia, it shows the unlimited lack of scruples — and common sense — of the European "leadership." Of course, such measures will be unpopular, to say the least, and populist or nationalist governments may reject bailouts by unilaterally deciding upon bankruptcy. These risks may lead to unleashing a panic, a bank-run, with people draining ATMs and banging on bank windows to withdraw their savings *en masse*, thus causing a chain of bank failures. This sort of crisis will be much worse than that of the 1930s. The sums involved are vastly greater, the global economy is much more fragile, and, globally, culture is much less resilient.

The shenanigans in Cyprus — as well as scandals like the collapse of MF Global, in which investors' funds were confiscated by managers — brings into relief the incompetence, megalomania, and unheard-of greed of those in elite positions in financial institutions.

These are the new oligarchs, with power and connections in finance and government; sociopaths like Jon Corzine, Jamie Dimon, and Henry Paulson operate with no consideration for their professional or moral responsibilities to the shareholders and employees who put confidence in them, not to mention the law!

In her book *Third World America*, Arianna Huffington summarizes contemporary capitalism as follows:

> It's not that capitalism isn't working. It's that what we have right now is not capitalism. What we have is corporatism. It's welfare for the rich. It's the government picking winners and losers. It's Wall Street having its taxpayer-funded cake and eating it, too. It's socialized losses and privatized gains.

President Dwight Eisenhower, as he was leaving office, talked honestly about the danger of a military-industrial complex taking power; but in the end, it was the *financial* complex that posed the greatest threat. Wars are possible through the Federal Reserve Money Machine, and while the military-industrial lobby conducts its business offshore, Big Finance runs the country.

Politicians of the Left, Right, and Center are unwilling to confront this elite, or perhaps don't understand it exists. They get elected by promising miracles and delivering a shabby program of *panem et circenses*: subsidies, welfare goodies, imbecilic entertainment, and easy credit; none is willing to speak the truth and announce the blood, sweat, and tears that will be necessary to refound our nations on a sound basis once again. And *après eux, le déluge* ...

Most fundamentally, our civilization has lost sight of the true nature of wealth — natural resources, which are so often hidden from us by the abstraction we call "money." Reality will reassert itself in the coming years, as we experience the end of the financial system.

Kenza is no longer able to make ends meet each month.

She has five hundred dollars a month, including government subsidies, for groceries, diapers for the baby, and children's clothes. Before, she could make it. She is still buying the same products—she's good at making lists. Sugar has gone up, cooking oil has gone up, bread and flour have actually doubled. She racks her brain to find alternatives. She is obviously not the only one having problems with money, since many of her neighbors are selling furniture in the classified ads. There are some really good deals out there: a nearly new sofa for a hundred dollars, a plasma TV screen for fifty dollars! Other people are selling their jewelry. The price of gold seems to be rising lately.

Kenza's husband Mikael has two jobs, one during the day and another, undeclared, at night, "to put the merguez [sausage] in the couscous" as they say in the local slang, but he's afraid the factory may close after the news of the latest layoffs. It seems that the new Chinese owners merely want to copy processes and technology and then shut the money-losing plant. He tries to reassure her by saying that the unions and the government will not allow this to happen. She's not convinced...

In the evenings, the electricity sometimes goes out. It's because of privatization. It seems the state is selling everything off: historic buildings, islands, public services, concessions for managing health insurance. Even unemployment insurance (its name has been changed) has been sold to a private group—it appears the group belongs to the President's brother. Some heads need to roll, as Kenza and Mikael say. The children went to bed early; the television is no longer working. They have nothing to do with themselves but make love.

<<the world is run by very different people from what is imagined by those who are not behind the scenes.

benjamin disraeli

politician

//1804–1881//

<<through the combined force of bayonets, marketing, and television, the western model of civilization has imposed itself on the universe, substituting having for being and commodities for values. In its liberal version, and in its marxist approach, mass production and mass consumption have become the principle engines of society, both an economic and social form of regulation, and a cultural project. every human society has had to embrace the religion of this way of life, which assimilates well-being to the maximum possession of the maximum number of things and bows before the golden calf of the private automobile, plastic wrap, the hamburger, and nuclear electricity.

jean-paul besset

politician

/1992/

<<fascist centralization was never able to achieve what has been achieved by the consumer society.

pier paolo pasolini

filmmaker

/1922–1975/

<<the american people have got to go about their business. We cannot let the terrorists achieve their objective of frightening our nation to the point where we don't conduct business, where people don't shop.

george w. bush

politician

/october 2001/

Global Culture

THE HUMAN BEING is an exceptional animal. He is aware of himself, and aware that he is aware of himself. He is capable of incredible extrapolations, projecting himself into the future, foreseeing potential dangers, and reacting in time. If a human being as an individual has so many capacities, however, what is his behavior like in society, in the midst of his culture?

Cultures, fashioned by their environments and by the shocks they have undergone over the course of ages, may well be neither equal nor morally equivalent. However, one must admit that the only objective criterion for measuring their effectiveness is to ask: *Are they able to survive?*

A culture that survives in its environment for centuries is eminently respectable, however barbaric it may seem to a foreign observer. Such observers are often impudent enough to judge it by their own ethnocentric criteria, which may only be valid in a specific context. Cultures that have *not* survived — which were unable to defend themselves against invaders and internal enemies, which were unable to remain dominant or foresee catastrophes — can only be observed, in the best cases, in museums or history books.

How does it stand with our own culture? Are we able to understand the problems with which we are confronted? Are we able to act effectively for the goal of our collective survival?

First of all, I think it is increasingly erroneous to speak of "cultures" today. Globalization has gradually turned local cultures into a big global one; though it has many aspects, regional variations, and subcultures, this global culture has become dominant and imposed its values upon most of the West (and increasingly, much of the world). This has not happened without damage, without the destruction of local traditions and customs. Of the some 6,000 languages in the world, half are no longer taught and will disappear within a generation. The real "Clash of Civilizations" is between global and traditional cultures, some of which will fight to the death to avoid disappearing. This is tragic, because in the disappearance of distinct societies and peoples, there are so many irremediable losses for the cultural and genetic patrimony of mankind.

So much of global culture comes out of the United States and benefits from the dynamism of that country, from its military victories, its movie industry, and genuinely efficient pragmatism. But the global culture is not at all uniquely American. Its strength lies in allowing the addition of elements from different cultures (Italian pizza, Turkish kebab, Japanese sushi, French perfume…) and transforming the working classes into consumers, thus eliminating the social barriers that once separated producers and consumers. The electronic-gadget industry and the study of frivolity are essential elements for understanding this global society (for which Michel Clouscard and Jean-Claude Michéa have presented valuable analyses).

In the post-WWII years, society evolved away from strict moral doctrines to permissiveness, from traditional and repressive "fascism" (as critics liked to call it) to a new society of unhindered enjoyment, with post-'60 indulgence disguising the economic degradation of the working classes.

This culture is now moving increasingly towards economic liberalism: it acknowledges that market law directs the economy and human activities. It is also libertarian, as it puts personal freedom, individualism, above all else, including morality. Karl Marx already saw this in his time, writing in the *Communist Manifesto*:

Wherever the bourgeoisie has come to dominate, it has destroyed all feudal, patriarchal, idyllic conditions. It has pitilessly torn asunder the motley bands that attached man to his natural superior, leaving no other bond between man than naked self-interest, inexorable "cash payment." It has drowned the most heavenly ecstasies of religious fervor, of chivalrous enthusiasm, of philistine sentimentality in the icy water of egotistical calculation.

I don't feel any real nostalgia for feudalism or the caste system, where men were separated by birth into different social groups and had little hope of changing their material conditions. But one can't help but admit that within two centuries, traditional social structures and conditions have been radically changed.

Consider, for example, the peasants who, by working the land, were the source of all wealth. In the 20th century, the peasantry of Western countries was converted into an industrial (and post- industrial) workforce; so many of their folkways disappeared, or else became cultural displays for tourists. This historical phenomenon has radically changed the relationship between man and his natural life-surroundings, has alienated him from the fruits of his labor, and caused him to lose sight of the interdependency of all the components of nature. Life has become a matter of artifice, an illusion of living disconnected from the earth, no longer aware of the natural equilibrium. This is why global urban culture has nothing but contempt for rural and traditional life. It has become normal to believe that, before the era of industrialization and development, the populations of Third World countries lived in conditions more miserable than today. The contrary is true. Of course, there were no hospitals or modern medicine, and child mortality was high (as in Europe at the same time). But the many narratives of the first voyagers to distant lands concur regarding the lack of poverty, relative material abundance, and good physical health (due to natural selection) that prevailed in the "New World." Like the European peasantry, these populations produced essentially all they consumed and were self-sufficient. The very notion of poverty certainly did not have the sense it does today in our commercial world. According to the African specialist Bernard Lugan, the word "poor" did not exist in most African languages: its closest equivalent was "orphan." Men in traditional societies possessed little but did not consider themselves poor, insofar as they were all bound in a network of social relations, organic communities, and extended families structured as clans. What are today considered *economic* functions correspond to what were then *social* functions.

The first great snag for our new global culture comes from the fact that economic functions cannot entirely respond to human needs. These derive from man's brain, which was fashioned in three great evolutionary stages: reptilian, mammalian, and human. Three types of needs correspond to these stages: physical and emotional needs, and the need for meaning. Man feels fulfilled and happy when these three types of needs are being satisfied. Passive consumption cannot answer all of them. If we want to be physically, emotionally, and intellectually happy, we must be active in these three domains; this can only be accomplished by socialization and the experience of an activity or work that provides meaning.

The great error of socialism was claiming that individuals are not motivated by self-interest and competition. Even when people do something out of love or generosity, they often expect something in return, if only recognition and consideration. The great error of any capitalist ideology is to think people are *only* motivated by materialism and immediate personal interest. Most people set a value on their families and friends that can't be expressed in monetary terms, and they are prepared to make sacrifices — even give their lives — for those they love.

The second fundamental snag for the dream of globalization comes from the fact that life in a global culture involves being ruled by a system that, while appearing to function well, is bound to be unhealthy. This system bears within itself the seeds of self-destruction. Few and weak values and founding myths, management by an increasingly corrupt oligarchy, unbound praise of individualism, futility, and stupidity — this is called "decadence."

Great powers in History, such as Egypt, Persia, Rome, the Spain of Charles V, the Ottoman Empire, France under Louis XIV or Napoleon, Victorian England, Imperial or Nazi Germany, the USSR, China, or the United States of America all required a common founding myth, which gave their people the strength to devote their existence and give their lives in the service and for the glory of their cause.

In Imperial Rome, there reigned the myth of inevitability and the primacy of Roman civilization in relation to others, considered barbarians. The USSR defended the myth of the classless society. Having theoretically removed social and ethnic classes through the Revolution, the Soviets' claim to authority rested on their having created an egalitarian society that fulfilled everybody's needs: they had eliminated excessive wealth and allowed every citizen, even the most humble, the opportunity to improve himself and live in security and dignity. Over the course of decades, and many disenchantments, this powerful myth lost credibility in daily life. At the end of the 1980s, no further great common effort was possible, and the superpower collapsed.

In the United States and the West, the myth is that of the middle class: everyone can dream of obtaining, through honest toil, a simulacrum of landed nobility, symbolized by a freestanding house with a bit of land large enough for a lawn and a parking place. Moreover, the concept of "middle class-ness" is sufficiently vague and flexible to allow persons of genuinely different social classes, having nothing in common but an automobile, to be spoken of in this same way. An automobile is an extension of the personality, a symbol of social success, of seductiveness and sexual potency, a central element of modern civilization — and only possible thanks to petroleum. Without that, the dream collapses.

There are, of course, other Western myths: the omnipotence of the market, which always has a miracle solution for every problem;

that capitalism and democracy are, by definition, the best possible systems; the religion of "human rights," which can justify any action, however malicious, anywhere in the world in the name of a "good" cause: neocolonialism, mass immigration, meddling in the internal affairs of other countries, bombings and invasions of sovereign nations, theft of resources, the kidnapping of children from their culture for adoption, etc.

These myths are constructed on a basis of verifiable truth. After all, the growth and supremacy of the West over a period of centuries *is* impressive. Improvements in our quality of life *are* evidence of the well-founded nature of the values conveyed by these myths. But is this due to our value system, or merely to our access to cheap and abundant fossil fuel? It always comes back to this same question. And now that a country like China, not very democratic or capitalistic (in the liberal sense of the term), is getting along extremely well without these Western values, one may wonder whether a strong causal connection ever existed between liberal democracy and economic success.

The value system tied to global culture has nothing to do with justice, or even being nice. It favors the search for the greatest power and the greatest personal wealth possible. Being rich and powerful is not, in most cases, connected to altruistic attitudes but to narcissism and egotism — that is, sociopathy. It's neither good nor bad, it *is*, but it's interpreted as if it *must* be good. This system gets people to believe that if we all behaved in egotistic and atomized ways (if the worst opportunists, sociopaths, and crooks were put in charge politically and economically) and finally if the rich got richer, this would be good for most of us. It is constructed on a profession of faith, on a sort of religious or magical thought, and not at all upon empirical observation or reality. The system's lucky break was to have coincided with a period of abundant, cheap energy. One of the effects of this faith is to define short-term profit as the ultimate and only objective. This is why companies are supposed to be competitive: to make a profit in order to survive and reward their shareholders. The well-being of employees and any other parameters not directly useful in the short term are neglected.

As in the feudal age, when the sons of lords were trained in war beginning at youth, the children of the well-off classes learn very early on how to be competitive and maximize their profits. Business schools are nothing but factories for creating champions of short-term profit. With long teeth and sharpened claws, the intriguers are ready for anything, servile to the powerful and pitiless with the weak: we have educated generations of war criminals. These CEOs, CFOs, and traders, though they don't chop off limbs with machetes or gas civilians, nevertheless provoke economic dislocations such that millions of lives are ruined. It would be interesting to have a magistrate propose defining *financial crimes against humanity*, crimes as serious as those judged at Nuremberg in 1946. One can imagine that a populist government, faced with public anger, might charge popular tribunals with hearing such cases.

It is easy to see that this model is insupportable in these times of crisis. It's not that it uses industrial processes or market forces to determine prices, or that it is founded on competition and self-interest. The problem is that this system does not recognize the need for limits — limits to the exploitation of resources, limits to competition, limits to inequality, etc. It's like driving a car with an accelerator but no brakes. Modern industrial society is not only ecologically unsustainable but also socially unsustainable. It results in poverty: material poverty in poor countries and emotional poverty in rich countries. The culture of consumption creates false needs, false desires for power, status and wealth instead of satisfying the genuine needs of the senses. This culture constructs an illusion of scarcity so people can satisfy their emotional needs by the act of buying. Finally, it provokes real scarcity in poor countries, where there are already too few resources to cover basic needs: food, drinking water, health, and education.

Whose fault is it? Who built this system?

Westerners born after 1945, known as Baby Boomers, are probably the most irresponsible generation of all time. Sorry, dudes, but here's why. Born into a period of rapid growth, Baby Boomers benefited from a powerful and rich welfare state bringing them education, leisure, and infrastructures beyond historical comparison. All this was the work of the preceding generation that had experienced the Great Depression, the Second World War, and reconstructed everything in the course of the thirty glorious postwar years. The Baby Boomers never really had to strain themselves: too young for the last colonial wars (with the notable exception of the Vietnam War for Americans), never having difficulty finding work, they benefited from all the feats of technology and medicine and spent their youth enjoying themselves and experimenting with drugs and "free love" against a backdrop of rock music. They even allowed themselves, following the "summer of love" and the European "revolutions" of May 1968, the luxury of questioning all that Western civilization had achieved over millennia. Casting aside all morality as an obstacle to immediate enjoyment, they found themselves making money in the 1980s and '90s, and now they are in the driver's seat, showing off their lack of education, their incompetence, and their contempt for the past. Like spoiled children, these Americans and Europeans born after the Second World War have squandered natural and cultural capital for their petty enjoyment. Worse, after accusing their parents' generation of "racism," "fascism," and even "genocide," the Baby Boomers, now entering their dotage, *demand* that their retirement be paid for by the following generation (which is much more deprived than they were.)

The result of these past forty years is the construction of a system founded upon egotism and exploitation, which has filled our hearts with greed, indifference, and violence. Fear, hatred, anger, conflict, and violence are the natural products of a system where wealth is subtly (but ever more visibly) transferred from the poor to the rich, and where the media show the world the immense luxury in which the rich live. The poor are afraid of being unable to escape their poverty, and envy the rich. The rich are afraid the poor will take their wealth by force, or through democratic political methods.

To maintain these wealth differences, walls of various sorts are built. The rich increasingly live in gated communities, and elite groups are working to create institutions and means of doing business that are unaffected by national democratic governments. You only have to look into the Bilderberg Group, the B'nai B'rith, the Trilateral Commission, Skull and Bones, the Bohemian Grove, or similar groups and webs of influence to perceive the attempts at creating a powerful superstructure above the world's nation-states. But then, creating a world government, for example, or putting billionaires in charge, will no more resolve our problems than endless G8 or G20 meetings.

We live in an economic apartheid system where sections of town — and, in some cases, entire countries — have become ghettos for the poor. No one wants you if you are poor, unless you accept being a wretch. The world is divided into three great zones: *rich countries*, where corrupt and corrupting oligarchs reign over progressively stupefied and distracted masses; *emerging countries*, usually undemocratic, where corrupt but not necessarily corrupting oligarchs reign over masses reduced to slavery; and finally *poor countries*, where the very idea of a state only exists episodically. In this latter world, by far the hardest but not necessarily the ugliest, corrupt-and-corrupting oligarchies dominate masses that are kept in poverty and ignorance.

The difference in revenues is considerable: in 2003, the revenue of the 225 largest fortunes in the world was equal to the total revenue of the world's poorest forty-seven percent, i.e., 3.4 billion people. What do these 225 persons do that is extraordinary and indispensable enough to justify such a difference?

Global culture maintains the illusion of wealth by promoting lifestyles that will never be attainable for most of the world, because there are simply not enough resources. In any case, the reality is that over fifty percent of the planet's inhabitants live on less than five dollars a day, and all the advertising in the world will not give them a car, a big house, or meat at every meal — rather, it will frustrate them.

Consumer culture does not understand the meaning of "enough." Millionaires want to be billionaires; billionaires still want more. Everywhere, the rich, able to travel like nomads and with lawyers specializing in finance, pay practically no taxes in comparison to their revenue and their fortunes. (This is becoming increasingly visible on television and the web.) The hatred of the poor for the rich is already considerable, but has not yet taken concrete form.

This will not be long in coming.

Between the rich and the poor is the middle class, and they are having a rather bad time right now. On the one hand, they are under economic pressure from outsourcing and competition; on the other, they are beginning to feel the effects of inflation and have seen their savings pulverized by the ups and downs of the stock market. Finally, they have been in debt for quite a while in order to buy houses or apartments, or sometimes simply to maintain their social status. Having enriched themselves during the first thirty postwar years, for the last thirty, they have been doing nothing but getting poorer and watching their purchasing power dwindle.

Above all, the middle class is suffering psychologically. Advertising sells the idea that qualitative needs can be satisfied quantitatively. It is obviously impossible to satisfy emotional and spiritual yearnings through consumption — at least, beyond the very short moment of satisfaction that a purchase procures, but which soon gives way to a feeling of boredom, dissatisfaction, and even depression. Consumption is a sort of addiction in which the victim requires his *fix* ever more frequently. This syndrome is maintained by shifting fashions, themselves reinforced by a sort of general feminization of society. Advertising sells both illusions and fear. Not only does it indicate that being happy requires being beautiful and rich, but that if you are not, you are a *loser*. From infancy we are bombarded by millions of advertising messages on television, in magazines, and in the street.

These messages create a lot of pressure and command us to be *like the rest*. This is extremely difficult to resist. You only need to have children to observe how early this constant propaganda influences them — and how effectively! Cuban leader Fidel Castro understood this when he declared in one of his speeches: "Advertising constantly distills its poison, giving birth to dreams and illusions, desires impossible to satisfy."

The infantilization of the population is advancing quickly, thanks especially to, quite literally, the promotion of ignorance and stupidity in popular culture — simply watch any music television channel or "reality" show for a while, and you can almost feel your brain cells scream in agony! Deprived of his sense of responsibility, a citizen can no longer be anything but a docile consumer, obedient and immature. Perversely, the educational system is helping move us in this direction, since it is getting ever less effective. Children's food is too fatty and sugary; everybody watches too much television (twenty-eight hours per week in North America!); the urban and suburban environments are not favorable to sensory development and stimulation; distraction by advertisements, smartphones, instant messaging, online social networks, and video games is constant; overstimulating leisure activities are overabundant; children don't learn to appreciate calm and silence; and finally, alas, teachers are failing to encourage and inspire the brightest students. The function of school is no longer to teach subjects or how to learn and think critically; it is to *institutionalize* children from their earliest years. The most gifted learn to obey and perform, while the rest are progressively prepared for a life of unemployment or precarious, underpaid dull trades. A genuinely educated person, by contrast, is someone with a free mind who is eager to explore the world on his own. If his choice is to obtain well-paid work, why not! But the current educational system only succeeds in producing graduates with no other choice than to join the labor market on the terms decided upon by their future masters. They teach us that financial success is more important than personal fulfillment, that having a career is more important than family life, and that failure is not an option. No one wants to be a loser. The crux of the problem is that, since the aim is to prepare a person for being an immediately productive link in a great economic machine, instead of acquiring universal knowledge and developing a large horizon of thought, the student receives knowledge which rapidly becomes obsolete due to technological change.

Another effect of modern education is that the last generations of the West — Generation X, the children of the Baby Boomers, and, even more so, Generation Y, their children's children — have been deprived of stories, myths, and well-defined traditions, which humans have cherished for hundreds of thousands of years. These children are badly prepared for living outside the artificial system constructed by the petroleum civilization: they have themselves become industrial products, placed since birth in a social context where they are evaluated, classed, and enclosed in a series of institutions that prepare them for a life of work, production, and consumption. Even if the wisdom of the ages were set before them, one is doubtful of their ability even to understand it.

As for science, what is it good for any longer? The most brilliant minds are increasingly mobilized to create consumer products, very profitable temporary treatments for chronic and recurring illnesses, or to manufacture products with planned obsolescence, in order to assure their replacement every few years. From shoes to washing machines: quantity and change rather than solid durability! Where did the sturdy, high-quality, good old "made in the USA" products of my youth go?

All this for the incomparable blessing of being offered 87,000 drink combinations by a coffee chain, or being able to click on eight hundred television channels. If you can choose between fifty different breakfast cereals — but only between two or three political parties, all with similar economic programs — then you have no real freedom. The illusion of "consumer choice" masks the tyranny of a tiny caste with similar and converging interests. Our leaders do not need to cook up plots in dark caves in order to know what is good for them. What is the difference between parties said to be "Right" and "Left" when all their cadres come from the same social class, have studied the same things together, and vote the same way on all economic subjects? Politicians, when they are not bogged down in sordid sex or money scandals, hardly make sense any more in this consumerist world. They are all subject to the market and only get ruffled over social and hygienic subjects of secondary importance: gay marriage, treatment of illegal aliens, anti-tobacco campaigns, etc. If there is a significant division, it is between globalists and anti-globalists, but the latter remain, for the time being, of marginal following.

And it is amusing to observe a society consisting essentially of docile office employees that adopts the fashions of "primitive" cultures: tribal tattoos are intended to make men seem tough; little hearts, dolphins, flowers, Chinese characters are for women — if not arrows on their lower backs or above their buttocks pointing to their butt (presumably meaning *enter here?*). Piercings, strange clothing, unusual holidays, tribal membership... One must be *different*, just like everyone else.

Everything is designed for immediate entertainment: constant amusement, pornography, drugs. Consumer culture makes us focus on having instead of being, possessions instead of relationships, appearances instead of well-being. This pushes us toward egoism, egocentrism, constant competition. In all areas, you compare yourself with the highest, idealized levels that you can never attain, engendering considerable confusion and frustration. The result: problems like mental illness, divorce rates, addiction to drugs and other substances, and, increasingly, crime and despondency.

In 1970, seventy-nine percent of American college students said their goal was a more meaningful life. In 2005, the same poll showed that the aim of seventy-five percent of students was to earn a living, but eighty-one percent of these admitted to feeling an *existential void*. Thirty percent of workers report being workaholics, accustomed to their emails, Blackberries, iPhones, and other electronic gadgets supposed to make them more productive. Fifty percent of workers report not spending enough time with their children and their families, while forty percent say they do not have enough time for themselves and their own leisure activities.

So it is not surprising that our society suffers from a very high level of psychological illnesses, such as anxiety, insomnia, and depression. A doctor friend of mine summarized the problem well:

> We are prisoners of a vicious circle: we do alienating and meaningless work that creates a depressive state in the worker; a medication allows him to go on working; the work affords the worker the means to buy the medication; the doctor who prescribes the medication is required to do so and remain in the system because he has to pay back the loan he took out to finance his studies, not to mention his annual golf club fees.

The media jump from one sensational story to another without stopping, never making a fundamental analysis or allowing time for reflection. For the greater part of viewers, their brains long dulled if not lobotomized, this entertainment is enough. But acute minds easily perceive the influence of the media in question. In our consumerist world, where money is venerated, the least criticism of the commercial system and the excessive accumulation of wealth and stuff is a sort of heresy. Every politician, professor, or citizen who speaks against consumerist society endangers his career and can expect to be heckled, accused of extremism, ridiculed and ignored. The few dissidents work outside the media system, like Beppe Grillo in Italy.

The life of Westerners is getting further and further away from nature. Less home cooking, more processed foods, more fast food, less physical exercise. While a minority swears by organics and fitness, the majority buys pre-prepared, preheated food — an industrial, nutritionally unbalanced excrescence that requires enormous amounts of energy to produce and whose ingredients have traveled thousands of miles. Between such "Frankenfood" and pollution, is it any surprise that cancer, diabetes, and heart disease are increasing? Obesity is growing, and life expectancy is declining. Add to this that fear and violence are ever-present in our whole culture: they permit you to sell films and win votes. Extremely violent acts are represented everywhere: on television, on the news, at the movies, in video games... Sixty percent of U.S. television programs contain violence, in spite of psychologists' repeated warnings of the harmful effects this can have on behavior.

The reduction of the West to a "digestive tract with a sexual organ" is well advanced! You only have to look at a bit of television — filled with profligacy, frivolous game shows, "reality." Should anyone be surprised that higher-minded immigrants from traditional societies *do not want* their children to assimilate: they simply don't want them to become as degenerate as us! But they don't succeed. Like the Borg from *Star Trek*, global culture assimilates everything in its path — "resistance is futile." "Tittytainment" is propaganda designed to protect the neoliberal capitalist principles that direct globalization (as defined in 1995 by one of its theoreticians, the neoliberal ideologue Zbignew Brzezinski). To resist it, you have to know how to be an ascetic, how to cut yourself off from the world — or you take up arms against it like the Taliban. It's impossible! Faced with this onslaught, the anti-globalists look paltry indeed. As for leftists, wealthy pensioners, petty bourgeois fashion victims, and youth cultists, they are incapable of imagining anything but their *idées reçues*, their pre-programed thoughts. They preach the soft fascism of political correctness (which is getting less soft all the time). They are asleep, cradled in sweet dreams of social equality, human rights, universal solidarity, and other such illusions.

The most frightening effect of global culture is the loss of the social bond. This bond can only survive urban anonymity with great effort. Before, it was best to maintain good relations with your family and neighbors in case you got into trouble, financial or otherwise. But now, the welfare state frees us of interdependence and responsibility. The rites of passage, which gave structure and meaning to life and social positions, are being replaced by fashion. Even the system of social protection has become so bureaucratic and incomprehensible that it favors the lazy and the dishonest, to the detriment of those who actually need a safety net. Finally, the lack of moral sense and responsibility of political leaders and captains of industry is so flagrant that no one can any longer be seriously expected to obey laws and authorities, or to show the least civic feeling.

Globalization also changes people's sense of identity. In a nomadic society based on clans, a person's identity is bound with that of his family, clan, or tribe. In agrarian societies, identities and loyalties are defined in relation to the authority of the monarch and religion. Finally, in industrial societies, identity is constructed upon a real or mythical national culture and a generally homogenous ethnic composition. But since a great change has taken place in these last few years because of mass immigration, which has brought us, for better and for worse, a mixture of cultures living side by side, getting along more or less (depending on the countries and immigrant groups involved). In fact, in the past, migrations took place either toward relatively empty countries (Australia, America) or by invasion; since the 1970s, however, we have passed to immigration on a massive scale for labor, economic, demographic, or (post-)colonial reasons.

Immigration has stopped being a matter of "minorities," as it was in the 1960s; it has become a matter of new *majorities* in neighborhoods, cities, and eventually countries. It's a phenomenon on the rise all over the world, and particularly in Europe and the United States.

The working classes of local extraction in the affected countries, which move out of certain areas, do not do so because of "racism," but in order to regain security, not merely physical but also relational; they seek the feeling of being "among one's own." Those who aren't able to leave the neighborhood often sink into despair, as they do not feel "at home in their home." At any given moment in any given territory, some cultural model must predominate. And if immigration and the birthrates of immigrant populations cause the natives to become the minority, they feel socially and culturally insecure. The immigrants' territories are not "ghettos" in the strict sense of places assigned to people. They are unstable zones where the law of the state is replaced by new local customs or organized crime.

In 2000, a UN report proposed various immigration scenarios in order to anticipate the aging of Western populations. The report suggested that a country like France accept 89.5 million additional immigrants between 2000 and 2050, i.e., 1.8 million per year. A real plan of colonization, assuming this is not a bureaucratic hoax! And then the same blackmail: the authors of the report threaten that if this level of immigration cannot be counted on, it will be necessary to raise the retirement age to seventy-five.

In reality, the working classes do not try to separate themselves from foreigners as long as these are in the minority in their neighborhoods, if they come to work in a time when there is no unemployment, or if they accept a certain degree of integration, considering the native customs as the standard. When this is not the case, the immigrant must often accept work that is close to slavery and terrible living conditions. This immigration, often illegal, is encouraged and manipulated by industries that want to drag wages down and bust unions that are not yet under their control. They are helped by useful idiots: immigrant aid societies and *bien pensant* movie and television stars. The wealthy classes do not see the problem in the same way, not being confronted with it and having a tendency to idealize the foreign culture according to its festive and culinary aspects. The wealthy, themselves buffered from the negative consequences of mass immigration, often encourage racial and cultural mixture — not simply as a matter of a friendship or marriage between individuals but as an ideological good in itself. Didn't Rousseau already discuss this in the 18th century? "Distrust those cosmopolitans who seek far from their own country duties that they scorn to fulfill at home; a philosopher loves the Tartars in order to be dispensed from having to love his own neighbors."

No population wishes to become a minority in a territory where it was once the majority: not a White American, not a Frenchman, not a Belgian, not an Algerian, and not a Tibetan. As the anthropologist Claude Lévi-Strauss wrote, "It is the differences between cultures that make their encounter fruitful." Demographic displacement is something altogether different.

Sociologist Alain Soral explains the genesis of this system in his book *Comprendre l'Empire* ("Understanding the Empire"). He describes the growing power of the West and, in the course of the last two centuries, the rise of networks of domination incarnated by an international finance cartel; the instrumentalization of Helleno-Christian humanism, the infiltration of states by these networks, the exacerbation of antagonisms... Soral describes an attempt to impose a supranational power by stealth. He also raises the question of popular revolts against this elite, which, from crisis to crisis, is both more powerful and more fragile, since it is increasingly arrogant and visible.

Our economic and cultural system is in an advanced state of bankruptcy; in a world that will soon be short of resources, it will be increasingly incapable of responding correctly to problems it generates. Our culture and society, following the example of the Mayans, the Romans, the Vikings of Greenland, and many others, has become dysfunctional just before its collapse. The paradox of the present system is that, in order to maintain itself, it needs to develop personalities and cultures incapable of making it function over the long term. Now, what works is what constructs a civilization and helps it survive: foresight, wisdom, intelligence, discipline, rigor, rectitude, courage, honesty, compassion, and generosity. We are in dire need of these qualities, and, above all, we need leaders of men. But I fear that our culture does not produce any of those anymore...

So we are unable to count on anyone but ourselves. As usual.

Matthew has no more money.

He lost the job his uncle found for him through personal connections. It's so bad that getting up early every morning is hard. He knows he is spending too many nights playing video games, but he can't help it—the new *BodyKill VIII* is just too cool! Thirty-two years old, Matthew lives with his parents, and that annoys him because they are always getting on his back. Sometimes he'd like to take a girl out, but he is way too shy. And besides, girls like guys with plenty of money and a big car. For him, fun means chatting online with other gamers or going to smoke joints with his buddies.

But what he really dreams of is one day becoming a rapper. That would be really gangsta! He'd be loaded and get the chicks. But as for the pressure of always having to work and earn money, he's really had it with that. What's worse, his parents didn't even pay for his vacation in Ibiza this year, the assholes! They're taking it easy. They had cushy jobs with the government, and they always knew how to live: vacations by the sea, skiing, and everything. If the bastards would only croak, or, at least, go rot in some retirement home, he could get their money—if there's any left. An only child, Matthew was always spoiled, especially by his four grandparents, then by Brigitte who married his maternal grandfather. Well, he's not going to sell everything he has on eBay. That would not be cool! But he really needs money for new clothes. And what is going on out there with the supermarkets empty and everything falling apart? He knows his father has a gun in his room. If they stop him from getting what he deserves, he'll blow them all away.

<<declare this an emergency.

come on and spread a sense of urgency. and pull us through.

and pull us through. and this is the end. this is the end.

of the world.

muse

musicians

_apocalypse please

/2003/

Unforeseeables

THIS IS A CHAPTER for which I shall certainly be considered paranoid! But since the principle of this work is to reflect on the world situation, without any *a priori* assumptions, I'm willing to accept that. Paranoia, at least, has the merit of allowing us to imagine the unimaginable — and this is useful, for sometimes the unimaginable plays dirty tricks on us.

The problems we are going to be confronted with are serious. It is our own fault that they have arisen. They are all a question of human nature. We are collectively the cause, and we can do something about them.

But something unforeseeable may also happen that escapes us, that throws in our faces all the hidden consequences of our culpable insouciance.

Nature has some surprises for us. In itself, this is nothing new.

The problem is the risk of a collision between natural and industrial catastrophes.

And *this* is new.

Ordinary natural events have not always been anticipated by the designers of our production and distribution systems: hurricanes, floods, volcanic eruptions, tidal waves, earthquakes, etc. If the effects of these events can be serious, their impact, up to now, has been local. Since the Fukushima disaster, we have begun to realize that such events can have a whole new dimension when they crash up against our already unstable industrial systems.

Our entire system has been conceived as if there were no need to worry about extraordinary natural events with long-term consequences.

I am speaking here of very rare natural events that are able to cause total destruction within an area extending up to hundreds of square kilometers and engender climatic changes on a global scale lasting several years. They happen perhaps once in a thousand years: small meteor or comet impacts, large volcanic eruptions, or unusual solar activity.

Our whole industrial system rests on the idea that these events are so rare that they can be considered outside the realm of possibility.

Except…

Except that being very improbable does not mean it's impossible.

The most worrisome risk of collision between natural and industrial disasters lies, however, elsewhere. It lies in the ill-considered manipulations of living things.

The Return of the Repressed

Modern medicine is one of the most magnificent human conquests. Our species has overcome pain and sickness. We have eliminated polio, smallpox, the plague, cholera, typhus, tuberculosis; we know how to treat the great majority of infectious diseases as well as a large number of rare diseases. Even cancer is no longer always fatal. In spite of the illnesses we provoke by our own behavior, we can take satisfaction in the progress we have made.

We even have a tendency to consider ourselves omnipotent in the face of micro-organisms. And yet the illnesses they cause can return quickly if the magnificent sanitary structure we have built goes missing, or if it is no longer accessible to everyone.

Viruses and bacteria are not going to give up so easily. They are plotting their revenge.

Two factors are working in their favor. First of all, the enormous growth of the human population and its density in cities offer a large number of human bodies for these organisms to develop and reproduce in. Second, by being exposed to antibiotics, bacteria end up becoming stronger, as is the case with Salmonella, E. coli, Campylobacter, etc. Mutations and variants are being observed in illnesses such as AIDS and SARS, and even mad cow disease. Viruses are found which pass from animals to people by mutation, like H1N1, H5N1, or other flu viruses. We will have reason to regret the allergic effects and weakening of the immune system caused by pesticides, pollutants, and hormonal disrupters.

This is not trivial. Spanish flu killed over 40 million people in the world in 1918 and 1919. That is far more people than died in the First World War. In 1348, more than thirty percent of the European population died following a particularly virulent outbreak of plague in urban areas. Seventy-eight percent of the world now live in slums, without toilets, without running water, without sewers; new illnesses are quickly going to find fertile ground for development. According to the WHO, a global epidemic is entirely possible.

In June 2001, the U.S. government conducted a simulated epidemic as an exercise: Operation Dark Winter. It tested the resilience of the American health and hospital system in the case of a national epidemic. *Results showed that the whole system will quickly collapse.* In the simulation, the virus was not contained; in only four days, it had propagated itself beyond the nation's borders, provoking the same chaos around the world. This is because developing a vaccine takes time. In any case, the hospitals would quickly run out of beds and caregivers, the doctors themselves being among the first to get sick, as the recent movie *Contagion* and the zombie flick *28 Days Later* vividly and realistically portray.

If such a virus were let loose in nature by an enemy state or a terrorist organization, the effects would be devastating. A totalitarian state or its elites, afraid of losing their status or simply wanting to reduce a population that consumes too many resources, could use a virus against its own people. It's a scenario that cannot be ruled out.

After all, if dictators like Hitler, Stalin, Mao, or Pol Pot could give the order to kill a part of their own population, what assures us that it would be different today? The commanders could choose to have vaccinated in advance those they designate for survival.

Paranoia on my part, no doubt, but another reason to keep an eye on The Powers That Be.

At a certain time and in a certain context, paranoia is a survival instinct.

Chris knows God will triumph.

It is his duty as a believer to lead God's struggle for his brothers, humiliated and under occupation around the world. He had a revelation during his last trip home, and he has since developed contacts with other believers in the neighborhood where he lives.

He doesn't trust in the methods of his brothers and sisters. Assassinations, arms, and explosives seem paltry to him. He has other plans.

His job in a biological research lab is very useful for him. Chris has worked hard in the lab of his research center. He has studied virus samples taken from Asian poultry. He got lucky: he quickly found a very aggressive form of the virus, but with a long incubation period. This allows for very effective propagation, especially since the virus can be transmitted both through the air and via fluids. Chris doesn't think the virus will be deadly, exactly. He will know soon, since he cannot avoid exposing himself to it for long. He has accumulated a large quantity of the virus in test tubes. He is expecting to release it by brushing some of it on the door knobs of the hotel rooms he plans to visit in the next few weeks. He will also deposit a little in the airplanes he'll take. He's run up his credit card rather badly, but it's worth it. He's going to be doing a lot of traveling on his next two-week vacation:

London — Paris — Madrid — Miami — New York — Atlanta — Los Angeles — Vancouver — Montreal — Brussels — Frankfurt — Munich — Milan — Moscow — Zurich — Amsterdam — London.

God is Great!

<<i am not a progressive. progressives, they always end up with a treblinka or a gulag.

éric zemmour

journalist

/2011/

<<to save the planet and assure an acceptable future for our children, we do not need merely to moderate current tendencies; we must altogether exit from development and *economiscism*.

serge latouche

economist

/2001/

<<we must, we can, we will have a better world. and we have no choice.

graeme taylor

researcher

/2011/

<<the stone age did not disappear because there were no more stones, and the oil age will end long before the world runs out of oil.

sheik ahmed zaki yamani

oil minister

/2010/

Hopes

I GLADLY ADMIT IT: what you have been reading up to now has not been very uplifting ... Is there hope? Could humanity avoid the fates I've discussed in the past hundred pages? (I wouldn't be an honest researcher if I didn't consider the possibility.) Human beings are resourceful and inventive. Awareness can provoke positive cultural change and this, if added to reforms and technological advances, could pull our chestnuts out of the fire.

However, we must be clear-sighted and look at possible solutions rigorously and objectively. There is nothing worse than systematic optimists — those who think that every problem has a simple solution requiring little effort. I call them the *Just-do-its*. Such optimists talk a lot about what one can *just do*, without defining who this "one" is: The rich? The poor? City dwellers? Public authorities? And through what means? You often hear that "one" could do this or that, if one really wanted to — that one could feed 12 billion people, that it's enough to use Canadian oil, or oil that hasn't been discovered yet (but which surely exists off the coast of Alaska, Brazil, or the Falkland Islands). We just have to develop cold fusion, a hydrogen-based economy, use tidal energy, capture electricity from lightning; we just have to convert to all solar power, or all wind power; we just have to change the kind of light bulbs we use, ride bicycles, etc. *Just do it!*

Besides the possible defiance of the laws of physics assumed by these expressions of hope, such arguments are often heard from the lips of amateurs, journalists, and activists — but rarely scientists, geologists or engineers. In a supposedly secular world, faith in the goddess *Technology* and the god *Progress* allows all alarms to be brushed aside with a wave of the hand.

Will scientific progress bring us miracle technologies? It is improbable *a priori* for two reasons: the first is that discovery is by its nature uncertain; the second, more fundamental reason is that the problem is only secondarily technological. It resides first of all in our social, economic, and political organization.

Long-term considerations are absent from our global cultural system. Industrial agriculture, the systematic neglect of resource renewal, the political contempt for regulating births . . . none of this has to do with technological limitations. The horizon of economic calculation stretches to a dozen years at most. Beyond that, predictions are no longer incentives. As for the calculus of democratic politics, it is limited to election cycles: didn't former U.S. Vice President Dick Cheney say, swaggeringly, "our way of life is not negotiable?" How can you get voters to accept a permanent rise in agricultural prices in order to prevent a crisis whose full extent is not yet known? How can you get companies to forego easy profits in order to guarantee the sustainability of the economy in twenty years? How can you get consumers to see that their lives would be improved by changing their behavior?

And yet it has only been ten generations (1750) since the world was governed largely by absolute monarchs, and slavery was normal. Globally, almost no one knew how to read or write, and, to a great extent, life was nasty, brutish, and short. We *have* changed. So, we will be able to change again.

Is this a pipe dream?

Social changes often begin with technical innovations that create new political, economic, and social dynamics. Firearms eliminated the advantages of the aristocracy on the battlefield; railroads allowed regions tucked away in the interior of continents to become developed; the internet allowed the creation of new communication networks beyond the media controlled by large economic groups, and put people and businesses in touch around the world.

Societies also change because new ideas appear. Historically, religions like Hinduism, Buddhism, Christianity, and Islam have tried to raise men above tribalism and ancient morals; nationalist, revolutionary, and separatist movements — which have united the masses in common projects, or even the ecological movements of our day — emerged as soon as the need for new meaning was felt. "Nothing in the world is more powerful than an idea whose time has come," said Victor Hugo.

Another World Is Possible

We can appeal to various sources of energy as a substitute for oil. Theoretically, there is a great number of these, but the possibilities they offer are still limited.

> Coal is available in relatively large quantities. It is quite polluting, contributes to the greenhouse effect when burned, and its extraction involves releasing methane.

> Natural gas, which consists essentially of methane, propane, and butane, would make a good transitional source of energy. Natural gas is easy to get out of the earth and easy to transport, but dangerous if care is not employed in handling it. This gas is often used for heating, fertilizer production, for improving petroleum extraction, and for making synthetic gasoline (although that process requires a lot of energy). World reserves of natural gas will also start to go down between now and 2050.

> Nuclear energy is costly and problematic because of the treatment and storage of nuclear waste, and because of accidents. Since the first nuclear reactor was put in service in 1957, 9,000 tons of radioactive waste have been produced; and though this is, on the whole, a rather small quantity and volume of material to manage, no one wants it buried near them. This energy cannot be substituted for

oil or the consumer products currently derived from oil. However, in the short term, nuclear energy could be a transitional solution, since a uranium atom produces 10 million times as much energy as the combustion of an equivalent amount of coal, and 2 million times as much as its equivalent in oil. So it is a useful energy that for a few decades longer (until the uranium runs out) can furnish electricity without producing greenhouse gases.

> Nuclear fusion is often cited as a future "miracle energy" — clean and limitless. In reality, besides the fact that it has never been realized under anything approaching normal terrestrial conditions, its production would require enormous quantities of energy. Nothing escapes entropy.

> The situation with hydrogen is even worse. Hydrogen has extremely low molecular density; therefore, it's voluminous. It is also strongly corrosive. So, for stocking and transporting it, you must liquefy it under high pressure, seal it up perfectly, and never have an accident with it on pain of producing a spectacular explosion. And since there are no hydrogen mines, it must be produced by dialysis, a more expensive process in terms of energy than the energy it produces. This is also a question of entropy...

There are more realistic hopes in concentrating on renewable energy, furnished by wind, sun, vegetables, and the soil.

> Woods, carefully managed, could be an excellent source of combustible energy and construction material. Badly managed, you get massive deforestation.

> Biofuels derived from beets, maize, potatoes, sugarcane, etc. have weak yields and require dedicating agricultural land to their production.

> Solar energy, although promising, has a limited yield and requires, for the construction of solar panels, materials that are becoming rare.

> Hydraulic energy is more competitive, very efficient and clean, but it requires a heavy investment. Dams need regular maintenance in order not to fill up with sludge and become useless after thirty years or so.

> Wind energy is very cheap, but only works thirty percent to forty percent of the time, since wind conditions are rarely optimal.

> Biomass generates natural gas through fermentation of agricultural waste. This requires intensive agriculture, itself dependent on oil.

> Other energies such as thalasso-energy, geo-thermal energy, marine currents, also have their advantages and their limitations.

These technologies are the starting points for some very promising efforts. In the Emirate of Abu Dhabi, the *Masdar* initiative expects to invest 200 billion dollars in the production of renewable energy between now and 2020 in order to replace entirely the production of electricity and water desalination (today dependent on oil) with photovoltaic electricity. There are massive wind energy projects in the North Sea, such as the German *Baltic One* project, with its twenty-one giant wind turbines that can supply 340,000 homes. In Germany, sixteen percent of energy produced is from a renewable source. Other wind projects are planned on Europe's Atlantic coast and on the north-south axis of the American Midwestern plains. Immense stretches of solar paneling are planned for North Africa and the American Southwest (Texas, New Mexico, Nevada, California). Following the example of Germany, Denmark, and Spain, Asian countries, including China, have also begun massive renewable energy projects — raising the price of the raw materials necessary to realize them, however.

Nanotechnologies are promising as well: they allow for the construction of machines the size of a micron (one millionth of a meter), for working on matter at the molecular level, and for extracting minerals in a more efficient and less costly way (in low-grade mines and with less ecological impact). It is possible that we shall create catalyzers to perform the function of enzymes, and chemically break down pollut-ants. New, extremely light and resistant materials may be created, as well as new batteries storing more energy, requiring less rare metals, and polluting less. We may be able to develop new windows capable of automatically managing insulation and temperatures, and never needing to be washed.

There is also good news in electrical-network-management tech-nology. It is improving thanks to the reduced risk of massive cut-offs and the appearance of smart boxes that allow better analysis of electri-cal consumption.

The internet is another technology that allows groups of people scattered across the world to interact, learn, open themselves up to new ideas, discover new horizons, and see the world as intercon-nected. It allows people to go beyond official "truths," finally silencing that "truth" Napoleon knew so well, of which he said, "History is but lies agreed upon." Today, it is possible with a little work to discover information often hidden from us or filtered by the mainstream me-dia. Thanks to the internet, awareness is growing. Users can gather information and learn how to act for themselves and for their families and to influence decision-makers and politicians. Civic activism can then come to life in all sorts of forms: boycotting, lobbying, protesting and political mobilization.

Advanced technology is not the only thing that allows for change. More traditional techniques are sometimes much better adapted for rehabilitating dying or damaged ecosystems or improving their productivity. Subsistence agriculture founded on permaculture and biodynamic agriculture is suited to low water, fertilizer, and pesticide consumption. Permaculture, popularized by agronomists like Bill Mollison and David Holmgren, allows agricultural land to be *created*, which copies the kinds of relations that exist in nature between differ-ent types of plants, while conferring greater productivity upon them.

We have also observed how, after the collapse of the USSR, North Korea and Cuba reacted to the new reality, deprived of oil and industrial agricultural. North Korea, with its centralized organization, suffered a gigantic famine, which caused several million deaths. Cuba, by liberalizing agriculture, maximizing agricultural surface area (on the roofs of buildings, in parks, and vacant lots, etc.), and using permaculture techniques, succeeded not only in supporting its population, but also in increasing the production and quality of its food.

As for housing, "passive houses" allow natural sunlight and heat to be taken advantage of, as in traditional architecture. Such techniques have been left behind due to cheap heating and air-conditioning; modern architects have long indulged in constructed buildings that are difficult to heat, cool, or air out.

We have become familiar with economical light bulbs, air turbines, and solar panels, recycling of household waste and paper, the gradual suppression of plastic bottles and bags, hybrid or electric cars, carpooling, "slow food", organic food ... But these habits will have only a marginal effect if we do not learn to live with the least possible consumption of fossil energy.

We must be realistic — *renewable energies are not compatible with the scale of systems developed by reliance on abundant fossil energy.*

Embracing Inefficiency

Instead of trying to get a car to run on something other than gasoline, it is time to reflect on a way of life without cars. The social structure is going to have to evolve; we're going to have to get rid of bad habits and accept limits: we cannot, for example, make commercial airlines fly on electricity, just as we don't mold titanium turbines with electricity. It is our habits and culture as a whole that we must change. Without new values, we will not succeed.

This explains how inefficiency has come to be admired in ecological milieus. As James Howard Kunstler, a brilliant critic of the modern urban, social and financial system, puts it, "Efficiency is the quickest road to hell." An inefficient economy is more chaotic, indeed, more complex in certain respects, than an efficient economy that reduces the number of species cultivated, concentrates processes by augmenting their volume, and thus increases its own dependence on them. What we think of as technological complexity is really a simplification of flow. Now, the ecology of a prairie is not efficient. Numerous varieties of flowers and grasses keep the soil fertile and healthy. A single species cultivated in monoculture is certainly "efficient" … but will exhaust the soil's nutritive elements, facilitate erosion, and rapidly destroy the soil for good. All of nature is an "inefficient" system!

Besides inefficiency, we must learn *sufficiency*—being satisfied with enough, taking care of real needs rather than false desires. Measuring one's own life by quality rather than quantity, by relations rather than things, is one of the keys to happiness, to which we may add imagination and the refusal of shackles and dogma. Let us be creative in finding solutions to problems, in discovering a healthy satisfaction in ways of life closer to our deeper nature, in order to promote positive models. We must learn to become a culture worthy of the Russian word непобедимый — *nepobedimyi*, i.e., *invincible*. We must learn to become invincible.

We will have to learn to live with greater simplicity and frugality. Simplicity does not mean living badly or in poverty. It is enough to have what one needs and not desire what one doesn't. As for cities and urbanism, the Romans knew how to construct five-story apartment blocks with reinforced concrete, and their empire was crisscrossed with roads. The ancient Chinese, 3,000 years ago, already had a flourishing trade thanks to their network of canals and their science. A civilization without oil can exist and thrive.

But the current world population and its programmed exponential growth prohibit any turning back. Aid programs for the so-called "underdeveloped" populations presuppose massive growth in GDP and food resources over the entire world. The question is not reducing growth but redirecting it toward certain and renewable resources. Agricultural production will have to double within the next thirty years, and this unprecedented productivity will have to be maintained indefinitely. Now, we do not know how to react in the face of the programmed loss of soil and resources. The challenge is to manage the contraction. The only possible response to such a challenge involves massive investments in research, irrigation, soil conservation, the organization and exploitation of marine resources, etc. Then the question will be not whether change is technically possible (undoubtedly, it is), but whether our governments possess the will, the vision, and the competency necessary for coordinating a global effort to face these problems — and whether we have the time needed to do so before a major crisis arrives and we blithely head into a collapse of our economies and civilizations.

The experience of these last decades leads one to doubt it.

Jack drives an hour each way to work.

He only has time for McDonald's. Smoking calms him down, though. One of his few pleasures is his annual vacation to the shore in August; to get there, he spends ten hours in traffic jams both ways. He's had so many tickets and accidents that they've threatened to revoke his license. He yells at his children and even slapped one once. He also likes to watch football games on TV. He doesn't give a damn about ecology and similar liberal crap.

Melany eats organic foods, is careful about her water consumption, and recycles plastic, aluminum, paper, and glass. Downtown, she walks or rides her bicycle and takes a plane only twice a year to go for a weekend to Cabo or Marrakech, and once a year for her winter vacation in Thailand or Bali. She votes for the Green Party. She knows she is just one link in the ecosystem, but she tells herself her little gestures are important in the permanent struggle for a better world. She does not hesitate to condemn those who do not do their part, notably her colleague Jack, whom she also suspects of voting right-wing.

Of the two, it is Melany who has, by far, the larger "carbon footprint."

By contrast, Mamadou, a peasant in the Dogon area of Mali, has a minuscule carbon footprint. Especially since he lost his farm. He followed the government's advice, which, under pressure from the IMF, has urged peasants in his region to plant cotton. He had to go into debt to buy pumps to irrigate his crop. The first years went well. But massively subsidized American cotton is rapidly becoming so cheap that Mamadou had to sell at a loss. The bank quickly became insistent about his late payments and ended up seizing the farm. It looks like the land is going to be used for an apartment project. Now Mamadou has nothing.

Fortunately, his uncle and his uncle's family took him in, in their village. There is no cotton here: only traditional agriculture, and some raising of chickens and guinea fowl. On the other hand, the rules are strict: you don't eat if you don't work, and you cannot marry and have children until you have proven that you are a responsible adult by passing one of the traditional rites. This year, in spite of the dryness, the village produced a good surplus that will be sold in Sangha, the neighboring village. With the profits, the village is buying a solar pump in order to improve the provisioning of drinking water. The future is looking good, in spite of the thieves who steal the chickens. Last month, one of them got caught and was immediately judged by the tribal leader. He was stoned to death. No one came to claim the body. Food is a serious matter.

<<it's the end of the world as we know it. It's the end of the world as we know it.

It's the end of the world as we know it, and I feel fine.

r.e.m.

musicians

_document

/1987/

<<one wild card is how angry the american people might get. unlike the 1930s, we are no longer a nation who call each other <mister> and <ma'am,> where even the down-and-out wear neckties and speak a discernible variant of regular english, where hoboes say <thank you,> and where, in short, there is something like a common culture of shared values. we're a nation of thugs and louts with flames tattooed on our necks, who call each other <motherfucker> and are skilled only in playing video games based on mass murder. the masses of roosevelt's time were coming off decades of programmed, regimented work, where people showed up in well-run factories and schools and pretty much behaved themselves. in my view, that's one of the reasons that the u.s. didn't explode in political violence during the great depression of the 1930s—the discipline and fortitude of the citizenry. the sheer weight of demoralization now is so titanic that it is very hard to imagine the people of the usa pulling together for anything beyond the most superficial cer-emonies—placing teddy bears on a crash site. And forget about disci-pline and fortitude in a nation of a.d.d. victims and self-esteem seekers.

james howard kunstler

writer

/2009/

PART II

THE COLLAPSE

<<all right we are two nations.

john dos passos

author

<<why take part in a rat race? only a rat can win a rat race.

graeme taylor

researcher and writer

/2011/

<<the roof, the roof, the roof is on fire,

we don't need no water let the motherfucker burn, burn motherfucker burn.

rock master scott & the dynamic three

musicians

/1984/

Mechanisms of Collapse

HISTORICALLY, WE ARE WITNESSING the death of the ideology of progress. Since the 18th century, thinkers and humanists have affirmed that utopian, socially and economically perfect, civilizations are possible. Voltaire thought that reason could bring justice and reforms. Condorcet saw in history an inevitable march toward justice and equality. These are the basic ideas that inspired the American (1776), French (1789), European (1848), and Russian (1917) revolutionaries.

At each new stage of civilization, at each new form of society, the following three conditions must be met:

> a new way of creating meaning from the new reality (economic, social, structural …) and a new way of interpreting this reality;

> institutions that respond to the social aspirations of the population, in other words, a new social contract;

> a new technology that permits increased productivity.

The industrial era could only appear in the 19th century because these three conditions were met:

> A rational ("enlightened") and productive vision of the world emerged, which gave a new meaning to life.

> A new social contract was put in place, more complex than the preceding, and resting upon democracy and individual liberties.

> Science, technology, and especially fossil fuels brought a hitherto unimaginable increase in productivity.

Industrial societies were thus more dynamic and creative than the agrarian societies that preceded them, because they encouraged permanent economic development. Agrarian societies found their meaning in the monarchic and religious system, which symbolized the continuity of order and natural cycles: the rhythm of life was composed of an unchanging revolution of the seasons and the tradition of faith in God. By contrast, industrial society has faith in progress: the individual should improve his life by work, invention, and creativity; and societies should always grow, extend themselves, and innovate in order to survive and flourish. Even service economies depend on the flow of energy and resources; for example, mass education, which is a very significant investment in technical capacities and social capital, is only possible through a will to centralization and through the wealth constituted by the exploitation of natural resources.

In an agrarian society, the economy is governed by social relations — rights, permissions, and obligations toward others, which were themselves informed by status and social class. Markets were only secondary, and their only goal was to facilitate the exchange of goods. In a world where faith and duty were the highest values, commerce represented a low and immoral social status. This is why in the great monotheistic religions, such as Christianity and Islam, lending at interest was forbidden between believers. This worldview is quite the opposite of that of an industrial society, where material wealth is socially valued. Societies are governed by financial transactions and by access to capital, which is necessary for the initial investment in industry — purchasing machines, constructing factories, putting in place industrial processes, etc. The purpose of markets is not only to facilitate the exchange of goods but, above all, to increase capital. The entire economy is in the service of a financial system designed to support an infinite expansion of capital. Capital grows above all by lending and by return on investment. Money is created by debt and, because interest can never be entirely repaid, money must constantly be created, all the way to infinity. Consequently, infinite growth and expansion are not just beneficial but entirely necessary. In a world with limited resources, this system inevitably ends in collapse.

The way of looking at the world and the meaning assigned to reality by individuals and institutions in the agrarian era were suited to a society of local, poorly connected economies with few people and a lot of resources. The industrial era, however, has rapidly transformed the world into a global village, highly interconnected, with a very large population and increasingly scarce resources.

This system has become dysfunctional, cannibalistic, and destructive. Its end is nearing, for it is obsolete. Its collapse is inevitable.

Why do certain societies collapse? Few people can imagine that the rich and powerful societies in which they live might collapse. But societies are dynamic systems, which constantly shift their equilibrium in response to internal changes and external influences. Major changes create tensions that can be constructive and creative (new ideas and technologies) or destructive (wars, invasions, uprisings and civil wars, epidemics, natural catastrophes, declines in agricultural productivity or energy). If a society does not succeed in adapting itself to destructive changes, tensions can become uncontrollable crises; and if nothing corrects the situation, the society starts to disintegrate.

All societies in history have had to confront such crises. This is why the vast majority of past societies no longer exist in their original form. Among recent examples, some have declined slowly, like Imperial China, while others have declined rapidly, like the Soviet Union. And others, like Great Britain, have transformed themselves, evolving from feudal monarchies into industrial societies and post-industrial mass democracies.

In certain cases, the process of collapse was so catastrophic that even sophisticated societies could only regress to a less complex system. The disintegrating Roman Empire saw its system of government, laws, order, infrastructure, roads, aqueducts, sewers, and commercial system disappear within a few years. While the cities and the countryside collapsed into poverty and chaos, the population rapidly diminished, and knowledge was lost. Certain parts of Europe regressed drastically and for a long stretch.

There are also cases where civilizations (e.g., ancient Egypt and China) have succeeded in surviving multiple invasions, famines, and civil wars. In spite of extreme tensions and massive destruction, they were able to adapt to changing conditions. They assimilated invaders or assimilated to them, they accepted new ideas and continued to function with almost the same fundamental culture and institutions as before, sometimes for millennia. It can happen that societies are confronted with so many problems — especially when these call into question the fundamental beliefs of their culture — that they cannot adapt, eventually disappearing amid famine and war. Their populations suffer the worst physical and psychological suffering imaginable.

In his book *Collapse*, the American author Jared Diamond speaks of the *conscious choice* to disappear: elites preferring collapse and the disappearance of their entire people rather than having to pay the political price of change and adaptation to the new ways of thinking and living. The Mayan Empire, the Vikings of Greenland, and the Easter Island civilization saw their societies collapse in a very short time. Shocks can come so suddenly and unexpectedly that they lead to the total disappearance of a population. Jared Diamond studies the reasons societies survive or disappear. He identifies five causes of collapse:

1   Environmental damage;

2   Climate change;

3   Hostile neighbors;

4   The end of help and support from friendly neighbors;

5   The failure of leaders to find constructive responses to problems and to give meaning to a new reality.

Although each situation is unique, one historically frequent cause of social collapse is the convergence of more than one of these factors. They weaken society and provoke internal unrest or civil war. External invaders quickly profit from these weaknesses to attack and destroy it. The most frequent problem is scarcity of resources, often caused by population growth and unsustainable habits. In agrarian societies, it is a matter of the scarcity of drinking water, food, wood, or other essential materials. Villages and cities, originally established in places with abundant resources — fertile soil, rivers rich in fish or forests full of game, etc. — saw their populations prosper and grow, using ever more resources and working ever more land, cutting down trees, polluting rivers, killing off all the game, and catching all the fish. Over time, thanks to demographic pressure on the land to produce sufficient food, the land is degraded, eroded, exhausted, or turned into desert. Productivity sinks. The price of access to resources grows quickly, for they must be sought ever farther away, or wars must be financed in order to loot the resources of other peoples.

The maintenance costs of an expanding society quickly get too high. This is the case with every empire studied by Paul Kennedy in his celebrated *The Rise and Fall of the Great Powers* and by Joseph Tainter in *The Collapse of Complex Societies*. Empires extend their power over territories in order to control resources, but the costs of empire also rise. There are roads and lines of communication to be protected, storehouses and ever expanding logistical chains to be secured, frontiers to guard, regional bases and garrisons to maintain against the will of the local populations, and, finally, police operations against people who must be governed by force. A bureaucracy must be put in place to manage everything, and it quickly becomes enormous and inefficient. So much expense kindles greed, which creates a culture of corruption and power struggles at all levels, further increasing costs and the resistance to change.

This is exactly what happened to the Roman, Chinese, Ottoman, and British Empires — and what is happening today to the American

Empire. In the long term, if these costs become prohibitive (that is, if they consume more energy than they bring in), the population will begin to suffer the effects of resource deficiencies. It is at this moment that most societies go to war with their neighbors in order to appropriate the resources they lack.

Conflicts often begin when populations start to think they have different objectives from their neighbors, and when it has become socially acceptable to resolve conflicts by force. Violence becomes all the more routine insofar as people's real needs are no longer covered, and as cultural and ethnic traditions encourage it. Well-known cultural factors are then put in place that trivialize violence and focus it on a well-identified target: feelings of superiority, devaluing others, authoritarianism, a monolithic culture, a dogmatic ideology, etc.

Sometimes civil wars, consciously or not, allow population levels to be regulated downwards. The example of the 1994 Rwandan genocide is instructive. It was generated by a combination of crises: ecological (overpopulation and a drop in agricultural resources), economic (hunger and inequality), and political (civil wars, etc.), as well as an upset ethnic equilibrium. Mass murder was most extensive in the poorest regions.

Finally, lowered resilience is another factor to be taken into account. An all-too-affluent society, not used to hardships and physical and intellectual effort, is often quickly corrupted, and its reflexes dulled.

It no longer knows how to value what it obtains too easily. It tends to create a narcissistic, materialistic, and lazy culture, which generates a less competitive young generation preoccupied solely with immediate enjoyment.

The *coup de grâce* is often given by a change in equilibrium of some sort. Distraught and overwhelmed, these civilizations give up the fight and totally disintegrate, finally disappearing.

If all this reminds you of a civilization near you, it is because you have understood the situation in which we find ourselves.

Considered over the long term, 200,000 years of human existence, the current industrial era is only a brief moment. Mechanization has allowed us to grow and consume renewable and unrenewable resources at a rate that cannot be maintained. When these resources come to an end, and major ecosystems start to crumble, we will have met all the conditions for a collapse of a global industrial society.

The Perfect Storm Is Approaching

This perfect storm, unleashing global crises, can begin any time and anywhere, since the system is composed of chaotic dynamics from now on. If we study the cases of Cambodia, Rwanda, Yugoslavia, Afghanistan, Iraq, Somalia, and the Soviet Union, we see that in these last few years, local societies have partially collapsed, provoking famines, secession, civil war, economic ruin, and sometimes even ethnic cleansing and genocide.

The epic of human history can ultimately be viewed through a prism of eco-analysis, which shows that energy sources determine the structure of human economies, political systems, and cultures: the transition from a hunter-gatherer to an agricultural way of life occurs through the mastery of agricultural and livestock breeding; the accumulation of a surplus makes possible the growth of the population, technological developments (writing, tools, etc.), and a sophisticated system of specialized social classes.

When a civilization collapses, it is replaced by a simpler one — lighter, less densely populated, less complex, but more resilient. The schema below, taken from the book *Evolution's Edge* by the Canadian researcher Graeme Taylor, shows how a crisis can evolve:

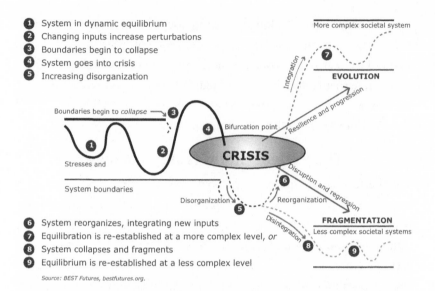

1 System in dynamic equilibrium
2 Changing inputs increase perturbations
3 Boundaries begin to collapse
4 System goes into crisis
5 Increasing disorganization

6 System reorganizes, integrating new inputs
7 Equilibration is re-established at a more complex level, or
8 System collapses and fragments
9 Equilibrium is re-established at a less complex level

Source: BEST Futures, bestfutures.org.

There are two ways of getting out of such a systemic crisis.

Society can evolve downward. The system collapses; irreversible damage is done. Civilization then regresses toward a less complex system, which finds a new point of equilibrium similar to what we knew before the industrial era. Here the questions are: what amount of stress can our society bear before regressing, and will this regression occur suddenly and rapidly, or gradually? The process of disruption and regression can take the form of the following sequence of events:

> A phase of deflation (recession) followed by hyperinflation and the end of most paper money;

> Rises in the price of raw materials;

> International tensions, wars over resources;

> Rupture of the global economy, breakdown of long logistical chains;

> Mass unemployment;

> Collapse of the electrical grid;

> Collapse of water distribution;

> Collapse of evacuation systems and water filtering;

> Collapse of law enforcement;

> Fires, panics, looting, and violence;

> Total loss of control by the government;

> General chaos, ethnic cleansing, famine;

> Serious sanitation crises, sicknesses, epidemics;

> City dwellers fleeing to the countryside;

> Collapse of the hospital system and medical care;

> Steep drop in population;

> Return to order by exhaustion and the grouping of individuals around small organized nuclei;

> Return to an economy based on local agricultural production;

> Reconstruction of society based on a simpler and more local model.

Society could also evolve *upwards*, developing new ways of functioning on a global scale by changing its culture and its manner of functioning.

These are the mechanisms of collapse.

We have a choice to make between these types of society, and there is not much time left.

David is doing well.

He made a fortune and racked up job titles: mayor of his village, president of the regional council, national deputy and European deputy, not to mention positions on the Board of Directors of several large private and public firms. He succeeded in earning more than 200,000 euros per month—not bad for a socialist! But something is bothering him. His usual message about feminism, homosexual marriage, the regularization of undocumented workers, anti-racism, etc., no longer seems to work on his electorate. It seems to be because of the crisis. But what crisis? All indicators and all the experts have pointed to a recovery! And the airplanes David takes are full, just like the luxury hotels where he lands in Strasbourg, Brussels, or Washington. In his view, if people start voting for the rising "populist" party—due to his experience acquired in 1968 and his membership in various Trotskyist movements, he knows that the party is truly part of "the extreme Right"—it's because the ethnic composition has changed. All these Africans, Arabs, people from all over the world, have driven his old constituents out of the neighborhood to live in the center of town (at least those who have the money).

David pays a visit to the President of the Republic. Though he's from another party, he's an old companion of David from the Lodge. He should be able to offer advice.

"…my dear David," says President Dominique Wolinsky, "you are coming face to face with a real problem. If you play the 'Clash of Civilizations' card with anti-Muslim and anti-immigration talk, you will have the 'politically correct' crowd on your back accusing you of flirting with the extreme Right, not to mention the construction industry, starting with the Murdokk Group. And since they control the big TV channels, Murdokk will make you pay. Then there are the restaurants and the rest of the service industries, which need black-market workers to stay competitive. If you are conciliatory, like a good leftist, you are going to get beaten by the far Right. You know I have this problem at the national level as well. Washington has warned me: if I want the UN job and my consulting gigs after my second term as President, I'd better get re-elected. They aren't playing 'Mr. Nice Guy' anymore in DC or Brussels: the old days of full employment for life are over. More austerity, more austerity ... Despite my self-respect, I'll have to cave in."

"But then we're finished; we won't be re- elected!"

"No, don't worry! Our American friends have figured out a solution. You know, in 2000, when Bush Jr. was elected, well, nominated anyway... Or think about when the French people stupidly rejected the European constitution in 2005—even though it was what was best for them! We can't let elections affect our ability to govern."

"But...how can you get rid of democracy?

Influence people, yes, but..."

"Don't get so self-righteous! The important thing is that we understand that these crises are *opportunities* to strengthen the government and get done what needs to be done. We need to start presenting things, not as proposals, but as *fait accompli*. No one will complain, nor even notice. (You should read the book *The Shock Doctrine* by Naomi Klein, quite a clever girl, and pretty, too...) Look, I received a whole package of laws that Brussels wants me to get passed during the coming summer holidays. If we can reduce pensions and unemployment insurance, we could cut the budget in half... It will be like a turkey-shoot. Your friends on the Left have already accepted it, just like my conservative ones! And then ... did you see the general intelligence reports? It's no joke: it seems that Saudi Arabia has no more oil reserves. It's no longer 200 billion barrels the towel-heads have got, but nothing, zero, *nada*!... You don't look like you get it. Let's be honest, without the Saudis pumping, things are going to get more ... difficult. We're already bogged down in Libya and Syria with NATO ... and we're going to have to intervene elsewhere. China doesn't look pleased with this. You remember the news about that submarine, the USS *Nebraska*, that went down last year near Taiwan? Well, it wasn't an accident... And these projects I get wind of—Venezuela, Nigeria, Iran... With our four fighter jets, we are going to look ridiculous! Again.

Oh, by the way, you should tell that ass Bertrand-Henry Lévy to shut his big mouth for once. Everybody knows the Russians aren't exactly behaving nicely in the Caucasus, but calling for humanitarian air strikes against Russian bases in the region! I swear, it's simply too obvious who butters his bread. Well, I'll let you go now; I've got two young things my wife arranged to come over for us this evening ... so, good luck, David."

David gets in his car to return home. Suddenly, his chauffeur slams on the brakes. A cobblestone smashes against the passenger-side window. It shatters. An accident? No. A demonstration. And it's getting nasty! "Trash the elites!" he hears The car is stuck behind a burning police cruiser. A bit stunned, David realizes that his chauffeur has fled. David is afraid, for the first time in many years. He gets out, but trips and falls; his obesity doesn't help. "Wh...where's the police?" he asks himself, picking up his glasses. Someone shoves up against him: "Look, it's that pig David Droy! Yes, it's him. It's *him*! The deputy with the Swiss watch collection! Yo, hand over the Rolex, you bastard! Hey, brothas, let's do him!"

David's last coherent thought was that he had urinated on himself.

On account of the murder of David Droy ... eviscerated, emasculated, and charred, all rolled-up inside a bus tire ... President Wolinsky enacted European emergency laws forbidding any potentially violent demonstration.

<<you are very, very dangerous people indeed. your obsession with creating this euro-state means that you're happy to destroy democracy. You appear to be happy for millions and millions of people to be unemployed and to be poor. untold millions must suffer so that your euro-dream can continue. just who the hell do you people think you are?

nigel farage

politician

_speech before the european parliament

/2010/

<<no one is going to feel sorry for the united states, just as no one felt sorry for the ex-ussr.

dmitri orlov

engineer & writer

/2008/

<<for the men who rule our world, rules are for other people.

naomi klein

writer

/2007/

Consequences

ALL OUR LIVES, WE HAVE BEEN TOLD that our economic, political, and moral system was the best in the history of humanity. We
live with the belief that contemporary ideas are the most evolved that
have ever existed. We burst with self-satisfaction at the notions of the
"rights of man," "humanitarian intervention," "minority rights," "freedom and democracy," without ever having doubts or questions about
the basic soundness of these beliefs or their workability. What if this
self-assurance is only a luxury, permitted by the massive use of cheap
fossil energy?

In reality, we live in an increasingly dangerous world. We don't always see this, for in the West, we still benefit from a varnish of comfort
brought to us by a complex and effective infrastructure. Now, while
this infrastructure is resilient in the case of local or minor events, it is
extremely fragile at the global level — particularly once a point of no
return has been passed. This point will be reached, in my opinion, by
the convergence of catastrophes I discussed in previous chapters, the
consequences of which we shall now study.

The Financial and Economic Crisis

The financial crisis of 2008 was announced to us by the media as one
cyclical movement of the market among many others. According
to modern economic orthodoxy, a recovery always follows a crisis,
however serious. But when you look more closely at the real state of
finance and the economy, you see that it is untenable.

The debt levels of Western countries, chief among them the United States, is significant. In this context, the continued and expanded issuance of fiat currency is going to create considerable inflation. The prices of imported goods — raw materials, natural gas and oil especially — are going to rise, making transportation and commerce in general more difficult. Companies are going to go out of business. Unemployment could reach fifty percent of the active population. Total consumer purchasing power is going to sink steeply. Governments are probably going to have to choose between austerity measures — which will be unpopular and will slow down the economy further — and a headlong rush by accumulating more debt.

Very quickly, the United States, via its intermediaries in Europe and its influence on credit ratings, is going to put pressure on the eurozone to make sure European countries are the first to get into trouble, although their situation is not, in fact, worse than America's. A number of European countries are going to be put in trusteeship, with severe austerity programs. Some will go bankrupt and be forced to return to their old national currency. Sooner or later, the United States will no longer be capable of continuing its policies, and will be forced to admit that its debt can never be paid off. The consequence may be a unilateral default, with the nationalization of banks and strategic industries, and the creation of a new dollar backed by some sort of benchmark (such as a precious metal); or it may be hyperinflation, with the euro and the dollar meeting their ends by no longer being accepted in payment. In any case, it will have a great effect on the real economy, and Europeans' and Americans' standard of living will sink rapidly and deeply.

Asia and China will not be spared by the consequent drop in consumption in the U.S. and Europe. The crisis will spread to the other countries of the world. Some will face mass unemployment and have to fear revolts and revolutions. From one country to another, the effects can be very different, ranging from a peaceful change of power to bloody repression, or the establishment of authoritarian populist regimes with the nationalization of industries and assets.

The problem in the West is that the overwhelming majority no longer works in agriculture and trades, and even industries have been delocalized. All that's left are office jobs and petty service jobs, which, like so much of the legal and financial industries, are no longer going to be of any use. If you think your employment is precarious today, just wait!

The heavy immigration of the last forty years, including illegal immigration, has meant that a whole class of basic trades, wrongly considered "unskilled," dirty, and lacking in prestige — cleaning, maintaining and restoring infrastructure, the food industry, transportation and logistics, mechanical work and construction, medical work, plumbing, electrical work — are now constituted by persons likely to return to their countries of origin if a serious crisis hits or ethnic tensions arise, depriving the economy of their competence and work capacity. This will be the case with Latin Americans in the United States; Africans, Indians, Pakistanis, and Eastern Europeans in the UK; Africans and North Africans in France, Belgium, the Netherlands and Italy; Turks in Germany; Ukrainians in Poland, etc. Everybody is someone else's foreign immigrant! A certain number of well-assimilated will, no doubt, choose to remain, and we must hope that they will be treated well. But other parts of the immigrant communities, already trouble-makers under normal economic conditions, may cause such problems that they will either assume power locally as gangs or mafias, or else simply be eliminated by rival gangs or by groups of citizens no longer afraid of laws that protect the dishonest and/or violent minorities. Such troubles and migratory movements are very difficult to forecast, especially as they depend on changing local conditions. A confidential document of the European Commission, intended only for its closest collaborators, contains the following:

> We expect a steep rise in inflation, a raise of prime interest rates and a
> massive increase in the price of the most important raw materials. The

combination of rising unemployment and the rolling back of benefits in the member countries will reinforce the risk of violence. In the medium term, we must reduce social security to a minimum, even if this provokes revolts and violence.

Similarly, a CIA report of March 2011 warns the government of

the possibility of civil wars in several of the EU countries which, with their significant immigrant populations, are considered weak and close to decline. The risk of troubles increases every year, especially through the criminalization of a margin of the Muslim population, which represents 70 percent of the prisoners incarcerated in Spain and France.

The Social and Political Crisis

With such an economic crisis, it is quite probable that governments will push to use the threat of total collapse to grab even greater power (officially in order to protect the citizens from themselves) by establishing security measures and depriving them gradually of their liberties. This is the path to national servitude under an oligarchic elite denounced by men like Alex Jones, Noam Chomsky, or Friedrich von Hayek — all of whom echo Benjamin Franklin — "Those who are prepared to abandon their essential liberties for an illusory and ephemeral security deserve neither liberty nor security."

According to Pierre Laurent, Director of the International Monetary Fund in Geneva,

The depression is going to be terrible, filled with despair and extreme violence. The millions of unemployed will demand from politicians what they have promised. These politicians will keep acting — above all, out of ignorance — in the exact opposite way that they should, in order to satisfy the expectations of their electors.

In times of hyperinflation, people must immediately spend their salaries or retirement funds in order to buy goods of intrinsic value. Purchasing power will go down from one day to the next. Badly invested fortunes will be pulverized.

In contrast to the Germans or the Russians, who still retain their collective memory of periods of hyperinflation, and to Southern Europeans or Latin Americans, who have recently known periods of heavy inflation, it will be hard for Americans to live in a world where the once all-powerful dollar is no longer worth anything, and their country is no longer a global power. The population will rapidly sink into poverty. Hundreds of millions of middle-class people will lose their savings and employment. Billions of Third World poor will find themselves facing famine. The conditions for a revolt will all have been met. These insurrections and revolutions will be sudden and unforeseeable. Who in 1788 would have predicted the French Revolution? And who would have predicted the arrival of Robespierre and Bonaparte?

And if you think the police will intervene, you are kidding yourself. During the 1992 Los Angeles riots, a very localized event unleashed by a verdict perceived as unjust by part of the population, even the police, confronted with the size of the riots, limited themselves to a particular area and waited for the mêlée to cool off by itself. Whole neighborhoods were thus left without protection until the National Guard and Marines intervened to stop the rioting. In France in 2005, during the suburban riots that began in Clichy-sous-Bois, the police preferred to lock down the problematic areas and stay out of them so as not to worsen the situation. One could conclude that if more serious revolts or large-scale unrest were to occur, the policemen might prefer to stay at home to protect their own families rather than perform their duties.

As most people do not own their place of residence outright (that is, they have them mortgaged), we could see a wave of defaults on these loans; consequently, the banks could take ownership of a tremendous amount of real estate. Similarly, people without income (and they will be the majority) will quickly be confronted with inevitable eviction if they don't find a solution quickly, especially since hyperinflation is likely to involve very high interest rates. Quite probably, given the number of cases that will occur, people will simply no longer pay their rent or mortgages and become squatters in their habitations (whose value will be close to zero in any case). And if they are evicted, they will simply move to another of the many empty houses or apartments that will increasingly be turned into dirty, insecure refugee camps. The result is also an increase in poverty levels. This process has already started: in the state of Tennessee, for example, since the beginning of 2011, twenty percent of the population has been living using food stamps.

The United States, which has considerable military power, will be tempted to use this last asset to seize sources of raw materials, or simply to provoke wars in order to rally the people against an external (or internal) enemy and galvanize the economy, as it did in the late 1930s. Beware the wounded beast! Other more visibly authoritarian countries, such as China (above all) or Russia, may also hope that military adventures could procure them an advantage. Regional wars for the control of resources will become frequent. Bigger wars might be unleashed in an attempt to revitalize the economy by arms spending and territorial conquest. Nuclear and world wars cannot be excluded. And it is not impossible that certain countries may implement programs for the physical elimination of the poor and deprived, perceived as unproductive, unnecessary, and not able to be fed. If you think such things too monstrous to be possible, open a history book.

The Crisis of Logistics and Food Chains

One does not necessarily need conspiracies by malicious governments to reduce the population in case of a crisis. The very structure of the system might just do that.

Think for a moment about the state of food distribution, as well as the distribution of most other goods in the world. We have destroyed craftsmanship. During the past twenty years, a few great commercial groups, dreadful predators, and capable negotiators have taken advantage of the immense economies of scale available to them, thanks to their networks of cheap suppliers and the great volume of their own purchases, to propagate themselves *everywhere*. These groups have been welcomed by consumers with open arms. Installed in strategic areas, at the crossroads of the great transportation routes around every city, they have signed off on the disappearance of a large number of small businesses. Collectively, we have agreed to destroy part of our local economic fabric in order to save on goods, which are often of poor quality and/or unneeded. We did not think too carefully on what we were destroying, for these small businesses maintained relations with local food producers, who have now been absorbed by great agricultural enterprises or who have retired and not passed on their knowledge to the young. In the West, in emerging countries and even in the poorest countries, food is bought in supermarkets supplied by trucks, often refrigerated, which drive thousands of kilometers between factories, centers of production, logistical centers, etc. In the United States, sixty-four percent of goods are transported by highway. In a world of scarce resources and expensive fuel, this may not remain possible for much longer.

Every major industry relies on "just in time" delivery. The concept is simple: thanks to tight coordination between a company and its subcontractors, manufacturing is carried out in the most efficient possible way in order to minimize inventory, freeing up storage space, minimizing the risk of obsolescence, and maximizing profits. Pieces necessary for making machines are ordered frequently, but in relatively small quantities. The risks to such a system are delays in supply, the disappearance of suppliers and subcontractors, or strikes. The delay of a single part can shut down the whole system. This risk is usually acceptable because of good management and because subcontractors can be quickly replaced, temporarily or permanently, with a minimum of planning. Alas, this will not be the case in a time of major crisis. When suppliers are not able to supply — whether from unemployment, closure or sickness — the whole system will come to a halt. This is just what happened on a small scale in 2011, when the tsunami that struck Japan caused the closing of a number of factories in Europe.

What is true for industry is also true for the supply chain of consumer goods. In large-scale distribution, thousands of subcontractors, producers, transporters, and logistical workers operate in a coordinated way in order to get food onto supermarket shelves. What you see on the shelves is practically all that the supermarket has in stock. Thanks to powerful computer systems, all this runs like clockwork: precise, efficient, profitable. But at the least problem, the system finds itself under pressure. In case of a major crisis, it stops completely. We have seen in the course of panics, like that of the summer of 1990 following the invasion of Kuwait by Iraq, that supermarket shelves were emptied within a few hours of all their stocks of rice, pasta, water, and milk. With an alarmist media, any panic will be quickly amplified. Fifty percent of the world's population lives in cities, and is totally dependent on these complex supply systems for energy, food, communication, water, transportation, medicine, spare parts, as well as for the evacuation of garbage and waste water. In the Western world, less than two percent of the population is involved in food production (agriculture, hunting, and fishing). This two percent feeds the other ninety-eight percent. You think that's bad? It gets worse. A good part of our food comes from monoculture farms from poor southern countries, and few of these are capable of self-sufficiency with respect to food. When a major crisis (water scarcity or otherwise) hits, they'll stop exporting and/or revert to subsistence farming. (Yes, we won't get our bananas anymore.)

In normal times, the average Westerner returns home to a refrigerator full of food, working electricity, working toilets, working heat, working telephones, a working internet connection; his salary is deposited directly into his account, and his bills are paid automatically. We have built an efficient and complex economic machine which is being extended ever farther across the world. If the machine stops, commands are no longer transmitted, trucks no longer make deliveries, shops quickly empty out, gas stations shut down, the police and firemen no longer perform their functions. If electrical lines break, who is going to repair them? If there is no more gas, how will the harvest be gathered or transported to the supermarkets? The typical family has a week's worth of food at home. And after that? Where should one go to look for food? Is the state going to be able to feed everyone? Will the search for food remain peaceful? When will the average Westerner become desperate and begin looting the shops, his neighbors, the cities, and then the countryside?

The United States Army is preparing to face such a scenario with the exercise Unified Quest, which lasted throughout the year 2011. Its object was to study the implications of — to quote the document itself — a "large-scale economic breakdown inside the United States that would force the Army to keep domestic order amid civil unrest." This exercise included putting in place internment centers for millions of Americans, centers which shall increase the capacity of the refugee camps that FEMA already had put in place during the first decade of this new century.

The Food Crisis

A global food crisis is going to occur thanks to a convergence of factors. First of all, the end of cheap oil will mark the death of modern agriculture, which cannot exist without tractors, combine harvesters, water pumps, automatic irrigation, and a vast number of other machines. It takes 1,500 liters of gasoline per inhabitant per year to feed a Westerner. To produce a calorie of food, the equivalent of ten calories of fossil fuel is needed, whether directly (fuel) or indirectly (electricity, etc.). With the exhaustion of the soil, the predicted phosphate impoverishment and more expensive fertilizers, pesticides, and herbicides, this form of agriculture that consumes seventeen percent of our energy will no longer be able to produce as much. Moreover, there is a global fresh water shortage. Many agricultural regions are originally semi-deserts transformed by water pumped from subterranean aquifers or brought from distant rivers. Mechanization has greatly reduced the numbers of farmers, who are increasingly elderly persons. The average age of a Western farmer is fifty-five years, and only 5.8 percent of them are under thirty-five. It is to be feared that when the greater part of these retire, their valuable know-how will be lost.

The situation is not better for farms in poor countries, which, as discussed earlier, are also geared toward intensive monoculture. It's sad to see that everywhere in the world, perfectly durable and self-sufficient communities have been undone under the economic pressures of globalist and hyper-liberal dogma. And just as this knowledge is on the point of being irretrievably lost, we are in greater need of it than ever before. Add in climate change, and you have the picture of crucial but incredibly fragile economic activity. If the price of oil goes up, more and more farms are going to have to shut down. Elderly farmers are going to prefer to give up their occupation. Large scale operations will have to raise their prices. The population is going to see prices explode. If in the West household food expenses are ten percent of income, they are fifty-eighty percent in poor countries. If prices go up permanently, and production goes down, there will quickly be famine on a world scale.

Rich and poor will have to leave the cities to find food or attempt to farm on their own; but with little available land, a lack of water and competence, the process could become a disaster. It will require decades for millions to learn to farm like their ancestors; in the meantime, there will not be enough for everybody. This will be an enormous food crisis, the greatest famine of all time, resulting in the deaths of hundreds of millions — perhaps billions.

Countries that import ninety percent of their food, like Egypt, are going to collapse with unheard-of rapidity. The survivors will migrate on a massive scale, like a cloud of locusts, and provoke (voluntarily or not) a whole series of destabilizing problems in the receiving countries. They will spread the crisis farther and farther. The humanitarian NGOs or the United Nations won't be able to do anything about it: there will be no food stocks to distribute. It is going to be a catastrophe.

The Social Crisis

In the face of these new developments, most of the population will react at first with apathy and resignation, waiting in vain for help and assistance, as they have been used to doing all their lives. The socio-economic problems we thought we had solved — social inequality, racism, etc. — are going to come back and hit us in the face. In this world, competition for increasingly scarce resources will be fierce.

Civilization is a thin varnish, built up painfully over centuries; when it is removed, you discover egotistical, violent, and cruel human beings. Take a normal person and put him out in the cold, the rain, amid hunger and thirst, take away his comfort and habits, his television, beer, booze, cigarettes, and other drugs, and you will soon see the savage within. First, he will show irritation, then (very quickly) violence or a degree of degradation unthinkable a few days before. And if you think fraternity and the social bond are still there after decades of consumerist, hedonist, narcissist, egocentric culture, you are in for a big surprise. A society that encourages the immediate satisfaction of our basest desires and whims can only, in a crisis situation, transform itself into a horde of violent psychopaths. In cases of state collapse or revolution, one can easily observe violent behavior of which people would have believed themselves incapable: horrible massacres, rapes, looting, gratuitous torture, forced enrollment in militias, child soldiers.

Where will such people go first? Supermarkets, convenience stores, gas stations — which will create a wave of panic. Then these hordes of normal people turned criminals will loot the most conspicuous apartments and villas of wealthy neighborhoods: the Upper East Side in New York City, Knightsbridge and Belgravia in London, Vaucluse and Bellevue hill in Sydney, Barrio Salamanca in Madrid, Neuilly in Paris, Uccle in Brussels, Cologny in Geneva, the Goldküste in Zürich, Beacon Hill in Boston, the Gold Coast of Chicago, Beverly Hills in Los Angeles, etc., moving gradually to the less wealthy neighborhoods. Then they will leave the cities to loot suburban housing estates, and

finally end up in the countryside where the food is. A large fraction
of the population will want to flee the violence and will try to get out
of the cities any way they can. Public transport will quickly become
saturated and then unable to function. Highways will turn into giant
traffic jams where violence will break out. A vast number of famished
and exasperated people arriving in the same place at the same time:
it's a recipe for disaster! This will be like an exodus, probably larger
and more dramatic than that of 1940 in France, or that of 1945 in East
Prussia. Vacation spots like Megève, Gstaad, Deauville, Saint Tropez,
Aspen, the Hamptons, etc., known for their wealthy residents, will
quickly become prized destinations for the hordes of looters, who
will soon come up with the idea of organizing in gangs for greater
efficiency. Recruits of all sorts will join these bands, ready to obey
any order in exchange for the promise of a daily meal. There will be
famine, violence, destruction, rapes, deaths, illnesses. Anarchy, even
temporary, will lead to confusion and disorientation. Gangs, mafias,
bands of thieves, private militias will violently and rapidly fill the
vacuum left by the state's powerlessness.

If you are reading this book, you belong, in all likelihood, to a
social group of a certain material level that will make you, your family,
your house or apartment targets for these people. It will be those who
have nothing vs. those who don't have much. If you possess something of value (water, food, gasoline, gold…), others are going to want
to take it from you. Your life and those of your family members will be
worth very little to a mob of hungry, thirsty people (already selfish and
rude under normal conditions). Even a simple light on at night could
mean you have something more than others. Sooner or later, as in one
of those bad zombie movies, they will arrive at your door — famished
and ready for anything.

The Sanitation Crisis

Such a social crisis will also provoke a rapid collapse of public electrical networks, for, under the conditions described, who is going to
work to keep the central stations operating or to repair broken lines?

If electricity goes off for more than a week, we will quickly be confronted with serious problems, because an electrical network is very complex and hard to get started again. Most cities are going to lack drinking water, because the pumps will stop working quickly without electric power. Communication will quickly break down, because the telephone stations can only continue for a week or two on their generators. No more internet, no more alarms, no more security cameras. Most heating will no longer work, because natural gas requires pressurization, which is provided by electrical systems. It will no longer be possible to call the police or the fire department — assuming they still exist. The population will be left to its own devices, and will have to face crime, storms and fires.

Without electricity, hospitals and clinics — already saturated by the number of wounded, the lack of care personnel, theft of materials and medicines — will no longer be able to provide intensive care or anything that requires machines. Many patients will die after a few weeks. Without water, hygiene in the cities will rapidly collapse: toilets will no longer flush, garbage will pile up, people will drink dirty water (contaminated by organic waste and the accumulating masses of solid waste), the corpses of those who have died, whether naturally or violently, will no longer be evacuated, cholera will start to rage again.

The Nuclear Crisis

In the case of a serious social crisis and economic collapse, who is going to turn off the nuclear power stations? The engineers and security personnel are trained to manage accidents, acts of terrorism, armed attacks, etc., but not the simple fact that no one is showing up for work any longer! What are the procedures if personnel is lacking, or in the case of an extended crisis? How will combustible substances and radioactive materials be isolated in the case of long-term emergency closures? If there is one thing you can actually do right now, it is write to your representative (mayor, congressman, president, king, CEO, etc.) or local media and ask that an inquiry determine the risks in case of a major crisis and precisely what measures will be taken.

After all, these guys are people, too, with families who will be contaminated just as any other person if an accident occurs. In your letter, mention Fukushima and Chernobyl a lot! We cannot let hundreds of abandoned nuclear reactors melt down one after another, expelling deadly radiation into the air and rivers!

When Will These Crises Happen?

Listening to political debates, no one in power seems to take such scenarios seriously; if they are spoken of at all, it is only in the most generalized of terms; and politicians always arrive at the same conclusion — more growth will solve all problems (yippee!). It may not be only a question of ignorance or blindness. Sometimes, announcing a crisis amounts to provoking it, precipitating the events one wishes to avoid. After all, it was by seeking to reform the Soviet Union that Mikhail Gorbachev hastened its demise.

When I address conferences or talk to people who ask me for advice, the question that inevitably comes up is *when?*

When are these crises going to arrive? How much time do we have left to prepare? Certain financial, economic, social, and political crises have already begun, and their effects can be felt, and not just in Greece and Cyprus. Other crises, like those of energy or logistics, have not yet begun as the English-language edition of this book was being prepared in 2013. Still others, such as the climatic and environmental crises, have such long-term effects and are so hard to foresee that it is impossible to say when we will feel the first effects.

It is possible that technological discoveries will hold back the inevitable for a few years, a few decades, perhaps even long enough to pass the problem along to our grandchildren... But I doubt it. All these problems are exacerbated by population growth, by unforeseen climate changes, and by the collapse of ecological niches. Any of these major crises will have repercussions on the others, which then, in turn, damage the global system, which becomes more fragile, more unstable, more unpredictable, until any event, however seemingly small or insignificant, can trigger the collapse of the whole rotten structure. Just because an event has not happened, does not mean that it will not ever happen.

I'll stick my neck out—the crisis will occur between now and 2020. We don't have much time left.[1]

---

1   See last chapter.

Michael's business
has closed.

It's impossible to manufacture anything with the transportation crisis. The *coup de grâce* was that war in Asia, which killed all hope of his parts arriving. He doesn't know what he is going to do to pay off his mortgage, but this week he has more pressing problems. The news on television said there will be a lack of foodstuffs in the stores, but there is no need to panic because the army will assure provisioning. (Obviously, everyone panicked.) The shops were empty in a few hours. It seems there were more than a few dust-ups, and even some serious injuries. People are stupid; we just have to wait for the state to do its job, and there will be rice, pasta, bread, and water again. Right?

Michael opens the cupboard. There isn't much … some cans of tuna, a package of pasta, some sweets … enough to hold out a few days but not more. What's this? The electricity's off! This is getting more frequent. Last night the news reported on the unrest in the United States: Detroit, Chicago, Atlanta, New Orleans … the people panicked after noticing the supermarkets were empty. There were images of looting and of police firing on the looters. It made quite an impression. On the web, videos are showing American citizens firing on their neighbors to protect their property. It looks like the President is going to declare a state of emergency, but with a large part of the armed forces bogged down in conflicts just about everywhere, he's going to have a hard time maintaining order. Michael says that tomorrow he is going to pack up the family and go to his mother's place in the country.

When he wakes up, there is no more water. No coffee. No shower. The bags are packed. Michael's family gets in the car. The neighborhood gas station is closed—no more gas. They only have half a tank. That will have to get them 180 miles. But it looks like Michael is not the only one to think of leaving the city. A gigantic traffic jam awaits—it takes them two hours to drive six miles! People are getting hot under the collar. Some fights break out on the side of the highway. Finally, they start moving a bit … but, halfway there, the tank runs out. After spending a day waiting for a supply of gas that never comes, Michael and his family decide to continue on foot.

*

Maurice is pacing like a lion in a cage.

Now at home, he's depressed since he and ninety percent of the personnel of his company were let go without indemnity, in spite of his fifteen years' seniority. His lawyer tells him he is going to hit the jackpot in court, so badly was the law flouted. He can't stop dwelling on his having done nothing wrong, that he has always been a model employee, motivated, devoted, working late at night, always ready to leave on business trips over the weekend so as not to waste productive time. Perhaps he could have given more, sold more, should have been more productive? He can't understand it. Everything was going so well.

His wife is encouraging him to move about, to go out more, get involved in athletics, look for a new job. A new job with twenty-five percent official unemployment figures? Impossible! Or should he become a street sweeper? Anyway, he hasn't noticed any street sweepers about in a while. Ugh! Still, she convinces him to go out a bit. Since the price of bread has doubled, he's in need of cash, and none of the ATMs seem to be working. He goes to the bank where at least two hundred people are lined up to get to the teller. It appears that maximum withdrawals have been set at fifty euros per person per day. That's annoying, but not as much as the stock market: his savings have lost sixty percent of their value in just a few days! Maurice tells himself it will go up again; after all, he has invested very conservatively, in transportation, food, distribution… People will always be hungry, and they will always need supermarkets and someone to produce yogurt, coffee, and chocolate for them. That the supermarket by the highway was burned down last night, like the school the day before, did not bother him too much; the worst that can happen is that the state will end up taking care of us.

*

Max is in good hands.

He's been recruited by a private militia led by "The General," an old Foreign Legion officer or mercenary in Africa or something. Anyway, Max gets hot meals and is respected—feared would be a better word—by the whole neighborhood. He only carries a baseball bat, not like the "officers" who have bullet-proof vests, pistols, and assault rifles. These seem to be The General's buddies, guys he worked with in the Middle East, Iraq, Libya. Max is not exactly sure where those countries are, but they must be somewhere near Algeria. Muhammad, his squad leader must know; he's Algerian, a Kabyle, in fact. It's all the same to Max—he doesn't know the difference anyway. Max's job is auto mechanic, not geographer. Things are heating up at the moment. It looks like a Comorian gang wants to take over one of the neighborhood parks. Max's gang has planted potatoes there, which have to be guarded against thieves. Anyway, it's all a lot of fun.

*

Mike can't find any more diesel for his machines.

He tried to get some on the black market, but even at the exorbitant price at which he found it, there was not enough. A combine-harvester is a gas guzzler! Too bad: his harvest is going to rot on the spot. This year, there will be nothing. And all those town people coming to the country, dirty, exhausted, soaked with perspiration—they look like refugees! But what the hell is the government doing? What is this business about civil unrest? All they have to do is send in the army! Besides, the army has fuel. Why don't they give him some so he can bring in the harvest? Anyway, if he sees one of those city folks approaching his garden, he's going to get out the rifle.

*

Kenza has become friends with the girlfriend of the local gang leader who controls the neighborhood.

That allows her to leave her apartment without trouble—sometimes they even open the door for her, or help her with her heavy suitcases. In the next neighborhood over, controlled by Sheik Abdel-Khader (formerly Jean-Pierre), she only has to put on a veil and, with the few words of Arabic she knows, she can get around without trouble. She can also go about (by paying a little bribe) in The General's territory—a tough bastard, but fair and predictable.

With her trade—mostly meat, alcohol, and cigarettes, payable only in gold, silver, or jewels—Kenza is starting to get good at the game. Her husband, Mikael, has lost one of his two jobs, but the other, with a security company, is really good for him since it is paid in foodstuffs—especially potatoes and vegetables—which allows his family to eat, and to sell whatever is left over. If only tap water came back and their children could go to school, things would almost be alright.

*

Matthew convinced the police that the murder of his parents wasn't his doing.

He had a rock solid alibi. The sister of one of his video-game buddies said that he was with her. Anyway, the police didn't ask too many questions. A burglary gone wrong, that's so common these days. Matthew still hasn't got his parents' money; it seems their accounts are blocked or something like that. But with the cash he has on hand, he's going to buy the coolest video game ever, *Road Warrior Infinite*, which just came out.

But is the department store over there still open? All these people in the street. What a mess! And what a racket! It's the dead of winter, and it's freezing outside. As far as food goes, he's alright; his parents had plenty of pasta and canned food, but what he's missing is soft drinks, and there's none left at the supermarket. He's spotted the old woman from across the stairs who always has soft drinks in her shopping basket. Maybe she'll give him some. He can buy one from her

… or he can just take it. After all, he's tired, he wants his soda, and what he wants he must get right away.

It's been a month that the supermarkets have been empty.

The food is only available on the black market at exorbitant prices. Elodie's husband has not found work and, with the state having stopped all welfare payments, he has spent everything on alcohol. For Elodie, it's clear: she can no longer put up with her children's cries of hunger. She has sold off everything of any value, but the money only lasted a week. She has tried in vain to find a job, but there are none anymore. The first time a man offered her food for an hour's pleasure, she had refused. Outraged. Now she doesn't even feel disgusted anymore.

✳

James Bockingstock III doesn't give a damn

about what's happening.

He took his private jet just before the troubles started and left for Argentina. He made the right decision buying that farm in the pampas. A fine mansion, fifteen gauchos and their families working for him and 2,000 head of cattle. No suburban punks causing trouble there. He shipped his gold bars, the family jewels, and the artworks there as well. The rest? Well, it's just a cost of doing business. Too bad about his Jaguar XJ13, though—he was fond of it. Too bad about his posh apartment—if the building doesn't burn, he'll recover it someday. Too bad about his house by the sea and his stock- market investments... Anyway, he has gotten so rich and lived so well during these last twenty-five years that spending some time playing gentleman farmer in the pampas suits him just fine. And if his country, now left behind, burns down, well, that's just too bad.

Paul feels like a winner.

A stock trader before the war, he loves his new job operating an M1A2 Abrams tank: action, teamwork, the satisfying hands-on aspect of the work, the visual side, the satisfaction of work well done, no pushing paper ...

François is a brilliant fund manager.

He saw the crisis coming and short-sold everything for the past three years. He's loaded. But now everything has blown up... He was able to flee to the countryside, but he knows it would have been better to buy a property farther away from the highway. Still, François hasn't done so badly so far.

He's spent the last week of chaos in this house, admiring his works of art and drinking one bottle of wine after the other. He has found some great vintages that he had forgotten about while buying more fashionable wines. On the other hand, he will soon have finished the little bit of food he had put aside. This evening, he wrote a letter to his children who are both at the University of Boston, and from whom he has had no news since the beginning of the crisis and the closure of the airports. His ex-wife, on the other hand—he doesn't give a damn where she is, although she left a message on his answering machine saying she was near the border and was going to try to get across in spite of all the refugees.

The house next door is burning. There are cries and gunshots. He watches from his window as the dirty, dilapidated bunch, armed with baseball bats and crowbars, enter his garden. The sound of a window breaking, furniture being pushed aside. Shall he use his .38 revolver to defend himself? There are too many of them! He doesn't want to suffer. He finishes his glass. Slowly, but without hesitation, he raises the barrel to his temple.

<<whoever thinks exponential growth is possible in a finite world is either a fool or an economist!

kenneth boulding

economist

/1910–1983/

<<the soviet union was much better prepared for economic collapse than the united states is. the american economy is going to evaporate like the morning dew. its population expects to be fed, housed, defended, and guided, when it is going to be abandoned to its fate. Upset and disoriented, it will look for someone to blame.

dmitri orlov

engineer & writer

/2010/

<<we are in a period of the somalification and madoffization of the world.

jacques attali

economist

/2010/

<<in the decades to come, we are going to experience hell.

richard heinberg

writer

/2003/

The World of Tomorrow

THE POST-COLLAPSE WORLD will be completely different from the one we know, so different that it is, perhaps, pointless to try to describe it. Economic collapse and its consequences can best be studied in the experience of countries that have undergone great crises in the recent past: the Soviet Union, Argentina, Zimbabwe, and Weimar Germany are a few examples. Certain tendencies can be identified. It is also interesting to read science-fiction authors or look at movies that depict a post-apocalyptic world. We may mention Neville Shute's *On the Beach*, William Gibson's *Neuromancer*, René Barjavel's *Ashes, Ashes*, David Brin's *The Postman*, James Howard Kunstler's *World Made by Hand*, Albert and Allen Hughes's *The Book of Eli*, John Hillcoat's *The Road*, George Miller's *Mad Max*, Larry and Andy Wachowski's *The Matrix*, Terry Gilliam's *12 Monkeys*, Alfonso Cuaron's *Children of Men*, Arnaud Lerrieu's *Happy End,* among many others, as well as the television series *Jericho*, *Survivors*, and even *The Walking Dead*, along with sensationalist fare like *Doomsday Preppers*, and *The Colony*.

The Role of the State

With the economic collapse, governments will be unable to function. They will have no more (or very little) revenue and will be totally discredited. With the energy crisis, the governments of large countries will no longer be able to control their territories. It is possible that the state, or organizations claiming to be the state, will continue to exercise a form of government over a reduced territory while waiting for the end of the crisis. *De facto* autonomous regions, those not plunged into chaos, will preserve a relative degree of authority thanks to their organization and the maintenance of order.

Businesses and Trade

Long logistical chains having broken down, all businesses will become local once again and will try to obtain the parts and materials they need on the spot. In those businesses that do survive, because they produce useful things, salaries will be paid sporadically or in kind. Such salaries will likely not be enough to live on, and people will have to cope with this, as is already the case in Greece since the downturn of 2011. Wealth will consist in access to assets and physical resources like food and drinking water, and to intangibles such as relations and networks. Even if you have physical gold and silver, which will likely be recognized as money, real wealth will consist above all in *know-how*: understanding how to cultivate a garden, how to locate a spring or digging a well, how to find batteries and solar panels, etc. In contrast to the industrial farms, which will have to reduce their acreage due to lack of fertilizer and gasoline for their machines, the small farms that survive will do very well thanks to their knowledge and manageable size.

Many craftsmen (e.g., blacksmiths, carpenters, shoemakers, instrument makers, etc.) make tools that today are considered obsolete, but which will become useful again; they possess know-how that will allow them to continue producing, if they find themselves in a secure environment.

Those who have land can permit certain families to settle on it and be nourished in exchange for their work. It will be in the interest of these land owners to know how to defend their domain against looters — they may even employ militias. It will be a return to a sort of feudal system.

The day when the ATMs stop working, banks close, and the stock exchange shuts down, people will still have needs. So there will, of course, be exchange, trade, and barter. We will see people trying to sell everything they have that is not vitally important; toys, furniture, and clothing will be considered worthless assets in this context, whereas other assets will suddenly be worth a great deal: rifles, ammunition, wood for heating, food, medications and medical supplies, soap, etc. We will see people like you and me sifting through trashcans. Moreover, in a situation of hyperinflation, no one will want paper money. Why exchange something useful, say, bread or a scarf, for a pound of dollars or euros that are no longer worth anything?

The Law

In the context of an economic collapse, it is quite possible that the judicial and police systems will soon be totally absent. After a shorter or longer period of chaos, a new order will gradually be put in place. Laws, prohibitions, and their enforcement will become local again. The legal code will be easy and quick to read. On the other hand, in the absence of a penitentiary system, punishments will be swift and severe. No one will be concerned any more with the psychological reason for criminal acts, but only the acts themselves and their consequences for the community. Finally, there is a great risk that the egalitarian society of the 20th century will disappear and that a redefinition of the ideas of citizenship, rights, and duties will leave a large part of the population outside the decision-making process.

Trades and Occupations

The trades and occupations that continue to exist will be much less numerous, less varied and specialized than those we see today. They will be determined by competence and concrete, immediately useful knowledge (most credentials and the "killer résumé" will cease to have much value). First of all, there will be the trades involving primary production:

> fishing, agriculture, gardening, hunting, and gathering will be done by those who possess the know-how and the traditional tools, and who have no need of machines that require gasoline or oil;

> the production of alcohol and drugs will be very lucrative, for persons used to those substances will be even more desperate than they are today, and a large part of the population will need to forget the trauma they have suffered;

> stock breeders, trainers, shearers, and slaughterers of animals, as well as those in the food preparation trades — butchers, bakers, pastry makers — will flourish;

> trades related to cereal production, such as milling, will once again be important.

Then, the trades related to caring for man and beast:

> doctors or medical aides capable of treating the commonest illnesses, capable of carrying out surgical operations or treating wounds with massage or manipulation (sophisticated and efficient operating theaters will no longer be available, and neither will complicated medications);

> midwives and obstetricians;

> herbalists, botanists, old-fashioned pharmacists and other trades involving knowledge of medicinal plants, their effects, and how to apply them;

> veterinarians who know how to care for animals and assist with their birth.

Among the most important trades will be those related to making and fixing tools, clothing, and machines:

> artisans of all kinds, rope makers, saddlers, weavers, dyers, carpenters, ironworkers, glass blowers, potters, etc.;

> metal workers, substitute part makers, machine makers, and repairmen;

> solar-panel repairmen, wind-turbine repairmen, battery makers, and others concerned with sources of electricity;

> masons and stonecutters, woodcutters and woodworkers, house builders, and repairmen.

Other trades will be those involving access to resources:

> trades requiring knowledge of safe places (hiding places, grottos, etc.);

> trades requiring knowledge of how to get access to water (well drillers, etc.);

> trades involving managing access to natural resources that can be tapped through manual labor (getting old salt, coal, copper, and asphalt mines running);

> trades involving knowing how to recuperate things of value and knowing where to find them (digging through abandoned villas and cities that have become open-air mines for materials, parts, etc.; this will require competence in cabinetmaking, scrap-iron working, masonry, as well as foremen to manage all these manual laborers and unskilled "hands" who help with the heavy lifting);

> trades involving the knowledge of how to use hand tools.

Another important category will be educational trades, probably involving apprenticeship rather than intellectual training.

Itinerant trading involving boats, barges, or carts will probably be a dangerous profession, but very lucrative. Less risky will be markets that will be installed locally or regionally, where communities can exchange goods, parts, agricultural products, seeds, etc. All these trades, rare today, will surely be the salvation of those who can master them — at least insofar as they are not threatened by looters and thieves or put under the control of organized-crime syndicates. For this reason, another important category will be security trades: people able to ensure the safety of goods, tools, territories, and persons. Policemen, soldiers, prison guards, etc. will need a source of revenue and will use their skills by exercising violence, either by defending or attacking. (Some of them know how to create a need for their own profession: if you do not employ them to protect you, they will likely be the ones attacking you).

Undoubtedly, many other trades will also exist. But they will all be much more "primal," much closer to the real sources of wealth, than today. It is imaginable that service professions will disappear — or be limited to prostitution, for example, which for many women may become the only means of survival, as was the case in the large cities of Europe throughout the 16th and 17th centuries. There will be no more office work, no more white-collar employees as productive units in long logistical chains of production. As for those unable to be useful in any special way, their only recourse will be physical labor; it will be very difficult and monotonous for former civil servants, marketing and communication strategists, accountants, bankers, lawyers, notaries, politicians, psychologists, academics, journalists, social workers, etc.

The Family

Although many families today have fallen apart, atomized, or involve only one parent, many will get back together. Several families may group themselves into common manors or clans in order to share resources, costs, and the tasks related to heating, housework, security, and the education of children, as well as the search for and production of food.

Travel and Transportation

With the high price and scarcity of oil — perhaps even its effective disappearance in many regions — our travel habits and our means of transportation will change completely.

Air travel will be the first to disappear, with the discount airlines leading the way. All civilian and military aviation will follow. Using a motor-powered vehicle will become a luxury reserved for the wealthiest people, who can still afford gasoline. The culture of the middle-class SUV or minivan will vanish altogether. In the absence of continual maintenance, road conditions will no longer be assured. This regression has already started in the United States, where, according to the Department of Transportation, eighteen percent of the highways are in poor condition and twenty-nine percent of bridges have structural weaknesses and are in a dangerous condition. Once roads and bridges have been abandoned, our transportation system is finished. Without automobiles, ground transportation will be carried out essentially on horseback, with donkeys or dromedaries, or by wagon. The railroads will work with steam or electrical trains, which can keep going for a while yet, as long as tracks can be secured against theft and attacks. Maritime transportation, especially along rivers, although reduced, can continue to exist. The most efficient means of personal transportation will be the bicycle. A large part of the population has bicycles either working or in a reparable state. With carts in tow, the bike will be the 21st-century means of transportation. Great care will be taken of them.

The Cities

Over the recent course of history, the urban way of life is the factor that has most changed people's living habits. And what changes! Detroit, the "Motor City," was the seventh richest city in the world in the 1950s. Today, the population of its downtown area is out of work, mostly illiterate, and living amid the ruins. Without automobile transportation, towns will rapidly change their appearance and way of operating. First of all, we will see the end of suburbs and industrial zones, which will quickly give way to pastures for cattle, sheep, and goats. The fate of the suburbs will be tragic: they will be filled with the unemployed; they will be looted and then systematically dismantled under the control of gangs or organized crime. Gradually, nature will take over again, as it has done in the town of Prypyat, near Chernobyl.

Downtown areas will contract and become more densely populated. Survivors will regroup in order to better defend themselves and use the remaining resources more efficiently. Many towns, artificially constructed in the middle of nowhere (Milton-Keynes, in the UK, among thousands of examples, comes to mind), will empty out rapidly; so will vast regions opened up only through automobile traffic. The scarcity of electricity, broken elevators, and inadequate water pressure will make the upper stories of apartment blocks uninhabitable. Skyscrapers will be gradually abandoned, remaining as witnesses to the days of abundant fossil energy. The cities that will best be able to survive are those with obviously strategic locations: near ports or bridges, on the major travel routes, easy to defend, etc. Parks and their lawns will be transformed into gardens, but will not produce enough to nourish everyone; hierarchies will be established, often by violence, to manage access to them. Generally speaking, the population of cities will live amid filth, and their numbers will diminish rapidly. Cities with hydroelectric plants, or close to remaining fossil resources, such as Dallas, Texas, or Ploieşti, Romania, will enjoy extraordinary advantages because they will be able to continue operating their water purification stations, sewers, water systems, electricity, etc. These cities will attract everyone else's envy and greed.

Religion

The crisis will mark the great return of religion, as well as religious violence. Religions organized on a global scale will have problems maintaining cohesion and internal structures; sects will multiply. Certain religions will try to give simplistic explanations of the crisis and the sufferings of the world. Groups that imagine themselves to be the strong arm of a vengeful God will be full of passionate intensity.

On the other hand, once the worst of the crisis has passed, the fact of living in smaller communities closer to nature will bring about a return of mysticism and natural spirituality, perhaps even Paganism. A re-enchantment of the world will occur, replete with symbolic stories and tales of the marvelous, as nature will again become a site of meaning, and not just a resource for exploitation.

Racial and Ethnic Tensions

Unfortunately, when times are tough, humans have a tendency to look for someone to blame, rightly or wrongly. Such scapegoats are often found among religious, ethnic, racial, social, or behavioral minorities. Once the social net disappears, and in a situation of chaos and anarchy (whether spontaneous or encouraged by authorities wishing to maintain power), victims are quickly chosen:

> Immigrants, who risk having blame focused on them through the amalgams: *immigrants = job loss; immigrants = drug traffic + crime; immigrants = lower salaries.* In other words: *immigrants = the cause of the crisis;*

> For refugees: *refugees = costs; refugees = new illnesses; refugees = eat our bread,* etc.;

> A religion or religious group, stigmatized because of its practices, real or imagined;

> A racial or ethnic minority, often immigrants or refugees with different customs;

> Well-organized minorities enjoying a lot of material success thanks to networking and powerful lobbies, increasingly conspicuous. Once you draw the equivalences *Wall Street Bankers = crooks* and *Wall Street Bankers = majority Eskimo,* it's easy to draw the invalid conclusion *Eskimo = crooks.* (And bankers can easily be replaced by lawyers, media, politicians, big business, or any other social or professional category at risk of being designated the source of the problems);

> The Baby-Boom generation. The young especially will curse their grandparents and show very little consideration for them once

they are left penniless due to the collapse of the economy and welfare state.

Alas, there is nothing new under the sun. The real danger is not so much spontaneous violence, which is rare and marginal, but rather demagogues taking advantage of it all. Politicians are always ready to seize any opportunity for strengthening their power. The possibility of mass persecutions, ethnic cleansing, even genocide, cannot be discounted. The risk will be greatest in fragile, ethnically diverse societies with racist undercurrents.

Sanitary Effects

Many of the medical and sanitary advances of the 19th and 20th centuries may be lost due to lack of crucial medications — factories no longer working and supplies no longer being available. With stress and privations, people's immune systems are going to be weakened. Opportunistic illnesses, such as viruses, will spread quickly and will probably kill more than civil unrest and wars. Especially in cities and refugee camps, we can expect sanitary crises and epidemics that will cause millions of deaths.

Psychological Effects

Beyond the physical effects of an economic collapse, the psychological effects will be enormous and traumatic. Millions of people, who used to be rich, will not understand how and why their wealth has evaporated. In modern times, fortunes are, at bottom, nothing but abstract representations, series of os and 1s in a computer; when bank computers fail, financial fortunes will cease to exist. These people, tucked away in their lovely but useless villas, prisoners in their luxury apartments, without food or water, are going to be caught destitute. The shock will be especially strong when they recognize that without money, their influence on others is no longer what it was. Worse, the rich, or those perceived as such, will be blamed for the situation and will be targets of popular vengeance; they will suffer humiliation and violence.

The poor and lower middle class will be hit hard by the death of the "nanny state." It will be in the interest of retired persons, the handicapped, and sick to have families to look after them. But paradoxically, those at the greatest risk will be those who enjoyed professional success. Everything these people worked and conspired for over the years will no longer exist: their income and savings will evaporate; their apartments and villas will be worth next to nothing; their cars will no longer run; all their status symbols will disappear. This category of persons will tend to take to drink, abuse drugs, or commit suicide. And we are talking here about dynamic people with useful skills and experience. They will be a significant loss for society. How will they learn to redefine success without the ability to produce and consume? It will be the worst possible time to fall into depression, for we will have the greatest possible need of their mental and physical resources in order to get back on our feet and act.

Scenarios

The collapse scenarios we shall have to face over the coming years are difficult to predict with precision, for there are many of them. And so much uncertainty is due to the nonlinear dynamics of human nature and unforeseen external events. In fact, human history is often determined by threshold effects. It's like a pregnant woman: we know the progressive, more or less rapid process that ends up putting her in that condition, but a woman cannot be *half* pregnant or *gradually* pregnant. It is an either/or binary. Similarly, a molecule of water will change its state once it accumulates or loses a certain fixed amount of energy: suddenly, water is vapor, or it is ice. There are unforeseen elements that have enormous consequences in a favorable environment, while they would have been insignificant otherwise.

Examples are numerous: the assassination of the Austrian Archduke at Sarajevo in 1914, the storming of the Bastille in 1789, the Boston Tea Party of 1773...

So what are the most probable scenarios for the next few years? Below, I imagine a few. Though some might seem impossible or bizarre, we shouldn't forget the dramatic, unforeseen turns history has made over the centuries. The scenarios I propose can be graphed, with the horizontal axis representing the size of the catastrophe, the vertical axis — its rapidity:

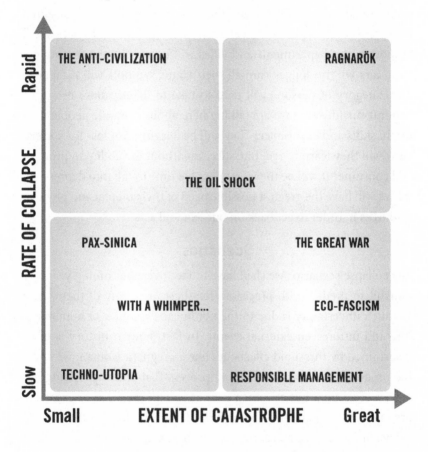

Techno Utopia

It's the End of History

The promise of liberal capitalism delivers worldwide. Financial crises come and go, but, in general, the world experiences steady economic growth. The massive debts of Western states are a burden, but these are countered by the discovery of massive oil reserves off the coast of Brazil, guaranteeing affordable oil for the foreseeable future. Chinese and Indian manufacturing power the global boom.

Not everyone benefits, though. International finance operates on an almost unregulated basis, and boom-and-bust cycles regularly wipe out unwary investors. Ordinary people occasionally face outright disaster, but the very wealthy continue to prosper. The world has its first "trillionaire" (in U.S. dollars) — an Indian financial and media magnate.

With general prosperity comes political apathy. Celebrity divorces, outlandish fashion, and electronic diversions are far more interesting to the masses than economics or government. "Smart clothes" are the newest rage, outfits that can change color according to the wearer's mood (determined by body temperature and an aggregate of social-networking status updates).

Social observers and pollsters conclude that people are, in general, satisfied. Political agitation is rare. Wars are almost entirely a thing of the past, and authors and talking heads praise the "end of violence." A few "Chavist" guerillas in Latin America and jihadists in Afghanistan give the world's militaries something to do, but the insurgents are more an object of pity than a threat.

Though a few media progressives bleat about inequality, severe global poverty is a thing of the past. Genetically modified foods and lab grown meat allow the entire world to be supplied with water and cheap, ostensibly nutritious food. Obesity is going global. With basic needs met and a (more or less) efficient global administration, the world population stabilizes around 10 billion people.

This population boom allows a dramatic increase in productivity. The global marketplace grows even more integrated and interconnected, as societies are defined by increasing consumption and trade. The quality of life for people around the world rises more dramatically in a shorter period than at any other time in history.

Market-friendly environmentalism integrates seamlessly with the global economy, as new technology allows for significant reductions in the amount of electricity and fossil fuels consumed by industry, transportation, and housing. Nearly forty percent of energy now comes from renewable sources. Defying pessimistic predictions, the international press reports that "global warming" was simply a short, abnormal phase in the long pattern of climatic cycles of the Earth. With no serious resource crises on the horizon, global corporations and governments prepare to launch the first colonizing and mining missions to the Moon and Mars.

Most important, perhaps, the great dream of the international elite is finally realized as a culturally and politically interdependent world finally yields to an efficient global administration. Based out of Jerusalem, the world government is headed by figures such as Henry Kissinger and Jacques Attali (or at least their brains preserved in vats of amniotic fluid connected to a mainframe computer.) The new leaders are able to act without much interference from the rump national governments. However, this regime is keen on preserving elections and parliaments as part of its efforts in "democratization." No one seems to care. Voter non-participation reaches levels of almost eighty percent, and mandatory voting — done digitally on smartphones and smart TVs — is seriously debated.

Despite global unification, economic growth, and increasing lifespans, the people of the planet Earth are gripped by an undefined malaise. The vast majority are on some kind of pharmaceutical anti-depressants, and self-medication through alcohol and legal (and illegal) drugs are so commonplace as to pass without comment. The latter, however, has no political outlet, and is thus funneled into ever more bizarre subcultures or electronic simulacra. After all — there's no profit to be made in rebellion.

Of course, out on the fringes, there are still a few neo-Malthusian prophets of doom talking about the impossibility of infinite growth in a finite world. No one takes them seriously. As one public intellectual repeatedly puts it, "They haven't learned anything." Everything works out for the best — in this, the best of all possible worlds!

2. Responsible Management

The Wheel Turns

The financial crises never really ended in the developed world. Western governments were forced to implement severe austerity measures and strict spending controls. Governments collapsed in the face of public outrage, and even the eurozone finally broke apart.

Faced with angry voters, politicians turned on the financiers deemed responsible for the crisis. Thanks to the work of the new "International Tribunal for Financial Crimes," many of the most successful investors and financiers from the 1980s onward were put on trial. Vast fortunes were surrendered to the state. As the debt-driven financial system collapsed, American voters turned on the Federal Reserve, and the once untouchable institution was dissolved. A new, gold-backed dollar was instituted. It was worth 1/100 of the retired "greenback," but this devaluation allowed the American economy to regain its footing and begin a slow recovery.

And besides, the damage had already been done. The American standard of living was gutted by a decades-long, quiet recession; some regions declined to Third World status. Still, though there is occasional civil unrest, the American sense of patriotism coupled with an aggressive national-security state allows the country to hold together. Troops from the National Guard and even the United States Marines become familiar sights on the country's streets, as the military takes on a more prominent role in what is delicately called "domestic peacekeeping."

Meanwhile, millions of people in Africa and Asia die because of droughts and climate irregularities. Scientists conclude that they underestimated the effects of global warming, and various developed nations collaborate more seriously to ensure climate security. A great series of nationalizations ensues around the world, especially of banks and large distribution companies. This hinders economic growth but creates a stable food supply.

The sudden scarcity of resources causes the mostly White nations of the West to implement repatriation programs for their Latin American, Middle Eastern, and African populations. As the welfare state is largely abolished, millions "self-deport" back to their countries of origin. Millions more are enticed or compelled to do so through largely successful "de-immigration" programs. After a period of turmoil, the Third World actually benefits during this time of crisis from the return of skilled workers from the West, the repudiation of debts, and higher prices for raw materials and food.

Largely driven by economic and ecological concerns, a world government slowly begins to take shape. Mostly represented by the G20 and a Security Council of ten nations from the UN, the new global administration aggressively moves to limit greenhouse gas emissions. Oil is rationed and has been declared a "common resource of humanity" on the model of water.

Oil-producing nations, especially in the Middle East, are outraged by this new global order. However, the new UN Army, largely composed of a working partnership between the American and Chinese militaries, discourages resistance. With developing nations having secured their needed resources, the world settles into impoverished stability. The Western standard of living plunges to about the level of China, but changing lifestyles make this easier to bear. For the first time in centuries, Westerners flee the cities, and agrarian life and values become more prominent.

Of course, the global government and a rather authoritarian world order are not without their critics. However, most people do not see any other alternative. The global administration is able to effectively weather a series of environmental problems, including a severe hurricane season in the American Southeast. Better management of land

and food stocks allow for a successful response to what historians begin to call the Great Drought. Finally, the effective institution of a Chinese-style One Child Policy over all of Africa, India, Latin America, and the Middle East—abundantly financed by private patrons and put in place under the threat of severe economic and military sanctions—creates a drastic fall in the birth rates. It is estimated that the world population will stabilize at around 8 billion, eventually falling to six.

The world is hardly prosperous, but at least it is peaceful. And besides, say many observers, things could have been far worse...

3. Pax Sinica

The Chinese Century

On the 20th of May, the First Secretary of the Chinese Communist Party and President of China proudly announced the creation of a new Asiatic Co-Prosperity Sphere. The members included Japan, the Unified Korean Republic, Vietnam, Laos, Cambodia, Myanmar, Thailand, and Malaysia.

The new economic and political order was enabled by China's crushing victory in what their propaganda ministry called the "Lightning War" against India, Australia, and New Zealand. Though critics pessimistically mutter about huge scores of civilian causalities in Indonesia caused by chemical weapons, there is no denying Chinese hegemony over the entire Pacific. Indonesia itself is put under Chinese military occupation. The Anglosphere's Pacific outposts of Australia and New Zealand are transformed into Chinese protectorates at the small price of guaranteeing delivery of raw materials and fishing rights to Beijing. Most Australians and New Zealanders are relatively satisfied with the new arrangement, considering it inevitable. As for India, the "world's largest democracy" quietly realigns with the Chinese world bloc, joined by second-tier powers such as Russia and Brazil.

The roots of the Chinese victory lay in its quick response to a systematic crisis caused by a slowing economy and unemployment. Recognizing the extent of the crisis, the Chinese leadership crushed dissent ruthlessly using both internal security forces and the military.

Unencumbered by domestic political considerations, China exploited the West's weakness caused by the global economic crisis. China forged a long series of military and mutual-support alliances with its trading partners in Asia, Africa, and the Middle East. At the same time, the Chinese aggressively developed its power-projection capabilities — with the help of technology from export-hungry countries such as Israel and Russia.

The rise of Chinese military power went almost unopposed by the West because of its own serious political situation. The collapse of the eurozone and demographic tensions within the ancient nations of Europe largely crippled the Continent's military power. As for the United States, disastrous military blunders in Syria and Iran pointlessly expended scarce resources, while alienating potential allies. From Angola to Zimbabwe, Third World nations openly renounced the American world order and put themselves under the protection of the Chinese Navy in the Indian Ocean.

When a conflict finally erupted between the American and Chinese militaries, the United States was simply exhausted. An incident between the Chinese aircraft carrier *Zheng He* and an American spy ship escalated into a short but intense naval battle between the titans. After the loss of several submarines, the United States had threatened to attack targets on Chinese territory. China responded by putting its nuclear weapons on high alert, which quickly forced the American political establishment to back down.

China also exploited America's demographic weaknesses by helping to instigate race riots in Los Angeles, Oakland, Atlanta, Washington DC, and Detroit. Faced with more pressing domestic considerations and crippled by an inefficient political system, America retreated. Uncle Sam eventually withdrew from its bases in Korea and

Japan, claiming that these were "cost-cutting measures" or efforts in "democratization." The truth was that America could no longer afford to compete with a serious military competitor in the Indian Ocean.

The Chinese government also exploited the atmosphere of crisis during what became known as the Great Drought. China used its vast stockpiles of rice and cereals to assist Asian and African nations, saving an estimated 150 million lives. African nations, who supplied the labor force for Chinese agriculture and even some industry, took the hint. Pakistan and even India also accepted Chinese aid after a disastrous conflict over water resources in Kashmir. By the end of the decade, long-lost Taiwan was peacefully reunited with the People's Republic.

By the middle of the 21st century, China found itself as the most prominent nation in the world. As the exhausted populations of Europe and the United States grasped for alternatives, China's efficient model of market authoritarianism looked ever more attractive.

Of course, after droughts, resource scarcities, and military conflict, the global population has fallen considerably, sinking to 4 billion. But the world is, at least, at peace under the new order of *Pax Sinica*.

4. With a Whimper and a Bang

The Return of History

In theory, the financial crisis that ripped apart the West in 2008 should have led to important changes. However, the governments of the world largely left the existing system in place. Enormous amounts of money were spent, but no one knew exactly where it all came from — other than the printing press. While some banks went under, others were recapitalized.

Still, as promised, consumption ticked up, stock prices rose, and most people thought the worst had been avoided. Many complained about news of record-breaking profits for multinationals and big banks and outlandish bonuses for CEOs. The case of one cheeky Wall Street trader who got a "bonus of a billion" on Christmas made headlines around the country, but there was no serious political momentum behind reform as long as the economic figures remained generally favorable.

However, in the absence of systemic change, the underlying instability of the financial sector quietly grew worse and worse. The price of gold continued to rise, as countries with a budget surplus bought more and more of it — as did the few savers who saw inflation destroying their fortunes. The price of $10,000 per ounce was breached … then quickly surpassed.

When the long-expected hyperinflation finally arrived, Europe's periphery was hit the hardest. Portugal, Ireland, and Greece were put under direct IMF control. Considerable unrest broke out, and the European Central Bank and the EU decided on a plan of direct aid to their populations, to be financed by a new European tax.

The American government responded the only way it knew how, with more "quantitative easing." Though this round was ostensibly directed towards small businesses and homeowners overladen with debt, observers quietly noted that the money ultimately went to the banks. The American press largely ignored this slow-motion fiscal collapse, choosing instead to focus on a "sex tape" scandal involving the President. While the masses were glued to tabloid TV, the global economic and political situation spiraled out of control.

The bottom fell out when the price of oil, increasingly negotiated in the Chinese yuan, rose to $250 a barrel. Economic instability in China led to shocking crackdowns by government security forces (there were rumors of hundreds of thousands of casualties). Meanwhile, the so- called American "middle class" began sleeping at the office or in their cars to avoid having to commute. Prosperous suburban neighborhoods transformed into bankrupt war zones plagued by crime and nonexistent public services. Europe experienced similar turmoil, but the impact was cushioned by widespread public transportation.

As politicians railed against "austerity" and cuts in government outlays, Western populations began to experience something much more painful—scarcity and market failures. The savings of lifetimes were consumed overnight by rising prices.

Helpless to deal with the economic crisis, populist politicians seized power in Europe and Latin America with promises to restrict immigration and protect national resources. The European Union imposed an outright moratorium on immigration. The United States took a more militarized approach, creating minefields and machine-gun turrets in the new "No Man's Land" of the U.S.-Mexican border.

As the West retreated inwards, the Global South's precarious stability collapsed. Civil wars erupted in Mexico, Ethiopia, Mali, Senegal, and Kenya. In Asia, the conflict between India and Pakistan crippled regional growth. Pakistan was further roiled by a low-intensity conflict within its own borders following the withdrawal of NATO troops from Afghanistan. China and the United States did what they could to prop up the Pakistani government and secure the nation's nuclear arsenal.

Historians called the decline of Western economies the "Great Destruction." GDP regressed in Europe and the United States by an average of twenty percent, reaching as much as fifty percent in some regions. Thanks to domestic markets, China was able to limit its decline and even maintain weak growth in some areas, but its dream of swift development was shattered.

The West paid heavily for its refusal to invest in renewable energy and infrastructure. World agricultural production collapsed because of rising fertilizer prices, and widespread starvation occurred throughout Africa and the Middle East. In Egypt, outright famine led to a bloody civil conflict.

Fleeing the devastation of the Third World, refugees stormed the borders of Europe, where newly elected populists did their best to keep them out. Ethno-nationalism returned, as countries shut their borders and turned on foreigners. Europe was "united" only through mutual suspicion and hatred. On the Israeli frontier, the "most moral army in the world" wasted no time in gunning down what the government called "illegal infiltrators." In the United States, food riots in cities such as Detroit, Atlanta, Los Angeles, and Washington DC led to outright counterinsurgency efforts by the military. In certain regions, the military cut off and bombed the so-called "lost areas" as if they were part of a foreign country. Rising violence and cultural clashes led to an increase in terrorism, religious fanaticism, and even new forms of narcotics, as people everywhere tried to escape experiencing the end of what they took for granted.

In the next few years, the United States invaded Canada to secure oil resources (using some "national security" or moral pretext that few can remember). The American military, already used to suppressing its own population, felt no compunction in dealing harshly with foreigners. Nationalists, non-White immigrants, and xenophiles fought in the streets of Europe, as Britain and France plunged into a bloody civil war. Spain, Italy, Romania, Hungary, Bulgaria, Poland, and Greece elected ultra-authoritarian regimes that carried out deliberate campaigns of extermination against their African and Middle Eastern populations. The figures could never be verified, but people spoke of tens of millions dead.

Russia actually emerged from the global chaos in a strengthened position as it fought and won a brief war with Ukraine over control of the Donbas mining region. Thanks to its relatively sparse population, its strong agricultural capacity, and its resources in gas and hydrocarbons, Russia gradually expanded its sphere of influence over Eastern Europe and the Nordic countries.

With no one to restrain them, India and Pakistan finally waged a war over control of agricultural resources. The question of Pakistan's nuclear arsenal was resolved with the destruction of Delhi, Jaipur, and Mumbai. However, India eventually prevailed and exacted terrible vengeance by deliberately reducing the Muslim population in the Indus Delta. Over 200,000 died so India could exploit the new land.

China's authoritarian social system was able to maintain order in its territory. Once again, the Middle Kingdom drew in on itself. The Communist state deliberately reduced its own population, while ensuring no serious challenges emerged to government authority. While globalization was set back, communication networks were maintained by falling back on older technologies, like long-wave radio or satellite communication. "Globalization" became a meaningful concept only to the rich who could afford to pay for such equipment.

Towards the end of the century, a number of nation-states collapsed into smaller independent regions better able to function. These included Australia, Indonesia, India, Canada, the United States, France, Spain, the UK, and Mexico. The African nations descended into complete anarchy. Countries like China, Brazil, Argentina and Russia came close to disintegration, but were able to maintain their territorial integrity.

Switzerland, Iceland, Norway, Sweden, Finland, the Boer Republic, Botswana, Namibia, and even New Zealand were able to ride out the storm thanks to their isolation and self-sufficiency in food and energy.

The new global economy saw the return of the "city-state" as a viable political structure. City-states formed an oasis of comfort, security, and technology in the midst of violence and chaos. In regions that possessed oil, refineries, industrial capacity, and an adequate agricultural base, they became quite powerful. Among the most prominent were the Republic of Libreville in the former Gabon, the independent town of Dammam in Arabia, the Houston-Austin conglomeration in Texas, the Sultanate of Brunei, the town of Mosul in Kurdistan, Bahrain, and others.

After a century of instability, a chastened humanity lived in a world with less technology, less energy, and less stability. Wars over resources eventually petered out, due to exhaustion rather than moral sentiment. Nuclear weapons became inoperative simply because the infrastructure could no longer be financed. The global population eventually settled at about 2 billion people. Weary and scared, they dedicated most of their energy to survival.

5. The Oil Shock

A Supply Crisis Puts Civilization on a New Course

People once referred to the "third oil shock" of late 2007 and early 2008 when the market price of crude reached record-setting levels. Today, one hundred dollars a barrel seems quaint, if not impossibly cheap.

Following the death of King Abdullah of Saudi Arabia, the new King Aziz launched a reform program in the Kingdom. More importantly, he announced that Saudi Arabian oil reserves had been overestimated by a factor of ten. There were not 200 billion barrels left to be extracted, but only twenty. The result was instantaneous. The price of oil shot upward, doubling in six months — then doubling again in three. This market event led to a devastating rise in transportation costs and prices for consumer goods. The Global South suffered the most, with the populations of several nations either revolting or emigrating *en masse* to the West.

China and the West were forced into an Energy Cold War, as each side waged proxy wars and financed revolutions to destabilize suppliers and ensure drilling contracts. Neither side won any meaningful victories, and the struggle only worsened the supply deficit.

The economic crisis that followed was long and had profound consequences — some of which were quite positive. In America and Europe, activists revived an old slogan, "*We don't have oil, but we have ideas!*" Renewable energy became an economic necessity, rather than an ideological axe to grind. As a result, both China and the West pursued alternative forms of economic organization and energy supplies. The global population eventually stabilized at around 5 billion people. After a lengthy slowdown, the world economy began to recover — and this time, it was on a sustainable course.

Although the price paid was high, the world's energy future was more secure since civilization was less dependent on fossil fuels. And it all occurred due to the momentary bout of honesty of a Saudi king.

6. Ecofascism

The Rise of the Deep Greens

The Great Global Depression was characterized by an ecological catastrophe and economic regression. In response, right-wing nationalists (derided as "fascists") and left-wing environmentalists (mocked as "hippies") both challenged the political establishment in Europe. Though the two groups hated each other, they had much in common. Both featured charismatic, blunt, and brash leaders who had contempt for mainstream political discourse. And both were characterized by an impatience with parliamentary procedure and an eagerness to find authoritarian solutions to everyday problems.

The trend was slower to develop in the United States, but eventually even the Tea Party dropped libertarianism and grew statist "green leaves." In some nations of Europe, Green Parties became a dominant political force with the rise of "Deep Green" coalitions in France, the UK, Germany, Italy, and most of the Nordic countries.

Green governments gradually abandoned nuclear reactors and turned to renewable energy — especially solar and wind power. Once looked at with suspicion, these efforts met with success and proved effective as job creators. Before long, Asian nations and even North and Latin America were aping the Greens' energy policies.

Because renewable energy limited vulnerability to oil-price shocks, the financial and debt crises were minimized. Broad segments of the population were employed in great public works, limiting unemployment. Governments also used environmentalism as a justification to impose taxes and regulations to limit greenhouse emissions, pollution, and the overuse of soil, water, and fertilizers.

In contrast to other governments of the past, the Deep Green leaders were more concerned with protecting national resources than pursuing economic growth for its own sake. They showed a willingness to reduce welfare payments and coupled this with commitments to border security and even forced repatriation. The latter allowed them to co-opt some of the support from the "disreputable" nationalists. Large majorities endorsed these policies and returned most of the parties to office with mandates for even more decisive action.

Eventually, Deep Green parties arrived at the conclusion that individualism itself was the problem. Governments must have the freedom of action to face the issues of the day. Democracy was too haphazard and messy. Again, the public seemed to agree.

Eugenic theories, which had been suppressed as a wicked "pseudo-science" since the end of the Second World War, re-emerged. It became common sense to think that a reduction of the world's population was necessary, and that the most efficient way to accomplish this was to limit births. A permit was required to have a child. A point system was implemented to give priority to the gifted. According to the "Mink Amendment" of the U.S. Constitution, national policy was designed "to avoid having that great mass of dull, obese, and useless people reproduce themselves." European legislation was similarly blunt.

Deep Greens showed a willingness to use tactics that a prior generation would have called ruthless. In order to limit demand on the welfare system, the mentally handicapped and those with Down syndrome were systematically tracked down and euthanized. Seniors over the age of sixty were barred from the public health system. The euthanasia of the severely ill was made free and immediate, unless specifically forbidden by the family. It was, however, the epidemics that had the greatest impact in limiting populations. These came out of nowhere, disproportionately affecting the poor, who could not afford the vaccines.

Gradually, and despite the ephemeral resistance of (mostly religious) groups hostile to this new world order, the human population
fell to 2 billion. Educated opinion concurred that this was an appropriate figure for sustainable and permanent human existence.
Practical science and human consciousness had undergone a
revolution. Instead of trying to master nature, men of the new century
understood that they should try to live in balance with Mother Earth.
Though some still object to the eugenic measures that have reduced
the population, few have qualms with the positive consequences. Even
critics admit that much good has come out of some evil.

7. The Great War

World War III Finally Comes

The United States of America suffered a crisis of confidence in all its
institutions. The government responded with repression, even to the
point of no longer measuring unemployment, lest bad figures hurt
public morale. As few trusted the banks, the stock markets, the news,
and the government, investor confidence collapsed. The European
economies also suffered, and the global supply chain, based on Asian
manufacturing and American consumption, was disrupted.

Barack Obama disappeared from the political scene even more
rapidly than he had appeared a dozen years before. He was replaced
by a populist, right-leaning administration. Many wondered if they
had been properly voted into office; no one could deny that they possessed vocal supporters.

The new regime attempted to solve the economic crisis in one
stroke by repudiating American debt with the claim that "foreign
interests" had imposed it on the American people. A new, gold-
backed dollar was issued. The administration also announced that the
country possessed huge, hidden gold reserves sufficient to back the
new currency. However, no one was allowed to confirm this assertion
independently, and the international press was suspicious.

The government's second step in confronting economic recession targeted unemployment. The President re-instituted conscription and raised the number of active-duty personnel in the military and the newly created "Homeland Security Force" to over 10 million men and women. The unemployed of all ages, eager for guaranteed food and shelter — and a smart-looking uniform — volunteered assiduously.

The new President attempted to win support for his controversial regime by waving the flag and baiting China. "Chinese manipulation" was a staple of American political rhetoric, and international summits were marked by confrontational theatrics. The regime complemented this with a massive armaments build-up. Washington doubled its defense budget within four years. The media were put on notice with "The New Patriotic Act," lest they "publish poisonous material that weakens the American people's resolve."

Most of these policies failed. The economy remained sluggish, outside the defense sector. The new dollar was never fully accepted at home or abroad, and alternative currencies became prominent. The right-leaning regime also antagonized African-Americans and Latinos by stripping them of their government privileges. Many Whites felt emboldened to engage in causal racism.

Still, the international situation remained stable ... until Israel launched an attack against what they called "terrorist" bases in the oc-cupied territories. The conflict escalated to the point that Israel reoc-cupied the Sinai region and bombed Cairo and Damascus as warnings to the enemies of the Jewish state. Iran responded with missile attacks; though there were not many Israeli casualties, the Israelis felt that a critical line had been crossed. A long-planned campaign against Iran was launched by the United States and Israel, including the use of tac-tical nuclear weapons. Though there were timid protests by Europe, China, and Russia, most of the world felt they had to accept this star-tling use of force.

But while the American international position was strong, its domestic situation was crumbling. The new "blueback" currency continued to decline in legitimacy as rumors spread that the government did not have enough gold holdings to back it.

The United States and the rest of the world might have still recovered from this instability. It was "some damn thing" in Asia, however, that instigated World War III. Pakistan, still allied with China but under the *de facto* control of an Islamist coalition, launched a surprise nuclear attack against India. The Indian response was equally devastating.

More than 100 million people died on both sides in less than a week.

The American government, desperate to secure domestic support, used the pretext of the Chinese-Pakistani alliance to impose a unilateral blockade against the two nations. Washington also used a combination of diplomatic pressure and military threats to force other nations to repudiate their oil-export contracts with China. The Chinese viewed this economic aggression as an act of war, but undertook no military action.

Ultimately, it was a naval conflict that sparked the greatest conflagration in world history. The Chinese navy began escorting oil tankers from the Persian Gulf, leading to battle with American ships enforcing a blockade of certain Middle Eastern ports. Under ambiguous circumstances, the Seventh American Pacific Fleet clashed with a Chinese escort force. When Chinese airplanes responded, American bombers based in Guam and Japan bombed military airbases in China. Abandoning restraint, the Chinese mobilized the entirety of its armed forces. The North Koreans prepared their military for attack as well.

The President of the United States, fearful of a conventional struggle with the enormous Chinese military and its allies, acted decisively. In a speech to the nation, he announced that the United States was forced to defend itself against a critical national threat. During the address, the U.S. launched the initial full-scale nuclear strike against the People's Republic of China and the Democratic People's Republic of Korea.

Within a few moments, more than 500 million Chinese were killed by over four hundred American nuclear warheads. The Chinese responded with an attack of about fifty warheads, as well as conventional strikes against American bases in Japan and the Pacific. The North Koreans launched a suicidal assault on the South. They were stopped, but not before Seoul was completely destroyed.

The conflict devastated Asia and North America and plunged the entire world into chaos. More than 200 million North Americans and a billion Asians would die from various causes as a result of the war. Casualties also included many Canadians, who died from radiation and accidental attacks.

The economic, ecological, and psychological effects set the global economy back by decades. The electromagnetic pulses of nuclear weapons led to the failure of most computers, electrical networks, and information systems. The resulting collapse of transportation networks for food and medical supplies led to millions of casualties around the world, even in nations that had nothing to do with the conflict. Instead of conquering new frontiers of space, science, and technology, the people of Earth had to painfully rebuild what World War III had destroyed in just a few moments.

8. The Anti-Civilization

And The Return of the Tribes

Rather than a retreat into the nation-state, the economic crisis resulted in even larger governmental units. NAFTA in North America provided the basis for the eventual North American Union that absorbed Canada, the United States, and Mexico. In Latin America, the trade union Mercosur gradually became the South American equivalent of the EU, mostly under the leadership of the regional superpower Brazil. The EU itself, far from collapsing, actually expanded, eventually including the countries on the southern shore of the Mediterranean. Turkey became a base for the European Union to gradually seek control over the entire Middle East and Southern Caucasus.

The new Federation of Asian Nations (FAN), under Chinese and Indian leadership, included most nations of the region, even Japan.

Russia regained political control over the dictatorships of Central Asia, Belarus, and Ukraine. The continent of Africa and its vast resources was a source of conflict between the great blocs, but disputes were limited by a tacit but well understood agreement that such conflicts never expand beyond African issues.

However, the real story of global society was not the breakup into regional blocs, but the division of the world's population into three classes. Today, these classes largely ignore national and regional boundaries. The first class, the wealthy global elite, benefits from planet-wide economies of scale and capital gains. They live in the regions most protected against climate change, pollution, and civil unrest.

The middle class, mostly concentrated in the cities, is slowly being squeezed economically. Social mobility is all but eliminated as the bourgeoisie can rarely escape their status as office drones. In desperation, they turn to intense electronic entertainment and substance abuse, or simply become obsessed with their meaningless jobs.

The great fear of the middle class is being fired and suffering banishment to the suburbs of the poor, the vast "third class" that subsists in walled-in areas. The multicolored global underclass has little in common with the "working class" of ages past. The new planetary *lumpenproletariat* is largely illiterate, violent, and controlled by ethnic gangs and organized crime.

In response to this unstable social system, governments around the world limited political speech to only "constructive criticism." Frequent financial or moral scandals are usually co-opted by suspiciously timed terrorist attacks that serve to remind people of the "real problems." The justification of all the regional blocs is the same — "growth." In the name of growth, industries and governments continue to aggressively pursue resources, even in the midst of eco-logical disaster.

There is resistance from outside the system, however. Though few are willing to confront the supranational governments directly, new communities are forming in rural areas around the world. These are termed "Fractions," and they justify themselves as attempts to preserve certain traditions and ways of life.

Fractions have entrenched themselves in the Alps, the Black Forest, the Scottish Highlands, the Apennines, the Rocky Mountains, the Rif, the Balkans, the Urals, the Altai Mountains, the Himalayas, the Andes, and Tierra del Fuego.

Ultimately, this strategy of survival outside the system and revolution from the periphery is proving enduring. After the depletion of marine ecosystems, other ecosystems started to show signs of fragility and instability, before disappearing, one after the other, in just a few years. Food crises were severe (and still are), and each region has, more or less, transformed itself into an insular and paranoid police state. Cries of "Eat the Rich!" are heard, and often taken literally. With no sense of cultural unity or ideological justification to fall back on, the global system of regional blocs is collapsing with startling speed.

By the end of the 21st century, world population has been reduced to less than half a billion. Only those belonging to the Fractions, in fortified villages and farms across the globe, seem to have any hope of surviving and rebuilding civilization.

9. Ragnarök

The World Ends in Fire ... and Is Reborn

Hindus believe that human civilization spiritually degenerates in the course of the *Kali Yuga*, the Dark Age. In Northern mythol-ogy, *Ragnarök* is a prophesied End of the World involving a series of events, including three successive winters without sunlight followed by a great battle in which most gods and men die. A series of natural disasters follow: the world is submerged by the waves and destroyed in the flames. But after these tribulations, there is rebirth. The remaining gods help the only remaining couple to repopulate the world. These myths were in the thoughts of many as the great crises unfolded. At first, it just seemed to be a financial problem. The banks were swallowed up, one after another, and governments seemed confused and impotent.

The real cause of the catastrophe, however, was something entirely unexpected. One night, a little "second moon" appeared in the night sky. NASA and the Russian Federal Space Agency announced that it was an uncharted comet, which had hitherto escaped the notice of observatories. They claimed the probability of its hitting the Earth was about ten percent, though that estimate kept being revised upwards as it drew nearer.

Peoples around the world interpreted the comet through various religious or cultural traditions. In a way, it came out the world's archetypal nightmare.

There was a sudden burst of religiosity, mass suicides, panics, debauchery, massacres, and murder-for-hire to settle old scores. The Russian, Chinese, and American governments launched nuclear rockets to try to intercept or redirect this comet, but it was already too late. For a time, all wars halted and combatants on all sides watched the sky.

A final desperate strike was successful only in part. The comet was hit by a missile and fragmented ... but its deadly intent was unaltered.

One part of the comet hit planet Earth on the northern coast of the Red Sea near Jeddah, Saudi Arabia, which it instantly vaporized. Everything within a radius of three hundred miles, including Mecca, was burned to a crisp (though the black stone of the Ka'aba was not damaged, and many began to speak of a miracle). Another piece of the comet, the largest, hit the Earth around the Gulf of Guinea, creating a wave almost one mile high, which destroyed nearly all life within a radius of 750 miles. The third and fourth cometary fragments hit the Mato Grasso region of Brazil and La Paz in Bolivia. Hundreds of millions lost their lives in a few minutes.

Though most of humanity survived the impact, the comet's fragments sent thousands of cubic meters of dust and ash into the atmosphere. A thick cloud blanketed the Earth, blocking out the Sun. Over the course of the following decade, temperatures fell considerably.

Today, the winters are extremely cold and wet; harvests are reduced to almost nothing; and what little does sprout can barely maintain itself. Most of the world's flora and fauna is endangered, if not extinct. Everyone fights for the kind of resources we once took for granted. A simple can of food is a priceless bounty, as it means living another day. Those who have survived — who can say how many we are? — are concentrated in the regions not cloaked in darkness or in the underground shelters.

Mankind is at risk of disappearing entirely. It was only we, the "paranoid" men and women who had prepared for catastrophe, who didn't get swept up in the tumult. We survivors, who remained in radio contact during the years of chaos, have organized ourselves into communities. We are the new leaders of humanity. We will repopulate the Earth, as was foretold in myth.

President Wolinsky has a serious problem.

Following the revolt and destruction caused by the invasion of downtown areas by inhabitants of the inner cities, the government has been evacuated to a command post in a secure location. The Army Central Command had been put on red alert. But no one foresaw that Wolinsky's own security—bodyguards, secret-service staff, and the rest—would reroute the presidential plane to a little rural airport like this.

They keep asking him:

"Where's the central bank's gold? We know you had the gold transferred to a secure location. If you don't want to spend your last hours in horrible suffering, tell us quickly. Marcel and Saïd here would just love to show you what they learned to do in Lybia..."

"You don't have any right! You won't get far!"

"Don't worry about us, pal—Mister President, I mean to say. We know everything's fucked. Even the army doesn't control anything anymore. That's what happens when you fuck around while your friends are stuffing their pockets. If you don't give us what we want, we'll let Marcel and Saïd work on you. They'll think of something medieval."

"Stop, I'll tell you ... I'll let you take it all ... but there isn't that much gold, you know ..."

"We know. But it's enough for our projects."

"You won't get far. As soon as you try to spend that gold—there are a few tons, after all—you're going to get caught!"

"Don't worry about us. We don't plan on going shopping with it."

General Hermann Schponz is Commander-in Chief- of the Bundeswehr.

He knows that the history of the world will be changed in the next few hours. He must present the Chancellor with plans for a lightning offensive to resolve the dramatic situation in Germany. Since the world crisis degenerated into a war in the Middle East and all its oil wells came under Chinese control, there hasn't been more than two months' worth of oil in the country's reserves.

The plan he has worked out with his strategic advisors is risky but bold—a surprise seizure of the Romanian wells at Ploiesti by Col. Mustapha Golügolü's 7th Fallschirmjäger division, later to be relieved by the panzer divisions based in Kosovo. Russia seems willing to accept the German takeover of the Balkans in exchange for an agreement giving them *carte blanche* in Ukraine and the Caucasus. The more things change...

Chris regrets what he did.

The virus has done more damage than he ever imagined. The chaos resulting from it has been enormous. Millions in the large cities were quickly infected. The collapse of the hospital system ... then of the entire economy ... plunged the world into a violent spiral. Michael, sick in bed, is awaiting the inevitable in his room at the Cabeza Negra Inn where he is hiding out. The buildings are getting burned down one after another by looters from the nearby suburbs. He's afraid. He'll be burned alive, like so many others.

He also knows that his killers are his fellow Brothers of God.

Lt Col Sandoz knew it would be a difficult journey.

His mission was to secure the northern frontier of the Canton of Geneva with his reinforced, mechanized infantry battalion. He was mobilized to help out the frontier guards, completely overwhelmed by the first waves of refugees. With the massacres of Grenoble and Lyon, all of France seems to have hit the road in order to pour into Switzerland. There were a thousand refugees the first day, 2,000 the second day, and 5,000 the third day, just before the government decided to close the border. But many succeeded in crossing the fields or simply forcing their way through. At the Ferney-Voltaire post alone, 1,500 French refugees have already gotten through forcibly.

From now on, no one is to get through—those are the orders. With the same thing happening in the Jura mountains and Basel, it's obvious that it's impossible to let everyone in. The crisis and the massacres began after a French TV network, Télé Mille Montagnes, started instigating Nigerian refugees to take revenge for the thousands of years of oppression and crime on the part of Whites.

These refugees were taken in during the terrible war between North and South Nigeria. More than 10 million landed in France and were stuffed into emergency "welcome centers" on the borders of large cities. It appears that a conflict between two gangs in the Lyon region unleashed a series of revolts and looting, involving several murders. The inaction of the French authorities, already overwhelmed with the problems of Pakistani and Egyptian immigrants, allowed the incidents to multiply rapidly. Incitation by a TV personality, calling for justice against the "chalk faces," was all that was necessary to turn their looting operations into murder raids. Rapes and massacres involving dismemberment and torture multiplied in the center of Lyon, literally stormed by tens of thousands of refugees. Then the same happened in Grenoble, and rumors broke out about similar incidents in other cities. But in Marseille and Lille, at any rate, the Islamic militia, well trained and disciplined, quickly turned things around, massacring the looters and protecting the civilian population. Be that as it may, the few journalists who have gotten out of Lyon are talking of 200,000 dead.

The White population seemed to almost let itself be massacred, docilely. Some have even paid, in money or sexual favors, for the privilege of being killed with a bullet through the head, cleanly and without suffering. They called it "buying a bullet." After fifty years of being taught—by the state, by the churches, by the media—that they are guilty of racism, sexism, colonialism, and other sins, the French preferred to die rather than fight.

It won't be like that here, Lt Col Sandoz tells himself. This isn't California or Rwanda! There won't be any excesses or internal unrest here! His colleague Major Bittrich and his special unit have already (in one night, with the help of the Cantonal police, and with impressive efficiency) rounded up all the illegals and non-Europeans of the Canton and transferred them to the interior of the country. The plan is to expel them—but where? With the pogroms taking place in the Italian Social Republic and its Austrian ally, they will have to go to either France or Germany; but this doesn't seem realistic in light of the chaos in both countries.

Lt Col Sandoz chases these thoughts away. The units of his battalion are positioned all along the frontier, keeping its heavy equipment and artillery in reserve close to Meyrin and Cointrin Airport. He will not use them unless a specific position is in danger of being overrun. What worries Lt Col Sandoz is Captain Droz's reserve company. Those twenty-year-olds have never been trained how to manage civilians or refugees. He doesn't know if they will obey orders, and he doesn't want to have to use drastic disciplinary measures... As a security precaution, he has asked lieutenants Ben Hamed and Biagetti (who are in charge of two squads of military police) to prepare their men and women for possible employment as execution squads. The telephone rings.

"Sandoz here."

"Lieutenant Chevalley here; Ferney post. We have a problem. The refugees are packed in and have advanced into the forbidden perimeter. We have given two warnings, but they are still advancing. Some of them are armed. I'm asking you to confirm the orders."

"One moment…"

He presses a button on his post's control screen in the commander's vehicle.

"Sandoz here; infantry battalion 19; give me Brigadier Wicht."

"GHQ 2nd brigade, Wicht here."

"Brigadier, the refugees are starting to cross the frontier; can you confirm orders?"

"Sandoz, we must apply the plan. Orders to open fire confirmed."

"Roger; over and out."

This is shaping up to be a very bad day.

<<how can we dance when our earth is turning? how can we sleep when our beds are burning?

midnight oil

musicians

_diesel and dust

/1987/

<<it is incomparably easier to be what one is than to imitate what one is not.

louis XIV

king of france

1638–1715

<<a man must choose. this is where his strength lies: in his power of decision.

paulo coelho

author

_o monte cinco

/1996/

The Moment of Decision

SO THE QUESTION IS: WHAT SHOULD YOU DO?

Perhaps at this point in the book, you are feeling depressed and impotent in the face of so many factors you cannot control, master, or even influence.

However, you have a lot of possibilities and you can act in several ways:

> You could go into politics and try to change things. This will take a long, long time. You would need several years to infiltrate the inner system in order to become actively involved (while taking care not to be devoured). In ten or twenty years, perhaps, if you are talented, patient, and have perseverance and luck, you *might* be able to change the laws and get important messages across.

> You could become a citizen-activist in the NGO sector or in grassroots movements, in order to touch the sensibilities of other citizens and gradually change things, one person at a time.

> You could change yourself by transforming your vision of the world and your way of life.

> Or you could just do nothing, thinking that any measures you might take would be laughable in comparison to the immensity of the problem: either the crises will not come about or you have faith in the ability of the government and civic leaders to overcome any problem they are faced with.

All this is very well, but it is not the way to make a decision! You must begin by evaluating all the factors, possibilities, and probabilities. But none of these evaluations will give you an *exact* result. No one can predict the future with certainty, still less when we are dealing with the convergence of enormous factors on a global scale. It is impossible to calculate the probability as a percentage, nor can one assign a precise moment when a collapse-like event might occur.

We must, instead, call in the aid of an analytic scheme common in risk management. On the vertical axis we show the only two possibilities we are able to consider: either the collapse occurs or it does not occur. The other axis represents your state of preparedness: either you are prepared or you aren't. On the quadrant formed by the intersection of these possibilities, we can determine four results.

First of all, let us imagine that the collapse does *not* occur:

If you are not prepared and the collapse does not occur, your life remains unchanged; everything stays as it is now. If you are prepared, you will have spent time preparing; you will have spent money; and you will probably look silly to your friends, who will consider you paranoid or an environmental nut. But apart from some cost to your ego and some expense in time and money, the difference between the two situations is not great.

If the collapse occurs, however, we have two considerably different situations:

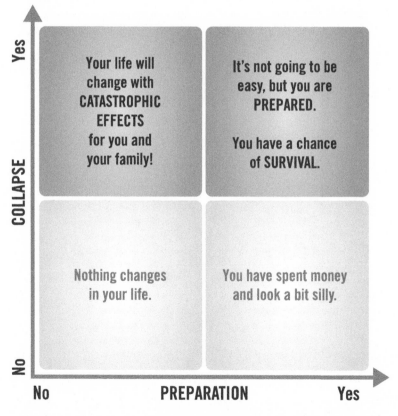

In this case, if you are not prepared, you are at risk of being hit by all the consequences. You risk losing everything suddenly: your way of life, your fortune, and perhaps your life itself. Moreover, the day there is no more food on supermarket shelves, when you have no more clean clothes, when you smell bad, when your house is too cold or too hot to live in, when the garbage and the excrement are starting to stink, and you are in the dark as soon as night falls — it will be a bit late to take action. On the other hand, if the collapse occurs and you are prepared, things will still be tough, but you will have a chance at survival.

The decision is yours.

François-Xavier is a high-level employee in a multinational based in the U.S.

He has done a lot of traveling over the course of a brilliant career: Africa, the Middle East, Europe, North America... He feels he ought to live apart from the swarming multitude. He has convinced his wife to buy a house, not in the suburbs like everyone else, but out in the mountains—a pretty, wooden house, chalet-style, on a fairly large lot on the bank of a river. The choice was not made according to survivalist criteria, but above all because of the price (half that of the suburbs) and because of the fresh air. Gradually, the house has been refurbished, the garden improved so the children can play in it, the grounds surrounded by a fence, etc. Then, seeing signs of imminent crisis, François-Xavier bought chickens and, after a fox had made his dinner on them, built a sturdy coop. He has added a garden and a greenhouse for vegetables that don't naturally grow at high altitudes. He expects to buy some hogs. He's become friends with his farmer neighbors, especially through his children and the local school, but also because he participates in the life of the village. He has even become president of the local shooting club.

<<three minutes without breathing, three days without drinking, three weeks without eating.

survival principle

<<most people cannot imagine a future any different from the present.

chris martenson

biochemist and writer

/2010/

<<leading humans to civilization required several million years, while a return to the neanderthal would take less than a week.

frédéric beigbeder

writer

/1997/

<<who's talking about winning? what counts is surviving.

rainer maria rilke

poet

/1875–1926/

<<even the most colossal encounter is never anything but the scale in which, today as always, the weight of men is measured.

ernst jünger

warrior & writer

_storm of steel

/1920/

PART III

SURVIVAL

<<civil defense first of all requires a certain self-assessment. do we want to survive? do we want to save our essential possessions? protecting the country does not depend only on the army: we are all summoned to this new task. we must prepare starting now.

albert bachman

swiss spy

_civil defense

/1969/

<<we are the domesticated animals in a zoo called civilization.

laurence gonzales

journalist

/2005/

Survival Attitudes

WHAT IMPACT DOES DANGER have on a human being? What mental preparation is necessary in order to acquire an attitude that will increase your chances of survival?

The Structure of the Human Brain and Its Consequences

About 500,000 years ago, our ancestors' brains went from a volume of 400 cm^3 to about 1,200 cm^3, finally reaching its current volume of 1,400 cm^3 about 150,000 years ago, at the time when *Homo sapiens* walked the African plains. Despite technological progress, the human brain has retained a structure bound to that remote age. It is important to understand that, under stress, we act as our Stone Age ancestors did. Faced with an unfamiliar or dangerous situation, the brain and body apply a simple program. It is a mechanism that has accompanied us for millennia and allowed us to survive rather effectively, considering that man is not a particularly powerful, swift, or agile animal. This ancient programming prepares us either to flee or to defend ourselves. Through an effect that scientists call the law of similarity, our behavior is a function of a situation's appearance rather than the reality. For example, faced with a free-roaming lion, any normal person would either flee or try to hide. No one would waste time on conjectures! For our brain, if what is in front of us looks like a lion, it's because that's what it is!

To simplify matters, the brain responds to danger by giving the body orders — the heart rate increases and hormones, such as

adrenaline, are secreted by the endocrine system. Their effect is to reduce the transmission time of nervous reflexes. These reactions allow
us to concentrate on the immediate danger. Sometimes such concentration is excessive and causes tunnel vision, which can make us forget
the rest of the environment and the other dangers it contains. But
since lions do not roam the streets in our comfortable existence, and
we are hardly ever exposed to such dangers, we are led to believe that
the danger is no longer there. This causes us to react quite irrationally
when a real danger arises.

An especially bizarre example was told to me in Zimbabwe, where
I lived for a short while in 1996, about two Japanese tourists traveling
in Africa. They apparently were so used to seeing cuddly, innocuous
animals at the zoo and on television that they did not hesitate to get
out of their cars in the African bush in order to photograph themselves right next to a group of lions devouring a carcass. No need to
complete the picture ... the lions were particularly well-fed that day.

Things like that happen because, though our brains have developed a good reactive system for responding to dangerous situations,
evolution has not yet allowed us to adapt to the sensation-saturated
environment of modern societies. This is why security specialists have
noted that modern man's typical reactions to danger are either panic
or paralysis.

With training, man can recover his reflexes and learn once again
how to respond to danger, with neither panic nor paralysis, with quick
reflexes and without inducing tunnel vision. This essentially mental
preparation is one of the three key elements for survival represented
in the following drawing:

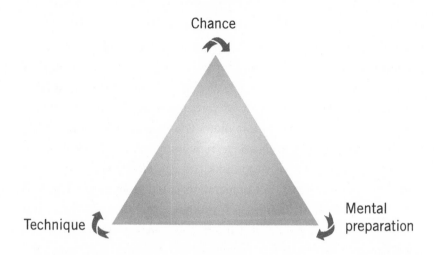

Luck

Luck is a series of probabilities favorable to us. It is important to know how to seize opportunities when they are offered to us. But we must be aware that it is a chance factor, not very important in a survival scenario. Luck is estimated to account for only about five percent of survival. This is why it is important not to bet too heavily on this element; rather, one should take its opposite into account — *bad* luck. Remember the Persian proverb: "When luck is against you, you can break your teeth even on jelly."

Technical Ability

Technical ability is all of one's know-how, competence, and acquired aptitudes relating to a domain of activity. In the case of survival, it concerns survival techniques: observation, shooting, certain types of handiwork, etc. Technical ability can be acquired by training and repetition — the more you repeat a movement, the more sure you become of how to execute it. After several thousand repetitions, the movement comes almost automatically. Survival experts estimate that forty percent of survival is a matter of mastering techniques.

Mental Preparation

Mental preparation, along with attitude and outlook, is the most important element, accounting for fifty-five percent of the factors of survival; it largely determines the success or failure of actions or techniques. Mental preparation allows you to seize opportunities that luck offers you. Mental preparation allows you to overcome more rapidly the effects of losing your bearings, remaining calm and clear-headed, using your adrenaline rush to think and act quickly and correctly. It would be illusory to think preparation could overcome a hundred percent of the effects of intense stress, but it can attenuate them; and above all, you will not be left without a response when you are faced with an unknown situation. During the 2011 tsunami in Japan and the 2004 tsunami in the Indian Ocean, as revealed in films, some people reacted to the first signs of danger and sought refuge in high places, while others did nothing, as if hypnotized, or else tried to hide in unsuitable spots.

To prepare yourself mentally, follow these three phases:

> **Phase One: realization.** To be able to confront a situation, obviously, it must exist and be perceived as real. We can prepare by imagining what our reaction would be in the face of a direct danger such as a lion, a natural disaster, physical aggression, etc., and thus improve the effectiveness and speed of our reflexes. On the other hand, in view of indirect or long-term dangers, such as economic crises or ecological collapse, our reflexes only take hold too late, when the situation is already too far advanced. So we should first confront the problem globally, with serious personal reflection on the subject. You see why it has taken so long to get to this point in the demonstration; if you have reached this stage of the book, it is because you are in the midst of this phase of reflection and realization. Now you can begin to familiarize yourself with possible scenarios and imagine your own. Decide which seem the

most probable to you and, once you have made a selection, you will begin to perceive these as challenges to overcome.

> **Phase Two: accepting the problem.** This phase will allow you to accept and validate your reflection, to feel the problems in your guts. This is very important, because you are going to consolidate your reasoning and develop your arguments while continuing to question them and, if the case warrants, revise your scenarios. You must allow yourself enough time in this phase, because you will probably go through (as I did before you) Kübler-Ross's five stages of denial, anger, bargaining, depression, and acceptance. This means that you will start by denying the problem — *No, collapse will never happen; humanity will know how to react, and there are always solutions!* Then you will get angry at those who have put us in this situation: politicians, industrialists, Baby Boomers, et al. — *They're all a bunch of bastards!* Then you will start bargaining — *Maybe we could influence the system, take part in politics, change everything from the inside, or buy more efficient light bulbs?* After this comes depression — *In the face of such immense, insurmountable problems, we count for so little; it's too late; we are doomed; those efficient light bulbs are a joke...* Finally, you will accept that you can react, find solutions, put them in place, and that you only need a little organization and outside help to get there. Bravo, you are on the right track! A good tip for speeding up and documenting this process is to keep a logbook in which to enter your thoughts, reflections, and feelings. Do not hesitate to deepen your knowledge on subjects that interest you by reading books and articles, talking with your friends, or asking advice from experts. In order to manage all this information, take notes, make lists and start to sort out your priorities. Little by little, you will have a large part of your solutions.

> **Phase Three: putting solutions in place.** Once you have a list of ideas and solutions, you must put them in place concretely to

enable you to face the problems connected to the scenarios you believe probable and possible.

A Few Basic Rules of Survival

I want to share with you the rules of survival I have collected from much reading and sharing of personal experience with a number of survivalists, explorers, and adventurers. These rules are general enough to apply to any situation or environment. Take note of them, reflect on each of them, discuss them with your friends, consider them a challenge, try them out, and keep those that seem relevant to you (if not all of them).

These rules are:

> On all occasions, be here now.

> Look — and believe what you see. If it looks like something is dangerous, that's because it most likely is dangerous.

> Avoid impulsive behavior. Think — do it quickly, but think.

> Remain calm and concentrated. Learn to control your breathing.

> Stay hydrated.

> Avoid or learn to control the four poisons of the mind: fear, confusion, hesitation, and surprise. Do not succumb to depression or defeatism. Have no fear of fear: fear is your friend, if you know how to master it.

> Set yourself small goals that you can achieve one by one. This will give you confidence. Believe in your chances of success, however small they may be.

> Learn to know yourself, your heart, and your body. Learn to be realistic about your strengths and weaknesses.

> Learn to know your environment and the natural world around you. Learn to respect the laws of physics, the forces in nature: energy, speed, distance, mass.

> If you have doubts, listen to them.

> Learn from your mistakes and those of others.

> Have backbone, but be flexible, be firm but pragmatic, humble but determined. Do not let anyone or anything tame or break your spirit.

> Reflect, analyze, plan, be decisive, and make correct decisions.

> Do not put more energy in a task than the benefits you will gain from it.

> Celebrate your successes; learn to appreciate life and to be grateful for every little thing.

> Know how to see the beauty in each situation, in nature and those around you.

> If you believe in God(s), pray.

As with anything, survival depends above all on the experience acquired by practice. Train yourself to go beyond your comfort zone, where you will learn endurance, strength, agility and the ability to withstand heat, cold, thirst, hunger, and pain. The more you exercise in a safe and controlled environment, the fewer surprises and suffering you will have the day you are confronted with a real survival situation.

Henry is in deep shit.

He knows he has to get out of town before the riots degenerate into complete chaos and carnage. He knows he stayed too long, in hopes of finishing his medical exams.

Bad luck: he lives in one of the wealthy neighborhoods, and it's clear that the police are no longer present anywhere. The bands of looters are getting together. Shots and cries can already be heard in the streets. He's got to think quickly. He mustn't panic. What resources are available? What is the best way to flee the neighborhood and rejoin his parents in their country home?

He puts on his walking shoes and jacket, takes a Swiss Army knife from his room, and grabs a well-sharpened kitchen knife. Oh, yes! Grandfather's M-1 Garand rifle; he thinks he knows where to find a few .30–06 cartridges. There they are, in the bottom drawer of a cabinet. A backpack—quick, fill it up—two water bottles, cereal bars. If only he had foreseen this when the bad news started... STOP! No time for useless reflections. Quick, a plan. Grab the equipment; done. Shall I try to negotiate with the looters? No, that won't work. Defend the apartment? Bad idea. Flight is the only sensible thing. Leave the apartment by the outside fire-escape, follow an alleyway west ... How do I do that? Compass! In the big desk. Quick, quick.

Henry hears cries and fighting from the stairwell. Time to get out. Henry thinks of his late grandfather who was in the Marine Corps; he survived the assault on Iwo Jima, for heaven's sake! What he's going through now ain't nothing compared to Iwo!

Let's roll!

<<the soul of a castle is its drawbridge.

rené char

poet

/1907–1988/

<whatever you do or dream of doing, audacity has genius, power and magic.

johann wolfgang von goethe

writer, poet, & politician

/1749–1832/

Sustainable Autonomous Base

IF YOU HAVE READ TO THIS POINT, you have a precise idea of the dangers that await us over the coming years. You have also begun to understand the attitude necessary for survival, no matter what situation you find yourself in.

This is good, but it is not enough.

Our goal must be to create a way of life that will allow you to survive, but that is also pleasant, full of meaning — that might even allow you to live more fully than you do now. This will not mean opulence and material comfort as we know them today, but it will mean a more authentic world, closer to natural human needs. Such a world cannot come about *ex nihilo*; we must create it.

While I was reflecting on what had to be done to survive the upcoming years, I read the various survival manuals available and had lengthy conversations with American survivalists and "preppers" on internet forums. Among these people, some have, for decades, been preparing for catastrophic events — including the biblical Armageddon or the invasion of the United States by the Communist hordes! (Hey, I admit that in my teen years I was a big fan of John Milius's *Red Dawn!*) Most preppers are more down to earth, however; they anticipate that a convergence of factors will provoke the economic collapse of their countries. Thanks to these conversations, and to interviews with a few autonomous communities in France, Britain, Germany, and South Africa, as well as reading books like *How to Survive the End of the World as We Know It* and *Patriots* by

James W. Rawles, I arrived at the conclusion that the only way to make it through the collapse is to settle in a place distant from potential trouble spots and acquire as much *sustainable autonomy* as one can with regards to water, food, and energy — and all the while integrating oneself into the local community. Rawles calls this concept the *American Redoubt*.

And thus I began my project to prepare for the economic collapse. I documented my thoughts and actions and, seeking a formula that could summarize and provide a framework for my work and advice, I came upon the book *G5G: Déclaration de Guerre* by Michel Drac, Serge Ayoub, and Michel Thibaud, which defines the concept of a Sustainable Autonomous Base, or SAB. I quote the authors:

> A Sustainable Autonomous Base is a secure space — this is what will be most scarce in the near future. We must construct a sound economy, rather than a maximally productive one. It should be an economy of physical production geared toward stable and solid solutions, in contrast to our over-financialized, virtual economy solely preoccupied with profit. We want stability; we want the long term; we thus want rootedness. We want to reconstruct autonomy, but also permanence. We want to see a future for ourselves and our children. We want a foundation, a ground, a base, a land. We want a true Sustainable Autonomous Base. A permanent base. Our motto: rootedness, autonomy, permanence... The political gesture is a foundation for mental and territorial rigidity. We *demand* this rigidity: it means that we will not bend, we will not bow.

It was from this concept, which the authors graciously permitted me to borrow, that I developed a program constructed upon seven fundamental principles. These will allow you to put in place an SAB, *your* SAB.

The seven fundamental principles are:

1   Water

2   Food

3   Hygiene and Health

4   Energy

5   Knowledge

6   Defense

7   The Social Bond

In the coming chapters, we are going to cover each of these principles. We will also see how to choose a location for your SAB as well as the different ways it can function from day to day.

Miguel worked his whole life as a concierge.

He bought himself a house in his native Portugal. Over the years, according to his means, he and his brothers, along with a sister and cousins, transformed this old country house into an SAB. He has put an abandoned well into working order, redone the roof, installed several cisterns for collecting winter rainwater and is thus able to face the increasingly dry, hot summers. His cousin is a tile setter, and was able to redo the bathrooms with the help of friends from the next village, as well as install a septic pit. They have also worked to construct a small henhouse with a thousand chickens, which one of his brothers manages, while his wife takes care of the garden. Miguel thinks that by the time he is sixty, this place will allow him to spend his retirement comfortably and, in case things get rough, let him shelter his family.

<<when the well is dry, we know the worth of water.

benjamin franklin

inventor, businessman, & politician

//1706–1790//

<<the dogmas of the quiet past are inadequate to the stormy present. as our case is new, we must think anew and act anew.

abraham lincoln

politician

message to congress

/1862/

Water

Water is indispensable to life; you could say water *is* life. To establish an SAB, a whole hierarchy of needs must be satisfied, the first of which is water. But let's first remember that the hierarchy of human needs is constituted of five levels, according to the celebrated scheme of Abraham Maslow. His research showed that human beings try to satisfy each lower-level need before thinking about the needs on the immediately higher level. This is why one can speak of a hierarchy or pyramid. For example, it is preferable to satisfy physiological needs before the need for security; this is why, in a situation where our survival is at stake, we are ready to take certain risks.

These five levels of needs are:

> physiological (breathing, drinking, eating, sleeping);

> security (of body, of employment, of health, of property);

> love and belonging (friendship, family, intimacy);

> esteem (confidence, the respect of others, self-esteem, achievement);

> self-realization (morality, creativity, problem-solving, etc.).

The day public utilities no longer work, you will only be able to count on your own preparation to supply your needs for water. You can improvise a lot of things, but not water. Water is hard to create; it must be found. Water is the key resource to master in an SAB, because it allows life, it allows food to be raised and prepared, and because without water, you have nothing. This is where we must begin.

Water for human consumption and for irrigation is increasingly difficult to obtain in this world. Over eighty countries, representing more than forty percent of the world population, are already facing water shortages. Infrastructure costs connected with water have increased sharply: it must be pumped from deeper levels or sought at greater distances. Water quality has deteriorated because of pollution, contamination with waste water from growing cities, from industry and from agriculture. Ecosystems are dying one after the other. One billion persons in the world lack drinking water, and 3 billion have neither water on tap nor a way of getting rid of waste water. Eighty percent of infectious diseases are water-transmitted. It is not for nothing that water has been called "blue gold." Most people in the West, along with those who live comfortably elsewhere in the world, are used to unlimited quantities of excellent drinking water: for their baths, showers, toilets, washing machines, dish washers, pools, lawns, and gardens. In the great majority of cases, such water is drinkable. If the distribution or filtering of this water were to stop, not only would the reservoirs empty out quickly, but the population and industry would soon have to seek water from open sources such as rivers, swamps, lakes, etc. Obviously, rainwater could be saved. But such water must be stocked and transported, especially if you install your SAB in regions where rains are seasonal or the climate dry, which may increasingly become the case in the world thanks to climate change.

You will need drinking water, but also clean water for your animals and to water your garden and your crops. And you will need water for hygienic reasons. Water is called "potable" (i.e., drinkable) when it satisfies certain criteria that render it suitable for human consumption. The standards in this area differ according to place and time and are, of course, informed by particular contexts and cultures.

They determine the question of access to water, because good water is essential to economic and human development. Water is also the vector for a number of parasites, bacteria, and viruses. One must take precautions before drinking water in the wild. An apparently limpid and pure water can hide micro-organisms or pollutants. Prudence is called for: across the world, more than 22,000 persons die each day from drinking unhealthy water.

Here are some of the possible contaminants and their consequences:

> bacterial contamination, which can cause such illnesses as cholera, typhus or dysentery;

> contamination by viruses (infectious hepatitis, etc.);

> contamination by parasites that are the origin of fevers and diarrhea, which cause complications if not treated quickly;

> contamination by parasitic worms (larvae swimming at the surface of the water; they can also get through the skin during bathing), which cause schistosomiasis, whose symptoms are abdominal pains, skin eruptions, anemia, and chronic fatigue;

> contamination by chemical pollutants (heavy metals, insecticides, hydrocarbons, etc.) with harmful effects (toxicity, neurotoxicity, cancer), especially in the case of prolonged consumption;

> contamination by algae or other toxic organisms in suspension.

Water, even when fit for consumption, is never simply H_2O. It can contain many dissolved salts, such as calcium and magnesium salts. It is then said to be "hard." Spring water, for instance, contains various quantities of these salts; it can have, therefore, various levels of "hardness." In France, the water of the Massif Central, the Vosges, the Armorican Massif as well as the Ardennes is soft, with less than two hundred milligrams of salts per liter. In the Parisian basin, the Alps, the Pyrenees or the Jura, this concentration can reach 9 hundred milligrams per liter. Check out what the level in your area is. For a person in good health, drinking hard water is not dangerous. Anything called spring water is naturally fit for human consumption. The only treatment useful for such water is aeration, decantation, and filtration.

You need a lot of water for drinking, cooking, washing, irrigating crops, and watering animals. If, on a world average, a human being needs between twenty and fifty liters of water each day, just two or three are sufficient for drinking each day; that's less than a gallon, but it's still a lot — and it's heavy if you need to carry it. This is the absolute minimum. Five or ten additional liters are needed for cleaning and cooking. Your SAB should have enough water for these needs, but also to water the garden and the animals, etc. In an ideal situation, you should try, in fact, to find fifty to seventy liters of water per day for each person.

Sources of Water

> **Spring water.** This is the best possible source of water for an SAB. A freshwater spring is often potable and of much better quality than the fluoridated or chlorinated water you get in the city, but it may be useful to get a laboratory analysis of the chemical and bacterial composition of the water. If you chose a rural SAB, access to a spring, preferably on your own property, is very important and will certainly be one of the main criteria for choosing your location. It was for me. It is important to verify that the spring flows all year round (sometimes a source will run dry during the hot, dry months, and it may freeze in the winter, although this is rare). Your location will be even better if the spring water can be canalized through the force of gravity to supply your house and garden directly.

> **Wells.** These are an excellent source of water, but they require a pump, manual or electrical. A good solution is a photovoltaic or wind-driven pump feeding into a water tower or cistern, from

which the water will then be lead by force of gravity into the house or onto the crops. You might use a water-level regulator to avoid having the cistern overflow: when the water level reaches a certain point, the pump shuts off. This is not expensive and works well.

> **Precipitation.** Rainwater is easy to collect in containers (water tanks, cisterns, drums, etc.) and can easily be used for irrigation, bathing, clothes washing, and sanitation. If it is filtered, it can also be used for drinking and cooking. One must be careful to use only clean containers for collecting rainwater.

> **Rivers.** Water can be pumped from rivers, streams, ponds, swamps, lakes, etc. It is essential to filter such water in order to make it potable.

> **Sea and Ocean Water.** If your SAB is by the ocean or on a boat, seawater is obviously an inexhaustible source, but it must be desalinized. For this one must invest in some rather costly materials relying on reverse osmosis.

In any case, verify whether any waste (especially toxic waste or anything polluted with heavy metals, intensive agriculture using pesticides, etc.) is being discharged from factories upstream from your spring, aquifer, or river. It is important to do this research before buying any property. Afterwards, one must remain vigilant about any suspicious and potentially polluting activity.

Water Treatment

One of the ways of making water potable is to treat it. There are three stages involved. First, pre-filtering, which allows for the removal of organic and solid particles. The water must be passed through a filter or tissue (several cotton t-shirts, bath towels, blankets, etc.). Then, it must be treated with chlorine with the help of purification tablets (Micropur© or similar), which kill bacteria. (These tablets are easily found; you should carefully verify the dosage.) Finally, the water must be filtered again through a ceramic or carbon filter

(Berkfeld©, Berky©, Steripen©, Katadyn©, MSR©, Aquamira©, Culligan©, PUR©, Water Sentinel©, etc.). Some of these are great for fixed usage (my preference is Berkey©), some are ideal for carrying, like the Katadyn© — choose the best combination for your usage. It is important to keep enough tablets and filter replacement parts in stock. A substitute for chlorine is ultraviolet radiation treatment. Pasteurization can also be a good system: the water must be heated to between 149 to 194 °F (65 and 90 °C) for a short period, which will kill the microbes. It is not necessary to boil water a long time. There are pasteurizers on the market that can be used for water, milk, and other liquids. You should buy the necessary materials in advance and test them, as well as locate the primary, secondary, and even tertiary water sources near your SAB. Make sure to have enough containers to carry water — bottles, canteens and the very useful jerrycans — should the need arise.

If you live in an area without easy water sources available the whole year through, you must arrange for a lot of rainwater storage capacity, with large-volume plastic or concrete cisterns or tanks. To collect rainwater, you can use angled roofs, tarpaulins, etc., with different sized funnels that channel it into your storage places. In an emergency, one of your first thoughts should be how to store water. In the worst case, there is always toilet water and water-heater tanks: but these will only last a very short time. In the most extreme cases, it is also possible to boil rainwater, or recover swimming pool water by adding a little bleach (a drop of 7–10 percent bleach for each liter of water to be sterilized). In the worst of worst cases, you can drink your urine or seawater. Obviously, this is neither a sustainable nor an enjoyable system! But in the collapse, millions will be reduced to such methods. You, on the other hand, are preparing to be autonomous and sustainable during the coming "interesting times."

Wilhelm has installed his SAB in an old farm on the edge of a forest in the Ardennes.

He has fixed it up over a period of years with his buddies and is quite proud of the result: a stone wall around his little property (6,000 m²), a vegetable garden, access to the forest for firewood, a little wind turbine for electricity, a few rifles for hunting and protection. Above all, he has dug a well that is always full, and there is a river not far away. The first time he tried drinking well water, he got sick (he did it under normal, non-emergency conditions so he could be treated if the contamination was serious; it wasn't, apart from one night spent on the toilet). The water is fine for the garden, but not for human consumption. Since then, he has installed a large ceramic filter. It cost a lot, but will be worth it the day the public water supply gets cut off (their area is no longer considered sufficiently profitable by the new Brazilian owners of the local water company). For greater security, Wilhelm's SAB has several ceramic replacement filters in reserve.

Maurizio wanted to install his SAB in his urban apartment.

In fact, he hasn't gotten far with his preparations. On his balcony and the roof of his building, he has installed basins and old bathtubs to catch rainwater. He then filters the water through bath towels and uses Micropur purification tablets to render it potable. On the whole, this is not the greatest solution, but he has a better plan than most of his neighbors. Fortunately, there are several persons in his apartment who belong to a neighborhood association called "social solidarity" (before the crisis, it was considered to be far-out and far-right). The street was quickly secured thanks to a small militia they helped to raise; a service has also been put in place dedicated to finding food and recovering anything that might be useful. There is even a retired doctor in the building across the street from his (the one that hasn't been burned, that is). Since the river is in the part of town under gang control, they get along by collecting as much rainwater as they can. A market is being organized thanks to "runners" who bring food from the park (now a giant vegetable garden) in exchange for metals and various objects of value. The neighborhood has become a haven of peace thanks to the security service organized by some ex-skinheads. In short, they are getting a working society back on its feet. After a serious clash with a neighboring gang for territorial control, there was a difficult period, but the war between gangs close to the river ended up leaving that area empty and destroyed; it was easily brought under control. With access to river water and the installation of manual pumps, the neighborhood is coming back to life. Now it is a zone of peace and industrious organization, helping to extend survival further and further.

i'm dividing things in two, the rich will have food and the poor will have appetite.

coluche

humorist

_revue de presse

/1980/

<<we are what we eat.

jane goodall

naturalist

/2008/

Food

DURING A VACATION IN ICELAND a few years ago, my girlfriend and I were looking forward to enjoying some fresh fish, since fishing is the largest industry of that beautiful country. We were disappointed. We were barely able to eat any fish, even in fishing villages. They explained to us that fish caught in the Atlantic Ocean were prepared, frozen, and wrapped on board the trawler; as soon as it docked, the fish were loaded directly onto a plane and sent to be sorted in London, Paris, Milan, and Frankfurt. We ended up fasting, in order to avoid eating frozen hamburgers for the whole vacation.

This was a reminder that in the modern world, the essential part of our food is routed from its source of production to our plates by an extremely complex—and fragile—system of supply. We have seen what can happen to this system in the case of a serious crisis and panic.

For this and other reasons, food is the second fundamental principle of an SAB.

How do you feed yourself in a time of crisis? The ideal is to be able to produce your own food, which means having a garden, raising animals, and being able to conserve a surplus for unproductive seasons. But since you can't do all this in a day, you must begin by stocking food right away to guarantee reserves in case of an immediate crisis. Even when, later on, your SAB is perfectly autonomous and capable of permanently supplying the needs of its inhabitants, you must have stocks in case of bad harvests or a lack of nutrients.

So, what should you stock up on and what should you grow? There are three rules to follow concerning food:

1   Stock up or grow what gives you good, balanced nutrition. You must eat healthily in order to have the energy necessary for long workdays. Nutritional balance also assures effective metabolism and a better immune system. Sick persons and children must have the best possible nutrition to guarantee, respectively, their best chance of recovery and proper growth.

2   Why abandon your gourmet habits, especially in difficult times when you'll appreciate life's little pleasures the most? Why sacrifice what you like and deprive yourself? Varied agriculture and a good complementary stock will give you high-quality, natural products with a taste and variety that will allow you to remain the gourmet or gourmand that (I hope) you are.

3   Store what you eat and eat what you store. This should encompass the previous two rules but also prevent waste.

Nutrition

The basic principal of long-term survival is good nutrition. Not only will it allow you, your family, and the other inhabitants of your SAB to satisfy your hunger but, above all, you will preserve your health, re-inforce your immune system, and gain physical and mental strength. Nutrition refers to the process by which a living being transforms foodstuffs in order to ensure its own functioning. It includes anything of nutritional value, that is, anything the ingestion of which is necessary for survival, good health, and growth. There exist many different nutrients divided into two main categories: macronutrients and micronutrients.

Macronutrients. A living organism draws its energy from carbohydrates, fats, and proteins. Energy is measured in calories. A group of organs ensures the extraction of energy from the digestive system, which transforms carbohydrates into glucose, proteins into amino acids, and fats into fatty acids. Each of these transformations is divided into several functional blocks. For example, the transformation into glucose occurs through 1) digestion, 2) hormonal regulation, and 3) use and storage in the liver, fatty tissues, or muscles. Carbohydrates are found in foods such as vegetables, rice, pasta, or bread. They are necessary for the body, and their concentration in the blood must be maintained at a relatively high level because the brain entirely depends upon them. On average, the adult brain requires a daily input of 130 grams. In practice, this amount is surpassed by a large margin: the average being 220 g to 330 g for men and 180 g to 230 g for women. The excess is stored in the form of fat. Fatty matter, or lipids, are found in vegetable oils or animal fat and make up, in the ideal case, twenty percent of one's daily intake in nutrients. Proteins, whether of animal origin (meat, fish, eggs, etc.) or vegetable origin (legumes, soybeans, cereals, etc.), are an essential component of the body and perform a great number of roles. For example, a single hair is composed of keratin, which is a protein; combined with another protein, collagen, it is responsible for making your skin strong, healthy, and elastic. An ideal human diet should not surpass the 35-percent level in protein.

Micronutrients Micronutrients such as minerals (calcium, magnesium, phosphorus, potassium, sodium, iodine, zinc, iron, manganese, etc.) and vitamins provide necessary components for the proper functioning of the human metabolism. A person deprived of them will develop illness and deficiencies that will weaken his body. The essential vitamins are: A, C (ascorbic acid), B1, B2, B3, B5, B6, B7, B8, B9, B12, D, E, K, and various forms of carotene. In short, you will not acquire the physical condition and mental concentration necessary to survive by eating potato chips and drinking sugary soft drinks!

For good nutrition, here are some basic rules that you can start applying now:

> Eat principally the fruits and vegetables of your region that are in season. Inform yourself about what grows at your latitude and in your region each month: besides being less expensive and coming from nearby, this will provide the best nutritional quality, for it is picked at the perfect stage of ripeness and will not have spent time in a refrigerated truck, ship, or airplane. Thus, you will assure yourself the best source of macro- and micronutrients each day.

> Eat a little of everything rather than a single type of food. Variety permits better nutrition and favors a regular passage of food through the system, which is important for preserving healthy intestinal microorganisms and efficient digestion, as well as for avoiding constipation, which can cause medical complications.

> Eat cereals (wheat, corn, rice, etc.) in moderation, legumes (lentils, green beans, peas) in sufficient amounts, along with a few nuts (walnuts, hazelnuts) and seeds (sunflower, pumpkin, etc.).

> Use herbs and aromatic plants according to taste (rosemary, thyme, basil, sage, etc.).

> Eat a few dairy products, but not in excess; favor fresh, unprocessed milk.

> Eat fresh ocean fish and seafood if you are near the coast, or freshwater fish if you are close to lakes and rivers.

> Eat meat and eggs.

> If you are a vegetarian, replace meat with mushrooms and legumes.

> Use a variety of oils, if you can (vegetable, olive, sunflower, walnut, tarragon, linseed), with a preference for olive oil, especially for cooking.

> Use salt (iodized) and spices, but not in excess.

> Avoid refined sugar, sweets, and sugared drinks in general.

> Avoid pre-cooked, processed foods.

> Avoid products to which you are allergic, even slightly. Don't forget that you may have to consume products in a different context from what prevails today: no more hospitals!

Stocking Food

Once you have understood what constitutes good nutrition, you will have to stock up on what allows you to have enough healthy food for a period of time. Imagine that your garden does not produce enough to feed everybody — if the grains you planted don't grow, if the harvest rots, or a parasite destroys it. Stocking additional food will be useful to you in such cases. And until you have established a regular little farm in your SAB, your food supply will be your only reserve.

Let us start by calculating how much food you will have to store. You must start by making a list of what one person consumes in a month, based on the needed calories. In the appendices, you will find a typical list that you can modify as you wish based on your calorific intake (not everybody needs the same amount — we are of different sizes and have different metabolisms). Another source of useful information is the Church of Jesus Christ of Latter-Day Saints (the Mormons), who advise their followers to learn nutritional self-sufficiency and how to stock food for three or even up to twelve months. Their websites give great advice on this subject. Once you have determined your needs, you just multiply the sum by the number of persons and the number of months you think you may have to hold out and start building up your reserve. Among the foods on the list, some merit special mention:

> **Rice** is one of the best foods to keep in stock. It doesn't take up much space, contains a lot of vitamins, and is very rich in nutritional elements. Stock brown rice, if possible, and if you want to

vary the taste, vary the types: Indian, American, Chinese, Italian, etc. *A priori*, you must reckon on two to six pounds per adult per month. Rice can be stored for five to ten years according to type, but I've tasted much older rice, and it was just fine. Buy a lot more in order to feed refugees or for exchange.

> **Wheat** is another basic foodstuff. You must plan on twenty to fifty pounds of it per person per month in all its forms. These include whole-wheat pasta, which takes up little space and can be kept a very long time (up to at least thirty years, in contrast to flour which can only be kept for three). Pasta is also ideal for exchange. Whole wheat can be kept a long time, but it must be ground, which means you must have a portable mill. Without a mill, you can eat your wheat whole by letting it soak in water for thirty-six hours and then boiling it.

> **Maize** can be kept for up to ten years in the form of grain, which is far longer than in ground form (polenta, etc.). You must stock five pounds per person per month.

> **Legumes** (lentils, soybeans, beans, peas, green beans) are an excellent source of protein. Stock at least six pounds per person per month (more if you are a vegetarian).

> **Oats** are a useful cereal to complement wheat. Stock about two pounds per person per month. It lasts about three to five years in the form of oatmeal or rolled oats.

> **Fats and oils** are used in cooking and provide a good selection of vitamins. Butter, peanut butter, and mayonnaise are examples of fats. As for oils, think about olive oil, but also stock sunflower oil, vegetable oil, flax oil, etc. Do not let oil cook for too long. Stock a minimum of one liter per person per month. It can usually be stored for about four years.

> **Milk**, in condensed form or as a powder, can be kept up to five years, and you must stock two pounds per person per month. Do

not buy pasteurized milk, which cannot be kept as long, unless you consume it frequently and thus circulate your stock rapidly.

> **Preserved fruits and vegetables** are the cornerstone of your diet and should be stocked in large quantities in the form of jars, cans, etc. These preserves can last a long time if they are stored correctly. The quantity to stock will vary according to your diet, but you should reckon on thirty pounds of vegetables and twelve pounds of fruit per person per month.

> **Preserved meat and fish** are a highly prized source of proteins and fats (especially fish conserved in olive oil, etc.). Stock two kilos from each category per person per month.

> **Salt** is important as a condiment, but also for preserving food. You should stock very large quantities. Think about how much salt you think you will need and then stock at least five times as much. No, make it ten times that much. Salt is cheap in times of peace and calm, but quickly becomes impossible to find in a crisis. It is not for nothing that the word "salary" comes from the Latin word for salt. Salt is valuable in hard times since it can only be found on the edge of salt marshes or in mines. The good news is that salt can be stored indefinitely. It may be worth your trouble to inform yourself about natural salt deposits close to your SAB. At the very least, figure on two pounds of iodized salt per person per month. Also store enough coarse salt for preserving meat and buy a salt lick, which will be appreciated by a number of animals.

> **Sugar** is one foodstuff that is very difficult to make on your own, so it can be worth the trouble to stock a large quantity. However, using sugar is not very advisable in a world without dentists, and it is better to use honey, molasses, maple syrup, or unrefined sugar such as the brown variety. Sugar can especially help you make preserves, and will be a valuable exchange item.

> **Meals ready-to-eat** (MREs) are essentially dehydrated rations designed to take up little space and be stored for long periods. Easy

5

to find in travel and mountain-climbing shops, such rations are very useful. Stock at least three months' worth.

> **High-calorie foods** such as nuts and their derivatives, like peanut butter, will come in handy.

> **Nutritional supplements** will provide you with vitamins and other essential elements that you may be lacking. Ask a nutritional specialist or simply look at the composition of each of the foods you consume and compare the result to a diagram of a recommended daily intake. Determine what is missing. Get the necessary supplements at a drugstore and multiply the dosage by the number of people and the time you may be in need.

If you have special needs, now is the time to prepare for them. Might babies be around? Stock the necessary baby food (as well as diapers, medications, etc.). Do you intend to lodge elderly parents in your SAB? Think about getting the things they like and need.

Finally, remember to stock your favorite "comfort foods," those that will give you a lift at difficult moments. If you're crazy about Nutella or chocolate, buy and store a lot of it! If your peccadillo is duck *foie gras* with whortleberry jam, stock up! If you like a certain type of tea or brand of coffee, get lots! In short, the idea is not to survive on bread and water. You must also know how to live! And if you like rice and green beans, so much the better.

How to Store Food

When I was at university, a friend who had done his military service as a cook in the Italian Army told me that in 1980 he was still using boxes of preserves stamped with the fascist seal of the late 1930s; apparently, no one died of food poisoning! If you preserve and store your food properly, you can considerably prolong its edibility. Many foods can be conserved for over thirty years. A dry environment free of mildew and kept at a constant temperature no higher than 68 °F (20 °C) is perfect for storing cereals, rice, and preserves (jars or cans) for years; and despite a drop in nutritional value and a slight change in the taste, the foods remain edible.

For starters, don't go too fast. Since you will have to rotate foods as a function of their expiry date, and your budget will perhaps not allow you to buy three month's or a year's worth of food at once for yourself and your family, go about it gradually. Start by establishing a reserve of three months and rotate it. Use the FIFO (First in, First out) method to rotate your reserves. Then, little by little, as determined by your means and tastes, begin accumulating more. A good method is to buy a tiny bit of food for your stock each time you go shopping. Another solution is to make a precise list and wait for discount sales to acquire what you lack. You can also buy in bulk to get a better price. I got myself listed as a grocer with a food warehouse and thus benefit from warehouse pricing. Another good process is what is called the "copy canning," which means that, when you buy your weekly or monthly groceries, you buy twice the amount (or what you can afford), which you will store away.

As for actual storing, install shelves in a dry room that remains at a constant temperature (a cellar, barn, loft, or store room). Ideally, the food should be protected from light and be kept in cans or other closed and labeled plastic or metal containers. Ensure the food is protected from rodents and moths by putting the most fragile foods (cereals, rice, etc.) into special air-tight food containers, and make regular inspections for any traces of infestation. Close tightly the rooms where you keep your food and, if you can, prevent theft with padlocks, chains, etc. Besides rodents and thieves, you must also keep your stock from being confiscated by the biggest thief of them all — the authorities! In a time of crisis, it is possible that the authorities will try to requisition all stocked food to distribute or sell. This is *your* food stock. If you want to give it away as charity or share it, this is your choice; confiscation is not only unjust, but can leave you at risk of going hungry. This is exactly how the Soviet government proceeded in Southern Russia and Ukraine in the early 1930s, causing the death of millions of peasants as a result. If you are concerned about this, stock your food discreetly, do not always buy from the same store, pay in cash, and do not talk too much about your project. To prevent burglary, you should also hide your stocks in more than one place: under beds, behind bookcases, in old freezers (which you can bury), in an old camper, etc. Don't laugh! Take the possible whims of a totalitarian and confiscatory state very seriously. It has already happened, and it can happen again.

A good sort of practice is to train yourself by buying a month's worth of food and, during this month, eating nothing more than what you have bought. Note what you lack and what you have left over, as well as what you dislike. Thus, you will acquire experience in the preparation and cooking of meals made from the food you have stocked; you will also understand your mistakes and what can be improved. Take note of how you feel. If you feel sluggish, tired, or are in a bad mood, this is likely because what you bought is not nutritionally balanced; you need to work on your list some more. Don't underestimate the impact of food on your mood and physical and mental abilities. You'll need to be at your best when times are tough.

Make Your Own Preserves

You can also preserve food yourself that you have bought fresh or harvested. This is the best option anyway, and the only one that can guarantee a long-term survival capacity. Preserving usually involves slowing the oxidation of fats (which cause food to become rancid); preventing the development of bacteria, fungi, and other microorganisms; and fighting the ravages of animals, especially insects and rodents. Food preservation should take into account all biotic factors (microorganisms, animals, germination, etc.) that can cause deterioration. For example, dried fruit, walnuts, and hazelnuts, as well as grains and legumes (green beans, lentils, etc.), can be stockpiled in a cool, dry place (barn, loft, etc.) without suffering damage, and thus be preserved. Certain fleshy fruits, such as apples or pears, can be kept for several months in a fruit cellar (a cool, dark, and well-aired place maintained at a constant temperature).

There are several ways to prepare food for conservation:

> **Vacuum-packing.** You must use a device that sucks the air out of a plastic sack into which the food has been placed. This allows the food to be kept fresh for a certain time (several months).

> **Dehydration** (drying, in the sun or in an oven). Fruits (prunes, apricots, figs, dates) are cut in sections and dried, or else dried whole.

> **Canning** permits the preservation of foods in air-tight containers for a long period, and without any other particular conditions. In a cellar or cabinet protected from light and heat, canned goods keep for a long time. The process relies on sterilization at between 239 and 250 degrees Fahrenheit (115 and 122 degrees Celsius).

> **Preserves** are made by mixing foodstuffs (usually fruits) with an ample portion of sugar and boiling them for a few minutes (to keep the taste of the fruit: 750 grams of sugar for one kilogram of fruit). The jars should be sterilized by boiling before being filled to the brim; and it must be closed when still hot in order to drive out the remaining air, which prevents moisture from forming.

> **Cold storage** allows one to slow or even stop the proliferation and action of microorganisms and to preserve the food for a rather long time. Refrigeration — lowering the ambient temperature to between 39 and 46 degrees Fahrenheit (3 and 8 degrees Celsius) — permits conservation for four to 10 days; this should be distinguished from freezing (between 32 degrees Fahrenheit and -4 degrees Fahrenheit or 0 and -4 degrees Celsius), which allows longer conservation (between three and 12 months) and deep freezing, which keeps foods at below -4 degrees Fahrenheit or -20 degrees Celsius for several years. These techniques require either a refrigerator/freezer (and thus electrical energy) or a natural

environment at these temperatures (e.g., mountains in the winter or arctic regions).

> There are also **chemical-preservation techniques** — with alcohol or salt (salt curing or pickling), smoking, acidity (vinegar), oil, sugar, fat, etc.

To make your own preserves, you will have to equip yourself with pots, seals, tanks, and containers made out of plastic or metal. A vacuum machine can also be useful. Practice making preserves, and never eat a preserve that smells bad or comes from a container that looks swollen, in order to avoid botulism and food poisoning.

At first sight, preparing and stocking food for months or even years for yourself, your family, and all those who will join you, or even in order to feed refugees, sounds like a colossal effort. But if you begin doing a little at a time, it is not so difficult or burdensome. Considering that the price of food is going to go up appreciably in the coming years, it will be a significant source of savings. I have drawn up a list of products to be ordered over the internet, to be delivered directly to my SAB, and which I will send off at the last minute. This list contains all sorts of perishable products that cannot be stored for a long time (bananas, pasteurized milk, fresh fruits, and vegetables). The day we go on high alert, the order goes off and, with a little luck, it will be one of the last to be filled and end with delivery to a sorting center. If it doesn't arrive, I'll know the situation is really bad.

Hunting, Fishing, Vegetable Gardening, and Animal Husbandry

Even if your food stock serves you well in difficult times, sooner or later it will run out. So it is necessary to know how to hunt, cultivate, and breed healthy, fresh food in order to have maximum autonomy. In the Soviet Union, ten percent of the agricultural land, allocated for individual gardens, generated ninety percent of agricultural production destined for domestic consumption. It was these gardens, nearly all of them cultivated according to the techniques of permaculture, that saved the lives of millions of Russians when the Soviet Union collapsed. Only so many people can live on a given area of land. There must be a balance between land and its inhabitants. A lack of balance always brings catastrophe. Be very careful about the number of people you accept into your SAB, and also about the number of people living in the surrounding communities. Do not let a disequilibrium develop.

One way of partly meeting one's nutritional needs is *hunting*. You should begin your training now by, first, acquiring a hunting permit from the proper authorities. You should also begin learning how to hunt and with various weapons (rifles, bows, crossbows, etc.) and how to prepare your catch once it is killed. (The subject of weapons will be treated in the chapter on defense.) In any case, you will have to adapt to the quarry of your region and understand the hunting techniques that are most appropriate for each species.

If you live near the sea or a river, *fishing* can be an excellent source of food, fish being the best kind of animal protein and the best source of omega-3 and -6 oils. As with hunting, arm yourself with the necessary permits and tools proper for the type of fishing you choose. Another way of having abundant fish is to make your own fish pond. A pond that's one hundred square feet and three feet deep is enough, and it's easy to make. You must, however, carefully choose the aquatic plants best adapted to the fish you intend to raise. There are numerous sorts of aquatic plants suited to the depth of your pond. For example, water hyacinths, aquatic forget-me-nots, or water irises are proper for shallow ponds. For deeper ponds, you might choose pickerel weeds, arrowheads, or water lilies. Equip yourself with the proper tools for fishing for the species of your region (lines, nets, etc.).

Your principle source of healthy, varied, and balanced food will certainly be your *vegetable garden*. First of all, you must determine the surface area you will need in relation to the surface you have available. The advantage of having an SAB in a rural area is obvious: more space, more cultivable ground, and better access to water. In the city, you will have very little space on your balcony or terrace to develop a sufficiently large cultivation area. Once you have determined the minimum surface area, you can reserve the remaining surface for husbandry or pasturage. You should know that animals require more space to produce the same quantity of food. At a minimum, you must allow 550 square feet of vegetable garden per adult under permaculture (a thousand square feet per person would be preferable). Permaculture gives you the maximum possible healthy yield, is effective against pests, and does not damage the soil. It is useful to leave fallow an extra section of a few square meters per person, in order to rotate crops from one year to another. Do not hesitate to reserve one part of your garden for flowers, which will attract good insects and bees (useful for pollination). Ideally, for a family, plan on some 10,000 square feet. Such a large surface will allow you to grow all kinds of things all year round and raise a surplus that you can preserve or trade. Use a wide variety of fruits, cereals, vegetables, and herbs. In this way, you will insure yourself against any plant sickness striking a particular plant, which can destroy an entire year's crop; even in the worst case, only a small part of your garden will be affected. Plan on species that sprout early in the spring and others that only sprout in late autumn; thus you will have something fresh to eat most of the time. In this spirit, inform yourself about what grows at each time of the year in order to know when to sow and when to harvest each root or vegetable.

Buy seed stock now and maintain three times as much as you expect to use. Thus, you will have a store on hand, and you will not be left empty-handed if you must restart a crop that did not sprout. For greater autonomy, recover seed from living plants and make sure the seeds you buy are organic (and not genetically altered or hybrids, since these are modified so as not to sprout more than once). Stock your seeds in a dark, dry place in rodent-proof metal containers. Remember to cultivate the foods you enjoy — but in moderation! As an adjunct to your garden, or if you live in town, you can also grow vegetables and small fruit trees in pots and large tubs. This is very useful if you wish to have a few oranges or lemons, where the trees would suffer from frost. A greenhouse can also help you grow fruits which would normally require a warmer climate. A greenhouse of one hundred square feet is a good start. If you have wet areas on your land, you can also plant wild rice, which will attract migrating birds that can add to your food supply.

To improve the productivity of your vegetable garden, you can use natural or organic fertilizers. Organic fertilizers are vegetable matter (compost or other vegetal waste matter). They can be made from plants cultivated or prepared for this very purpose (such as nettle manure or algae) or manure piles (composed mostly of vegetal litter and half-digested vegetal excreta).

To sow, cultivate, maintain, protect, and, finally, harvest the fruit of your labor in your garden, you will need good tools. Buy all the necessary tools in a specialty shop, and only buy high-quality items: remember that you are going to have to use these tools for a long time, and you will not easily have anyone to repair them or any place to go to buy others. Avoid all tools that require gasoline, electricity, or modern technologies. Think of it as if you were living in the 19th century, or even the Middle Ages. What worked then will work tomorrow: seeders, scythes, billhooks, saws, wheelbarrows, hand mills, etc. Also remember to get replacement parts for your tools (handles, axe heads, etc.).

Protect your crop against pests that, if they are annoying now, will become deadly enemies when your survival depends upon your agricultural production. With all due respect to vegetarians, to get cereals and vegetables, rats and harmful insects must be pitilessly destroyed; this genocidal mission requires frequent attention. Having cats or dogs specialized in rodent hunting is a good idea. Prepare traps for mice, rats, and moles. Buy the material necessary for making wire and picket fences to protect your crops from the depredations of larger animals (boars, deer) and smaller (hares, squirrels). Also protect your animals (poultry, rabbits, etc.) from fox and wolf attacks.

Having a cat who likes hunting mice is a good idea in an SAB, as is a guard dog. It will be even more important to fight insects. The best solution for this in a world without pesticides could be organic, with the help of other insects and plants. Beetles pursue aphids, nematodes infect and kill slugs and weevils, etc. To protect your fruit trees, install bird foils, reflective paper or Mylar strips; attach old CDs to branches with fishing lines or install bird nets. For the interior of your home, choose plants that provide visual comfort, but, above all, clean the air.

If you have space left over after installing and protecting your garden, animal husbandry will help you meet your needs for animal protein in the form of meat, eggs, or milk. Certain animals are useful for their strength (oxen, donkeys, etc.) or for riding (horses, etc.). As with everything else, improvisation will not work. You must know each breed and all the peculiarities of the animals you wish to raise: their proper food, their natural rhythms and life cycles, what care must be given them and, if necessary, under what conditions they can be prepared for consumption. Most animals today are super-specialized and selected for maximum efficiency in producing meat and milk. Unfortunately, these Frankenstein animals are sometimes unable to reproduce, or lack basic instincts (nesting, etc.). They are neither nutritionally healthy nor able to live on their own. If you want to raise animals to produce eggs, milk, wool, hide, or meat or for plowing, you must select healthy animals adapted to your region, climate, and type of soil. Ideally, you should choose local breeds with good genetic diversity, and which do not require the constant presence of a veterinarian. So choose carefully: heritage breed chickens (rather than industrially selected breeds) are able to lay eggs, reproduce, and provide good meat for consumption; healthy rabbits with a varied genetic patrimony; pigs, sheep, goats, cows that can caper and frolic, and provide good meat, milk, wool, etc. Looking for such animals will give you occasion to meet many farmers in your region and establish contacts that will be useful later. When you are buying animals, pay attention: you must have all the authorizations and follow all health and other regulations. Take care to ask the sellers questions about the animal's health, age, breed, and reproductive capacity (look to see if it is castrated). Consult a veterinarian or expert, especially the first time. But it is up to you to choose: buffaloes, bison, cows, pigs, goats, sheep, chicken, rabbits, emus, ostriches, geese, turkeys, llamas, alpacas, mules, donkeys, horses... Finally, learn to keep your animals on your own land: provide walls, fences, or barriers. Keeping animals is no game. Although the result can be excellent (fresh eggs in the morning), the daily work required can be significant. A cow requires more work than a pig, which requires more than a sheep or chicken. In all cases, learn to care for your animals and treat them as well as you would a human (well, sort of) in all areas, including when you must slaughter them to eat or to cut short their sufferings in case of sickness or an accident.

Again, it is from practice that you will learn and develop know-how. Start by thinking small: a few square feet for a garden, a few fowl or rabbits. After a while, enlarge the terrain, plant more, develop your technique, try raising a sheep or a pony... Gradually, you will become more experienced and self-sufficient. Even if you are rich and someone manages your farm for you, learn to do everything yourself. Your manager will not always be there, and it is better to practice before someone makes a mistake with terrible consequences.

In general, take inspiration from nature and its laws. Practical agriculture cannot limit itself to a technique or production goals. It must view the whole environment in which it is inscribed with a real sense of ecology: water management, reforestation, the prevention of erosion, care for humus and soil, respecting and preserving biodiversity, etc. The agriculture practiced in your SAB will thus become a regenerative force for the soil, and your local production will be healthy and nourishing.

Are you ready to become a farmer?

Created in 2008, the "Francilière" association has the goal of defending France's heritage and culture.

Established in the Burgundy region, its projects are covered with the dual objective of conserving and transmitting the values that are at the heart of European civilization and the people who forged it across time. The foundation declares that it "participates in safeguarding and favoring the permanence of the environment and the common heritage of the European peoples." It pursues this goal while respecting natural balances and with a constant care to foster fraternity among its members. One of its callings is to promote and support the creation of a place for meeting and exchange. Its seven founders renovated an abandoned rural site, which they renamed "La Francilière." This site, organized as a community, is entirely similar to an SAB. It is a place that accepts permanent residents, but its vocation is also to accept tourists, which permits it to be self-financing. All year long it welcomes individuals and families into a warm and convivial atmosphere. Internships and themed residencies are offered within the framework of the association's cultural activities. According to its members, it defends a "certain idea of France" that "under the combined effects of immigration, demographic decline, and a fashionable ideology preaching universal crossbreeding, risks causing everything French to disappear from France in a short time." Practically, a household with sleeping quarters, living rooms, a kitchen, and toilets is equipped to receive a large number of people. A large garden and field are already being used to grow cereals and vegetables, thanks to techniques inspired by permaculture (complete with hedgehog shelters) and traditional agriculture. A food reserve, the fruit of surplus production in the area, has been put in jars and stored at a constant temperature.

<<the beginning of hygiene is to hate one's neighbors' germs!

réjean ducharme

artist

_wild to mild

/1973/

<<a great doctor is a curer who also happens to have learned medicine.

maurice druon

writer

//1918–2009//

<<a doctor helps one die more slowly.

plutarch

philosopher

//40–125//

<<as long as men die and want to live,

the doctor will be ridiculed—and well paid.

jean de la bruyère

philosopher

//1645–1696//

POINT 3

Hygiene and Health

HAVING SPOKEN OF THE IMPORTANCE of food and water, and
thus having studied the two essential needs for human survival, we
must now develop the theme of safeguarding human life. The third
fundamental principle of an SAB is the management of hygiene and
health.

Here, we come up against a major stumbling block of civilization.
Although one can easily establish efficient subsistence agriculture
independent of modern science and technology (with a source of
water, work, and simple tools and techniques), medicine is different. It is probably in this domain that our life has changed the most
over the last 150 years. We have gone from a perilous world of high
mortality—with short life spans filled with physical suffering, with
an uncertain, improvised medical system incapable of diagnosing and
treating illnesses—to a world where everything can be treated except
a few rare diseases or those caused by human behavior (cancer from
tobacco, diabetes due to poor nutrition, etc.) or the environment (car-
cinogenic pollution, etc.). We haven't achieved immortality yet ... but
modern medicine's ability to extend and improve people's lives, even
in very poor countries, is nothing short of astounding!

If the economy collapses, we will be confronted with the rapid—and perhaps permanent—disappearance of modern healthcare.
Even if a doctor is available, what happens if treatment becomes

impossible because pharmaceutical factories have closed, or the ingredients necessary to produce medication are inaccessible? In serious cases of social unrest, hospitals and doctors are often taken to task, or even destroyed and murdered by mobs who do not understand the implications of their actions, or that medical treatment cannot be given to everyone indiscriminately. In periods of turmoil in Rwanda, the Congo, and Cambodia, and to a lesser extent in Uganda, Togo, and El Salvador, hospitals were sacked and burned; often, patients and certain doctors who tried to protect them were executed by militias or angry mobs. This does not mean that such aberrant behavior would happen in the West, where the role of modern medicine has traditionally been held in higher regard. But who can be sure? In short, you should do everything you can do to remain healthy and out of hospital.

Good advice, certainly, but not always practical. And we must be practical; so let's start at the beginning.

In order to avoid being ill, in weak health, or wounded, you must never get sick, have accidents, and need medical care. It sounds obvious, but it's simply logical. First of all, you must prevent medical problems from occurring as much as possible. Then, if a problem occurs in spite of our precautions, it must be treated effectively. Priority should be given to treating the statistically most common problems, without neglecting the less common and more difficult ones. Finally, one must be realistic and honest: there are a lot of injuries and illnesses that cannot be treated without the help of a doctor with an operating room and modern medications. Lacking these, one must be prepared for the worst: a lingering death, terrible suffering. All the more reason to practice daily prevention.

How does one do this?

Not being able to undertake long medical studies at my age and become a specialized caregiver, doctor, or surgeon, I decided to converse at length with some friends and acquaintances: emergency personnel, surgeons, anesthesiologists, and Red Cross doctors. Moreover,

I have studied works on military and rural medicine. Two works in particular have been indispensable to me:

> *Where There Is No Doctor* by David Werner was published in 1977; Werner describes treatment methods in Third World villages. The book is extremely comprehensive and covers our concerns perfectly. This book and its companion, *Where There Is No Dentist*, are available for free download at www.piero.com.

> *68W Advanced Field Craft: Combat Medic Skills* is the combat medicine manual of the American Army, which has acquired a great reputation for its ability to save the lives of its soldiers. This well-illustrated manual explains how to treat injuries as varied as fractures, bullet wounds, burns, chemical poisoning, and radiation damage. It is a wonderful reference to have at home.

All the doctors I interviewed and all the works I read (listed in the bibliographical section) agree that prevention is the best way to avoid problems, that if a problem occurs, a doctor must be consulted quickly, and that if there is no doctor and no medicine, one must try a few simple techniques and hope for the best. What I write in this chapter is a summary of these interviews and studies. This will give you a start on developing a system to follow. You will quickly understand that you must investigate each of the elements yourself by reading books, taking courses, and talking to your doctor (and asking a lot of questions). Never try to provide medical or surgical care at home, as an autodidact or autonomously. Do not improvise where medicine is concerned. There is good reason for a medical student's long years of study and practice. As much as you can, in case of a sanitary or medical problem, consult specialists.

With these warnings in mind, let's put on our surgical masks and gloves, pick up our scalpels, and start the operation.

Basic Hygiene

Hygiene refers to all behavior designed to keep you in good health. You must know how to distinguish between good microbes and those that are pathogenic or can become so in certain circumstances (which good hygiene attempts to prevent or mitigate). Hygiene seeks to master the environmental factors which can contribute to weakening health, such as pollution, but also numerous risk factors intrinsically linked to one's lifestyle. Care of the body, physical activity, nourishment, work, and addictions have a universal impact on individual health.

Let's begin with lifestyle.

Four factors allow one to prolong one's lifespan considerably and make it more pleasant:

> Abstention from tobacco. Withdrawal should be quick... .

In an economic crisis, the disappearance of cigarette factories should help you kick the habit.

> Moderation in one's consumption of alcohol. (Let's define "moderate" as one glass of wine per meal).

> Daily consumption of mostly fruits and vegetables rather than fats and sugars. You must cultivate enough vegetables and have enough fruit trees available. Fats will be relatively scarce in your post-collapse diet, and while the latent sugars contained in cereals or potatoes are relatively welcome, refined sugars will be almost absent.

> Daily physical exercise. You are unlikely to miss out on this in your SAB!

Avoid acute or chronic pollution, whether biological or chemical, or from sound or light (these factors add to or multiply each other's effects), which are also a significant source of illness. Try to avoid these problems. Prevention is the best medicine. Good health, good nutrition, and a fit, balanced and enduring physique will be your best protection:

> Start by eating natural foods — avoid industrially produced meat, eat those vegetables that are in season and buy your food at the market if you can, all the more as it is less expensive. Eliminate snacks and junk food. Buy smaller plates. All this will require discipline, but will be an excellent investment.

> Practice an endurance sport as well as one that is rapid and intense. Walk or get at least half an hour's worth of activity each day. Lose your excess weight, but try to keep a five-to-ten-pound surplus, as this extra body fat will be a welcome reserve in a crisis.

> When you are living in your SAB, your physical condition will be very useful given what you will have to do (cut wood, fetch water, etc.). If you are already in shape, it will be one less thing to worry about.

Next, let us consider *washing and cleanliness* in general. Washing refers to the removal of undesirable matter, organic (grease), or mineral (dust or tartar) that can contain microorganisms. *Disinfection* allows the direct removal of certain microorganisms. *Detergency* consists in removing undesirable foreign substances that adhere to an item or living tissue by dissolving them. Washing generally involves four things: mechanical action (water pressure, rubbing), chemical action (the dissolution of certain materials, including fats), water temperature, which helps to remove contaminants, and, finally, the duration of detergent action. Good hygienic practices regarding the materials used in the food industry and the cleaning procedures applied after each item has been prepared allow healthy food to be produced, and thus permit longer conservation. The method and product to use depends on the nature of the undesirable foreign substances and the fragility of the object to be cleaned. For bodily hygiene, soap and warm water under no more than slight pressure is fine, but for equipment, more aggressive methods should be employed. Cleaning and detergents only have a temporary effect, of course, and must be repeated regularly. This is why one must be careful to wash one's hands with soap and dry them before cooking, handling food or a wound, or carrying out any other task involving the risk of infection or contamination. One must also wash one's hands thoroughly after using the toilet, handling animals or soil, coming into contact with excrement, chemical, or toxic products or playing with children. You must be careful to stock a lot of soap in your SAB.

Here is a typical example illustrating the need for cleanliness. A child has worms and scratches the area affected. Since he does not wash his hands, his fingers and nails are covered with hundreds of little worm eggs invisible to the naked eye. If he touches food, puts his fingers in someone's mouth, or plays with other children, he may contaminate other persons. If this doesn't sound too serious, imagine that the case involves a deadly bacteria or virus.

You must be able to *disinfect and sterilize* things. Disinfection consists in killing, removing, or deactivating microorganisms (parasites, bacteria) or viruses. When disinfection involves living tissue, it is called antiseptics; when it involves medical materials, it is called de-contamination. The effects of antiseptics and disinfection are limited in duration. Sterilization consists of eliminating *all* microorganisms from a material and conditioning the material to maintain this state of sterility. The principal methods used for disinfection and sterilization are chemicals, temperature and pressure (pasteurization, autoclaves), and, finally, radiation. If you are a doctor yourself, or have a doctor in your SAB, it would be useful for you (or him) to prepare the materials necessary for sterilizing medical tools—typically a small auto-clave—and a little vacuum-packaging machine to keep them sterile until their next use. Otherwise, boiling water and soap cover the great majority of needs.

One must adopt hygienic *behavior* and make it a habit. This does not mean becoming obsessive or maintaining the hygienic level of

an operating room! It simply means avoiding bacterial or viral contamination. Do not worry: with your agricultural activity, contact
with animals, life in the open air, you will have plenty of occasions to
immunize yourself. Remember that your work and good health are
indispensable to your family and the proper functioning of your SAB,
and that the less you are sick or weakened, the better everyone will
feel. Good personal hygiene is important not only for your health but
also for your mindset. Maintaining civilized decorum and cleanliness
is important. Be clean: wash your hair and hands, clean your nails,
shave. If you are clean, it will also be easier to get the respect of others. The difference between a disciplined, self-respecting person or
organization and a band of louse-infested refugees leaps out to any
observer.

You must take care never to let animals, which may have come
into contact with sources of bacteria or viruses, enter any of the rooms
of your house, lick children, or climb into your beds. If this happens,
clean the persons and objects that were touched. By animals, I mean
all animals, including those called domestic: cats, dogs, etc. Keep all
your animals clean and healthy, whether livestock or pets. Get a veterinarian to verify that they have no parasites, and then learn to make
this kind of verification yourself. The excrement of healthy herbivores
(but not cats, dogs, or pigs!) can be added to compost and used as
a fertilizer. You must ensure that no one, especially not children, do
their business on the ground in or around the home. Everyone must
be made to use toilets or latrines. Sheets, clothing, and linens must
regularly be put out in the sun, as in Mediterranean countries, since
ultraviolet rays in sunlight have great power to sterilize against many
microbes. Regularly check your bedding, especially if you experience
itchiness, for fleas, ticks, etc. Keep your hair clean and your nails
short, and treat any symptoms as quickly as possible. In case of lice,
ticks, mites, or bedbugs, make sure you wash your sheets, slipcovers,
bedspreads, and all bedding in boiling water. Tampons and all other
elements used to absorb blood, and which cannot be washed, must be

burned or buried deep and far from the garden or grazing fields. Be careful not to spit on the ground, not to urinate or defecate anywhere but in your toilet or latrine, and to wash your hands after every meal, every trip to the toilet, each time you touch an animal or an object that may have been exposed to bacterial or viral contamination. In case of illness, even a minor one, separate the sick person from healthy people. Clean your rooms often: floors, walls and underneath the furniture. Fill in holes that could house insects (roaches) and other animals (not to mention lizards, snakes, scorpions, and other warm-weather creatures). Keep things in order, for this will make it easier for you to find what you need. Leave shoes outside at the entrance to your house. You might consider wearing indoor shoes in the house.

Here's another example to illustrate the importance of cleanly behavior: a man ill with dysentery cannot control himself and defecates behind the barn wall. Without being seen, he covers the deed with a bit of soil and goes on his way. A little pig passes by, poking its snout into everything. This little pig still has traces of human feces on its snout when the household children play with it. Later on, one of the children gets hungry and cries. His mother takes the child on her knees and gives him a bit of the food she is preparing and returns to the kitchen. The poor women does not realize her hands have touched the child's and that now, by touching the food she is preparing, she risks contaminating the whole family. The next day, everyone wakes up with stomach pains and the urge to run to the latrines! One might smile at this story if dysentery did not kill 100,000 people per year across the world.

Hygiene is of great importance to *water and food*.

We have already described how to purify water. It is equally important to have pure water for cleaning food. You must watch out for bacterial or viral infection. Take thought to avoid any food that is spoiled or otherwise unfit for consumption; eating it could give you food poisoning. Also beware of cooked food that has been lying around for several hours. Try to eat freshly prepared food, especially if you are sick.

Persons with tuberculosis, colds, sore throats, and other highly contagious illnesses should take their meals separately; their plates, glasses, and silverware should be washed carefully, especially after use. You must always carefully wash your hands with soap before cooking, and wash your kitchen workspace. The most important point is to avoid any contact between animal or human fecal matter and the food you are going to consume. So when you are dressing animal carcasses, be careful with the offal, especially the intestines, so they do not contaminate the rest of the meat. Wash fruits and vegetables with water before peeling in order to eliminate parasites, microorganisms, worms, and animal excrement. Do not let fruits or vegetables touch eggshells that do not originate in egg-crates. Cooking should be done so as to ensure the destruction of any possible bacteria or viruses. Meat and fish must be fully cooked; vegetables and fruits that are steamed, cooked, or boiled for twenty to thirty minutes usually present no bacterial or viral danger. To conserve food, protect it with lids, cans, transparent film, or aluminum. Do not keep them at above 50 °F (10 °C); beyond that point, bacterial development accelerates. If you do not have a refrigerator, consider installing a cool room in your cellar. In any case, do not put sensitive products (meat, fish) in contact with those that might contaminate them (unpeeled fruits and vegetables). Thaw items in the refrigerator (rather than in the open air) in order to avoid the development of germs. Tools, cans, and jars used for conserves should be sterilized with boiling water after use. After cooking, clean your workplace, utensils, dishes, ground, and your hands, especially when you have handled raw animal products.

Finally, you must properly manage your *garbage*. For garbage, you should never use any containers you plan to reuse for keeping food. Then some good news: since you are going to recycle a large part of everything you use — organic waste for compost, wood and paper for heating, metal for recasting, etc.—you will have very little real garbage! Plan on having garbage bags of various sizes for sorting and storing plastic and other materials. Those you cannot sell or recycle can be burned or buried at a distance from your vegetable garden. The golden rule with garbage is never to let it pollute your grounds or (especially) your water supply—or those of your neighbors.

Toilets and Waste Management

No one likes to talk about it, but human waste must be managed, one's own and that of others. Indeed, the proper elimination of human waste is a fundamental element of good hygiene. If you have ever experienced a cut in the water supply to your house or apartment, you will quickly have understood how important working toilets are. The quantity of excrement produced by a normal adult quickly becomes a sizable problem. In fact, each adult will produce one liter of urine and over a pound of feces per day. Multiply this by the number of persons living in your SAB, and you will see that it rapidly becomes a significant quantity, a source of disagreeable odors and, above all, of potential illnesses. If you have access to a source of water with a pump, if your house or farm is equipped with modern toilets that flush properly, you can use them and consider yourself lucky. But if your toilets no longer flush properly, do not use them any more! You need another solution. Verify that if the sewers break down or overflow, the excess does not flow in the direction of your home. If sewers do overflow, it's time for some emergency plumbing, and it would probably be a good idea to block the access to the sewers.

The ultimate solution is to construct latrines or "composting toilets" outside. The good news is that for 12,000 years, we have known how to do this.

> Latrines must be, at a minimum, twenty meters or sixty-five feet
  from any habitation or water or food source (e.g. a vegetable garden). They should also be inaccessible to animals — especially pigs
  and dogs. This can be accomplished with a simple enclosure.

> Verify that the natural drainage beneath the latrine does not flow toward a vegetable garden, river, or other source of water.

> Dig a pit as deep as possible — a depth of three meters or ten feet or more is fine — to allow for the maximum amount of excrement and reduce the problem of flies and odor. Ideally, install a ventilation duct for odors and place it away from the latrine. It will act like a chimney and evacuate bad odors.

> Take care to arrange for a minimum level of comfort in case of rain with a roof and wind protection.

> Arm yourself with a bag of sawdust, wood shavings, or ashes to throw by the handful on your waste after each session. You will need a cubic meter per person per year of such material.

> Make sure to have toilet paper or newspaper, and ideally a pitcher of water to clean yourself and the seat (if you have installed one) or any "misses." Close the hole of the latrine until the next use.

> Teach everyone, especially children, to do their business correctly in these latrines.

> If the latrine fills up too quickly, before it overflows, dig another farther away.

> Wash your hands with soap after using the latrine.

The advantages of having a latrine are numerous:

> They save water. These "flushless" toilets avoid wasting between three and twelve liters of drinking water per use.

> They don't burden plumbing systems. Salts do not easily degrade in water. The bacteria and chemical substances we excrete require lengthy treatment to become harmless. So flushing will continue to increase the burden on any treatment plants that may still be running.

> They do not make the noise of flushing toilets. There is no problem of pipes freezing in the case of external toilets in cold regions.

> They reduce the risk of epidemics. Villages in poor countries that correctly use latrines almost never suffer epidemics, and their inhabitants do much better than those of the shantytowns that make use of "flying toilets." (Waste is placed in plastic bags and thrown as far away as possible from the hut: onto another hut, or even into a public street. Think about that.)

Water that has been used for various types of cleaning (dishes, linen, clothes, etc.) should also be disposed of correctly, that is, not into a river that can be used for other purposes. You can create filtering systems and natural drainage into the ground (with the help of rock strata, gravel, and sand) that will slowly but effectively filter waste water.

Oral and Dental Hygiene

The collapse of the economy will have one advantage: you will no longer have to go to the dentist! Other than the few remaining country dentists who still have the old machines that work with a pedal, most dentists will not be able to operate as their high-tech equipment becomes unusable or uneconomical. The bad news is that if you have poor teeth, bad dental care, or cavities, you will suffer the pains of a martyr and greatly miss your cleaning sessions with your old dentist as sweet moments of pleasure. Prevention must be emphasized, the goal being to avoid developing cavities. These are caused by bacteria in the mouth that transform sugars into lactic acid, which, in turn, attacks dental enamel, demineralizing it until a cavity appears. Many different types of food can cause cavities. If a cavity gets deep enough, it hits the nerve, which is quite painful, and can allow bacteria to enter the blood and nervous system. This can cause very painful abscesses, sometimes even death by blood poisoning and pericardial infection. An untreated cavity can be especially serious for a pregnant woman.

Fortunately, saliva allows the acidity level of the mouth to return to a normal level. Unfortunately, no one's natural defenses are able to fully counteract the effects of these acids; and some people are simply more susceptible to cavities than others. This makes prevention all the more important. Cavities are above all prevented by:

> **Good oral and dental hygiene.** Careful brushing twice a day (morning and evening) is imperative from an early age. Use a soft brush with a fluoride toothpaste and dental floss in order to prevent the formation of cavities between teeth. Once a week, rinse your teeth with a fluoride solution. If you have no toothbrush, it is possible to use a soft piece of wood in place. If you have no toothpaste, use a bit of clay or bicarbonate of soda (also commonly referred to as sodium bicarbonate or baking soda). If you have no dental floss, use vegetal fibers. Be careful not to injure your gums. If you do not have access to a toothbrush, sugar-free chewing gum can be used to promote salivation (which reduces acidity in the mouth) as you await the next mechanical brushing.

> **Fewer snacks and sugared drinks.** These promote bacterial activity and acidify the mouth. Sodas, syrups, and fruit juices are especially bad, since they are not only sugary but also acidic. Water should be the preferred drink, especially for young children.

> **An appropriate diet.** Prefer whole foods over processed foods, replace white sugar with unrefined cane sugar or honey, and decrease your consumption of foods containing sugar as much as possible. The good news is that unless you live near a source of sugarcane or sugar beet production, you will not be consuming much sugar anyway.

> **Regular trips to the dentist.** This will allow you to get cavities treated at an early stage. Dental lesions will then be kept to a minimum. Cavities cannot be healed; their progress can be stopped with cleaning and the sealing of the remaining cavity. Ideally, dental visits should occur every six months. Once a year should be

enough for an adult with few cavity or gum problems. While you are at it, verify that you have a good bite. This often has an impact on your other bodily functions.

Once living in your SAB, if you notice that your gums are swollen or irritated, continue brushing your teeth and cleaning between your teeth (flossing), and massage your gums with a toothbrush or your fingers. Wash your mouth with salt water for several days and eat mostly fresh green vegetables and fruits. If, despite an exemplary preventive regimen, a cavity develops and no dentist is available, redouble your efforts to keep the cavity from becoming larger. But if it does, and the pain becomes unbearable, there is only one solution — pulling the tooth. To do so, you will need a certain number of tools: a dental mirror to see behind your teeth, a hook to find cavities, and a speculum and wood to displace the tongue. Then you must wash your hands with soap, sterilize your instruments, and have the patient rinse his mouth until no traces of food remain. Verify by touching the tooth that it is, indeed, the cause of the pain and not something else (such as a broken jaw), and, above all, make sure you have the right tooth. Once it is identified, administer a mild analgesic (paracetamol) and apply clove oil. Equip yourself with cotton and gauze in case of bleeding. If you have any local anesthetic (lidocaine, procaine, etc.), administer it to the gums on both sides, close to the teeth, with a sterile syringe. Unless you have dental forceps, use pliers or a clamp to pull the tooth. Do not jerk it suddenly, so as not to break the tooth or the roots, which could become infected. (Note: some teeth have only a single root, some two, and the molars have four.) Verify the whole procedure by referring to an appropriate guide to dentistry. Once you have a firm grip on the tooth, act as if you have a stake stuck in the ground: manipulate the tooth in one direction and the other until it becomes loose and starts to come out more easily. Cover the wound with a disinfectant (chlorhexidine or clove oil) and place a little gauze on it, asking the patient to bite down for 30 minutes. This should stop the bleeding. Then stitch the wound as you would any other. You can only hope that the patient has not suffered too much (and that the experience doesn't do too much harm to your friendship). If after a few days the patient experiences pain in his tongue and sinus cavity, this means that the wound has become infected. It must be treated like any other infection, which we shall discuss below. Of course, if you have the tools and the know-how to treat a cavity by drilling and filling it, this is preferable to pulling the tooth.

So one of the first things to do in case of a serious economic crisis is to immediately visit the dentist for full treatment of cavities or other problems. Do not wait—your dentist could save your life. For that matter, put down this book, call your dentist, make an appointment, and tell him I sent you. Take heart: it won't hurt as much as having a tooth pulled.

Medicine

We must be realistic. The immense knowledge and know-how developed by modern medicine will not necessarily be there for us in a crisis. If we are lucky, a certain number of doctors, medications, instruments, and sophisticated machines will remain permanently in operation. If not, we will have to rely on more rudimentary methods.

Here are the two cases to consider: either you have access to medical expertise (you are a doctor yourself or you have a doctor, or at least persons with medical knowledge, in your SAB) or you are left to your own devices and must get along as best you can with the knowledge and competence you can acquire.

In both cases, here is what you should do *now*:

> Identify the doctors, hospitals, dispensaries, clinics, and pharmacies nearest you.

> Buy some medical-emergency manuals.

> Buy a few medical tools and instruments.

> Identify courses available at universities nearby or given by specialized organizations such as those that train humanitarian

workers who travel to natural disaster areas or isolated areas. You will certainly find specialized courses — evening or continuation education — on first aid, emergency care, and holistic medicine. Your goal should not necessarily be to get a diploma but to learn the basic ideas and, if possible, get a little experience. For example, you should learn how to administer an injection (intravenous or intramuscular), perform cardiac massage, apply bandages or medication for burns, set up an intravenous drip, etc.

> Stock up on medications that will allow you to treat a certain number of problems (see list below).

> Verify that you and all persons in your SAB, especially children, are up-to-date with vaccinations. See a doctor who can immunize you against hepatitis A and B, tetanus, poliomyelitis, yellow fever, tuberculosis, measles, etc.

To get started, let's look at a few basic principles of survival medicine:

> **Be aware of your surroundings.** Unless you are a doctor yourself, one might very well be difficult to reach. This is why you must learn as much as you can to increase your know-how and experience.

> **Use common sense:** if you know there is no doctor available and you don't know what to do, ask around. If no one can help you, call upon your good sense and improvise. For example, if a woman has given birth and continues to bleed, and you are thirty minutes from a doctor or hospital, take her there as quickly as possible; however, if you are *two days* away from help and cannot communicate, look up a childbirth manual and take the initiative by massaging her belly (perhaps the placenta has not come detached properly), while someone else goes for help.

> **Use what is most effective in modern medicine along with what works the best in traditional medicine.** This combination may be better than either one taken separately. Respect local traditions

unless you identify harmful methods. But if certain methods do neither harm nor good (e.g. in certain lands, there exists a belief that biting the serpent that bit you can help you recover), let auto-suggestion (i.e., the placebo effect) operate; it may help and, in the worst case, it will have no adverse effects. Work with local healers if there are any: midwives, veterinarians, retired doctors, etc. Learn and ask questions. Do not waste chances for learning or observing, but ask — e.g., if you are present at surgical operations. Get used to the sight of blood and wounds.

> **Lead by example.** If you care for your own health, others may imitate you, but if you make no effort, it will be hard for others to follow your recommendations. This goes for excess drinking, overeating, smoking, and sanitation tasks. If you give instructions to empty overflowing latrines, take part in this unpleasant but necessary task yourself; you will gain respect. Teach the people around you, especially once you are in your SAB, how to avoid getting sick, how to maintain good hygiene, how to care for oneself, and eat and drink in a healthy way. Learn to observe and ask the right questions: why does diarrhea occur? Why did this or that animal die? What could have caused these cases of malnutrition, depression, or other illnesses? Proper diagnosis is of the greatest importance. For example, a person has a cough that he thinks is a problem requiring treatment. Now, his real problem might be smoking. He must find the will to quit, and this is not a medical problem but a social and psychological one. What he needs is not medicine but a strong will, the support of his family and friends, and perhaps some practical advice on how to break a habit.

> **Maintain a proper balance between prevention and cure.** You must not fail to treat real problems on the pretext of preventive action. The treatment of a slight illness can keep it from becoming a serious one. Make use of treatment to teach and practice prevention. For example, if a mother of a baby with intestinal worms comes to have it treated, take advantage of the situation to explain

how such worms are caught and reproduce, and what must be done to keep them from returning.

Then you must learn to *classify* medical problems.

For all kinds of problems—whether they have a psychological, bacterial, natural, or viral cause; are due to an injury; or are chronic—there exist three categories of seriousness: slight, medium, and severe.

Treatment must be administered as a function of the type and seriousness of the problem. Let us be clear and pragmatic: everything serious (heart attack, impalement, amputation of a limb, deep or extensive burns, open fractures, poisoning, serious behavioral problems, etc.) will require emergency hospitalization. Even a very good surgeon cannot perform a liver operation without an operating room! So we must concern ourselves only with slighter categories and a few more serious cases. But whatever happens, consult a doctor as soon as possible if you can.

Shock Trauma

Falling from a ladder while picking fruit, cutting oneself while woodcutting, and spraining an ankle while running are all physical traumas that can occur in your SAB (indeed, these occurences will likely be common). You must also consider the possibility of more unusual types of injuries, such as bullet wounds. Shock trauma is a large category of trauma, direct or indirect: falls, puncture wounds, cuts, or blunt trauma, and these involve, in increasing order of seriousness: bruises, open wounds, hematomas, sprains, dislocations, and fractures. These injuries involve soft tissue (skin, fat, muscle), the skeleton (bones and articulations), and/or vital areas such arteries, veins, nerves, organs. Since the list of possible injuries and treatments is very long, let us take just three examples from among the many cases you should research yourself:

> In case of a cut, you must disinfect it with iodine or a chlorhexadine antiseptic, then stitch it with a sterilized needle and suture. If possible, administer a local anesthetic (e.g., lidocaine, procaine).

> If a foreign object is in a wound, you must also disinfect and, if possible, remove the foreign object with tongs—you might also use retractors to keep the wound open during the procedure. Sometimes, if the foreign object is too small or close to an organ that might be damaged, it may be preferable to leave it inside and try to prevent infections by administering antibiotics.

> For fractures, keep the limb immobile with a splint and recommend rest. Plan on having preformed splints for the neck, ankles, or wrist; you will find them at a pharmacy; they will also be useful for sprains. If you have an open fracture, it must be treated as a wound; try to put the bone back in place while removing bone fragments. *Good luck!*

For any surgical operation, always wear gloves, eye protection (glasses at the very least), a mask, and an apron. You must wash your hands before and after an operation and, if possible, disinfect them with an alcohol-based disinfectant. For pain, or in order to administer a general anesthetic, use morphine. The dosage is a function of the patient's weight: for a 70-kilogram or 154-pound adult, seven milligrams are necessary; for one hundred kilograms or 220 pounds and up, you will need ten milligrams. Morphine is administered by injection (into the fatty tissue under the skin). You must then bandage any wounds with the help of a homeostatic tourniquet and compress bandages.

The best way to avoid wounds is, of course, to prevent them from happening. Wear shoes outside, wear protective clothing when you are doing dangerous work, protect your eyes, protect your hands with gloves, wear a helmet, etc. Be prudent, attentive, deliberate, and careful.

Burns

A burn can be caused:

> by contact with something hot (solid, liquid, or gas);

> by contact with a caustic substance;

> by friction;

> by the effect of combustion (the action of a flame);

> by the effects of radiation (sunburns being the best example);

> by the effect of an electrical current (electrical burns);

> or by cold (frostbite).

There are three degrees of seriousness:

> **First-degree** burns are the least serious and most common. Only the epidermis is affected, causing redness. The area of the burn becomes sensitive, as with sunburn. Such burns require no special treatment since the skin retains its power of regeneration.

> **Second-degree** burns damage the epidermis and, to a lesser degree, the dermis. These burns involve the appearance of boils on the affected areas. The skin can heal on its own, provided the patient is careful to avoid infection.

> **Third-degree** burns are the most serious. They destroy all of the skin (dermis and epidermis). The damaged skin takes on a white, brown, or black coloration and becomes insensitive, dry, and subject to infection. In this case, there is no possibility that the skin can regenerate itself, for all of the living skin cells have been destroyed. If the lesion is large, a skin graft is indispensable for the patient's survival.

The basic treatment for a burn consists in moistening it with cold water, gently and without pressure. Do not pour water directly upon the burn, for this applies microbes on a lesion that has just been sterilized by heat. Moistening a burn limits its extension and consequences, as well as relieves pain.

In the case of a chemical burn, remove the clothes affected by the chemical and run plenty of water over the burn or affected area as early as possible, to remove the substance in question. If the substance gets into the eye, again rinse abundantly with water. A serious burn frequently provokes cardiovascular collapse, shown by an intense paleness of the skin (especially around the lips and eyelids), a rapid pulse, and the feeling of thirst. If the burn is extensive, and the patient must be transported, wrap him in a sterile blanket and keep him still in order to reduce pain. If the burn is on the back, transport the person face-down.

Frostbite is a kind of burn caused by the cold. It may be superficial or deep. Apply moderate external heat to the affected areas. This can be done by bringing the patient close to a radiator or fireplace, for example. This will lead to a remission in the affected area after a few days.

Eye and Ear Troubles

The main forms of eye trauma are: dust, contusions, cuts, and burns. Treatment differs according to the type of problem, but one must always act quickly.

> For dust, it is enough to rotate the eye so tears can wash away the dust in a natural way, but a more serious problem, like a cut or foreign body in the eye, renders this solution inapplicable.

> For a contusion, administer a pain reliever and hope that the hematoma gets absorbed naturally (as it often does). If pain persists, the eye must be thoroughly examined by an ophthalmologist, or else the patient may lose his sight.

> For a cut, the patient's head must be immediately immobilized; you should place your hands on both sides of the head, in order to eliminate the risk of losing the eye. One must be careful to leave

the patient in the position in which he was found. The eye must not move. If an object is lodged in the eye, do not remove it immediately. If possible, put a screen of some kind in front of the victim's eye so that he is not tempted to try to see what is going on around him, which would cause the eye to move and create complications. Reassure the victim. If there is no possibility of having the victim treated by an emergency ophthalmology service, and no doctor is available, anesthetize the muscles around the eye, administer sedatives and painkillers, and remove the object with sterilized tweezers.

> For burns, regular washing with clean water can limit the effects of heat or chemicals.

Be sure to have several pairs of corrective glasses on hand if you need them. Wear good-quality sunglasses to protect your eyes in case of heavy sunshine, especially on ground covered with snow, at high altitudes, or in the desert. If you are nearsighted and have a chance to get surgery, do not hesitate to do so. Procedures such as LASIK or the PRK will improve your sight. If you are astigmatic or have presbyopia, these will handicap you less than being nearsighted. If you wear contact lenses, be sure to buy a large number, along with bottles of the solution necessary to maintain them.

To treat auditory problems due to shock or loud noises, prescribe rest and hope that the internal ear (perforated eardrum, etc.) heals on its own. Avoid letting water enter the ear in such a case. If you wear a hearing aid, plan on having a backup and a large reserve of batteries.

Psychological Problems

Let us keep things simple, realistic, and pragmatic. Depression will be frequent. Everything you have known will get turned upside down. Social statuses will be in flux, and there will be a great deal of uncertainty. Even if you are well off in your SAB, things won't be easy. You may have witnessed scenes that have disturbed or traumatized you, or even lost those you loved. Since there will be no counseling center, you will need to be in friendly surroundings and speak to others. Above all, you must know how to distinguish that which is real from that which is imaginary. The best remedy is activity: cutting wood, fixing the roof, making sure everything is working, keeping busy with your vegetable garden, fields, animals, machines, etc. Depressed persons, or those with slight troubles (anxieties, insomnia, nightmares), will often find a good outlet in physical labor. Work by its very nature — tiring yet satisfying, and sometimes exhilarating — promotes better morale; when you've finished chopping a pile of wood, you feel like you've really done something! Avoid boredom and downtime. In any case, you won't have much of it in an SAB! Eat a good and healthy diet, get plenty of water and physical exercise, get rid of all behavior linked to alcohol, tobacco, or drugs. If you have time, get involved in group leisure activities or team sports. If a person shows signs of serious psychological problems with a potentially dangerous effect on others, he must be taken to a specialist. If there are none, you will have to make decisions of an organizational rather than medical order.

Bacterial Infections

The most common illnesses are caused by bacteria. Bacteria are microorganisms, some of which can lead to infections as they develop in the human body. You cut yourself with a knife while peeling a poorly cleaned fruit: bacteria pass from the skin of the fruit to the knife, then into your wound, finding there a propitious environment for reproduction — you have a little infection. An infection can be identified by a painful red swelling. If the infection gets worse, you may get a fever, experience more serious pain at the level of ganglia (under your arms, in the neck, etc.). Small infections can be treated by disinfecting the wound and applying a plaster or a sterile bandage to keep the wound from coming into contact with other sources of infection. Then you must wait. More serious infections are treated with antibiotics. If you have access to a doctor or pharmacy near your SAB, ask for the most appropriate antibiotic, but otherwise the simplest thing is to have a basic antibiotic on hand — co-amoxicillin. This antibiotic, derived from penicillin, works for ninety-five percent of common infections. Obviously, if you are allergic to penicillin, avoid using it and ask your doctor what other antibiotic might work for you. Co-amoxicillin is administered in 625 milligram doses, three times a day, for five or six days. Be careful with the dosage in the case of children: they take doses two or three times smaller in proportion to their weight. If the infection is very serious — e.g., a pulmonary infection (pneumonia) — you must go to a higher dose: two or three grams, three times a day, for ten or twelve days, preferably intravenously.

Pill-popping should become a thing of the past. First of all, after a crisis, if you have medications at all, they will be a rare commodity, and it is thus best to use them sparingly (and not to treat each and every scratch).

> If you have a normal fever with no signs of inflammation, rest, drink plenty of liquids, and take a little aspirin to relieve any headache.

> If you have a cough, drink water or inhale steam.

> If you have diarrhea, drink plenty of liquids, eat clean, healthy food, and maintain good hygiene.

For examples like this, antibiotics are not advised unless the illness persists or gets worse. Even in cases of colds and flu, which are spread by viruses, antibiotics will have no effect, so it's best to save your meds.

Fungal Infection and Other Parasites

Other microorganisms that can cause problems are microscopic fungi that parasitize the human body, especially the skin, in order to develop. There are also other parasites such as worms. In all cases, good hygiene and cleanliness is the best solution, and if an infection starts, you will often find the solution thanks to products (many of them natural) mentioned above (and in the bibliography).

Since you will be doing a lot of walking, take special care about skin conditions of the foot. Even with good hygiene, feet perspire profusely and must be carefully washed and dried, especially between the toes. Foot powder or talcum can be useful. Avoid plastic soles; prefer leather. When possible, wear open sandals to allow air to get to your feet. In the common dressing room or shower of your SAB, wear beach sandals. In general, never go barefoot.

Viruses

Viruses are different from bacteria. They are biological entities that use their hosts' cells to reproduce. Colds, flu, chicken pox, measles, and infectious mononucleosis are examples of relatively common human viral infections. More serious conditions, such as AIDS, SARS, bird flu, smallpox, and Ebola, are also caused by viruses. The power of a virus to cause illness is described in terms of virulence. Viruses have many different strategies and mechanisms for provoking illnesses. A virus penetrates a specific host cell and takes over its normal functions. At the cellular level, a virus can have various harmful effects: protein synthesis can be disrupted, viral particles can accumulate and cause the death of the host cell, which frees other viral particles and allows the virus to be disseminated. Given that viruses use the host's cellular machinery to reproduce, it is difficult to eliminate them without killing the host cell. Antiviral medications, however, allow the reproduction of the virus to be disrupted, vaccination lets one resist infection, and various medicines treat viral symptoms. Patients often ask for antibiotics, but these have no effect on viruses. Antibiotics interfere with the constituents or the metabolism of bacteria and thus allow for the treatment of bacterial illnesses, but not viral illnesses. So how do you protect yourself against a virus? First of all, increase your *immunity*:

> **Stop smoking**, since it makes the respiratory system more suscep-
> tible to infections and increases the risk of complications.

> **Lose weight:** extra fat tires the body, especially the heart, and an unbalanced diet weakens the immune system.

> **Eliminate all forms of refined sugar from your diet:** candy, fast food, sugared drinks with additives, artificial color, and sweeteners.

> **Avoid non-organic meats,** which are produced industrially (in factories and co-ops).

> **Eliminate anxiety.** Pray if you are a believer; philosophize; be *Zen-like* and sure of yourself. Limit your consumption of coffee, tea, and stimulants.

If a serious, virulent virus seems to be spreading in the population, try not to expose yourself to it. Stay out of the way, avoiding the urban zones principally affected. Avoid public transportation, train stations, airports, and all places people pass through heavily. As a minimal protection, wear a mask and wash your hands with soap often, especially before touching yourself (rubbing your eyes, nose, or other mucous areas). Ideally, wear protective glasses and gloves. In the case of a serious outbreak, this is the time to get into your SAB and not let anyone approach without going through a quarantine — a small building at the end of the garden with its own toilets, for example — for twenty days (typically). You will have to define the quarantine procedure that seems safest to you.

Finally, learn to identify the symptoms of a viral infection, and if, in spite of all your precautions, you are struck, rest and drink plenty of water. A good drink you can make for yourself is to dilute in one liter of water half a teaspoon of salt, two teaspoons of honey or cane sugar, and half a teaspoon of baking soda (sodium bicarbonate). Take aspirin or paracetamol for fevers and pain, and wait for the symptoms to pass. Aspirin is also very useful for moderating the immune system, which can react too strongly and cause the death of the sick person. During the Spanish flu of 1918–1919, the most robust persons died more easily. If you suffer pulmonary congestion, inhale expectorant vapors, which are good to have on hand. Above all, stay by yourself and do not infect others.

Nuclear, Bacterial, and Chemical Fallout

First off, you should not panic about the risk of atomic (i.e., nuclear, radioactive), bacteriological, or chemical contaminations. Your SAB will (in all likelihood) not be a target. However, having a Geiger counter on hand to measure radioactivity can be useful. In the case of radioactivity, stay inside, close the windows, and wait for it to rain, as precipitation washes away most radioactive dust. Then, clean the interior of your house. In the case of high radiation (nuclear war, etc.), you must remain inside longer and use your food reserves. In the end, you will eventually have to go outside again and, after having cleaned everything, take the risk of cultivating the earth again and pursuing your outdoor activities. There are really no other solutions, unfortunately.

In the face of a bacteriological contamination, one must react as for any other bacterial infection: avoid cuts, avoid contamination, avoid touching any corpses with your bare hands, etc.

Chemical contamination is a very isolated case which should not concern you.

As a precautionary measure, I advise having one or two ABC protective kits — you can find them cheaply as surplus items from Eastern Bloc countries — along with a gas mask, with two or three spare filters per person.

Chronic Illnesses

If you are afflicted by chronic illnesses that require a long period of medication or hospitalization, or if you are suffering from a very serious illness such as cancer, you will have problems that will only be exacerbated by the crisis. You must hope that your illness is not too serious. In any case, you will have to stockpile appropriate medication for the long term and, if possible, establish your SAB close to a place where the medications you need are produced. Consult your doctor, explain your theoretical scenario, and see what he or she advises. You may not like the response... Be sure to stock a lot of pain medication (aspirin, paracetamol, morphine, etc.).

Natural Problems

Allergies. If you do not know what you are allergic to, get tested by an allergy specialist. It is better to know beforehand than discovering for yourself the hard way. Then you must avoid anything that might cause an allergic reaction, especially among antibiotics and food.

Childbirth. Some experts advise avoiding situations that would require childbirth in an SAB, and to prevent them by instituting a birth-control policy (through condoms and contraceptive pills, if any are left), at least for a time. Even if these measures are taken, you will likely be confronted with "accidents" as well as pregnancies among refugees or neighbors of your SAB. You must be prepared.

In general, nature is well-designed, and, most of the time, childbirth will be easier than you think. A trained midwife or obstetrician can handle it. Even an inexperienced but resourceful person — if he has been present at just a few births and read a good book (with diagrams) on the subject — can successfully bring a child into this world. That said, when things go wrong, they can go very wrong.

In such a case, you must urgently find a doctor or get the mother to the nearest hospital, for the situation can quickly become dangerous for her and her baby.

If you do not have a midwife or obstetrician in your entourage, to prepare yourself you must read a guide, ask women who have already given birth, and stock the minimum tools and materials: hot water, soap, disinfecting alcohol, cotton, clean bandages, sterilized scissors, flashlight, straws — to blow mucus out of the mouth and nostrils of the newborn — sterilized syringes and needles, gloves, sterilized suturing equipment, two or three hemostats or clamps — to sever the umbilical cord — etc.

Children. Children frequently contract childhood illnesses (measles, rubella, chickenpox, mumps ...) and catch slight infections (conjunctivitis), which must be treated with reduced doses (100 to 250 mg according to weight) of the same antibiotics as adults use. To prepare for these eventualities, contact a pediatrician and consult a specialized book on the treatment of illness and infections typical of children and babies. Be sure your children's vaccinations are up to date and stock up on some vitamin supplements that promote healthy growth (especially A, B1, B2, B12, C, D, iodine and iron) in case of shortage or prolonged isolation. The most important thing for children, in all cases, is to get good nutrition, be clean, and get enough sleep.

Disabilities. For slight disabilities, which don't render the person incapable of taking care of himself, it is quite possible that with a little imagination, a good stock of necessities (catheters, replacement parts for wheelchairs, or hearing aids, etc.), and a few specialized medications, a handicapped person can get along quite well for a long while. Even the deaf, blind, and paraplegic will do fine if they have the know-how and caring friends and family in the SAB. Things will be very different, however, for someone suffering a handicapping accident *after* the economic collapse and *after* the disappearance of super-specialized medical structures that allow a seriously injured person to be treated, reeducated, and rehabilitated. Once again, prevention is key.

For the seriously handicapped, the mentally handicapped, the insane, and other persons requiring permanent help, I fear that survival may not be possible. In the course of my numerous trips to Africa, I have never seen persons with such handicaps — African societies, where one's next meal can't be taken for granted, eliminated them rapidly. One must hope that care personnel will have the humanity not to abandon these people during a collapse, letting them die of hunger amid their own filth, and that a dignified and painless solution can be embraced at the proper time. Does this sound horrible? It is.

Aged Persons. Old age is the condition to which we all hope to succumb … though not right away! Many bodily functions slow down with age, and many illnesses appear that are quite similar to the chronic ones discussed above. If there are aged persons with you in your SAB, be sure to have large stocks of medications for them. Otherwise, they will suffer or rely on the questionable effectiveness of natural remedies.

Corpses. Death is a natural stage of life. Today, we have rendered death almost invisible; in a post-collapse scenario, however, death may become ever-present. And however unpleasant it might seem, you must consider the problem of dealing with corpses. More specifically, you must learn the basic precautions in order to protect yourself from the infections or serious illnesses that a corpse can carry. If you must touch a corpse, wear gloves and, if possible, a mask, protective goggles, and an impermeable apron in order to avoid direct contact, especially if you have wounds or injuries. You can sterilize or burn your protective clothing afterwards. Put the corpse in a mortuary bag, if you have any, or in two large garbage bags (sixty to one hundred liters or more each), which can be taped together. A corpse should be buried or burned within three days (less, if possible) following death. If you bury it, this should be done at a minimum of thirty or forty meters (100 to 130 feet) from all water sources, dwelling places, or vegetable gardens in order to avoid contamination. The corpse should rest two or three meters (or the proverbial "six feet") deep in order to avoid animals tearing it up. Funeral rites can be carried out at that point. Mark the placement of the corpse and note the place and circumstances of death (for the authorities may come and question you some day). After each handling, wash yourself thoroughly.

Medication and Medical Equipment. Having succinctly reviewed a few of the medical problems you will probably have to face, you must establish a list of medications and medical instruments to have on hand. I would advise you to make two lists: the first will be for one or more first-aid kits you should have on hand, containing the bare minimum needed for treating minor wounds and stabilizing more serious wounds; the second should serve as a real medical field kit, which will become the dispensary of your SAB. It will be important to manage these instruments and stocks of medications in order to avoid using them incongruously or using too many of them. You will find a list of medical instruments and medications in the appendix. You can buy many of them at your local pharmacy. As a matter of discretion, you may want to go to a different pharmacy or spread the purchases across several pharmacies. (A trip to Equatorial Africa is a good pretext for explaining the purchase of such a quantity of materials and medications.) For certain medications, especially antibiotics and morphine, you will need a prescription. There is no miracle solution: either you explain your project to a doctor who is willing to write the necessary prescriptions for you or you must convince your pharmacist.

In the following table, which I have compiled with the help of doctors at the Cantonal Hospital of Geneva, Switzerland, I have listed some common medical problems and their treatments. Of course, this list is not exhaustive by a long shot. Be sure to verify with your family doctor or pharmacist whether the names given here correspond to the names and brands of the country in which you live (e.g., *Imodium* is a brand name for a loperamide-based medicine). Common sense — and my lawyer — tell me to advise you not to take any medication without consulting a doctor first!

SYMPTOM	TYPE OF MEDICATION
Allergy / Hives	Antihistamine / Loratadine (Claritin)
Conjunctivitis	Aminoglycoside / Tobramycin (as eye drops, ophthalmic ointment, or gel)
Asthma	B-Sympathomimetic (Salbutamol) or Glucocorticoide (Ciclesonide / Budesonide / Flutacasone)
Muscle Contracture	Relaxant / Tizanidine (Zanaflex)
Constipation	Bisacodyl
Diabetes	Insulin
Acute Diarrhea	Loperamide
Mild Pain	Paracetamol / Diclofenac

SYMPTOM	TYPE OF MEDICATION
Medium Pain	Tramadol / Buprenorphine / Codeine
Severe Pain	Morphine
Dyspepsia / Gastric and Intestinal Pain	Omeprazole / Pantoprazole / Ranitidine
Gout / Acute Monoarthritis	Ibuprofen / Colchicine / Prednisone
Hypertension	Hydrochlorothiazide / Lisinopril / Nifedipine / Enalapril
Infection	Co-amoxicillin
Urinary Tract Infection	Nitrofurans / Nitrofurantoin
Skin Infection	Cephalosporin / Cefuroxime
Lyme Infection (tick bite)	Penicillin / Amoxicillin Tetracycline / Doxycycline
Bacterial Infection (Gastroenteritis)	Quinolone / Macrolide Norfloxacin / Azithromycin
Herpes	Valacivlovir (or Valacyclovir)
Ear Infection (Otitis)	Ibuprofen (as eye drops)
Strep Throat (Streptococcal Pharyngitis)	Penicillin V or Macrolide
Pneumonia	Cephalosporin / Cefuroxime Tetracycline / Doxycycline
Sinus Infection (Sinusitis)	Ibuprofen
Ulcer	Amoxicillin
Urethra Infection	Ceftriaxone / Cefixime / Macrolide / Azithromycin
Chickenpox (Varicella infection)	Valaciclovir
Heart Failure	Metoprolol / Lisinopril / Torsemide / Spironolactone / Carvedilol / Enalapril / Valsartan / Furosemide / Eplerenone
Migraine Headache	Paracetamol / Ibuprofen

SYMPTOM	TYPE OF MEDICATION
Venomous Snake Bite	Antivenin Crotalidae polyvalent is an effective anti-venom for various poisonous snakes in North, Central, and South America, including rattlesnakes.
Nausea and Vomiting	Domperidone / Metoclopramide
Parasitic Worms	Anthelmintics: > Mebendazole against roundworms (nematodes), whipworm, hookworm, etc. > Triclabendazole against tapeworms (flatworms and flukes), Dipylidium, Echinococcus, etc.

Note that for many medications, their effectiveness rarely lasts for more than two years. And be very careful about using medications after their expiry dates. Some expired medications will have no effect; others can put you at risk. Ask your doctor for advice.

Take a first-aid course in order to learn the basic steps to be taken in treating a person in the case of accident or injury: secure, examine, alert, act, reassure. You will learn some useful techniques such as the Heimlich maneuver, compression for a hemorrhage, compress bandaging, positioning a patient safely on his side, cardiac massage, mouth-to-mouth resuscitation, and the half-seated position.

You will need to be healthy and strong to survive in a collapsing world. Start now getting your teeth and eyes checked, getting an overall medical checkup, etc. If possible, immediately treat any illnesses you can treat in order to eliminate them quickly. The most important thing is prevention, which starts with a healthy way of life. Also, be open to so-called "alternative" medicine that uses medicinal plants that you can cultivate. Observe and research which of these treatments work, and which simply don't. Finally, while assembling the team that can join you in your SAB, give a high priority to including a doctor.

And always remember to wash your hands!

Bjorn and his family have installed an SAB high in the mountains.

They have always liked mountain climbing, and buying a large chalet (a former vacation colony) in a rather remote corner of the mountains seemed like a good idea. Since then, they have stocked up on a lot of food and have plenty of spring water available. There is a river nearby, whose water is pumped and heated with energy obtained through solar panels. Bjorn and his wife have managed their SAB for several years as a little hotel for hikers. They have been able to follow the news of the world on the internet and, when the cities were becoming chaotic and unlivable, they welcomed a few friends who lost their mortgaged homes; these newcomers were slightly disoriented at first, but quickly adapted themselves to the simple, hard mountain life. For several months, everything has gone well. Winter and snow protected them from the large wave of refugees that devastated the plains. In the spring time, one of the children complained of stomach pains on the lower right side. They have read their medical guide and used a stethoscope on the child; it seems to be a case of appendicitis. They have to wait and hope the infection will pass on its own with the help of antibiotics. But if it degenerates into peritonitis, they will have to operate. No one knows how to do this. One of their friends proposes to go looking for a doctor immediately. Two others volunteer to transport the boy to the nearest village, where there will surely be a doctor. Fortunately, their 4x4 still has enough gas for the journey. A decision is made—administer antibiotics and make the expedition. Four healthy, armed men will take the car and transport the child to the village and look for a doctor from there. They'll take with them a few bottles of alcohol to trade, a first-aid kit, and a jerrycan with twenty liters of gasoline.

energy is eternal delight.

william blake

/1757–1827/

i invented a solar-powered flashlight. it has just one defect: it only works in bright sunshine.

andré franquin

_gaston lagaffe

//1924–1997//

Energy

VERY GOOD! YOUR SAB IS STARTING to take shape. You have identified water sources and made the water drinkable. You have created a garden with a few animals and stocked six to twelve months' worth of food for your family. Finally, you have filled your medicine chest and begun an exercise program to stay in shape. Bravo! Now you must make your SAB autonomous and sustainable for all your energy needs. Undertaking an energy project, however, can be like going off on a trip without any idea of the destination or cost. It may be fun for a little while, but very quickly reality catches up with you, and things can become expensive and problematic.

First of all, what are we speaking of? Energy? Electricity? Heating? Or something else altogether? Before answering these questions, you must imagine the lifestyle and level of comfort you wish to maintain in your SAB. This will influence your energy needs and thus the solutions for meeting them. If you want to live exactly as you do now — e.g. with all the lights on, air conditioning going full blast all summer long and heating all winter long, music constantly playing and plenty of trips in your SUV — you are going to have greater difficulties than those who prefer a sober, monkish life by candlelight!

So the fourth fundamental principle of an SAB is energy.

Let us see what your needs are. In the first place, everything depends on your geographical region. If your SAB is in a warm region (the Mediterranean, the Southern United States, etc.), your principal concern will be protecting yourself from the heat. But if your SAB is in a temperate or colder region (the mountains, the arctic zone, etc.), your principal care will be keeping yourself warm. Then we must ask if you want to be completely autonomous or still be connected to an electrical grid. Finally, you must not only calculate the energy you will need but also reflect on what you could save. In fact, by however much you can reduce your energy needs, you will also solve that much of your energy-production problem. The only free energy is what you do not need to generate!

So as not to have to study all possible cases, we shall imagine an SAB situated in a temperate region of Europe or North America with warm summers and cold winters, and which is, for the moment, connected to the electrical grid. We shall also take into account the normal energy consumption of a well-off family of two adults with two children, but which could accommodate up to ten adults in an emergency.

Let us start by covering the notion of thermal comfort and heat exchanges. Calorific energy, i.e. heat, always circulates from warm toward cold (remember entropy!). So when two bodies or materials of different temperature are put near each other, the warmer gives up calories to the other, more or less rapidly according to the nature of the material. One warms up at the expense of the other, which cools off. These changes take place in four ways: by conduction, or contact (a hand warms itself against a bowl of hot soup, a foot is cooled by a cold stone floor); by radiation (warming oneself in front of a fire); by air convection (the warmth provided by a radiator or the coolness of a breeze); and by evaporation (you cool off from perspiring). A good understanding of these four kinds of heat exchange can help you save energy. So let us try to make the living areas of your SAB, which for simplicity's sake we will call the "house," as energy-efficient as possible. A house that consumes little energy and manages it efficiently is called a *passive house*.

If you build a house, try to take advantage of the best possible orientation: use sunlight and take into account that (in the Northern

Hemisphere) the south side is always the sunniest. If the sun is too warm in your latitude, avoid windows facing south and cool your house with natural air conditioning thanks to the circulation of fresh air. Also, arrange to have the roof cast as much shade as possible. Make shade with tents, awnings, shutters or even fabrics, as is traditionally done in warm climates. Watch out for verandas and winter gardens that remain open to the house and continue to heat it during the summer months. Make as much use as possible of the plant environment: shade from trees, climbing plants (which add to the insulation), grounds that reflect light more or less, etc. You can plant greenery or a lawn on a roof or terrace, which will help humidify the air and reduce temperature differences in winter and summer.

If, on the other hand, you live in a cold climate, do the opposite: install windows facing south (consider the shade from any possible trees, buildings, mountains, etc.). Be sure to optimize the orientation of rooms, and make use of natural light, which will let you have better illumination all year round. In all cases, a judicious choice of construction materials according to their thermal, and not merely aesthetic properties, will be of great importance to your overall "thermal strategy." The differences will be noted in your energy consumption. You will also have to eliminate any unhealthy moisture caused by humidity. This can be done by ventilation, preferably natural, but if the "water" rooms (toilets, bathrooms) are insulated and without a window on the exterior, you will have to install an electric ventilation system.

You should also consider a "Canadian well," which is a system allowing ventilation of a building with air from outside, but whose temperature has been modified by circulating underground, bringing about heat exchanges with the cool earth. Thanks to inertia, the earth suffers less temperature variation the deeper it is. Thus, in the summer, the air will be cooled five to ten degrees Celsius, while in winter it will be warmed. This allows you to economize on heating in the winter and to have fresh air in the summer.

Old buildings from before the Industrial Revolution, especially in the countryside, were often well planned from the point of view of energy efficiency. This was because the people living in them had to warm themselves, and every log they could avoid cutting and transporting would save them effort. I enjoy hearing old peasants make fun, quite justifiably, of the absurdity and ugliness of modern buildings. Those suburban apartment blocks and industrial quarters will be quickly abandoned when energy becomes too expensive!

Once you have made use of the natural possibilities of your house, you must diagnose its energy performance in order to determine and locate problems and inefficiencies. You must be sure that the roof, walls, and floor are sufficiently insulated and that the windows are airtight. Also, identify any heat conduits that are not insulated, as they are a frequent source of energy loss. Verify that heating water (or any other water) is not lost through leaky joints. Also make sure that your hot-water heater and pipes are insulated. You might install a timer, which only heats the water when you need it, according to your habits: if you usually shower in the morning, heat the water an hour ahead of time and cut off the heating for the rest of the day. Finally, install the most efficient radiators you can find; there are many kinds: convection, radiation, inertial, etc., and their efficiency depends on the size and insulation of your rooms. It is usually easy and quick to acquire sufficient expertise in these matters.

Now that the living spaces of your SAB are well-insulated and energy loss has been managed efficiently, you must try to diminish your consumption of electricity. First, we should understand that the watt (symbol W) is a unit of energetic and thermal flux — a rate of flow and not a quantity. For example, a toaster with a power of 1,200 watts that operates for six minutes (i.e., 1/10 of an hour) consumes 120 watts per hour (Wh). If it operates for an hour, it will consume 1,200 Wh or 1.2 kilowatts per hour (kWh).

The watt is a small unit:

> A nuclear power station produces several billion watts (gigawatts per hour or gWh).

> A train engine has an average power of 4 million watts (megawatts per hour or MWh).

> A washing machine requires power on the order of a thousand watts per hour (kWh).

> A professional cyclist can deliver, at his maximum effort, a power of about 430 Wh, which might raise questions about the potential of cycle-slavery, if only the drugs didn't cost so much.

> A portable computer consumes about fifteen Wh.

> A normal, incandescent lightbulb requires sixty Wh; a low-consumption electric lightbulb only requires ten Wh; and an electroluminescent diode, or LED ("light emitting diode") needs only about two Wh.

So how do you reduce consumption, and thus watts used? Let's begin with equipment: refrigerators and freezers are large consumers of electricity, often more than the lighting in a house of normal size. Avoid large refrigerators of the American type and choose a smaller model. A fridge that consumes four to six kWh, for example, could be replaced by a more economic model that consumes 0.6 or one kWh at its maximum. You should also ask yourself if you really need a freezer. If you have learned how to conserve food, the answer is "no."

Second place on the list of champion energy-gobblers goes to your *dryer*. Dry your clothes by air, preferably outdoors, and if you cannot do without this machine, choose one that doesn't consume so much energy. Then ask the same question about your other domestic appliances. Keep those you consider indispensable; add a few that you will need (radio, etc.) and avoid *phantom charges*. This does not refer to a specter from beyond the grave, but to the invisible consumption of energy in your house: appliances such as dishwashers, televisions, CD players, microwave ovens, and cordless telephones, which use electricity even when not in operation. The products do not consume a lot of energy in waiting mode, but if you add them all up, you get an average of twenty-five appliances per household, which represents up to ten percent of annual energy use per household: between two and three kWh. To reduce or eliminate these phantom charges, plug as many of these appliances as you can into a power switch you can turn off when you are not using it. You can also tinker with appliances so as to turn off certain clocks and light signals. Also, see if you can replace electrical heating, which is getting increasingly rare due to the cost. Your stove may also be electric, and if so, note the level of consumption, which can vary widely — from one to twelve kWh depending on type (induction oven, etc.), the number of burners, and the other equipment included (oven, etc.). You can also change your light bulbs, replacing incandescent light bulbs with compact fluorescent bulbs or LEDs, which also last a very long time. Obviously, use common sense — turn out the light when you leave a room; avoid lighting a kitchen or a room with a dozen halogen lamps; and don't leave your lights on all day; etc.

Between the gradual replacement of your electrical appliances by more economical ones, the replacement of your light bulbs and elimination of what you don't need, you ought to be able to lower considerably the daily electrical consumption in kWh of your SAB. A reasonable goal is not to surpass a daily consumption of three kWh per person. For ten people, this would allow thirty kWh each day. But since this is a theoretical mean for the whole year, and you will need more in the winter (light, etc.) than in the summer, it would be prudent to figure a little higher and set a maximum of thirty-five kWh. Once these calculations have been carried out, you must figure out how to produce this electricity. Electricity is not a source of energy; it is energy that must be produced. Although there are many ways of generating electricity with renewable energy (solar, wind, hydroelectric, tides, sea currents, geothermal, etc.), few of these are accessible on a small, non-industrial scale. On the other hand, three of these methods are relatively accessible and easy to realize.

Micro-Hydro Electricity

A hydro-electric micro-station is like an electrical plant that uses hydraulic energy (the force of water) to produce electricity, but on a small or very small (pico-station) scale. This energy can be used to supply isolated sites (one or two houses, a studio or barn…). The working principle of a small hydro-electric station consists in transforming the potential energy of a waterfall into mechanical energy with a turbine, then into electrical energy by means of a generator. The capacity of the station once installed is a function of the water that passes into the turbine and the height from which it falls. Another important element is the regularity of flow. As a function of these three parameters, you can install either a micro-station (twenty to five hundred kWh) or a pico-station (less than twenty kWh). These solutions are not very onerous; they are easy to install, and they are clean and durable (they wear very slowly—but think about having a few turbines in reserve anyway). However, these are not solutions that can be made to work everywhere: you need a watercourse with a fairly even flow, which is not common since flow usually varies with the seasons. If the minimum flow is above zero (i.e., if the river does not run completely dry in the summer), you should take this measure into account in making your calculations. If you have no river, stream, or spring (which would have to be canalized in any case), it is still possible to create an autonomous system with two large basins, one higher than the other, and a wind- or solar-powered pump to carry the water back from the lower to the higher basin. The water will go back down and get pumped up again, and so on, allowing you to create a circuit to feed a micro-station.

If you have the means to influence municipalities close to your SAB, try to get a little hydro-electric station with a capacity of between 0.5 and one megawatts established in rivers in your area. This electricity will be extremely useful in the century to come, and you must hasten to carry out such projects, for who knows if it will still be possible to set up a hydro-electric station a few years from now?

Wind Energy

A wind turbine is a device for converting wind energy into mechanical or electrical energy. For millennia, windmills have turned wind energy into mechanical energy, usually in order to mill grain, press oil, or beat iron, copper, felt or paper, or even to pump water in order to dry swampy land, irrigate crops, or water cattle.

The criteria for choosing a place to install wind turbines are the size you envision, the power you wish to produce, the number of turbines and the regular presence of wind. The efficiency of a wind turbine depends on its placement. The capacity increases in proportion to the speed of the wind cubed. For this reason, sites are determined by the local wind speeds: a site with winds averaging twenty mph will be eight times as productive as a site that averages ten mph. The consistency of the speed and wind direction are two other important criteria for choosing a site. In fact, as a general rule, wind turbines can be used where the wind speed is above five and below fifty-five mph, a speed beyond which turbines must be disengaged in order to limit damage and the risk of breaking. The turbine's axis of rotation should usually be kept parallel to the direction of the wind. Certain sites close to obstacles (trees, buildings, complex escarpments, etc.) should also be disallowed because the wind there is too turbulent. You should know that wind turbines become less effective at high altitudes because the air is thinner. At 3,200 feet, the product of a wind turbine will be ten percent lower than at sea level. Finally, note that certain specific sites increase wind speeds:

> The sea or lakes are favored spots since there are no obstacles to the wind. Thus, even at low altitudes, winds are faster and less turbulent. The nearness of an escarpment, on the other hand, will create turbulence and cause wear and tear.

> When air rushes in between two obstacles, such as two mountains or buildings, it accelerates; the same occurs when it reaches the top of a hill. So these places are very appropriate for wind turbines. However, the surface area is usually very limited and can be subject to turbulence.

Wind energy can be very powerful in certain cases, especially in wind parks at sea, which can generate hundreds of megawatts but cannot function under all conditions. Denmark, the uncontested world champion of wind power, only produces twenty percent of its electricity through such power. In practice, the electrical power yield represents between twenty and forty percent of installed power. On the other hand, a small wind turbine, individual or domestic, with a power up to one hundred kWh, can be very useful. In this case a wind turbine, connected to a network or even an autonomous turbine in an isolated spot, can be used to produce electricity and run electrical appliances (pumps, lighting) in a permanent manner, especially in a rural environment. For example, a small wind turbine equipped with a solar photovoltaic module and a battery pack can guarantee the energy autonomy of a sailboat (lighting, instruments on board), which makes possible a marine SAB. In any case, you must take into account that the actual yield of your wind turbine will be far inferior to its theoretical yield. If it has a theoretical optimal yield of one hundred kWh, you should count on the average production being between twenty and forty kWh.

In cities, where it is difficult to get powerful air currents, smaller equipment can be used. Roof wind turbines — which are generally small or medium capacity (up to six kWh, what your old refrigerator consumes) and specially designed for urban environments — allow you to mitigate routing problems and palliate electrical outages, but produce only a modest amount of energy. Small installations can be fed by a portable wind turbine, which can be useful, e.g., on board a boat.

Armed with these basic notions, you must now determine the wind potential of your SAB. If your SAB has a lot of space available, and the winds are constant and fairly strong, choosing to use a wind turbine can be very valuable. You must study the winds: determine any possible sea breezes or land breezes (in daytime, wind tends to flow from sea to land; at night, it is the other way around), and the different air flows found in a valley (hot air tends to rise during the day, while the cooled air flows down into the valley at night). Study regional winds like the Scirocco, Bora, or the Mistral in Europe, Chinook, Diablo Norther, or Chubasco in the Americas, Brickfielder in Australia, etc. If the wind is too violent, it is not useful. Consult meteorological statistics, talk to people who have lived in the region a long time, arm yourself with a map, climb to the most elevated spot you can find and make observations. Figure out what possible obstructions there might be to the wind (e.g., buildings, trees, and especially hills and mountains). The best spots are usually beside the sea and crests that always face dominant winds. Finally, and this is important, inform yourself about any building restrictions, especially environmental and zoning laws. Talk about your project with the neighbors and be open to their objections in order to avoid making enemies (people often react negatively to wind turbines, which they consider damaging to the landscape, noisy, or even harmful to animals or to health). In any case, it is not easy to get authorization for a small wind turbine (i.e., one to five meters [three to fifteen feet] in diameter with a yield of three to forty kWh). For large properties (farms, ranches, etc.), it will be much easier to get authorization; in this case, a wind turbine ten meters (thirty feet) in diameter, generating between forty and two hundred kWh, can be an excellent solution, if wind conditions are favorable enough. Also note the frequency and complexity of repair work, since a wind turbine waiting to be repaired does not produce any electricity. So carefully study the lifespan of the parts most subject to wear. Inform yourself about the possibilities for reselling excess production to public authorities; this could allow you to cut your own costs and make a profit on your investment.

To summarize: wind can be a good source of energy if conditions are favorable, but it cannot be your sole solution, since winds can die down for several days at a time. It can be useful for the inhabitants of a valley or small region to form a group and install a wind park to meet some of the local electricity needs. A wind turbine with twenty- to thirty-meter (sixty-five to one hundred feet) blades costs between $400,000 and $520,000, and can generate enough electricity for one hundred to two hundred households. Volume also allows one to employ specialists, who are dedicated one hundred percent to such sources of energy and maintaining and repairing the equipment involved (this is almost impossible to do on an individual level.) Thus, a wind park could be a strategy for transforming a village or small region into a super-SAB. We'll talk more about that later.

Solar Energy

Energy radiating through our atmosphere directly from the sun will be useful to us. It can be caught by solar panels, of which there are two kinds:

> *thermal* solar panels, called "solar collectors," trap the heat of solar rays and transfer it to a fluid medium;

> *photovoltaic* solar panels convert light into electricity. Photovoltaic solar power is commonly called PV.

In both cases, the panels are usually flat and about one meter square in size in order to keep them easy to install. Solar panels are the basic equipment for producing solar energy. Thermal collectors are more efficient and profitable at the moment than photovoltaic modules. Their price is much lower, and they yield around fifty percent, even if the energy they allow to be recovered is obtained in a less valuable form (hot water at a sterilized temperature instead of electricity). Thermal collectors are just as profitable in northern latitudes

(Northern France, UK, Belgium, Canada, etc.) as in sunny regions (Spain, Italy, Texas, Florida, New Mexico, Australia, Tunisia, etc.). On the other hand, photovoltaic panels are only profitable where there is no electrical grid, unless they are subsidized in some way. You must inform yourself thoroughly about the possibility of selling your excess solar-generated electricity to public authorities. You must know that only ten percent of solar radiation is transformed into usable energy (electricity). Although profitability is not our primary concern, it is a point you must keep in mind in order to choose the right project. In mountainous regions and those with heavy snowfall, solar panels can be inclined up to sixty degrees to allow the snow to slide off. The warm surface of a sun catcher will quickly melt any remaining bits of snow. (I can confirm this is the case, as I have roof installation on my mountain farm.)

Thermal solar panels ("solar water heaters") are panels in which water or another fluid medium moves in a closed circuit through tubes equipped with blades. To get the best yield, the whole ensemble is placed in an insulated glass box, which permits a sort of greenhouse effect. With significant sunshine, and if your need for hot water is moderate, a simple tube network can be sufficient. The fins, which form what is called an "absorber," are heated by solar radiation and transmit their heat to a liquid medium, which circulates in the tubes. Solar water heaters are used to produce clean hot water in a solar hot-water heater. For now, this is the most profitable solar-energy solution. Combined solar systems are starting to be developed, with the goal of producing both clean hot water and hot water for heating a house. Such systems allow savings on the order of 350 kWh per year per square meter paneling.

Photovoltaic solar panels are made up of small photovoltaic cells connected to each other. They can be installed on fixed supports or mobile systems that move to face the sun. In the latter case, electrical yield increases by about thirty percent compared to a fixed installation. Outside solar-power stations, fixed installations are found mainly on the roofs of houses or office buildings, either integrated into the roofing material or superimposed. In certain cases, panels are installed vertically on the facade of buildings, although this inclination is not optimal for producing electricity. Portable solar panels can be useful for camping or on trips; plan on having some in your SAB.

The principle by which current is obtained by the cells is called the "photoelectric effect." These cells produce direct current from solar radiation. The use made of the current differs from one installation to another according to purpose. Two types of use are worth distinguishing: where the photovoltaic installation is connected to an electrical network and where it isn't. Non-connected installations can directly consume the electricity produced with battery accumulators, in order to dispose of the electricity during periods without light (night, blackouts, etc.). Photovoltaic installations connected to a network inject the electricity they produce directly into the network. To do this, installations are equipped with alternators that transform the direct current to alternating current according to the characteristics of the network. This does not require installing storage batteries. The electricity is consumed the moment it is produced by the closest devices on the network.

It is also possible to configure a system connected to a network, but which also has batteries in case the network goes down. The value commonly used to calculate the capacity of a solar panel is one kWh per square meter of panel exposed to direct sunlight. In practice, the energy coming from the sun depends upon the latitude, cloudiness, the inclination of the sun (which determines the density of the atmosphere that light must cross), and thus the hour of the day. In the course of a single day, even without clouds, the electrical output of a panel varies constantly as a function of the sun's position; it is only at its maximum during midday, for a short period. It is just at this time of day that you have the least need of electrical energy, and if you cannot store the electricity produced in a battery, it will be lost.

The quality and lifespan of your solar panels vary considerably according to whether they are of the mono-crystalline or poly-crystalline type and according to the quality of manufacture. A high-quality solar panel, which is more expensive, can last more than thirty years.

What is the solar capacity of your SAB? As a function of your geographical position (latitude, altitude, climate) and orientation, you will have greater or lesser exposure to the sun. Cloud cover is also an important factor, since it diminishes the efficiency of solar panels: some regions are very cloudy, others get a lot of fog, smog, etc. Watch out for places that can get violent gusts of wind, as panels can be torn out of the ground.

If you want to cover all the needs of your SAB — thirty-five kWh in our example — you will have to install at least thirty-five square meters (375 square feet) of paneling. If you obtain eighty percent efficiency, you will need to add another seven square meters (seventy-five square feet) for a total of forty-two square meters — which would make for a rather large roof. The good news is that in spite of their rather high cost, photovoltaic solar panels are easy to install. But even if you have covered all the roofs in your SAB with panels, you will still have a problem: at night, when there is no more sunlight, you will not have any electricity. So you must consider batteries, which are very expensive, or keep plugging in to the public electrical grid, which defeats the purpose of full autonomy. A hybrid solution, like the one I have, would be to have photovoltaic panels plugged into the grid *and* have batteries as backups that you connect in case the proverbial shit hits the fan, and the grid goes down.

Heating

"Central heating" means that several rooms of an apartment or house are heated from a single point thanks to a heat generator, i.e., the boiler, and with the help of various forms of energy such as wood, coal, gas, heating oil, etc. To do this, you install one or more boilers in the boiler room according to the needs of the facility in question. In

most cases, the boiler is connected with piping to radiators or convection ovens placed in the rooms that need heating.

Given the kind of future for which we are preparing, heating with
gas, coal or heating oil seems like it would be heavily compromised
over the long term. If the boiler in your SAB is old or inefficient, this
is perhaps the time to replace it with something longer lasting. If your
SAB is close to a forest, why not heat it directly with wood? This is
a much cheaper solution than heating oil. In any scenario, the good
old wood stove in the main room remains an excellent solution for
the winter, since it heats efficiently, especially in the case of an isolated home. Hence the importance of effectively insulating the living
spaces of your SAB. Be careful not to heat your house to the point
where it turns into a sauna, and you are forced to go around in shorts
and flip-flops in the middle of winter — which happened to me in an
overheated apartment I once lived in. Lower the temperature to 66 °F
(19 °C) instead of the usual 70 °F (21 °C) and dress normally. Do not
overheat your sleeping quarters: people sleep better at a cool temperature (and in times of crisis, you will probably want to snuggle with the
wonderful creature who sleeps with you). For bachelors, there's always
the water bottle! A temperature of 63 °F (17 °C) or 64 °F (18 °C) should
be acceptable. At my farm, for example, I don't heat the bedrooms, so
that we sleep in winter at 15 °C (59 °F), but that's also because the walls
are well insulated from the sub-freezing temperatures of the outside,
and because the wood stove in the main living room radiates quite
efficiently. In general, err on the cool side and put on a sweater if you
are cold.

For auxiliary heating, why not plan on having a heat pump, which
can take the heat from the air, water, or ground and release it in the
places where it is needed?

As with all your projects, find out if there are possibilities of receiving subsidies or tax exemptions in your region or country. Use all
means allowed by law to economize, while you still can. And if you do
not care about the savings, you can always send me the excess money.

Cogeneration

Cogeneration means producing electricity and heat simultaneously, with heat being a by-product of electrical production, or *vice versa*. Generating electricity usually releases a great deal of heat, which dissipates into the surroundings. Cogeneration allows this heat to be channeled into heating buildings, sterilizing water, etc. The electrical energy is either consumed or put back into the public grid.

Let us take a practical example. In case your SAB simultaneously needs electricity and heat:

> a classic configuration could be a heating-oil boiler in conjunction to electricity coming from the grid;

> a cogeneration configuration would be having that same boiler generate electricity, while you use the heat for heating the house. Electricity can also be generated by solar panels (to heat water and produce electricity) and other renewable sources.

Batteries and Candles

Look around you: how many things do you see that run on batteries? Flashlights, surveillance equipment, computers, Geiger counters, etc. Stock enough rechargeable batteries of all types and get some chargers, including those that operate on solar power. It is better to overestimate your battery consumption. According to the U.S. Army, lacking a sufficient number of batteries is one of the major problems of modern armed forces. You will consume a lot of them — quickly.

If you have chosen an electrical system that stores electricity in batteries, handle them with great care; they are potentially dangerous objects because of the electrical charge they contain, but also because a battery is filled with acid (lead batteries, for example, actually contain sulfuric acid). You will have to stock empty batteries for recharging (without acid, which should be stored separately and safely), so as not to use up your batteries too quickly.

Stock lots of candles in all sizes; you will need them. A good-quality candle can be kept indefinitely, and short of learning how to make them yourself — which is not a bad idea — your supplies can serve you for a long time, or be useful as items for exchange.

I am often asked if it is necessary to acquire a diesel generator. This is certainly a very useful machine, especially if you get one able to generate between four and ten kWh, since it can supply you with electricity if all your other systems are down. But how much gasoline can you store anyway? Besides, a generator is very noisy and thus, in urban environments, can attract a lot of unwanted attention during bad times. It is a good auxiliary solution in the medium term, but certainly not over the long term if oil scarcity accelerates.

I do not know if an ideal system exists to cover the energy needs of your SAB. In any case, it seems logical that if you reduce your needs and consumption, and, at the same time, install an efficient system for generating heat and electricity, you can arrive at a reasonably affordable result that will last a long time and, perhaps, even be totally autonomous.

Do not hesitate to ask for advice from energy specialists. Have them explain the different options for your SAB, get a few estimates, go into detail and distrust rough estimates. For the installation, unless you have a lot of experience yourself, work with an electrician who knows how to manage everything connected with electricity. It would be stupid to burn down your SAB because you left some wires uncovered...

To complement the bibliography and links you find in the appendices, a good source of information is the site of the European Council for an Energy Efficient Economy, whose address is www.eceee.org.

Pierre has installed his SAB in the Jura Mountains.

He bought an old 9,000-square-meter farmstead with its own spring. The farm is kept by a friend of Pierre's, Lucas, who lives there full-time. Lucas is a veteran of the French Foreign Legion and has a passion for the six horses he is raising. He also manages the defense of the farm. It seems he has "kept" a fair amount of equipment from his time at the Legion base in the south of France. Around the farm, there is a 1,000-square-foot garden, a chicken coop, and several Icelandic sheep (which are good at enduring the winter cold). Pierre and Lucas have stocked enough food to feed ten adults for a year. They have reached an agreement with two other friends—Yassine, who is a doctor, and Marc, who is a mechanic—whereby these two and their families will join them in a crisis. So that the SAB can have energy autonomy, photovoltaic solar panels have been installed to generate forty kWh. But this will not be enough for complete autonomy. Thanks to the help and counsel of a Canadian specialist, the heating-oil system has been replaced by a cogeneration boiler with wood heating (pellets and shavings) as its principal source, as well as a miniature hydroelectric turbine (five kWh) at the spring. As a result, the boiler works on wood (easily available in the region), hydroelectricity and solar power, furnishing at once heating, hot water, and electricity. The SAB is at 800 meters above sea level, and Pierre insulated his farmhouse so it's nice and warm during the winter months.

Pavel has installed a large SAB in the eastern Ukrainian steppe close to Lugansk.

Since he has made a fortune in the computer business, he is able to spend whatever it takes to make everything perfect. He has bought immense grounds and employed two farming families to take care of the fields, cattle, and horses. He has laid in a great stock of diesel fuel to make the heating work, as well as electrical generators and agricultural machines. He has several fresh-water wells from which he pumps water with the help of energy generated by a large wind turbine. Surplus electricity, to which one may add the energy produced by photovoltaic solar panels, helps bring in enough kilowatts for the main house. But the farmers' houses are not autonomous for the moment. To heat all of them, Pavel has installed a system of wells, supplemented by a classic fuel-burning heater. Each house is also equipped with an old-fashioned stove in which wood or coal can be burned. In case of emergency, Pavel thinks he and his family will be energy-independent and that his SAB will be in good shape, no matter what happens.

Let's get back to Henry, still with his grandfather's M1 rifle. He was able to escape the city through the subway. He was frightened amid the darkness and the rats, but he pulled through. For a week he has been feeding himself with soft drinks and chocolate bars he got from a vending machine he broke open. He's tired but has to keep going. He hiked into the country without any precise goal, avoiding the congested highways, which seem to be at the mercy of bands of looters. From a distance he has witnessed scenes of unheard-of violence… Yesterday he came to a farm where they welcomed him. This farm, a great place, is kept by a community of old hippies and their children. They have everything they need: water, solar panels for heating and electricity, a large garden, goats—the works. They welcomed twenty or so people, all in pretty good shape before the crisis, judging by the cars parked outside in the lot. The leader and patriarch of the community explains to Henry that the place is organized like a commune: everyone works together and shares the fruits of their work—organic food and the rest. He explains that violence does not solve anything, and that the mind is more powerful than weapons. If he wants to stay, he must get rid of his rifle. Henry says he will think about it. After a night's rest—and after devouring a large plate of vegetables and salad—Henry decides to leave.

Just in time. The next day, the farm is stormed and occupied by a motorcycle gang. All the inhabitants are tortured and then killed, the women raped and enslaved, the stocks looted, and the farm eventually burned down before the gang decides to leave for another target.

<<he who possesses a trade is like he who possesses a castle.

berber proverb

<<it is impossible to add anything to a full container.

laozi

philosopher

//6th century bce//

Knowledge

THE GLOBAL ECONOMY has collapsed, the world has descended into bloodshed and fire, and you, your family, and, perhaps, your friends' families have taken shelter in your SAB: you have abundant water and food, you are taking good care of your garden and livestock, and you have a fairly good supply of medications. You also have hot water and electricity. You now have a lot of free time. But you can't get in the car and go to the movies, or vacation on the Côte d'Azur, or fly away for "spring break," or go party on Mykonos or Cancun! What are you going to do with your time? What knowledge will you start to develop now for the day when you will be in your SAB? Besides, what trade can be useful to you in this kind of future?

There are three categories to consider:

> **PROFESSIONS** — the know-how you will need — and which you must be able to teach and transmit to others.

> **CULTURE** — the essential cultural heritage, which is the basis of your identity, which can be taught, and which stimulates you intellectually.

> **ENTERTAINMENT** — game activities necessary to avoid boredom and keep your family and comrades from killing each other!

Knowledge is the fifth fundamental principle of an SAB.

Professions

By now you have a good idea of the skills required in your SAB: botany, herbalism, gardening, cabinet making, carpentry, shoemaking, mechanics, emergency medicine, etc. If these are important to acquire quickly, at least at a basic level, it would be useful to divide their study among the members of your SAB in order to obtain specialists in each. Some of these abilities will be tomorrow's best professions; they can become your profession starting today.

In any case, if your SAB project is serious, you must now begin preparing yourself and developing a hobby which can become your profession. One might imagine that, in a family, the husband can become a woodworker and the wife, a gardener (or *vice versa*). The children, too, in accordance with their age and strength, can contribute, learning (as a form of play or amusement) how to take care of little animals (rabbits, chickens, etc.) or performing simple tasks (collecting wood or dead leaves, removing snow, etc.). Be careful not to make such tasks too dull for children (or for yourself!). The aim should be to learn while playing, so why not make a fun family activity of it? It beats playing video games!

Be careful not to attribute too much importance to technology or gadgets. Among my clients, I have persons who eagerly equip themselves with everything that can make their lives easier: chainsaws and many other rechargeable electrical devices, 4x4s, tractors with massive stocks of fuel, all kinds of firearms. They stock everything necessary for a rural operating room, installing wind turbines, solar panels with batteries and alternators... but they never have the time to learn to use them. (Having a chainsaw is fine, but have you ever cut down a tree?) Dependence on technology can play tricks on you: what will you do if your wind turbine breaks down? How do you repair an alternator? How do you use all the tools you have bought?

When I began my preparations, I often injured myself, especially the first time I used an axe. It was easy for me to run to the medical center down the street to be disinfected and have my finger stitched by a professional physician. It is better to have these experiences *now*, and not when you might be isolated or alone in your SAB. The same goes for a generator or a car that breaks down. As the American survivalist James Rawles says: "Skills beat gadgets, practicality beats style, and if your hands are not callous, it is because you don't work hard enough."

In practice, this means that right now, you can begin to learn one or more professions besides the one you have now. To get started, why not consider some of the trades that existed in the 19th century and the first half of the 20th, and see what suits you? There is no sense forcing yourself to do something you hate. Try out several activities to find out which give you the most satisfaction. Perhaps you will even rediscover one of the professions you dreamed of pursuing as a child, before the economic machine forced you to choose a more remunerative career.

Culture

We must also choose which pieces of culture we want to take with us: which books, which artworks, what music, what movies we want to keep and transmit. The idea is to imagine that you are like Noah with his ark, but instead of preserving animal species, you must choose which cultural products you want to safeguard: if literature is your passion, fill boxes with books and create for yourself a good library; if you are a music fiend, furnish your SAB with the music you love; if you collect stamps or Lego, take your collections with you.

Thanks to electronic support, it is easy and cheap to digitize a huge amount of material; but this poses the question of whether such support will last, and whether computers will be able to read the data over the long term. I would advise a mix of support systems and multiple electronic copies, which you should renew regularly. Consider putting your hard disks and computers in a metallic cage (a Faraday cage) in order to protect them from electromagnetic impulses of solar or other origin.

But do not only consider what pleases you. Reflect on what defines your culture. If, for example, you think, like General de Gaulle, that

France can be defined as "a European people of the white race, Greco-Latin in civilization and Christian in religion," take with you the New Testament and the great classics (Homer, Plato, Socrates, Seneca, etc.). Think what it means to be, say, an American, a Brit, a Scot, an Australian, an Israeli, a Swede, etc., and consider storing in your SAB what you believe to be the key founding cultural texts, books, songs, movies, music, etc. of your culture. If you think that a culture is defined by its history, and this history in relation to that of the world, take loads of history books concerning the cultures of the world and ethnography. Or do both: it's up to you.

To cite my own modest example, I took a large number of history books (as that is my passion), a lot of French, Swiss, Italian, American, Russian, and German literature classics, and added to them a good number of dictionaries and foreign-language manuals (German, Russian, Chinese — you never know who will inva... er ... save you...), scholarly manuals for grammar, mathematics, physics. I hope to transmit the maximum amount of knowledge to my children, beginning with reading, writing, math, and physics. Finally, I took care to take books with the foundational stories of Western civilization: Greek, Egyptian, Celtic, and Nordic mythology, as well as more recent and regional stories and legends (from Iceland to Central Africa, including those of the Geneva region).

You will understand that learning about a culture is much more than a pastime. Knowledge and wisdom will help you, your SAB, and your extended community distinguish truth from error and make good collective choices. Literacy, general education, learning math and physics are all basic for not plunging into barbarism or regressing too far into "pre-literacy," which, in my opinion, would mark the end of humanity. I believe it is our responsibility as heirs to some of the most glorious and advanced cultures and civilizations in history, to preserve them and act as witnesses for this knowledge, wisdom, and experience. I hope that the world of tomorrow might arise from the ashes better, stronger, and wiser.

Entertainment

Since there is more to life than reading Plato or Nietzsche, you should also give some time over to amusements. Long winter evenings can be dull if you have nothing with which to entertain yourself. What you choose to put in your SAB will depend on your tastes and areas of interest. For some, it will be still more reading: adventure stories, romance, fantasy, or detective fiction. For others, it will be music: classical, jazz, rock, etc., stored in CD format, digitized on your computer, or on vinyl. Be sure to have enough energy for your stereo or portable music player. For others, entertainment will be synonymous with board games, cards, puzzles, etc. I think that, since it is possible to become bored with one's fondest passions, it is good to mix and match somewhat, and take various things with you. I encourage board games and cards, because they allow a change of social roles, which serves as an escape valve for the frustrations inevitable in a family or community. Role-playing can also be useful to this end.

The important thing is to take with you some of your passions and some of the luxury you used to enjoy. This will serve both as a connection to today's world and as a bridge to help you build the new one.

Oliver has transformed his villa into an SAB.

He likes to say he has "bunkerized" it. His villa is a house in a nice residential suburb. It is situated on the top of a small hill and is the last house on his street. There is a large lake three miles away, a sizeable river a thousand feet away, and a forest with considerable game on the other side of the hill. His wife loves to garden, and they have worked for several years on a small garden of 1,500 square feet. They also grow mushrooms (champignons de Paris) in their basement. They have stocked six months' worth of food and various supplies that could be useful in an emergency. Now that the crisis has come, they remain at home. Oliver is a former drill instructor, and he was able to keep a few firearms—assault rifles, sniper rifles, pistols—and several thousand rounds of ammunition. His wife Simonetta, a secretary in normal times, trains dogs for a hobby, and they now have several very good guard dogs. As soon as the riots began, they took in Simonetta's parents, Oliver's mother, father, and sister, and their respective spouses. Space is tight inside; but since they expanded the garden, they do have enough food. Oliver quickly contacted all his neighbors and took note of who was armed. He organized twenty panicked persons into a disciplined militia and rapidly taught them the concepts of an SAB. He helped them create vegetable gardens and store their food. He organized guard shifts and established a roadblock at the end of the street. Simonetta also helped train local dogs as guard dogs. With their knowledge and know-how, they have transformed their SAB: from just one villa, an autonomous community has emerged.

<<si vis pacem para bellum.

publius flavius vegetius

_de re militari

/5th century ce /

<<you can do anything with a bayonet except sit on it.

napoleon bonaparte

warrior & emperor

//1769–1821//

<<the aim of war is not to die for your country but to make the other bastard die for his country.

george s. patton

warrior   .

//1885–1945//

<<the price of liberty is eternal vigilance.

thomas jefferson

land owner, philosopher, politician

//1743–1826//

<<better to go with your head hanging than feet first.

michel audiard

filmmaker

//1920–1985//

<<to live happily, let us live hidden.

french proverb

Defense

HERE YOU ARE, ready for anything. You've got your drinking water. Your garden, which you have developed with great care and devotion, is finally productive. You've stocked a lot of food and acquired useful know-how that lets you work under all sorts of circumstances. You have installed a well-equipped SAB, sustainable in every way including electrical energy and heating. You are happy and satisfied with the result of so much labor.

Soon others will know about it. Soon other people, those taken by surprise, who did not prepare, who lost everything, who have nothing left to lose, those without any scruples and who are capable of anything ... well, suffice it to say, *some* people will think that it'd be much easier to take your SAB (eliminating you and your family in the process) rather than work hard for survival.

With this in mind, the sixth fundamental principle of an SAB has to be defense.

This is the great problem with the "back to the earth" agrarian communities that have come into fashion over the years. These communities are founded on philosophies close to those of the Pennsylvania Amish, who chose to live in the United States, a new promised land, solely with the tools and know-how that existed in the 18th century. True, in the event of a crisis, these groups can live very well off their extremely productive organic agriculture, and they have no need for electricity and mechanization. Yet they will not last long — being unarmed, non-violent, and pacifist, in the face of the violent armed gangs that will specialize in pillaging. These gangs, motorized with stolen gas, will carry out raids ever deeper into the countryside and with violence not so different from the *Einsatzgruppen* of the Eastern Front. Before these desperate criminals die of hunger or attrition, or are neutralized by honest citizens, they will cause great damage, destruction, and suffering.

Might you be their next target? Yes, especially if you are not ready.

Since the beginning of time, human beings have had to protect themselves from wild animals, harsh weather, and enemies. Man possesses survival instincts and self-protective reflexes, and his need for security, as we have mentioned, is the second level of Maslow's hierarchy of needs. The need for security is primordial for man, and he tries to protect himself, those dear to him, and his property from any danger of death, damage, or theft. In the case of an emergency or serious economic collapse, this need will quickly become an imperative. Limits imposed by law will quickly give way to the law of the strongest, the most cunning, or the most ruthless. You must do everything possible not to become a victim. It is not enough to surround your property with barbed wire and arm yourself with an old rifle in order to feel secure. You must take important measures to be able to assume as effective a defense as possible, whatever scenario occurs. We are going to try to become invincible!

What is Defense?

Let's agree on one thing: *absolute* security does not exist. It is not possible to prepare yourself for every risk. First of all, there are too many of them, and they are too different. Above all, there are parameters outside your control, and even if you master a certain number of them, the immensity of potentialities and possible combinations thereof render an attempt at technical mastery of all potential risks fatuous. In any case, there is no use being obsessed with security; a healthy relation to risk is an essential aspect of life.

As you were able to read earlier descriptions of possible future scenarios, the risks that might provoke an economic collapse are numerous, since they are tied to governmental decisions, human error, forces of nature, and other entirely unforeseeable factors that cannot be controlled. Is it useful, then, to attribute such importance to security? The answer is a categorical *yes!* Indeed, although many factors are unforeseeable, others are quite foreseeable, especially those related to human nature. And the elements influencing human nature can be understood and mastered, which considerably reduces the risks you have to take.

Let us take a simple example: say you are crossing a road. Your security could be compromised by an inattentive driver who could run you over. You have no influence over this driver. Although you know that there is a certain risk to your safety, you will still cross this road anyway. You are conscious of this risk, and you limit it by crossing over at a pedestrian crosswalk and paying attention and looking both ways. You could also foresee the possibility that a driver is distracted and about to hit you if you notice a car failing to slow down while heading in your direction. You could avoid the unsafe driver, or quickly duck behind a concrete pillar, or something like that.

Though we cannot avoid risk entirely, we take measures every day to reduce our exposure to it and minimize its potential consequences.

In this context, defense can be defined as a set of attitudes, physical and psychological preparations, know-how, and equipment that will reduce your exposure to risk.

Safety and security are not a generic recipe; they are *habits* and *ways of thinking* specific to each individual and each group preparing together. You must thus take into account the type of threat you face and its background and setting: you don't defend yourself the same way in the city as in the countryside, in Lagos as in Chicago; you don't protect yourself from a man as you do from an animal or the natural elements. And you might have to struggle against the prejudices of most of the people around you: to many, being prepared to defend yourself amounts to being "paranoid."

In reality—and more important than the opinion of those around you—defense is generally well-defined by law. Although the question is vast and not universally agreed upon by jurists and lawyers, one must recognize that the criminal law contains a whole arsenal of rules on what is permitted and what is not. A person unfamiliar with the law should reflect on what it means, in the legal sense, to defend oneself—in order to respect the law in all circumstances for as long as the state of legality exists.

In this chapter, we must clearly distinguish between self-defense in the world as it is today and self-defense during or after a societal collapse—when survival will be the one and only rule. We should start by briefly touching on the principle of "proportionality," which informs most legal systems and criminal statutes around the world. We will then think about the means at your disposal for defending yourself, your family, and your SAB.

"Proportionality" entails the suitability of a response to a particular threat. This might seem complicated, as with much of legal theory. So let's take an example. An individual, Jill, is returning from tennis practice. While taking the train, she is verbally attacked by Jack, a local thug, who wants her bag. In the eyes of the law, Jill cannot defend herself by striking Jack with her tennis racket, because the threat has remained at a verbal level. Striking someone with a tennis racket can cause serious injury and even death. Most legal systems consider that the potential damage (the theft of the sporting bag) and the potential bodily injury are not proportional. Now, imagine that, in a similar situation, Jack threatens Jill with a knife. In this case, a blow with a tennis racket would be justified, since an aggressive person with a knife threatens Jill's person and life.

Keep this principle in mind as long as the state assures order and security. In a period of total chaos, however, when the state has disappeared, your thought process must be totally different: everything will be permitted to stay alive, and the limits will be only those that your conscience dictates. (And there will be no more tennis practice.)

How Do You Defend Yourself?

To defend yourself effectively, you must first know what you are defending yourself *against*. Further on, we shall see how to defend ourselves against animals and the elements, but the greatest danger for man remains man.

The predator-prey relationship takes on vital importance in cases of structural insecurity. In a crisis, the population's dwindling respect for state authority will be quickly replaced by the law of Might Makes Right, which justifies all possible behavior. Urban predators exist and are getting bolder by the day, as demonstrated by the shocking attack on the outskirts of London in May 2013, in which a man was run down with a car and then beheaded.

The scenarios described in the first part of this book would create a favorable environment for predators, already used to living outside the law. If the economy collapses, the capricious law of gangs might replace that of the state. Gangs are usually organized hierarchically, and they respect only their own property; the property of others is treated as ripe for the picking. From that point on, the best solution will be to avoid these predators and leave the neighborhoods they inhabit, putting distance between yourself and their hunting grounds.

If we look more closely at the motivation and psychology of these aggressors, we will be better able to identify their different profiles and modus operandi.

Let's establish five categories:

The psychopath is not simply a person who's "crazy" (they can often appear perfectly civilized); and he is not necessarily from a lower social class (often quite the contrary). The psychopath is characterized by a lack of empathy with other people, indeed, by a denial of their individuality and worth. Social norms and ethics don't apply to him, and he is characterized by impulsive, antisocial behavior, which can extend to crime. Such people will be ready to do anything to survive, and by their violent acts, their dishonesty, and their attempts to satisfy their own needs at the expense of others, they can cause a lot of damage. Avoid them and avoid having any person who displays these traits in your SAB.

The lone aggressor is an individual who prepares his aggression in advance, who sets a trap. He will engage in violence only if he feels sure it will be worth it, and will give up easily if he perceives the victim is tougher than expected. That is to say, he is rational and calculating. Such cowardly individuals may well survive, for they can be ruthless and are capable of crookedness, crime, and murder. But in the post-collapse period, it will be hard for these persons to commit aggression against you in your SAB, as you will be far away and they will be numerically inferior. On the other hand, they may try to convince you to accept them, coming up with all sort of reasons and excuses. You must identify them — these are the types who are constantly up to no good and might brag about stealing from others — and you must reject them immediately, for once the worm is in the fruit, they could destroy your SAB from the inside out.

The unforeseeable aggressor is an unstable person who attacks you unexpectedly and for no reason. An impulsive fighter or a thief driven into a corner, a disturbed teenager or drug addict without his fix, he does not easily let go of his prey. In hard times, these persons will be quickly confronted with those stronger than themselves and rapidly eliminated. Try to avoid letting this task fall to you.

The organized gang of aggressors is a group of persons who plan attacks. Only taking action in situations of numerical superiority and when everything is favorable to them, they hope to get what they want quickly. In normal times, they give up if it is only a matter of theft (a phone, cash, etc.) and run away if things get violent. After a collapse, however, they will likely be more brazen. You will be protected in your SAB, but cornered in it as well. That is, you will not be able to flee gangs if they attack you, and you must defend yourself by putting such vile creatures out of commission — permanently, if possible — in order to prevent them from coming back with reinforcements.

Finally, **mobs**. People in large numbers are willing to do things they would never do as individuals. For unforeseeable, often trivial reasons, mobs take action, often gratuitously or opportunistically. Think of the vandalism and mayhem engaged in by fans of rival sports teams after a big game. Mobs are rarely tightly bound, but can have gregarious reflexes and behavior. It can be possible to reason with or calm down mobs; though often, the best idea is simply to run away. You can also prevail over them physically, especially if you discover their leader and succeed in isolating him, reasoning with him, or dispatching him. In a collapse situation, most people making up a mob will be looking for food and are not necessarily dangerous if encountered individually. A mob is not the worst danger, especially if you learn how to behave like a firm leader, decisive and resolute, and if you address the mob vigorously and with authority. (This can be learned and practiced.)

In case of emergency, it is best to adopt a safe distance from persons outside your family or your group of friends. Many persons behave irrationally in a crisis. Avoid being attacked by a desperate person.

In general, under normal circumstances, if running away is possible and doesn't have negative consequences, do not hesitate — flee. An insult or slight is not worth a response, in light of the physical and legal risks this involves. There is no dishonor in not exacting revenge on a dishonest man.

In a collapse, your priority at all times should be your survival and that of those you love. Safeguarding strangers is secondary and should only be undertaken if the risks are quite low. Apply the old saying: your children before your cousins, you cousins before your neighbors, your neighbors before strangers. Do not be a hero.

That said, it is not a wise choice to isolate yourself completely in an emergency. As far as possible, be generous with the people you meet. Try to help them, if your means allow, for one day you may need help yourself. Do not forget that beneath a chaotic exterior the person you are speaking to may be a doctor, an engineer, or anyone with a useful trade who might perfectly fit into your group and greatly facilitate your survival. It's not only a practical thing to do, but a moral one as well. Most people you will encounter, whether they are Christian, Muslim or have no religion at all, will act the same way.

Use violence as a last resort and only to defend yourself and your loved ones. Using violence aggressively is a sure path towards your own destruction, as there will be many ready and willing to defend themselves against you. In normal times, use the principle of proportionality; in a situation of lawlessness, then, after trying to avoid violence, be prepared to defend yourself *without proportionality* and *without pity* in the Afghan or Israeli style: two eyes for an eye, a whole face for a tooth!

From now on, you have the advantage of being aware of the dangers. What remains is to prepare yourself for them. It will be like everything we have discussed regarding survival attitudes: a little luck, a lot of technique, and, above all, mental preparation. Since luck is in the hands of the gods, let's start with the most important factor — mental preparedness.

First, accept that you must defend yourself. It's your right and your duty to yourself, your loved ones, your brothers-in-arms, and those under your responsibility. First, recognize your current reactions to stressful situations. Learn to deal with being physically hit or wounded (this can be done harmlessly by simulation during training). Learn to avoid tunnel vision; learn to breathe to control your heartbeat; learn to be relaxed with your body and sharp with your mind. Learn also how to assess a situation realistically after something stressful happens. Learn to learn from your mistakes. Finally, learn to have the humility and wisdom to ask for help and advice from others. This is how the best of the world's special forces (SEAL, Rangers, SAS, Foreign Legion, GIGN, Spetsnaz, Col. Moschin, COMSUBIN, GSG9, Sayeret Maktal, Shayetet 13, etc.) excel at combat: they train hard, are humble, and display no bravado — at least until *after* they've achieved total victory!

In all circumstances, face the danger. As the Swiss saying goes, "The blow that hurts the most is the one that comes from behind your back." If possible, always have your back to the wall in order to maximize your field of vision and see threats approaching. Above all, do not look like a victim. Have a strong posture, demonstrating with your look that you know what is happening and have seen what your attackers are doing. Be clever: if an attacker threatens you with a knife, for instance, tell him you have an infectious disease. Have confidence in yourself and your capacities. Use good sense: do not let yourself be provoked and distracted by people you do not know, move in groups if possible, avoid elevators, do not carry signs of wealth, visible objects of value, do not show off that you have the latest phone or anything that indicates you would be a profitable hit. Do not forget that in a crisis, even a brand new or ostentatious pair of shoes can also attract attention, so be discreet and inconspicuous. Pay attention — make a habit of noting the strategic points in your neighborhood and learn to notice changes or unusual elements. Locate the escape routes in your workplace and in your house. Leave the area as soon as possible in case of danger. Once again: do not be a hero.

In many circumstances, it is advantageous to take the initiative and look your attacker right in the eye. Learn to have a firm and de-termined appearance. Practice in front of a mirror if necessary. Do not have shifty eyes. Do not lower your head or draw in your shoulders; keep your back straight. Breath calmly and deeply, master your stress and fear. Be sure of yourself. If the attacker you are facing does not like your gaze, tell him politely that you are not looking for trouble, that you wish to be left alone, and that if you are left alone, everything will be fine. If he insists, tell him firmly, with a gaze matching his own, that you are prepared to defend yourself and that you "mean business". Do not provoke the attacker with sudden movements and, if you can, leave calmly. Remain sure of yourself and control your breathing.

If you must strike, do so quickly and by surprise, for example, in the middle of a sentence. Strike hard — harder than when you are practicing — and visualize an escape route. Remember that the aim of self-defense is survival and not victory or revenge; as Gichin Funakochi, the founder of modern karate, says, "When two tigers meet, one comes out injured, the other comes out dead." Neither result will be good for you.

If someone threatens you with a firearm, you must ask yourself whether what you are going to do will improve the situation or make it worse. In most cases, comply, keep your head down, lie on the ground. In the face of a firearm, the aim must be prevention and anticipating the situation. If gunshots break out in the street, quickly hit the ground or get behind a protective cover (a wall or the engine block part of a car).

Finally, keep a low profile, especially in preparing your SAB. When the economy collapses and panic breaks out, you do not want all your neighbors, friends, distant relatives, exes, et al., taking refuge at your place. Worse, you don't want a gang of looters, who hear there is a fellow prepared with plenty of food, showing up at your SAB to knock you off. Still worse, it is not in your interest that the government come and confiscate everything under a pretense of sharing it, keeping it off the black market, forbidding you the possession of dangerous material, or with any other "good intentions" that would leave you butt naked or force you to react in a drastic manner.

In short, be discreet. Pay for as many of your purchases as possible in cash, and don't talk openly about your project with just anybody. Do not make all the purchases for your SAB in the neighborhood where you live; this will prevent rumors from developing. Do not tell just anybody where your SAB is located. Above all, don't write a book on the subject! Once you are ready to imagine all the things that could happen, and have begun your mental preparations, you can start learning a few techniques.

Martial Arts and Self-Defense

In the movie *The Professional* by Luc Besson, the hitman character, played by Jean Reno, teaches his young pupil that one must first learn to fight at a distance before learning hand-to-hand combat. I believe one must do exactly the reverse.

First, learn to defend yourself with your own body, then with a close-range weapon, and only afterwards with a long-distance weapon.

Of course, one can perfectly well take a shooting course and learn karate at the same time. But the idea is that if you do not master your own body and street-corner self-defense first, learning to fight with a knife, pistol, or rifle won't be of any great benefit. Knowing how to hit a target at 1,800 meters with the help of a 50-caliber precision rifle is fine (indeed, it is excellent). But such know-how will not help you in a dark alley. It would be a case of "who can do the most can do the least."

Martial arts were invented by peasants at a time when carrying arms was severely restricted and reserved for soldiers and noblemen. The practice of a martial art allowed peasants to defend themselves against brigands or armed enemies. These martial arts, from countries around the world, have evolved to become sporting disciplines accessible to every normally constituted person. Enroll now and start practicing one of them.

Favor the "mixed" martial arts, for they focus on real situations. Among these techniques we may mention Systema, Sambo, Krav Maga, Hapkido, Thai Boxing, Yi Quan, and KAPAP, which are all excellent. It is essential to select a martial art in which you will learn to take blows. Too often we forget that everyone receives blows in a fight; you must thus learn not to be surprised or freeze up when you get hit!

For my part, I have chosen Systema, a fighting and self-defense technique developed for Spetsnaz (the elite fighting forces of the USSR) starting in the 1950s. It is a technique with the peculiarity of having no fixed rules, allowing all possible blows, teaching you how to take blows, and not imposing a hierarchy of levels or grades. In the past few years, Mikhail Ryabko and Vladimir Vasiliev further developed Systema, focusing on non-opposition (absorbing blows rather than trying to block them); control of the body, breath, and reflexes; and the ability of a fighter to rapidly throw off balance and neutralize his opponent, which allows one to defeat a numerically superior adversary.

Whatever martial art you choose, train regularly and assiduously. Complete your physical preparation with at least one endurance sport (jogging, bicycling, swimming, etc), which you should try to practice daily for at least 30 minutes. Take long hikes (two or three hours) as often as possible and engage in regular weightlifting sessions or another kind of strength training.

As you prepare your body, learn the ten basic principles of self-defense:

> **Run away**. If it is possible, avoid conflict.

> **Train**. Prepare your body and mind for difficult situations.

Repeat, visualize, practice sports, take courses.

> **Don't let yourself be cornered**. Disengage yourself, try to leave yourself space, either by repelling an attacker or drawing back. Do not let yourself be encircled by several opponents.

> **Attack your opponent's organs of vision, breathing, and mobility.** You must have a good idea of the incapacitation zones to aim for. At the same time, you must know how to protect your own sensitive zones.

> **Deliver a series of blows.** On average, it takes five to seven blows to bring an adversary to the ground and put him out of commission. You must learn to deliver blow after blow rapidly in order to destabilize your adversary and deliver an incapacitating shock.

> **Vary your level and techniques in order to favor surprise.**

> **Absorb blows.** You must psychologically accept that you will take blows and learn to absorb them without losing your balance or being shocked.

> **Hit hard and fast.** Once you have decided to use force, you must strike quickly and deeply. Aim for the inside of your adversary's body and not the surface.

> **Use the environment.** Anything can make an improvised weapon: a stick, a keychain, a pen, a rolled newspaper, a flashlight, an electronic device, a cup, a glass, a household tool, a stone, a fire extinguisher, an ashtray, a bottle, an iron, a motorcycle helmet, a chair, an umbrella, etc.

> **Don't get stuck in tunnel vision.** In spite of the stress of combat, do not fix your gaze solely on your aggressor; you must perceive your immediate environment in its entirety, observing the actions of other people and seeking out materials that could be of use to you.

> Finally, **don't go to the ground.** This a very unfavorable position, except in some rare situations where it is actually an advantage. If you are victorious, do not persist in attacking your adversary: neutralize him and evaluate the situation, looking all the way around you (360 degrees).

Above all, remember the strategic saying of General Sun-tzu:

Only a warrior chooses pacifism. Others are condemned to it.

Weaponry

If the rule of law disappears and the police are no longer there to protect honest citizens, you will have to have weapons to defend yourself. In fact, an armed citizenry is one of the few — if not the most indispensable — guarantees of a nation's independence. As we say in Switzerland: "An unarmed citizen is only a taxpayer."

Weapons often have a bad reputation, unfortunately, as they are harmless in themselves. It is up to the weapon's bearer to show himself fit for the responsibility he has assumed by owning the weapon. It is not knives or firearms that maim or murder, but the men and women who use them unwisely. As for accidents, they happen mainly to those who do not know how to use them properly, or who think they no longer have to follow the basic rules of safety. All weapons, whether for hunting or fighting, require that you learn how to use them and maintain them in a manner that is safe for yourself and others.

I want to remind you, once again, that you must start by informing yourself about the weapons legislation in your country and state. Laws vary greatly, and I encourage you to respect them in all circumstances when it comes to buying, transporting, and using weapons.

Weapons serve three purposes: 1. hunting, 2. deterrence, and 3. defense. In all cases, the choice of arms will depend on several criteria:

1 > **Versatility.** A weapon can serve many purposes, but no weapon can serve all of them; and so it is important to start with a weapon that can cover the greatest possible number of needs.

2 > **Robustness and quality.** A weapon must be able to withstand frequent use with normal maintenance and not break down, especially if there is no one around to repair it for you. Always choose a good quality weapon; even if it is expensive, the difference will be worth it.

3 > **Availability of ammunition and spare parts.** If you choose an exotic firearm with a caliber requiring an uncommon type of ammunition, you will quickly find yourself with a useless weapon, unless you make your own ammunition. So it is preferable to choose weapons with calibers corresponding to those that are most frequently used within your area and your country.

Here are a few types of weapons:

Cold weapons. These are knives, axes, tomahawks, etc., and are all easy to buy on the market and are usually not regulated in most countries. On the other hand, their use demands a lot of training and courage, for you must go hand-to-hand with your adversary. Moreover, you cannot completely protect yourself from a knife blow, and you can expect to receive painful and serious wounds. Choose a martial art that teaches the use of knives or other cold weapons; that way, you will learn the basics. Once again, avoid as much as possible situations in which you must use a knife to defend yourself; hopefully, a knife's mere presence will end a dispute before it begins. The knife is the survival tool *par excellence*: it is useful for practically everything and will be used every day, especially in a rural environment. Take good care of it and keep it sharp.

In an emergency situation, it is good for everyone to have the following knives:

> a pocket knife (Swiss Army knife);

> a multipurpose tool (Leatherman, Victorinox);

> a combat knife or a bush knife;

> a hatchet or kukri-type knife;

> emergency survival knife.

Improvised Weapons. This category includes weapons such as screwdrivers, pots, and pans, etc. You are limited only by your imagination and what you have around you. You can easily put a brick in a handbag or pouch to use as a scourge in an emergency. Do not neglect these means of defense, since they are easily available and have the advantage of not drawing much attention.

Bows and Crossbows. Easier to access than firearms, a bow or crossbow can be very effective, if you know how to use it and practice regularly. If you are short of time, choose a crossbow, for it is easier to handle. Bows and crossbows can be used for hunting and have the advantage of using ammunition that you can most often reuse or make by hand.

Firearms. Access to firearms is usually highly regulated. In fact, governments increasingly seem to view an armed citizenry as a dangerous threat. That is why owning a gun, pistol, or rifle has become more difficult in the past few years.

Before even approaching a firearm, it is important to know by heart four basic safety rules that were codified by Jeff Cooper:

1 > All arms are always considered loaded.

2 > Never let the muzzle point at anything you are not wanting to destroy.

3 > Keep your index finger off the trigger until your sights are on a target.

4 > Always be sure of your target and your surroundings.

The mastery of these rules will help you avoid a lot of problems and accidents. If you do not understand them, ask your firearm instructor to explain them in detail.

Using a firearm requires following a rigorous course of training. Without training, you will not even be capable of handling a firearm in an emergency, meaning your adversary will certainly overcome you, and you'll be wounded or dead. For this reason, you should enroll at a local shooting club. Take a course from an experienced instructor and get a handgun permit or hunting permit; you can then buy arms, ammunition, and practice in a safe and legal environment.

Prefer firearms with a caliber common in your area and easy to handle. Avoid exotic weapons, which won't be useful, even if they look impressive in movies. Being armed also serves to deter unwelcome or hostile visitors by making them think that they would do better not to come onto your property. A firearm with a strongly dissuasive effect is the pump-action shotgun: the characteristic *click-clack* sound when you load one is usually sufficient to make an intruder turn around and seek out easier targets.

I advise you to acquire, as quickly as possible, and insofar as it is legal in your country, at least two firearms: first a long weapon (rifle or assault rifle) with the caliber used by the army in the country where you live. Ammunition and spare parts will be all the more easily obtainable in case of unrest. Typically, this will be a .223 Remington or a .308 Winchester, which are the NATO standards. If these firearms are available in a fully automatic version (multiple shots with a single pull of the trigger), this is preferable, because it will give you more versatility. This is not obligatory, however, as most modern techniques do not require full-automatic, or suppression, fire. These calibers will give you the capacity to fire, aiming with high precision, up to two hundred or three hundred meters (650 to 1,000 feet), depending on the weapon's quality, barrel length, etc. This distance is sufficient for the defense of your SAB against common aggressors. Of course, with good training or specialized weapons with the proper sights or optics, one can aim with precision far beyond these ranges, even exceeding 3,000 feet. Sadly, it may be that the sale of such arms is not permitted in your country. In such cases, hunting rifles or carbines of smaller calibers — but still very efficient, like the .22 Long Rifle — can usually be obtained.

Next, you will need to acquire a handgun, which will be your secondary combat weapon in most situations. You must choose a robust pistol or revolver of good quality and with very common calibers such as .45 ACP in 9-mm Parabellum (9 x 19 mm), .38 special, etc. Handguns are also quite useful in urban environments, in enclosed areas (inside a house), and for targets no more than fifty meters away. (Statistically, the vast majority of engagements with handguns by police or security personnel are at less than ten meters/thirty feet). Above all, a handgun is a fallback if your primary weapon (i.e. your carbine or rifle) has run out of ammunition or has been incapacitated. It is important to buy a lot of magazines for weapons that require them (certain rifles, pistols, etc.). I recommend at least a dozen magazines for each of your weapons and ideally twice as many, if you can afford it, as these very valuable items could be used for barter.

I should make particular mention of the .12-gauge caliber pump-action shotgun. This weapon can be very easy or very hard to get, according to the laws of different countries. It is remarkably robust, relatively easy to use, and has great power and versatility. In fact, you can use it with a wide variety of ammunition grades, from small pellets to medium pellets for duck hunting to buckshot and slugs for larger quarry (such as boars) and anything in between. Although I did not begin my own training with this weapon, I now think that if I had to choose or could afford only one firearm, the shotgun is the best choice.

For hunting, you must acquire the correct permit before undertaking your local safari. You will learn quickly, in any case, that the weapons mentioned above are not ideal for hunting, and even if the pump-action shotgun is capable of shooting hunting ammunition, this is generally forbidden.

If you plan on hunting small game or even just eliminating vermin, a low-caliber weapon such as the same .22 Long Rifle carbine mentioned above is excellent for anything from a rat up to a hare, or even for that stubborn chicken you can't catch. Moreover, the ammunition is not expensive at all. Arm yourself with a carbine and a little pistol or revolver of that caliber. For slightly larger game, a light, rapid caliber will let you hit small animals at up to 300 meters (1,000 feet). For example, the .222 Remington for a fox, the .243 Winchester for a roe, and the 6.5 x 68 for an antelope. A rapid but heavier caliber will work for larger animals (deer and boar) at a long distance, like the .7 millimeter Remington Magnum, the .308 Winchester, the .30–06 Springfield, and the .300 Winchester Magnum. Some of these calibers are also used by the armed forces as elite sniper weapons, and they are effective with a good rifle and a good sight (Leupold, Schmidt & Bender, Nightforce, Bushnell, Zeiss) at up to 700 to 1,000 meters (or 2,100 to 3,000 feet).

For birds and larger game, the .12 gauge caliber is perfect. This is the most common caliber for hunting rifles, single or double-barreled, and is usually the one most people learn to shoot with. The whole variety of cartridges at this caliber is easily available, which allows you to hunt practically all animals allowed (duck, partridge, pheasant, etc.) with small pellet cartridges, as well as heavier animals such as boars, deer, and bear with cartridges known as buckshot.

Whatever weapons you equip yourself with, you must learn how to store and maintain them. It is fundamental to store one's arms and ammunition in a correct and safe manner, especially in a humid climate. You must avoid rust and anything else that can damage the mechanical parts of your weapons. All weapons, from knives to rifles, must be stored where children cannot get to them, in a locked armory or trunk at the very least. Ideally, store your guns and your ammunition in separate places. To avoid accidents, teach children early on that a gun is not a toy, that it is not used the way you see in movies, and that they must not touch it, but that, when they are a little older, they can learn the basics of how to handle one and, once they reach the legal age, they will learn how to use and shoot it. Progressive familiarization helps avoid an unhealthy fascination, all too common, alas, among certain adolescents who like to identify with Tony Montana in *Scarface* (!).

Ammunition must be correctly stored, in locked boxes sheltered from humidity (avoid cellars). In this manner, ammunition can be conserved for more than fifty years. And don't be afraid to store a lot of it. At a minimum, per person and per weapon, figure on the following quantities: 6,000 to 10,000 cartridges for each assault rifle or carbine, 2,000 to 3,000 cartridges for each hunting rifle and 1,000 to 2,000 for each pistol or revolver. This is a minimum requirement, as ammunition might soon become scarce, more tightly regulated, or significantly more expensive. Inform yourself about the materials necessary for making ammunition yourself: cladding techniques are well established, easy and safe, and can save you a lot of money in the long run.

It is obvious that between arms and ammunition, you will need a significant budget; all the more so because you must buy the ammunition necessary to practice (nearly one hundred cartridges per session). But this ammunition will be indispensable to you and will be irreplaceable in a world where access to manufacturers will be difficult. A stock of ammunition and replacement gun parts will be worth its weight in gold (likely literally), since ammunition is just as important as the weapon: neither is of use without the other. Remember when European colonialists sold weapons to African tribes; although they sold a lot of rifles, they sold very little ammunition. There was a reason for that. (Also, should you wish to stock up on ammunition for barter, be sure to only buy common calibers.)

Finally, a weapon in the hands of a novice is worse than useless — it's dangerous. You must learn to handle your weapon using plastic or metal practice cartridges. Then, you must learn to shoot at a shooting range. Invest in lessons with an experienced instructor and spend a good deal of time learning how to aim with precision. Learn to be a good shot. An experienced gunman knows when a trigger should be pulled — and *not* pulled — and how to live with the consequences.

Accidents most often happen to people who never practice, or who shoot so often that they become complacent with the safety rules. Re-memorize the four security rules before each time you handle a weapon: *always* remember that a weapon is not a toy, and that it is not dangerous *per se*. It is the user who can use it badly and be a menace to himself and others.

To perfect your defense, think about equipping yourself with what are called force multipliers. These are all the elements that can give you an advantage over your enemy: tracking alarms, vision, and coordination. See your enemy before he sees you thanks to long-distance optics, or infrared or thermal tracking. Getting alerted to an alien presence by alarms, or having the possibility to communicate with all the members of your team with a permanent connection, can give you a significant advantage. Opinions are divided on the use of these battery-gobbling high-tech devices. Over-equipped Western armies have trouble combating the Afghan rebels, who are lightly equipped but mobile and inventive. First World armies have probably become too dependent on technology. It's up to you to figure out what you want and can use.

Finally, in terms of your equipment, you must reflect on the circumstances and conditions in which you will be carrying arms (hunting, defending your SAB, etc.). I recommend, first of all, a belt onto which you can fix a sheath or holster for your handgun, one or two magazines for it, and your main knife. This belt can rapidly be put on in an emergency. Then, for rifles and other long arms, try out different types of bandoliers or vests — preferably in your instructor's presence — in order to find the type that best suits you. You must also plan on one or more magazines for your principal weapon, attached to your belt, a tactical vest or suspenders. There is an infinite number of models. It is worth the trouble of trying a few to find out which is the most practical for you. For hunting rifles or pump-action shotguns, plan on having a hunting pouch full of cartridges, or a cartridge belt or bandolier. If you need a backpack, a canteen, or other equipment, consider the conditions and the mission (reconnaissance, defense, etc.), for which one model may be better adapted than another. To avoid surprises and clumsy "epic fails," remember this rule regarding equipment: "train as you fight, fight as you train."

Always have eye protection (protective glasses) and ear protection (earplugs, etc.). Equip yourself with cleaning materials proper for each of your weapons and with discreet transport bags. Never stop practicing regularly and preparing yourself by imagining all the possible scenarios.

To conclude, a weapon is worthless without preparation for fighting: you must be physically prepared, and for this, you must live in a healthy way and consistently exercise with a varied and regular program over the course of your life. You must be materially prepared (have minimal equipment along with a plan B, a plan C, etc.). Above all, be mentally prepared for any scenario. Respect the law, of course, and in a case where you must use a weapon, remember the principle of proportionality — but also this old American saying: "Better to be judged by twelve than carried by six."

Organizing the Defense of Your SAB

The ideal is to plan the security of your SAB from the beginning. The first paradox with which you will have to reckon is that of discretion and defensive capacity. The more your house resembles a bunker, the more it will be recognized as a place where the owners or residents want to protect valuables, and the more likely it will be that an organized expedition is carried out against you. The better the location of your SAB is for defense — for example, on a hill like a castle — the less discreet it will be, and the more conspicuous from a distance.

Ideally, an SAB should permit a vision radius of 100 to 200 meters (300 to 600 feet), without trees, obstructions, or large objects behind which one could hide. This will keep people from approaching your SAB from behind cover and thus evading your surveillance. If your SAB remains undetectable beyond these measurements and cannot be seen from a public road, being hidden by trees or a forest, for example, your situation will be even better. You must ask yourself: in case of economic collapse, will the area where you live simply be subject to more break-ins, or might it fall under the control of organized gangs of looters?

If you have a large garden, make it less visible by surrounding it with hedges, flowers, and bushes in order to give the impression that it is mostly decorative. If a blackout occurs, even a small light could reveal your location. I remember that once at church, the local bishop told us that in times of trouble we should always look for a house with a light on at night. Although he was not using this allegory in the same context, it remains true that those who have an independent source of energy will attract all sorts of people, from refugees to looters. You will want to be better prepared than merely using blinds if you prefer your light not to be seen from the outside. Consider dark tarpaulins or weatherproof plastic curtains. Verify that no light can be seen externally.

Some people equip their property with external lamps (activated by motion sensors). That's fine, but this is another way that someone may find you. A more effective solution would be to install infrared lamps connected to a motion trigger. Thus you can "light up" the intruders without their perceiving it, unless they have infrared goggles like you.

If you can afford to buy a large plot of land, I recommend a system of defense on several levels. At the external level, install walls with barbed wire on top and thorn bush hedges, armed and grated access doors with an alarm system, if possible. This is very common in villas and gated communities in many countries like Mexico, Colombia, Nigeria, South Africa, etc. Then, at an intermediate level, the ideal would be a zone of trees large enough to hide the buildings that make up your SAB, with an area of 100 to 200 meters meters (300 to 600 feet) without any obstacles going right up to the house. At the interior level, plant a large thorn bush beneath each window. Ideally, install steel shutters, solid bars on the windows, an armored door, and a heavy chain able to stand up to vehicles a few meters in front of your main entrance, in order to discourage ramming with them. Replace all doors to the outside with reinforced doors.

Having one or more well-trained guard dogs is a good idea. Dogs are a very effective means of alert and defense, but require a lot of knowledge and responsibility. A dog also involves significant costs and food. So this is a means of defense reserved for connoisseurs. Always keep dogs and all other animals outside. If you have enough persons living in your SAB, put a security perimeter in place; keep it under constant surveillance by guards with a regular schedule of shifts, especially at night. This is fairly easy to organize, but, as with everything else, training and practice are required.

In general, you must first install preventive (passive) defenses. Identify the weaknesses of your SAB and how to overcome them and make them more secure. Define surveillance zones (windows, peepholes, observation posts in the garden, on a tower, or at the top of a tree, etc.). Then, establish control zones where you can act without being seen, and kill zones to lay an ambush and neutralize any intruder or aggressor. Finally, choose security zones as locations for retreating. They can be rooms with reinforced doors underground or upstairs. You might even construct a shelter, install hiding places or even a subterranean passage way to the exterior or to another building. In such security zones, stock whatever might be useful to you if you are forced to take refuge there for a period of time. If your security zone is a room protected by a resistant door, install a means of communication (battery-powered radio, telephone), water, some energy bars, a first-aid kit, torch lamps, materials for defense (weapons, ammunition, etc.). If it is a small hiding place, think about storing water, energy bars, a pocket lamp, and defensive weapons. As a mental exercise, imagine yourself in the place of the Warsaw Ghetto inhabitants one day in 1943, where they have come to deport you to a certain death. Where would you hide? With what personal effects and equipment? Andy Grove, former CEO of Intel, who comes from a family that survived the deportations, likes to say that "only paranoiacs survive."

As we have already mentioned, living in an urban apartment or SAB is not an optimal situation for your security and survival in times of crisis. Defending an apartment is difficult but not impossible. You dispose of better assets if you are the owner of your four walls. Start by strengthening the door you usually use with steel. Remember that the best of doors will not protect you if the lock or the wall around it are not equally solid. Plan on thick curtains and tarpaulins for your windows, since, once again, you will be a target if you are the only person around with lights. If you live on the ground floor or second floor, you must reinforce your windows, install bars and secure your blinds or shutters. In an urban SAB, the most dangerous moments are mainly when you enter or exit. Observe your surroundings carefully before entering or exiting and be on your highest alert. Over the long term, you cannot avoid having your apartment invaded by sufficiently determined people. This is why it is a good idea to set up caches for your food, weapons, and other important material. Such caches should be installed in innocuous places. Keep a minimum of food and objects of value available for possible intruders, because that keeps them from having to go away empty-handed, and, perhaps, they will let you live.

If you have transformed your villa into an SAB, you must think about reinforcing it and protecting all your doors and windows. Consider installing armored doors, but also reinforce your walls with the help of steel plates, if you can afford that. Always have a temporary solution in case of intruders, such as a "safe room" or "panic room." Keep it closed when not in use, storing your most important supplies, but also barricade yourself there, if necessary. The best thing is to use your basement for this purpose, or, in countries where they exist, like Switzerland, a radiation shelter (but ensure that the door can be blocked from the inside). As you cannot remain closed in forever, plan on being able to contact the outside world in one way or another (radio, field telephone, etc.). At this stage, it is important not to forget to secure the door of your garage if it is attached to your house. Children's rooms should be close to those of their parents. Finally, install caches in your house and garden. Hide your small valuables in unusual places. If you want to bury some of your bars of gold or silver coins as well as firearms in the ground, make sure to dig at least 1.5 meters (five feet) deep to avoid freezing and most metal detectors; and protect your goods from dampness with a hermetically sealed container. And, of course, remember the spot where you buried your treasure!

One very effective means of defense is also restraining the movements of a potential intruder or aggressor. Such restrictions are called barricading techniques. A band of looters will choose an easily accessible target rather than the one where they will have to overcome numerous obstacles. Barricading techniques represent a possibility for effectively limiting the movements of potential adversaries while increasing your own safety. You must be aware that this is not usually allowed under normal circumstances, and that it can represent a legal infraction. On the other hand, nothing keeps you from preparing such measures and applying them in a crisis once laws and regulations no longer apply. Among the means of barricading, barbed wire is easy to find on the market and not very expensive. You should always attach the barbed wire to the ground with concrete blocks and use at least three interlaced levels to get effective protection. Handle barbed wire with protective gloves. The primary function of barbed wire is to prevent access to a spot, or at least make such access difficult. The effectiveness of barbed wire is increased by adding "bells" (empty conserve cans containing stones or an electronic system) that can act as alarms.

Sandbags represent another classic and very effective barricading technique. They can be stored as empty sacks to be used in case of an emergency. Plan on buying spades to load sand (or soil, or gravel) quickly. The bags can be made of jute or plastic materials (polypropylene or polyethylene), which stand up better to sun and humidity. In due course, you can fill the bags with sand or gravel. You will need several thousand to cover a house front effectively and protect semi-underground shelters.

Another barricading technique is to use 200-liter (or 50-gallon) barrels filled with water, sand, or soil. Several such barrels will allow you to barricade a road or entrance very effectively. They are readily available and easy to handle when empty. Be careful not to buy barrels which have been used for dangerous or toxic chemical substances.

Finally, there are countless possible and imaginable improvised techniques for blocking an entrance, barring a road, etc. It is possible to use an old car or stone blocks as obstacles. Always keep in mind that you may have to remove these obstacles quickly to let in welcome persons or to flee.

A final point of organization is protecting your SAB against fire. Since the fire department may not be available in times of crises, you will have to handle this issue on your own. Plan on having enough reasonably new extinguishers on hand and learn how to use them. If you can, plan on a manual or electrical pump and a hydrant, so you can organize a little fire brigade. One old but effective technique is keeping buckets filled with sand handy all over your SAB to dowse the flames. If you can, fireproof as much of your walls and roofs as possible.

How to Defend Yourself against Animals

It would take a whole chapter to cover defense against wild animals in a natural environment, but that is not the aim of this book. Of course, it is possible that wild animals could wander onto your SAB area, but there is little risk of being attacked and devoured by them. And in light of your hunting and self-defense arsenal, rare wild animals should not present a problem. On the other hand, domestic animals could become a danger in times of crisis. This is what is happening in abandoned areas of the Ukraine, Mexico, and Nigeria, where wandering dogs rediscover their natural instincts and organize into packs. These will be dangerous to children and homeless persons. Avoid packs: a dog bite is painful and hard to treat under normal circumstances, and can represent a serious health risk (infections, rabies). If you are forced to face up to a pack of dogs, do not try to run away; stay where you are, remain calm, and avoid sustained visual contact. Try to appear larger and more menacing by augmenting your height and size, e.g., letting your jacket fall down your arms, which you can spread out to look like wings. An animal will always hesitate to attack a prey which seems to present a significant risk of injury. If attacked, defend yourself with blows to the muzzle, neck, and eyes.

In a collapse scenario, avoid areas near zoos. It is possible that the keepers (or animal-activist groups) will not have the heart to let the animals die of hunger in captivity, and will prefer to release them. Imagine lions or tigers at liberty in your town! In general, avoid animals you don't know: dogs, cats, reptiles, insects... This attitude will help you avoid plenty of injuries and illnesses.

Defending Yourself against the Elements

Defense against natural disasters or the elements is not "defense" properly speaking, since nature does not literally attack us. Still, you must prepare and equip yourself against all eventualities, whether usual (wind, cold, heat, rain, etc.) or exceptional (storms, natural disasters, etc.). Accustom yourself to cold and heat. Wear good-quality clothing, resistant, and functional. Judge clothing by its thermoregulatory properties: rapid drying, proper insulation, resistance to repeated washing and wear; select those that permit mobility, flexibility, comfort, and are relatively light. Think about having an appearance that lets you feel good and pass unnoticed. Choose colors that are suitable anywhere in town (avoid fluorescent pink!) or which do not contrast with the natural terrain (earth tones, or colors similar to the local vegetation). If possible, dress in three layers: one to regulate perspiration, the second to maintain warmth, and the third to protect you from the elements. Dressing in camouflage uniforms is a good idea after a collapse, because it will give a sense of cohesion to your team, but before that it is too striking, and serves no purpose. Get used to wearing hiking boots or military boots of the best possible quality. Make sure they are water-tight, impermeable, and have non-skid soles. Plan on having a backpack with which you can run, jump over walls, or fight. Good ergonomic design is essential, and you should test several before buying one. Plan on putting a bullet-proof plate in your backpack or another kind of bag to make yourself a shield in case of an emergency. Also remember mini-first-aid kits.

Alert Levels

How will you know when the collapse has gotten so bad that you must leave everything and take refuge in your SAB? You mustn't be fooled, for it wouldn't be expedient to leave on a false alarm! You must make an effort to stay abreast of what is happening in the world and around you: analyses of the crisis, conflicts, geostrategic positioning, etc. Skim the news on the social networks as well as on internet sites that you have identified as well-informed and reliable. All this will help you anticipate riots, revolutions, regime changes, etc. Talk about it with your friends, listen to what is being said on the street and do not believe reassuring statements by the political authorities. Learn to identify spiraling threats, i.e., the way in which violence increases: more frequent break-ins and kidnappings, the use of increasingly sophisticated tools by burglars (ramming vehicles, firearms, military equipment), increasingly sophisticated ruses for entering homes (disguised as delivery men or policemen), or organized diversions to attract the police somewhere far from the real target.

A good method for managing societal regression toward a serious crisis is to agree on a system of alert levels with your friends and the persons you plan to join in your SAB. Decide upon what each of these levels represents, and on the actions to be taken at each level. Here, I shall offer you a six-level alert system; it's up to you to adopt it, modify it, or take it as a model for developing your own.

> **Level 0** is the normal state: everything is going fine, you are safe in your house, in a family environment, with no particular risks. For the moment, this is the state of most people in Western countries.

> **Level 1** is when there is not yet any specific threat, but you start to ready yourself, both in daily life and in preparation of your SAB. You are conscious of your surroundings and observe the people around you carefully, but without any particular stress. This is the state in which you should be today when you go out onto the street, and the minimum level of operation to begin your preparations.

> **Level 2** is when a real crisis begins, and criminality increases in your town or region. Be vigilant when the first serious unrest arrives: if the situation becomes pre-revolutionary, or if there are large demonstrations or external threats. This level corresponds to a period where you can foresee neither the consequences of

important events nor society's reaction to them. This is the level of alert you would have had, for example, when the Berlin Wall fell, during the attempted Soviet *coup d'état* of 1991, or the 2005 civil unrest in France. This is the level of alert if a war breaks out between India and Pakistan, or at an onset of a viral contamination somewhere. At this level of alert, finish buying foods to stock in your SAB, especially those of short duration (milk, flour, medicines, etc.), check your essentials and survival kit, and pack your suitcases. Remain in contact with all members of your SAB at least twice a day, and especially with members of your family. With a little luck, the situation will improve, and you may lower your alert level again by one notch.

> **Level 3** is when there is a proven threat. You must focus on the danger and be ready to make quick self-defense and survival decisions. This level is reached when, for example, wars or revolutions break out, when panicked buyers empty supermarket shelves, and violence has begun. Do not wait: this is the time to leave immediately for your SAB. You will require the maximum amount of mental concentration and expect to confront imminent danger. Contact your family and everyone who is to meet you in your SAB, and leave. How do you prepare for this trip? Group those people who must leave with you, and if you are traveling in several vehicles, plan on a convoy with pre-established rendezvous points. If possible, stay in permanent or frequent communication. Plan on having a charged battery for your mobile phone. It would be good to test the departure plan at least once. Plan several routes in order to avoid obstacles or barricades (imagine that your city is surrounded by a military "sanitary cordon" to keep anyone from getting out). Have several departure plans involving traveling by car, by bicycle, or on foot. Take your passport and ID card with you as well as all your title deeds, especially the one for your SAB, and all other important papers.

> **Level 4** corresponds to generalized chaos. Your country is in a state of civil war, there is ethnic cleansing, brutal repression, an invasion, etc. If you have prepared, you would already be in your SAB, and this level of alert would be what you consider normal after the economy collapses. You must be on guard all the time and practice systematic surveillance of your surroundings. It would be important to rotate your guard in shifts in order to limit stress and tension on its members, which, after a time, can have an impact on health.

> **Level 5** corresponds to a large and sudden state of panic. This level may be unleashed by a substantial natural disaster, a nuclear attack, or a rapidly spreading virus. You may be surprised and thus unprepared and vulnerable. You must immediately leave for your SAB if you are not already there. If this is not possible, you must hide the best you can and wait for somewhat better conditions in order to get moving again. This is where your 72-hour survival kit will be indispensable to you.

The big question, of course, is how you are going to get to your SAB safely, especially when many other people are leaving the city for the countryside. This is one of the reasons you must either live in your SAB or leave for it as soon as possible. Plan on having in your garage at least twice the gasoline needed for the journey (rotate it every six months) and always keep your tank full. Since you will not be able to carry everything you need on your single, final trip, you should have already accumulated large stocks and as many useful tools as possible in your SAB. If you are counting on making the trip with all your supplies, you will need either a truck or a trailer. This is also where a Bug-out bag (BOB) will be needed. We'll cover this later. This is possible but complicated, because apart from a false alarm, you may only get one chance to head to your SAB. In general, accept that you must abandon your goods and your wealth. Your SAB can protect a good deal but, generally, choose the vital (your life, your family) over the ephemeral (stuff).

To conclude, you must consider the defense of your person, your family, your comrades, and your SAB as a right, a duty, and a general attitude that induces you to master your behavior, know-how, techniques, and materials. Anticipate as much as you can in order to become more vigilant and efficient in your everyday life. Practice regularly, both physically and psychologically, a discipline of self-defense; taking regular trips to a gun range is one good idea. Maintain good hygiene. Learn to be attentive to the details of your surroundings. Maintain a security budget, take a first-aid course, do not resemble a victim, and be discreet.

Finally, you cannot survive for long by yourself. You must establish a network, bind yourself to, and integrate into a community through personal, interdependent relationships. Do this in such a way that the people and groups around you have the least possible number of reasons for aggressing against you and will associate themselves with you for common defense.

You must create and reinforce a social bond.

James Edwards got to his Argentine estate alright...

despite a long trip involving being rerouted, then a chaotic arrival in an Argentina full of social unrest—it seems there has been a revolution, with a *coup d'état* and confrontations between various political groups.

The roads were full of refugees, especially coming out of the capital, Buenos Aires. But once he got beyond the main highways, they thinned out. The arrival went well; his staff were helpful and nice.

After a few weeks, things started getting a little tense. Servants stopped speaking in his presence, avoided his glance or even gave him defiant looks. "Damn, I am the boss, after all," James Edwards said to himself one day. "I'll go talk to Alfonso, the overseer!"

The next day, the estate was reorganized on a cooperative basis—a very rich cooperative! No one knows whatever became of James Edwards. Officially, he never arrived at the estate.

Nicholas has organized and equipped all the members of his SAB well.

Each member made preparations, after a period of unrest, according to a precise list. Each one has two sets of camouflage, clothes for the summer and winter, several pairs of good hiking shoes, a Kevlar helmet, a bullet-proof vest (level IIIA), and the team even has a badge for their uniform: the serpent from one of the first American revolutionary flags from the 18th century, with the motto "Don't Tread On Me." Everyone has a .223-caliber Romanian Kalashnikov and a 9mm pistol. Several hunting rifles and a pump-action shotgun complete the arsenal. The best shooter, Anna, the wife of one of the members, is equipped with a precision Remington 700 with a high-quality Leupold Mark 4 scope.

After the riots and social collapse, all the families got to the SAB in good time, except for one member whose car broke down, and who had to finish the journey on foot. Over the last few months, several refugees have even been added to the group after a rigorous selection process. So the SAB has a mechanic and a doctor, along with their families. Fortunately, the farm was planned from the beginning to take in twice the number of persons as those who participated in the original project.

One night, one of the observation posts gives the alarm. By radio, and quietly, the code for hostile intrusion is given. In fact, a group of cars and trucks is approaching with their headlights out. The SAB team follows procedure: it rises and arms itself silently while the guard starts moving into combat position according to the defense plan and standard operating procedures they have often practiced. In less than five minutes, the thirty adults of the SAB are armed and at their stations, some on defense, some protecting the children in the most secure part of the SAB, and some ready for interception.

The group of intruders is, indeed, hostile. It's a band of fifty or so men and a few women, all armed, some heavily, with rifles and stolen military supplies. Some are wearing helmets and bullet-proof vests. They force the roadside gate with a large crowbar and advance quietly over the access road to the property. It is precisely 0400 (4 AM). Suddenly one of the aggressors cries out: he saw something moving in the bushes. Too late! The SAB team opens fire in a coordinated manner. In a few seconds, six of the aggressors are on the ground. Others flee but are cut down by bullets. Their leader can be seen issuing orders from the roof of a 4x4. Car motors start. Suddenly the leader's head explodes: Anna, stationed three hundred meters away, immediately located him and, in spite of the darkness, was able to take aim without difficulty. One group of aggressors hesitates, and this is fatal to them: they fall rapidly. Some cry out in pain. Several cars accelerate along the path and direct themselves toward the main building house of the SAB. The first car is quickly riddled with bullets coming directly from the SAB and ends up crashing into a tree. Another advances at full speed and hits a heavy chain strung between two cement pins, which stops it. The car's occupants, stunned, get out trembling, but that does not last for long: they collapse, torn by salvos from the defenders' pump-action shotguns. Within a few minutes, nothing is left of the aggressors but the wounded and the dead.

Nicholas's team secures the area. The wounded are disarmed and placed under surveillance awaiting interrogation. Arms and ammunition are put out of the way. Recon patrols are organized to evaluate the danger in the area around the SAB. There are twenty-five dead and ten wounded among the attackers and one wounded by a bullet among the defenders. They are going to have to operate, and that will be difficult. Fortunately, Henrique, the doctor, has already practiced this sort of operation. His prognosis is positive.

In the abandoned automobiles, they find several traces of the band's recent robberies. According to the interrogation, they call themselves the "Savage Flayers" and have brutally attacked several farms in the region over the last several weeks. It seems that certain members have even practiced cannibalism. What is to be done with the wounded? None of them have particularly useful abilities and, in spite of their age (between sixteen and twenty-four), they are already too old to be reconditioned. Two days later a tribunal is set up, and the surviving wounded are judged and sentenced to death. It falls to Nicholas, as the elected leader, to carry out the sentence. Preparing to pull the trigger, he says to himself that it is a shame to waste precious bullets, but that he doesn't have the stomach to cut their throats one by one with a knife. Anyway, a bullet to the head, Chinese-style, is clean and painless: a rather merciful end for these characters. He quickly carries out the job.

<<order, and order alone, is freedom; disorder is what causes servitude.

charles péguy

_notre patrie

/1905/

<<the struggle of man against power is the struggle of memory against forgetfulness.

milan kundera

the book of laughter and forgetting

/1979/

<<speak softly and carry a big stick; you will go far.

theodore roosevelt

/1858–1919/

The Social Bond

BEHOLD: YOUR SAB IS READY! You have thought of everything: you have the means of living autonomously and sustainably. And whoever approaches you better have peaceful intentions if he does not want to be blown to bits!

But this is not enough. You cannot survive alone.

Imagine the most hardened survivalist hidden in the underbrush deep within a forest. He can hunt, cultivate a garden, create hiding places for food, and be armed and trained like Rambo. He will survive … for a time. Then he will get old and sick, dying alone. It is true that he will have defied the system and sheltered himself from the violence of a collapsing world, but to what end?

Although we all die in the long run, what is the point of living if not to have the hope of something that is greater than ourselves, whether in the form of healthy and intelligent children leading a worthwhile life, or in the form of a strong, well-balanced civilization to which we have contributed, and which will carry a part of us into the future?

I admit that this is a personal and, some might say, masculine vision of life's purpose. Yet you will surely concede that man is a social animal, and that he prefers to think that he will leave something of himself to his posterity rather than mere food for worms.

More specifically and beyond philosophy, the question of the social bond occurs in two simple ways:

> What will happen if a group stronger than you comes to exact violence against you? There will always be someone more powerful and determined than you. In this case, how will you survive alone or isolated?

> Can you imagine a life forever cut off from the world for yourself or your family? This life will be quite sterile inasmuch as the rest of the world (even if reduced to a primitive state) contains resources you will need, people with knowledge useful to you who are kind, generous, and honorable. It is desirable and positive to build communication and relationships with such people in order to reconstruct, little by little, a balanced and just civilization.

I am convinced that everything you have done up to now — the first six fundamental principles of an SAB — amounts to nothing if you are not able to foster a community. The social bond is the seventh and final fundamental element of a successful SAB.

Who Should Be Your SAB Companions?

There seem to be two schools of survivalist and prepping thought: those who opt for solitude, and those who love communities. The solitary individuals prefer to disappear into the wilderness, live in their log cabins, and reconnect with nature. This is a conceivable solution, but you will have to go very far — to Canada, the Rocky Mountains, South America, the Sahara, or Siberia — because elsewhere the population density and urbanism will make this option difficult if not impossible.

As for the communal approach: we have seen it. We are no longer in the dream of '60s or '70s utopias. We are now quite far removed from being all about "peace and love"; nor are we a rich society capable of financing a group of idealists going off to California, Kathmandu, or the Larzac to raise goats and smoke hashish anymore. There is also strength in numbers: to be able to survive alone is fine, but a good system of defense and a variety of skills are more easily acquired by a group of people.

First, the question of the family arises. Whom will you take with you? *A priori*, you will bring your spouse, boyfriend or girlfriend, and your children. This part of your family surely knows about your project and will be prepared.

What about the rest of your family? Your parents: are they up to making the journey or even understanding your approach? Your brothers and sisters and their families? Your uncles and aunts? Your cousins? And if each additional person wants to bring his family along — his parents, his other cousins, uncles and aunts — what will you do? Then come your friends, colleagues and acquaintances, all imploring you to take them in! It's going to get crowded in your SAB — especially if you multiply this process by the number of friends with whom you have built your SAB project!

The only solution is to be cold and calculating. Beyond the persons emotionally indispensable to you, you must choose rationally on the basis of the usefulness and morality of the person. What useful abilities does this person have? How much work capacity? What mental power? Will he cry like a baby because nothing is as it was? Is he a good person? You must know how to take account of the advantages and disadvantages of each extra person. This will be a difficult decision, but you must be firm. It is better to make the choice during the process of setting up your SAB in order not to have to make it after chaos breaks out, when you find yourself faced with your great lout of a cousin — useless, stupid, and lazy — begging you to save him along with his whole unbearable family! All the more reason to be discreet about your preparations.

Once you have resolved the matter of your family, you must reflect on which of your friends you would like to convince to join your SAB.

This is difficult to do in advance, since most people do not have the slightest idea how severe the problems that we have described in the first part of this book are. Going to them to propose their participation in an SAB may, in the best case, make you look paranoid; in the worst, it may look like a recruitment attempt on the part of a cult!

In any case, draw up a list of the qualities you would like to find in the people you would feel comfortable having in your SAB: self-discipline, useful trades, sense of humor, work capacity, honesty, sincerity, a good heart, etc. It's up to you; there is no minimal list. I advise you also to draw up a list of unacceptable behavior and attitudes, whose presence in anyone will cause problems: extreme individualism, dishonesty, egotism, hypocrisy, uncontrollable addictions or compulsions, sadism, etc. Once these lists are complete, look to see who would be suitable both among your family and among your friends. Discreetly approach persons with innocent questions concerning what they think about this or that political or social event, and if their answers show a good understanding of the problems in today's world, probe further. Begin describing your project, and if they share your interest, propose that they take part in it.

If your SAB project is already underway, or you have already put it in place with established rules, it will be much easier to convince someone to join you.

If your SAB is still at the planning stage, you will get a lot of theoretical agreement and politeness but little action (whether financial contribution or labor). This is normal: there are so many everyday chores, and many people will likely find an eccentric project like an SAB to be strange and off-putting. The collective SAB approach is even more difficult. A good number of half-built SABs have been aborted or suffered great delays due to a lack of collective involvement. The majority of the population today is too individualistic and under day-to-day pressures to associate with such a project. They would prefer to join an existing project and subordinate themselves to it.

For this reason, you will need to develop leadership skills. Good leaders are those who take the initiative and have natural authority. They don't simply say what needs to be done, but do it: they set an example!

A good leader must understand human nature, whose fundamentals have not changed for thousands of years. We have looked at Maslow's hierarchy of needs; to this we may add that human beings always try to avoid pain, seek pleasure, protect those they love and follow those who promise to realize their dreams. "A leader is a merchant of hope," remarked Napoleon judiciously. It's up to you to become the kind of a leader who sets an example and naturally inspires respect and esteem. It is an act of love for others.

The Internal Workings of Your SAB

One question that often comes up is: how will an SAB function once there is a significant number of persons in it?

A society is necessarily a differentiated system. Besides the informal hierarchy of abilities and task specialization, there is also a formal hierarchy as a reference structure, without which a group falls apart. An SAB needs concrete, not abstract equality: it will be brought about by the rotation of tasks, and by all members participating in the common good and collective security.

In any case, rules are necessary, and the simplest way to adhere to them is to create statutes (as in a constitution), then legal codes and regulations, which all members of the SAB promise to obey scrupulously. It's not a matter of regimenting everything! I have come across written rules everywhere on certain sites that might be described as SABs, even in the bathrooms, where men are required to sit when they pee! This level of detail is unnecessary, but I think that two sets of rules are required: one for regular circumstances and another for crises. In this way, you have rules adapted to the level of risk, and which leave a large margin of personal responsibilities to the individual. If possible, apply the following principle, "Each person's freedom ends where another's begins."

If, under normal circumstances, a person on guard duty falls asleep on the job, the consequences for the group will be slight: perhaps a fox will steal a chicken. In times of chaos, this dereliction of duty may lead to much more serious consequences. This is why the regulations must include punishments: light for the less serious lapses, severe for more serious behavior or lapses. Let us take a concrete example: in your SAB, Claire is married to Laurent, the only veterinarian. Handsome, muscular François seduces her. Claire and François have a fling; Laurent finds out. Mad with rage, he seizes an axe and kills François. What do you do? Do you try and convict Laurent of murder? In this case, the sentence might be, for example, banishment. Or, perhaps, you do not condemn him because you need his skills next season when the animals give birth. But that amounts to saying crime is allowed if the murderer is indispensable. A delicate situation, isn't it? Let us complicate the situation further by imagining that François is not a member of the SAB but a woodcutter, the mayor's son from a nearby village. What law applies? That of your country, which no longer exists? That of the angry crowd in your SAB? Or that of the village?

This example illustrates the importance of careful forethought in order to establish a legal framework, including rituals, if possible, to daily life in your SAB. Rituals would serve to accept a new member, celebrate the seasons' passage, harvests, remembering important moments, traditional local festivities, etc. These functions are ensured in industrial societies through other means; in a collapse situation, you will gain a new appreciation for the necessity and usefulness of ritual, both practical and spiritual.

Once the legal framework has been put in place, you must define the functions of the members in your SAB. Keep it simple, but differentiate between various functions:

> The leader makes the final decisions. This leader can be natural (the SAB belongs to him) or elected according to the rules foreseen by your code, which allows you to name the most competent (or charismatic) and the most appropriate person (whether based on wisdom, intelligence, intuition, etc.) to make decisions, resolve conflicts, and carry out justice.

> An "overseer" manages the details of production and stocks for consumption.

> An adjutant, or "gunnery sergeant," sees to it that everyone carries out the tasks assigned to him with the necessary speed and discipline. The idea is that the SAB should run like a clock, and that "gunny" applies consistent pressure so that everything is done correctly, just like the character played by Louis Gosset Jr. in the 1982 movie *An Officer and a Gentleman*.

> Then, educators should organize the instruction of children and the transfer of as much knowledge as possible to all members of the SAB: mechanics, medicine, veterinary medicine, plants and gardens, weapons, cooking, etc. Everyone in an SAB can and should be an educator according to his or her skills.

Carefully manage envy in people's perception of preferences and privileges. (The adjutant can quickly get everyone to agree against him — that's his role in a way.)

Finally, it is possible that we may have to thoroughly reassess those social relations that we have learned over the past three generations. The collapse of the economy and the chaos which ensues will force us to reflect a great deal on this problem and try new ways of living together: simpler, more natural, and probably more spiritual.

In this context, I will quote the French historian and specialist of Africa, Bernard Lugan, who explains how a simple society functions:

How were preliterate populations able to live without money? It did not exist because there was no occasion for it to exist. Barter was how goods of the greatest necessity were regulated. There were neither social security, nor insurance, nor retirement pensions. One's offspring saw to the latter need, according to a principle of direct mutual assistance from generation to generation. Communities were close in their way of life or survival — to their earth, their water, their seed, their knowledge, and their know-how. They built their houses themselves with the help of their friends and neighbors. They also answered their immaterial and cultural needs. They

constituted not a social agglomeration resulting from migrations but a social body where each individual is in the place where he is useful to himself
and others. It is the power of the social bond which, without guaranteeing
ideal relations, abolished solitude. The individual was not identified by his
mere physical or moral reality, but as a soul in the strongest sense of the
term, as a future deceased with an immortal soul in a very concrete sense:
he will live on as an ancestor.

Relations with the Outside World

Within the framework of creating ties with the outside world, your
aim is twofold: to improve your chances of survival and to contribute
to reconstructing a healthy and lasting civilization. It is obvious that
an organized and motivated community has better chances of sticking
it out in all matters concerning survival than an isolated SAB or an
individual. Imagine an entire village, a valley organized for optimal
production of food and energy resources, with pooling of resources
and know-how (veterinarians, doctors, stonemasons, mechanics,
etc.), creating better defense and undertaking works for the common
good.

One might even hope that the SAB concept be applied to an entire
community, a neighborhood, a town, a region and — why not? — an
entire country. I sincerely believe that countries like Switzerland,
Norway, Sweden, Iceland, Finland, Japan, and even Chile could become super-SABs. This sort of community is already being established
on the scale of cooperatives, villages, and little towns. These are the
concepts of *Résilience communautaires* in France, *Transition Towns*,
Post-Carbon Cities and *Relocalisation Projects* in Canada, England, the
Netherlands and Sweden, or *Belastbare Gemeinden* in Germany.

The cells of an organism, the corals of a coral reef — like the individuals in a bankrupt company, family members confronted with
illness, death, poverty, or the members of a society in crisis, which
must face up to a war or a civil war — can sometimes adapt themselves spectacularly well to complexity by innovating or summoning
new resources. I think that true resilience is necessarily collective.

Individuals die or migrate, but their society and civilization (in the broad sense) can endure and largely restore itself after a crisis. You must transform your SAB into a link in a network of SABs.

Here is the process that will make the community around your SAB increasingly resilient; it begins at the bottom and works its way upward:

> Form your team or the working group of your SAB out of people who share your ideas and values. In the very least, this will mean you alone, and at most, as many persons as you can integrate.

> Install your SAB according to the seven fundamental principles of the SAB described in this book.

> Put a plan in place to create bonds with the communities around your SAB: neighbors, local authorities, villages, etc. Start in a very innocuous manner in order to avoid frightening or upsetting them. First, establish neighborly relations: a little present to announce your presence in the region, a visit to the mayors of the surrounding communities, use of local talents for work necessary to your SAB (ask the cabinetmaker to make you furniture, the mason to repair an old wall, buy food directly from the producer or from the cooperative on the corner). Identify the religions practiced, local beliefs, customs, traditions as well as their origin and significance. In all circumstances, be polite and friendly.

> Evaluate the population of the surrounding communities. How many inhabitants are there? How many refugees? How many are under fifteen years old? Do they all know how to read?

Is there any way of establishing a school to continue teaching the children and not leave them with nothing to do? How many births were there this year? How many deaths? What caused them? At what age did the deaths occur? What might have prevented them? Is the population size increasing or decreasing? What problems are caused by this development? How many people are struck with chronic illnesses? What illnesses? Are they contagious? Is there a quarantine system?

> Evaluate local nutrition. What is the basic foodstuff of the region? Is it adequate, and where does it come from? Is it healthy and proper for consumption? Is it polluted? Is there any excess, usable agricultural land? Is there enough free land for possible future distribution? Who are the large landowners? How is food stored? Is there waste, and why? How many children are poorly nourished (underfed or overfed)? Who smokes? Who is an alcoholic? Who uses drugs? What is the social impact of these practices (marital violence, theft, etc.)?

> Evaluate sanitary conditions. What is the state of human habitations? Are they houses, apartments, farms, villas? How good are the walls and floors of these habitations? Are they clean? What animals are allowed inside? What sanitary problems do they cause? Under what conditions is food stored? Is it protected from rodents and harmful insects? Is it protected from all forms of chemical contamination, toxins, and other pollutants? What illnesses, human and animal, are common in the region? Where does the water come from? What precautions are taken to ensure that the water is potable? How do toilets and any possible latrines function? How many people know how to use them correctly? Are they working? Where is waste and garbage consigned? Why that place?

> Evaluate health resources. Are there local doctors or midwives? What is their role? Are there traditional healers? What are the nearest medical centers or hospitals? Are they operational? Are there any shortcomings in the matter of vaccinations?

> In case of relationship turmoil, show sincere empathy; provide emotional support and treat people on equal terms. Behave humanely with the sick, even if nothing can be done. If necessary, help put an end to suffering in the most appropriate and respectful way possible.

> Then, evaluate how important the sense of belonging is to a community. Do the locals even have that sense? Are some people excluded; is there hostility toward a group, an ethnic or religious minority, or anyone at all? If so, why? What are the historic or current leaders of that community? Who are the richest and most notable? How are they treated (respect, mockery) and why?

> Participate in local politics and — why not? — become an elected representative. Make an effort to understand the needs felt in your region, i.e., what people consider to be their biggest problems. Then, try to understand their real needs. Is there anything available to resolve them? Is there a will to do so? Finally, try to understand the human, material, and financial resources available for doing what is necessary.

> Make an inventory of the abilities in your region. Which farmer is cultivating what? What animals are being bred? What local industries are there? What are the local sources of energy (hydroelectric plants, etc.)? What trade does each member of your community practice?

> Take care of people; they are valuable: a good bottle, a few vegetables from your garden, a meal... Maintain your bonds, but in a natural and unostentatious way.

> Work with the local authorities to understand their plans in case of a natural disaster and identify the persons responsible for security (police, firemen, etc.). Offer to help them as a volunteer, but also by contributing to improve plans and capabilities.

> Contact the organizations responsible for drinking water, water treatment, and electricity and take an interest in their emergency plans. Do they even have any?

> Work to establish a coherent plan of resilience in conformity with the means at your community's disposal, then get it put into action.

> Connect this resilient community with others, then others still...
  Little by little, you will have mobilized a large number of people
  and resources in order to increase the resilience of a small region.

> Finally, always respect the property of others. A "private property"
  or "do not enter" sign should be respected, or you risk serious
  trouble, especially in rural areas. Learn local customs, respect
  them and do not try to impose your own. Remember that if you
  are a city dweller in a rural area, you are almost as much a stranger
  as if you came from the other end of the world.

Establishing a social bond takes a lot of time and requires a lot of
observation, empathy and discretion (you don't just arrive with your
list of questions and interrogate each inhabitant!), but in the end, you
will have the information needed to help people. And when the crisis
sweeps away the world, the community in which you are integrated
and find your place will be grateful to you for having started so many
projects destined to strengthen and protect them. You will have transformed them into a Sustainable Autonomous Base!

Then, one might imagine your region developing thanks to the installation of security, following Maslow's hierarchy: first food security
(food can be obtained in your region), then physical security (there
is no violence, thanks to locally raised militia), then self-accomplish-
ment (you can educate your children, work or participate in a common project). You can conduct business (barter and trade, etc.)... If
you succeed in doing that much, you will really have contributed to
humanity!

I believe you will discover in the process of creating social bonds
that communal solidarity founded on work as the creator of the
common good brings much greater and lasting satisfaction than
the ephemeral satisfaction of individualist consumerism. You will
discover the emotional advantages brought by a sense of community,
personal autonomy, the satisfaction of honest labor well performed,

intergenerational solidarity, cooperation, contact with nature, and
even happiness.

Race and Racism

Sadly, history is replete with misfortunes caused by racial hatred and
resentment. You must make sure that racism never rears its ugly head
in your SAB. Don't get me wrong. It's not that we are all equal — we
aren't. And without question, most people are simply more comfortable around people like them (whether they admit it or not). But what
is racism and where does it come from? We should remember that our
differences are so varied that there exists no simple hierarchy between
races. Is this race "superior" to that one? This raises the question, *in
what?* Moreover, no people has ever invented "self-racism"; surprise,
surprise, the "chosen people" always happen to be ourselves! In antiq-
uity and the Middle Ages, the slave was a member of the lowest social
class, but not a racial class: the vanquished became a slave, but he
could buy back his freedom under certain conditions. Whatever one
might think about the scientific validity of race, the fact is that the enslavement of African populations, first by Arabs and then Europeans,
as well as the ethno-nationalism and chauvinism of the two World
Wars, have all left a bitter taste in the West's mouth. For the last forty
years, it has been fashionable to point the finger at White people as
uniquely exploitative; but "racism," in the sense of a wish to dominate
or exterminate other peoples, no longer exists in Europe or the United
States, apart, perhaps, from a tiny minority of persons.

Alas, it is possible that racism of this sort will return in force due to
several factors. Certain maleficent groups have been able to instru-
mentalize public resentment for imaginary or exaggerated crimes
in order to create scapegoats. And the so-called liberals and multi-
culturalists, too, have contributed to racial resentment. The policies
of mass immigration, associated with an expressed preference for
institutionalized miscegenation, could effectively destroy all cultures
by rendering them uniform. Moreover, in uprooting and acculturat-
ing individuals, the ancestral wisdom of nations is being suppressed.

All of this risks recreating racist movements — first against Western populations, then as a White-European-American reaction against the populations of the Global South that have been implanted into the North on a mass scale. If one wanted to create the conditions for future civil wars, one could hardly have done a better job!

Now, of course, racism is quite unpleasant and offensive to modern man. We don't like judging people by *a prioris*, that is, things they cannot change. And in terms of analysis, sometimes race can whitewash more consequential differences: an Irishman and an Englishman, or a Ukrainian and a Pole at times hardly get along despite the fact that they are all White! And what will you say about a Fulani, a Fang, an Ashanti, a Baoulé, a Kikuyu and a Xhosa? That they are alike because they are all Black? This is both absurd and insulting! In many cases, culture, climate, environment, history and, above all, individual character can trump race.

The question that interests us within the framework of an SAB is not so much philosophical as *practical*. Are you increasing the risk of internal conflict because of racial selection? Are you depriving yourself of talents and abilities? Although the question of identity is fundamental, I encourage you to still consider each person with regard to the qualities and defects intrinsic to his individual character.

In general, you must be careful not to acquire a "siege mentality." Be mistrustful, defend and protect yourself, yes! But remain open-minded and know how to communicate, share information, understand what is going on beyond your own thought horizon. Know how to be generous and charitable by stocking food and essential objects (bars of soap, medicines, preserves), which you can give to refugees or people in need.

If you are a stranger to a community, it's up to you to make the maximum effort to integrate yourself into it and better assimilate yourself to it (it should be this way all the time anyway!). It is possible they will require you to prove your new allegiance and go through difficult rites of passage. Especially at the beginning, you must prove that you are worthy of confidence and capable of being a member of the group. For this purpose, you should leave behind certain notions about individualism and your own culture. However, it can be useful not to abandon your culture of origin totally, for every culture has some good and useful things and acts as a vehicle for wisdom. These are elements that will bring renewal and richness to the host culture.

Communication with the Outside World

When the world economy is in complete chaos, it is probable that the means of communication will suffer a significant breakdown. Is the infrastructure behind the telephone or internet going to be able to hold out very long? It may be that this is not important to you if you wish to remain isolated in your SAB. However, it is useful and even essential to remain in touch with what is going on in the world. It would be prudent to avoid resembling that Japanese soldier who remained hidden in the jungle on a tiny pacific island for twenty years, not knowing the war was over! More pragmatically, news from the outside world will inform you about possible dangers (nuclear or chemical accidents, pollution, natural disasters, wars, etc.); above all, it will be necessary to communicate with other SABs and other communities in order to form connections, gather intelligence, organize trade, ask for help, and work on reconstruction.

Plan on having several systems of communication in your SAB: first of all internal systems (which saves members from having to yell in order to call other members!), then external systems connected to nearby and more distant communities.

For internal communication, you can opt for very simple solutions such as installing an *ad hoc* LAN (local area network) that will allow you to communicate via Wi-Fi over a moderate distance with computers and telephones. The range can extend up to several hundred meters if you add a few relays. The only problem with this system is that a wireless network can easily be detected by anyone with a modern telephone (with a standard 802.11n receiver). Another simple solution is ultra-high frequency (UHF) walkie-talkies; modern models are hardly larger than a microphone- equipped headset. If you have enough rechargeable batteries, this system is excellent for tactical communication, and its range can extend up to five km (three miles). The field telephone, a product of military technology, is a little more powerful and allows radio communication of up to fifteen or twenty km (nine to twelve miles). You will have to stock a very large number of rechargeable batteries and, ideally, a portable solar charger in order to recharge the batteries directly in an observation post or during a reconnaissance mission.

For communicating over longer distances, the CB (citizens' band) is a frequency band allotted to radio traffic and open to everyone. (By extension, the word CB also designates broadcasters on the citizens' band; users are called CB-ers.) The frequencies used by CB are around 27 MHz. Anyone, without passing an examination or having any license, can buy a CB broadcaster-receiver, hook it up to an antenna, and receive and send signals. Conversations are described as "public," because anyone tuned in to that frequency can receive them. To communicate discreetly you must use coded or encrypted language. There are many internet sites that discuss radio and other communication; it can be worth the trouble to consult them and get a better idea of your exact equipment needs. Whatever communication equipment you choose, do not forget that you will need electrical energy (and detachable pieces) for everything to work. Figure these needs into your energy calculations, and figure on a lot — including plenty of rechargeable batteries.

So now you have mastered, in a theoretical fashion, the seven fundamental principles of an SAB, and what you must do to assure yourself a great deal more than survival. Whoever you are today, rich or poor, at the top or bottom of the social ladder, you will have the chance to start again at zero, and can do so in such a way as to count for something, or even take a leading role in the reconstruction of tomorrow's world.

Times are hard at the "Francillière," but morale is good.

The association's success has caused many motivated people sharing the same convictions to become voluntary exiles in the household. The first winter was difficult, with a lot of people sick and a stock of food that ran out much faster than anticipated. Everyone just hopes that the harvest will be good at the beginning of spring. All healthy persons are contributing to woodcutting, to enlarging the vegetable garden, and to sowing what can be sown. Relations with the nearby village and farmers are good, although a large number of refugees is starting to present a problem. Fortunately, a group of gendarmes—now without any hierarchy—has taken up position in the village, and is maintaining order within a radius of several kilometers. Since there is no gasoline available, they go on patrol on foot or horseback.

One day, when snow was falling heavily, a group of Senegalese refugees approached, fleeing a burning nearby town. They asked to be allowed to stay. They were exhausted and wanted a bit of food. It was not possible to feed these fifty extra persons permanently. An inventory was made of their professions. A vote was taken to accept Mamadou and his family, because he is a doctor. The vote barely passed. On the condition that Mamadou and his family accept the rules of the community, they can stay. Mamadou weeps tears of joy for himself, his wife, and their four children. It was a good decision: that spring, two cases of appendicitis were diagnosed and successfully operated. The other refugees, having no useful abilities, had to be on their way, and were escorted the next day to the edge of the SAB's territory, not without having benefited from a night of warmth, supper, and even a few rations. Perhaps another village further on can do something for them.

David and Rebecca have finally stopped running.

They had fled the U.S. for France following mass expulsions due to the war. They would have gladly opted for the U.K., but they are no longer accepting refugees, since that country does not even have the capacity to feed its own people. It is being ravaged by a civil war. After spending a year in a refugee center and being lucky enough to escape the pogroms of last September, thanks to the help from local farmers and fleeing through the countryside, they were finally received into an Islamic SAB on the border between France and Belgium. This communitarian SAB is well-organized, has enough food and good medical care at its disposal thanks to flourishing trade under the protection of the Emir of Lille and his militia (originally financed by Saudi Arabia). David and Rebecca were accepted following the principles of hospitality dictated by Sharia. They were allowed to stay if they agreed to convert to Islam. They didn't have to, but it was that or the road. It appears that Germany is doing alright thanks to Romanian oil, but that the roads are not safe. Moreover, the winter is approaching. They decided quickly: David is now called Daoud. A former Wall Street trader, he now cleans the latrines. Rebecca, now known as Rafqa, cleans the linens by the canal. They are happy to be alive.

Colonel Yonni needs to talk to the new recruits of the militia that has now grouped in the square.

Most are from central Tel Aviv, but some walked as far as Petah Tikva. They are young, mostly boys and girls between the ages of sixteen and eighteen, but there are some old men as well as commanding officers. In total, this year's "Kfir" militia under the responsibility of Col. Yonni—former Sayaret Golani and war hero—is about 2,000 men and women; they're ready for training before being sent to various commands across the country. The training was hard and painful, and Yonni wished he had more ammunition available for the fire drills. But he had to make do with what he could get his hands on. Motivation was high, however, and there were very few cases of dropping out—some recruits even lied about their medical conditions…

The situation is tough. Now a decade past the big collapse, Israel is struggling.

Sure, there were many high-tech weapons at first; sure, no one dared to attack across the border. Sure, there was a plan to withdraw from the most exposed parts of the occupied territories in the West Bank. Sure, it was painful to close the border to any immigration, including the Jews living abroad. The images of the massacres still resonated in the nation's collective memory, but that sacrifice had to be made: the country could not feed everyone. Sure, Israel did not suffer as much as other countries, but the situation was still difficult.

At first, the lack of petrol and spare parts was dire as the country's heavy reliance on motor transport and lack of railways caused very serious logistical problems. Surrounded by enemies, Israel could only survive by becoming completely autonomous—for water, agriculture, defense, and energy. That it succeeded without too much chaos was proof positive of the country's successful social cohesion, despite the usual "crazies" and their aggressive millenarian actions. Blowing up the Dome of the Rock mosque was not a smart move as this sparked a war with the country's neighbors as well as massive revolts from the Palestinian and Israeli Arab Muslims. They were managed harshly but fairly … and quickly had to choose: fit in, or fuck off into the Gaza-Negev-Sinai radioactive wastelands. The choice was quick.

No, Col. Yonni muses, as he finishes writing his speech, Israel was no place for individualism. Israel was where people, in their totality and with a common cause, succeeded in keeping the dream of their grandfathers alive. Hard work brought self-sufficiency in food and water; Israel is where we were able to maintain basic medical and bicycle factories; small-arms ammunition could be manufactured; and we generated electrical power for hospitals and other important matters. A small fleet of warships kept the coastline safe from the hordes of pirates that infested the Mediterranean. We kept trade open.

Times are tough, but we will live! Col. Yonni yells to the recruits to close his speech, amidst a roar of applause and cheering.

Wilhelm has taken in a lot of people at his farm over the last year.

To lodge refugees from large cities, he linked up with the neighboring farms and established an efficient network to supply food. In order to be fed and lodged, each refugee must agree to work and respect the few simple, collectively determined rules. There were a lot of people who did not, especially at the beginning. Between thefts and fist fights, many were banished. The few who tried to return in order to pilfer were received with blasts of buckshot or were beaten to death by others. This is because food is precious in these difficult times, and not everyone gets enough every day. Overall, they are pulling through. A group of doctors has organized a permanent station on one of the farms. A barter system has been put in place for trading fruit, vegetables, etc., and no one is dying of hunger. Recently, Wilhelm has received two new recruits on his farm, a young man named Henry, visibly battle-hardened but a good negotiator, and François-Xavier and his family. The latter was able to repair an old radio post that a neighboring farm had had since the 1960s, and was able to start communicating with other groups of survivors—some self-proclaimed SABs, others refugees, still others retired and semi-retired people—and the situation no longer seems so desperate. In fact, he discovers that even in large cities, neighborhoods are self-organizing and gradually beginning to restore order in spite of the difficult sanitation situation. He already had reasonably good contacts with the Emirate of Lille before it imploded from internal rivalries. The other day, one of his most recent radio interlocutors, Maurizio, explained to him that he is located in a town that is not doing too bad thanks to the trade which has developed along a river. Another SAB, the one whose leader is named Nicholas, has visibly extended its influence by having organized a large valley into an effective defensive system; agricultural production has generated a surplus that is distributed to other valleys and communities to help get them back on their feet. This region seems to have good contacts with Switzerland, which has been almost entirely able to preserve its territorial integrity, and which, like Norway, is working to organize itself so as to produce surpluses to help other regions get through the hard times. Solidarity between regions and groups of persons who have succeeded best is being created. Soon, messengers, chosen from among the most battle-hardened, are sent out in order to seal alliances between these groups and regions. Little by little, civilization is being reconstructed on the ruins. Although at least sixty percent of the world population has died in less than two years, hope remains.

<<when the weapons fall silent, their sound is replaced by the lamentations of the dead, relayed by the sighs of the living.

moses isegawa

writer

_abyssinian chronicles

/1998/

<<everybody knows that the dice are loaded everybody rolls with their fingers crossed everybody knows that the war is over everybody knows that the good guys lost everybody knows that the fight was fixed the poor stay poor, the rich get rich

that's how it goes.

leonard cohen

_everybody knows

/1988/

Where to Install an SAB

YOU ARE ALMOST READY. You have absorbed each of the seven fundamental principles essential to setting up an SAB. Your first — most important — decision was to take your own future into your hands and choose to *survive*. Now it is time to make your second decision, which will have a significant impact on the next few years of your life: you must decide on a place to install your SAB.

Having read this book up to now, you probably already have certain ideas. By simple logic, you can deduce what places are the best or least suited. You also know that a good place for an SAB cannot be chosen randomly on a map.

If, as we have defined it, an SAB is a place where one can live safely and soundly, it is not a matter of fleeing to a cabin in the woods. Instead, it is about finding an autonomous location, removed from as many dangers as possible, easy to defend, and with adequate organization and comfort: a place you like, and one that corresponds to your real needs. First, you must imagine it as a castle or monastery: a place of survival, but also one where you can live well. In my view, there are four possibilities for locating your SAB: the mobile SAB, the rural SAB, the urban SAB, and the off-shored SAB.

The Mobile SAB

Mobility, of course, means not having a fixed location, which offers greater ability to flee danger. Adventure-loving persons who concentrate on individualism often speak of this solution. But something that might be very nice on your vacation may no longer be so in a time of crisis.

The first serious problem with a mobile SAB is that you only have what you can take with you and transport on your motorbike, car, camper, barge, sail- or houseboat. Furthermore, there is a possibility of ambush as soon as you run out of gas, or if the road or stream is blocked. What will you do then? You will be forced to stop and remain immobile, except that there won't be the advantage of having chosen the spot, or of having stocked what you need to survive for long.

A variation on the theme of the mobile SAB is that of the "100-percent survivalist," a person used to camping and hiking, who is thinking of setting off into nature alone or with his family, with his backpack, hunting rifle, tent, survival guide, and bushcraft skills. Unless you have vast experience in this field, this is an approach that can turn into a total disaster from the lack of adequate shelter, ammunition, an unbalanced diet (essentially, game), few ways of taking care of oneself in case of accidents, etc. Too many things could go wrong, and there is no plan B if and when they do. Moreover, imagine the number of city dwellers who love to go camping, and will have the same idea as you: it could get crowded!

On the other hand, it is possible that having a sailboat or another kind of boat moored close to an SAB at a fixed seaside or riverside location could be a good means of transport, fishing, or, in the worst case scenario, a good means of flight. One might well imagine an SAB installed on a moored boat or barge, or, indeed, of having caches of food supplies along a coast or riverbank. Yet this remains an imperfect solution. If, however, you love the sea and choose to install an SAB on your boat or sailing vessel, you must consider the following points:

> In case of crisis, do not remain moored in a port. You do not know whether the authorities might try to prevent anyone from leaving. And remaining stuck in the port of a town may prove dangerous. It is better to hoist the sails early.

> A boat at sea, operated by an experienced sailor, can be a good initial solution for avoiding the most difficult moments of a crisis, and your mobility will give you the opportunity to head to a calm area not yet touched by turbulent events. Your capacity for autonomy would be determined by your water and food supplies. So, you would need a rather large and spacious boat in order to have sufficient storage capacity. Stock at least two months' worth of food. Also, invest in a small wind-turbine-driven or photovoltaic seawater-purification system. Thus, you will not have to stock months' worth of fresh water. But have a large reservoir anyway, in case your system breaks down.

> You must be able to rely on the sea worthiness of your boat easily, especially the hull. You may strike an object (tree trunk, whale) and have to repair it as quickly as possible with the means on board, or in dry dock. It will be much easier to repair a wooden or metal boat rather than one made out of advanced polymers (which require highly specialized tools). Think in terms of durability.

> Plan on having several maps, since a GPS navigation system cannot function without satellites, the lifespan of which you cannot control. Besides maps, learn to navigate as the great navigators of history did: without instruments, or only with basic instruments (sextant, compass, etc.).

> Make sure your boat can navigate in shallow water, for example, in the mouth of a river, so as to be able to conceal it. In order to do this, the keel must be removable. For greater discretion, a quiet motor offers an advantage.

> Equip your boat with a large fuel reserve, a good CB radio, and a high-frequency receiver.

> Reflect carefully on the equipment necessary to protect your naval SAB in case of a pirate attack. Can your boat flee quickly? Plan on having powerful high-caliber arms, which have a long range, and are able to pierce the hull of a light vessel and frighten thugs

(a .338-caliber Lapua Magnum rifle is perfect for this, despite the high cost of its ammunition). Do not underestimate piracy, and forget about characters in 17th-century "Jack Sparrow" costumes. There will be many pirates. Most fishermen will gladly convert quickly, in the Somali or Indonesian style. Do not underestimate the former naval forces of Third World countries (or rich countries), because these will also need to feed their crews. In all cases, distrust the night — the perfect time for attacks. Finally, plan your mooring point carefully.

> Remember to take many replacement parts with you for everything (motors, turbines, equipment, radios, GPS, etc.).

The Rural SAB

The best possible choice, in my opinion, is to install an SAB in a rural environment and take root there (literally and figuratively). The first and most important criterion in choosing a place for a rural SAB is good soil. To determine if the soil is good, you must gather information from local farmers and verify that the soil is not poor or arid. Look for yourself to see whether there is erosion, and how water drains out of it. Run a little water into the soil: if the soil soaks it up like a sponge, it is better than if it runs off in a stream. Also, determine what plants grow there: if there are a lot of fir trees, for instance, this is because the soil is acidic and weaker than that which houses maples; the latter prefer balanced soils, which are better for agriculture.

It's often useful to study pre-20th-century religious buildings in the nearest town, often a church, mosque, or temple. A small church, for example, may mean that the region is traditionally poor, and, therefore, that its agriculture is sub-par. A large, opulent church with a lot of ornamentation and decoration could be the sign of a traditionally rich community, and thus one with good soil.

Between two farmers with the same surface area to cultivate, the same tools, and the same amount of work, if one does better than the other, it is probably due to the quality of the soil. This method is not infallible, but it's a good indicator. After all, before the Industrial Revolution, rural wealth came exclusively from the land. Good soil will be located near springs, and will be productive. Spring water or aquifers must be abundant.

In the future (as in the past), good land will not be sold, not even for gold — what will you do with gold if you have no place to live? Remember that all wealth originally comes from the nourishing earth. In the same vein, also study the climate and precipitation. If possible, avoid areas where the winter is too long. Prefer regions with regular and abundant rainfall.

Carefully observe regions known for having particular microclimates, because this determines what can grow there, which animals are best adapted, etc. If possible, avoid zones that need a lot of irrigation or that do not have enough water available. Carefully observe the vegetation growing in areas that are not irrigated: if it is green and dense, this is a good sign; if it is dry and sparse, this indicates a lack of water. Always keep in mind that although one can make deserts flourish with technology, fertilizers, electricity, and water, as soon as the industrial system crashes, nature will reassume its normal state: the areas that will pull through best are those with rich soils and sufficient water. Also do extensive research on the natural disasters most common and possible in the region: what risk is there of earthquakes, hurricanes, storms, tornados, floods, landslides, avalanches, tidal waves, forest fires, etc.?

When choosing a rural location, look to see if the nearest community is resilient. A good indicator is the presence of agricultural cooperatives, and whether festivals and fairs are organized. These are signs of a population with a communal spirit that wants to keep its traditions alive. If you can, analyze or observe the age distribution in the region. If it is varied (i.e., if there are both the young and the old), and if there is a mix of rural professions, this is also an excellent sign.

Look to see if women have gardens. If so, then that is also worth noting. After all, it shows that there will be know-how and a tradition of subsistence cultivation, which areas of intensive monoculture will scarcely have. Agricultural production should be more than sufficient for the whole community and easily generate a surplus. Also, verify that the population density is not too low, especially if you plan on establishing yourself with young children in your SAB. They will need friends to play with and develop. Gather information on whether the surrounding communities have electrical generators (wind, little hydro-electric centers, etc.). This is an important advantage. Look whether the religious fervor is not too strong or extreme. In times of crisis, it may be exacerbated. Avoid finding yourself in a community of religious fanatics!

It is better to choose a region with low population density: a village will be better than a town, and a small town nearby is preferable to a large urban center. Evaluate the area carefully: a rural zone close to a large urban center is not necessarily more secure than the city itself. In case of complete economic collapse, it is possible that refugees will march for several days in search of food. So avoid being within 90 miles of any large urban center, especially the great metropolises (London, L.A., Chicago, New York, Washington DC, Atlanta, Miami, Paris, etc.), which are the most dangerous places. Avoid spots too close to prisons or asylums for the mentally incapacitated. These institutions may not be able to resist budget cuts, and it is imaginable that in cases where the inmates are not killed by their guards, they will simply be let go without any other resource than pillaging the region, alone or in bands.

Also be careful with the great motorways between cities. For example, the L.A.-San Diego, Boston-New York-Baltimore-Washington DC, London-Coventry-Birmingham-Liverpool, Brussels-Antwerp-Rotterdam-Amsterdam, Frankfurt-Köln-Düsseldorf, Paris-Lyon-Marseille, Tokyo-Kanagawa-Nagoya-Osaka, Hong-Kong-Shenzen-Guangzhou, Shanghai-Nanjing, Seoul-Busan, Madrid-Zaragoza-Barcelona,

Milano-Brescia-Verona-Vicenza, and Vienna-Budapest-Belgrade-So-
fia-Plovdiv-Edirne-Istanbul-Ankara axes may be taken by many urban dwellers fleeing the cities. These "refugee migrations" should be
avoided, since you are at risk of being submerged under thousands of
famished people whom you cannot feed, and who will quickly become
unmanageable and possibly hostile.

It is possible that the government (or what remains of it) could
expropriate your farm or house to convert it into a refugee center, thus
making you a refugee yourself! If this happens, it will mostly be in areas bordering cities, and not in more remote territories. These will be
spared because they are not served by the great highways, or because
they are difficult to access. If you are unable to live far from a city, at
least plan on choosing a less visible spot that would not be obvious to
a refugee or looter. If you choose to make your SAB a second home,
think about its accessibility in times of crisis. Will you still be able to
cross borders? Will you be up to making the trip with a full tank and
a few extra jerrycans? If the price of gas increases greatly, can you still
have the means of getting there often?

Above all, avoid installing your SAB in vacation centers known for
catering to the wealthy, because they will be one of the first targets for
looters. Avoid areas too close to chemical plants and nuclear reactors.
(This is getting increasingly difficult, since the number of reactors
is significant: 101 [+11 planned] in the U.S., 58+2 in France, 33+27 in
Russia, 15+76(!) in China, 20+25 in India, 23+9 in South Korea, 55+13
in Japan, 7 in Belgium, 5 in Switzerland, 8 in Spain, 16+4 in the U.K., 9
in Germany, 18 in Canada.) Also try not to be too close or downwind
from potential nuclear-weapons targets, such as large military bases
(e.g., the U.S. Ramstein Air Base, Germany, etc.). Another criterion,
of legal nature, is that it might be worthwhile to establish an SAB so
as to benefit from agricultural subsidies or low taxes. An even more
agreeable situation is a region where the government is not too curi-
ous or intrusive, and where the laws about hunting and firearms are
minimal.

Once you have considered these numerous criteria, it is up to you to make a list and decide on their level of importance. After all, you must compare the level of risk with the advantages or inconveniences of a plot of land, a house, a farm, or a castle that you are sizing up for constructing or installing an SAB.

The good news for all of us is that in our days, rural regions ideal for an SAB are often not very expensive places. Because of the rural exodus and consequent low population density, land prices in rural areas are quite affordable in comparison to cities, especially if you avoid fashionable spots. Selling an apartment in town, even a small one, can allow you to buy a very large property in the countryside. You can purchase entire villages for the price of a villa — but hurry before millions of people read this book!

Many other criteria enter into one's individual choice of land and property. We may note style, age, type of construction materials, whether a new building must be erected, or an existing one renovated, if someone is living on the property as a renter, whether you want to keep the renters or not, etc. It is impossible to list all the criteria exhaustively. Then there are questions of the heart: do you love the place? Would you like to go there a lot? To live there most of the year? In my experience, this emotional factor is also among the most important, for better or for worse!

The advantages of a rural SAB are numerous: more space for gardening, livestock breeding, the possibility of springs or freshwater wells, relatively low costs, better adapted in case of total economic and social collapse, better storage, an easier place to defend, lower risks from epidemics, less violence and fewer refugees.

The disadvantages are that rural life is difficult, and that effective defense of a large property demands organization and a suitable number of inhabitants. Relative isolation makes all transportation and trade more difficult.

The Urban SAB

Installing your SAB in town may make sense if you do not have the time or the means to install one in a rural area.

Cities have a lot of advantages: a dense environment with a number of important services and access to transportation infrastructure and efficient supply chains. This is exactly what hundreds of thousands of your neighbors depend on. And it is this system which runs the greatest risk in a major crisis or economic collapse.

Of course, if the economic collapse takes the form of an extended crisis and progressive deterioration, it is imaginable that a city could adapt by transforming parks and other green spaces into agricultural fields, like Switzerland and England did during WW2, and by organizing local militia to guarantee order and security, by putting in place local energy production, by organizing the efficient functioning of sewers, and the provisioning of drinking water, and also by putting in place programs of gradual reduction or limitation of the urban population.

The advantage of a city is that, *a priori*, you already know your neighbors and neighborhood. You are part of the community, you will have access to markets that spontaneously spring up for barter, etc. And it is in a city that one finds the greatest density of doctors and medical personnel.

But a city involves great disadvantages. Empty land is scarce. Thus there are limits as to what you can cultivate, and the amount of water and food you can store (in a basement, garage, or attic). Above all, cities will have to face massive sanitation problems. The risk of social disorder is also quite substantial. If the latter occurs, the law of the state will certainly be replaced by that of the strongest. These will be gangs, social riffraff becoming "big shots," surrounded by large-scale banditry, or even the state transforming into a mafia. If you have cultivated your roof, garden, balcony, or if you raise animals, these outlaws may find out. It will be hard to go unnoticed as someone who is prepared for the crisis, at which point you will become their prime target.

If you still want to install your SAB in an urban environment, you would be better off choosing a medium-sized town rather than a megalopolis, and it will be even better if the town possesses large parks, if it is crossed by a river, if there is a hydro-electric station nearby, if it contains one or several large hospitals, and has no dangerous ghettos.

If you have transformed your suburban house into an SAB, it is better for it to be the last address on a dead-end street, and for your vegetable garden not to be visually prominent (bushes will be useful for hiding it). Ideally, an urban SAB can be an entire block, with all inhabitants taking part in the project. A squat property can become an effective SAB if the "renters" agree to maximize their ability to live autonomously and organize the neighborhood around them for food production, water purification, waste disposal, the installation of an emergency medical dispensary, the generation of a little electricity, and the organization of defense. A neighborhood system and community, organized around shared objectives accepted by all, can succeed as well as a neighborhood organized and motivated hierarchically. It's up to you to find the organization and social bond adequate for an SAB to have a high enough quality of life. I develop how to set up an urban SAB in my second book *Rues Barbares* (*Barbarian Streets*), co-authored with Franco-American survivalist Vol West.

The Off-Shored SAB

You also have the option (using the same criteria of choice as for a mobile, rural, or urban SAB) to carry out your project in a country you think should be sheltered from serious troubles, or which, in your opinion, might not be affected. This is a delicate decision, for the choice of a country depends on what scenarios you think possible and probable. Asia, for example, seems to be a high-growth area, and to have a better future than Europe. But who can say whether tomorrow, under the pressure of a serious crisis, foreigners will not be expelled, and their property confiscated? For relatively low sums of money, you can acquire a lot of land in South America or in Africa, but who can guarantee you from ending up a victim of social revolts or ethnic cleansing as a "rich foreigner?" Even if you apply all the principles for installing an SAB, the greatest difficulty will be establishing strong social ties as a foreigner in another country: both on the local level (which you can influence) and on the geostrategic level (which you cannot influence).

It's up to you, but I do not advise emigration to any place where the culture, race, or ethnic groups are too distant from your own. To remind you of an old and wise Piedmontese saying of my grandfather's, "*Donne e buoi, dei paesi tuoi*" (choose wives and cattle from your own country).

Larry is very rich.

Not just very rich, but filthy rich. Since his passion is the ocean, he transformed his yacht, *Setting Sun*, into an SAB: a luxury SAB that can do twenty-eight knots! At least, for as long as there is gasoline… Larry's yacht is not a boat for your ordinary millionaire:

453 feet long, eighty-two cabins on five floors, jacuzzis that operate from large cisterns that collect and filter rainwater, a sauna, a gym, a wine cellar, a private movie theater, a basketball court (that can also serve as a helipad). Solar panels that furnish four hundred kWh of electrical energy, which is also used to pump and desalinate seawater. The crew is composed of thirty people, and Larry has employed a security team of five former Marines. When the crisis broke out, Larry was with a few friends on the Côte d'Azur. He cast off and decided to return to the U.S. by sea. His investment in a security team was rewarded when he had to repel an attack of Moroccan pirates off Gibraltar. He turned about and decided to set sail for a Greek island belonging to one of his friends. The *Setting Sun* finished its short cruise by being boarded and confiscated by the navy of the young Neapolitan Republic. Larry and his friends had to live in rather difficult circumstances for several years in an old apartment in Naples, suffering the jeers of the local urchins. Larry came out of it well, all considered. His billionaire friends who stayed in St. Tropez were captured, while they were attempting to get to the Nice Airport in a limousine convoy, by a hoard of famished unemployed men. The sight of their corpses hanging from the street lamps and eaten by birds is said to have been terrifying.

Florent has been elected as a one-year official of his SAB in the Vosges.

Everything has changed since the global economy followed that of the U.S. into the greatest depression of all time. Nothing functions as before: there is no work, especially in the cities, and the population revolted in the middle of winter following a cut-off of Russian and African natural gas. The governments, whose priority was paying back interest on their debt, could no longer pay the gas bills. The revolts caused serious malfunctions of infrastructure. Certain towns no longer have running water. Electricity blackouts are getting more common. The provisional Communist revolutionary governments do not control much, and most of Europe has plunged into great confusion. Fortunately, there has not been much violence and, to general surprise, immigrant populations have joined together rather fraternally with the European populations in a common struggle against big capital. Representatives have long since taken to their heels. However, because the world's currencies are no longer worth anything, they will not get far.

One morning, Florent receives an urgent radio appeal from a friendly German SAB in the Black Forest. It seems there has been an accident at the Fessenheim nuclear power plant, and that one or several reactors have exploded. (Later on, they learned that the revolutionary council in charge of energy, in their haste to bring the grid back up to please the masses, did not listen to the advice of the engineers, who recommended a shutdown and inspection…). In the course of the day, the Geiger counters show a rapid rise in radioactivity. Everyone must quickly go inside, and the building needs to be made as close to impenetrable as possible. All windows and shutters are closed and weather-stripped with industrial tape (also keyholes, joints, ventilation ducts, etc.). A long wait follows, which ends three days later with the arrival of rain. When the rain passes, the puddles show rather high levels of radioactivity, but it seems that the house was essentially spared. How will the harvest turn out? How long before they can expect to receive trustworthy news? How many additional sick people will there be because of this event? Florent realizes just how great his responsibilities are.

<<it wasn't raining when Noah built the ark.

howard ruff

investor

/2008/

<<this is your life, and it's ending one minute at a time.

chuck palahniuk

writer

_fight club

/1996/

PART IV

PREPARING ONESELF

<<luck is when preparation meets opportunity.

pierre e. trudeau

politician

/1919–2000/

<<this is your last chance. after this, there is no turning back. you take the blue pill—the story ends, you wake up in your bed and believe whatever you want to believe. you take the red pill—you stay in wonderland, and I show you how deep the rabbit hole goes. remember … all i'm offering you is the truth, nothing more.

morpheus

_the matrix

/1999/

<<fear is like fire. you can make it work for you: it can warm you in the winter, cook your food when you're hungry, give you light when you are in the dark, and produce energy. let it go out of control, and it can hurt you, even kill you.

cus d'amato

boxing trainer

//1908–1985//

<<the rigid man is a disciple of death. the intelligent, supple man is loved by life.

laozi

philosopher

//6th century BC//

How to Prepare Yourself

THE IDEAL PREPARATION for the economic collapse is living full-time in your SAB. For most people, this is impossible because of urban habits, employment, etc.

If you are stuck in a large city and must leave for your SAB suddenly, it is clear that you must stock most of your supplies in it in advance. Other than false alarms, you will only have one chance to travel to your SAB. In fact, in this world of real-time news on television, blogs, and social networks, the panic effect can occur quite quickly. Shops and supermarkets could be empty in a few hours, and the roads will be quickly filled with out-of-gas refugees.

We have seen what level of alert allows you a timely and coordinated departure. In general, when D-Day comes, whatever you have is what you will have for good. This is why you must begin preparing now — later on, it will be too late.

Do you have time to prepare? The answer is that it is impossible to know, but that it is better to be even a little bit prepared than not prepared at all. Does preparation require a lot of work? The answer is: *yes!* All the more reason to get started right away. In fact, you will notice that even if you devote all your time and an unlimited budget, you will not be able to accelerate the preparations indefinitely. You must allow time to understand what is happening and what you must do. You will need time to educate yourself about the courses you have chosen. As I like to say: one woman can have a baby in nine months, but nine women cannot have a baby in one month.

There is no single pattern or ideal model for creating and organizing your SAB; each SAB is established as a function of the needs,
budget, constraints, and peculiarities of its creator(s). For instance,
one celebrated actor has invested 10 million dollars in a luxury bunker
to protect his family from the arrival of extraterrestrials! Little green
men or not, do not fall into the trap of excess comfort, for once you
get used to it, it becomes a need rather than a want. Many people say
to me that having a car is a necessity in an SAB. In reality, we have
constructed our lives around cars, which is part of the problem!

Financial Preparation

Money is the nerve of war, and you will need means to finance your
SAB project. You must also ensure that your savings and investments
are as safe-guarded as they possibly can be in the coming economic
tumult. Remember the chapter on the end of the financial system
and the destined collapse of paper money? If you figure in increasing
inflation, you can see that your savings could literally be reduced to
nothing. Financial analyst Pierre Laurent summarizes this situation
perfectly when he says, "Today, the only strategy that allows you to
preserve the value of your patrimony consists of investing in gold and
silver bullion, raw materials, energy, agricultural land, and all tangible
assets unconnected to the dollar and based outside the U.S." I should
add, "and unconnected to the euro, and the yen, and all other currencies that are created by their central banks without any real collateral!"

I would also add that in the near future, investors will flee the markets for real values. At any moment, we could see a panicked movement toward gold. Above all, avoid government debt. Finance is an
industry that is well adapted to periods of maximum credit and debt
expansion, which benefits (at least in the short term) the stock, bond,
and real-estate markets. But in the coming decade, people will seek
real value, and not assets backed by all sorts of dubious debtors. So
avoid stocks, bonds, and shares in general, especially those of banks
and financial firms. Also, stay away from mutual funds, hedge funds,
and everything that is not liquid — you must be able to withdraw your

assets rapidly if necessary. I also advise you against liquidities in the form of paper money or savings accounts that could be lost when the bank goes under.

Here are some principles for building a sound financial legacy in an age of crisis:

> Save as much as you can and get out of debt. Do not contract any new debt. Reduce your costs, especially fixed costs, and try each month to set as much aside as possible.

> Convert your cash and liquid assets into gold bullion — at first, in the form of ingots, of whatever size you can afford. Keep them in a secure place, like a safe. Once you have established a hoard, another part of your estate can serve to buy more gold ingots that you deposit in a bank that offers a serious guarantee of its stocks of gold through regular inspections. Make sure that, if the necessity arises, you will be able to withdraw this gold in 24 or 48 hours.

> Regularly buy silver coins with the cash surplus from your income. These coins, like gold, will not merely be a hedge against inflation, but can serve as everyday money more easily than gold ingots.

> Sell your secondary or vacation home if it cannot be converted into an SAB, and do it before it is no longer worth anything because of demography (aging populations), because of the crisis, or — very soon — because it is impossible to take those low-cost flights to get there.

> If you are thinking of moving in two or three years, sell now and rent while you wait to move. A good trick for avoiding having to move is to sell your house to a real-estate company and rent it back from them.

> Develop a skill that will never be obsolete: medicine, gardening, plumbing, electrician, etc.

> Think of developing a second job from home, or alongside your principal job. Do not necessarily think big (though you never know), but a second source of income could be very useful.

> Ask yourself: what do you know how to do? What are you good at? What competence and knowledge do you have that can be used? Be aware that it takes at least ten years to get good at a trade. Consider training to become an installer of solar panels or wind turbines; go back to school to become a doctor or veterinarian. Think about trades that do not involve dependence on distant suppliers or require transportation and electricity; consider the kinds of trades and crafts that existed in the 19th century. Use these new abilities to generate revenue.

Prepare Yourself to Be Resilient

Preparation for surviving an economic collapse can be compared to that of a long voyage, in which you do not know the destination nor the time of departure. Initially, it is crucial not to get depressed or burdened with anxiety.

The best way of starting your preparation is to do what is easiest and quickest first. Then it becomes a matter of making your life fit your ideas. Preparation is the prudent and non-selfish act of an adult who wants to control the risks in his life — it is not the antisocial act of a recluse or paranoiac. At this stage, you know a lot. You must simply continue your mental and physical preparation.

We can add a few more ideas:

> Understand from the start that whatever you do will be insufficient, but that it is infinitely better than not being ready at all. If you are ten percent prepared, this is vastly better than being zero percent prepared. It is better to be ready one year early than one year too late.

> Acknowledge that you cannot foresee everything, even with un-limited funds, time, and consultants. It is impossible to foresee everything, know everything, cover all possible eventualities, etc. However, it is necessary to get started and prepare oneself.

> Whatever the subject, the goal, or the know-how involved, try your best not to depend on a single source. In turn, you will be truly resilient when you can rely not only on yourself but on your family, your friends, and your community.

> You must realize that you will not succeed in keeping one hundred percent of your present way of life and comfort.

> If you don't act for yourself, who will?

> Be realistic, align your thoughts with your actions. Do not spend your money on useless things (convertibles), but make room for little pleasures (music, food you like, etc.).

> Set short- and long-term goals for yourself. Make lists and cross out what you have already accomplished. It will bring you psycho-logical relief when one of the goals is reached.

> Start with something simple and easy, but do it! It can consist in buying a week's worth of food and putting it in your cupboard, taking courses, gathering information over the internet, etc. By doing things little by little, you will gradually learn everything while correcting your errors.

> Even if you like preparing by yourself or in small groups, make yourself available to others in your community — share with them your experiences, ideas, etc. Of course, to help others you must first help yourself. It's like an oxygen mask on a plane: they tell us to put our own on first, before assisting our children and neigh-bors. And you don't have to be an expert to share your experience. A community is strong and resilient because each member has these qualities. Start with your own project, then help your close

family, then your friends and neighbors. Next, all together, influence local political authorities ... then regional and national.

> Whatever happens, it is better to face problems surrounded by friends and people who respect each other, who are bound by love, admiration, confidence, and friendship. Like Greek warriors in a phalanx, you must be solid, advancing arm-in-arm. To this end, you must be able to have confidence in others, and that confidence must be merited. Conversely, your comrades must be able to have confidence in you, and you must deserve it. As with respect, to be worthy of it, you must earn it. *Do* exactly what you *say* you are going to do. Alas, we live in a cultural era where it is acceptable to have excuses for everything (not getting up in the morning, arriving late, not keeping deadlines, not caring about the consequences, etc.). This will be unacceptable in an SAB, and if your attitude is undisciplined, you will be quickly marginalized or suffer severe punishments.

> Remember that no tool is useful without training. Whether a rifle or gardening shears, if you do not know how to handle it correctly, it will be of no use to you. Worse, you could become a danger to yourself or others!

> Appreciate old technologies. The tools of yesterday — which worked without electricity and were close to indestructible — are precisely the ones you need. Modern gadgets work fine ... until they wear out, or you have no more electrical current, batteries, or gasoline.

> Don't be afraid to work up a sweat! Learn to do things by yourself, including making and repairing the tools you use. It is quite possible that the only person available to construct a palisade, repair a barn roof, shovel manure, work in the garden, and clean clothes will be *you*, and no one else.

> Choose your friends carefully. Associate with doers rather than talkers. Hard work will be necessary, so choose persons who share

your moral principles and philosophy of life. Drop the dishonest, complainers, the lazy and incapable. Find those among your friends who have useful abilities, those who share your desire to pull through, who are serious enough to stick it out and contribute to the well-being and survival of the group.

> Be flexible. Do not become infatuated with your SAB plan. If it doesn't work, change it and find an alternative. Have a plan B. If, for example, you plan to establish an SAB on an island in order to benefit from the excellent climate and extraordinarily good conditions for food production, wine, seafood, fish, etc., but then must evacuate the island because of increasingly frequent storms and rising sea levels, it would be to your benefit to have reflected on another survival plan. Take the example of a person unable to reach his SAB; perhaps, he has thought to establish a cache with a minimum amount of food, water, and gasoline somewhere. This will let him hold out long enough to resume his journey via another path.

> Be frugal and remember your grandparents' (or great- grandparents') way of life before the world wars. At the time, people made use of everything and squandered nothing; they were still happy and found joy in the little things in life. Take inspiration from their wisdom.

> Do no take unnecessary risks, of course. However, there are things you will have to risk *everything* for, such as your family and freedom.

> Be ready to leave quickly, according to the criteria of the alert schedule you have defined. It is better to risk losing a few days' vacation on a false alarm than finding oneself amid chaos, stuck in a giant traffic jam like all the people who tried to leave New Orleans before Hurricane Katrina and spent whole days on blocked highways.

> Ask yourself if you have confidence in the state, if you think state programs are necessary for your security, especially as concerns terrorism, public health, and agriculture. When the system begins to collapse, you can figure on government trying to show it still has authority and decreeing ever more draconian and authoritarian measures: mandatory vaccines, even population management by microchip implantation, etc. All this is probably destined for failure, for a structure as large and clumsy as a state will not be able to hold together for long in such a crisis. Be discreet and don't get yourself noticed; this period will pass quickly. In the case of a totalitarian or quasi-totalitarian dictatorship, the only possibility for freedom is to present yourself as a dutiful subject, while maintaining a free spirit and keeping up appearances. In other words, playing along with the Powers That Be, while preparing for the things that may come, may be your only option. Numerous cultures and organizations have succeeded in hiding their membership at the very heart of a society that was hostile to them. Avoid expressing extreme individualism or political opinions contrary to those that are dominant.

> Learn to be in sync with nature and follow the seasons. Be outside in summer to harvest and profit from nature. Spend the winter indoors, amid the warmth of your family nest, repairing whatever broke during the summer.

> Whatever happens, and whatever you do, put some passion into it! You have only one life to live, and you might as well live it in a fulfilling way and alongside great people.

Vehicles in Your SAB

People often ask me about the best vehicle to have in case of a crisis or in an SAB. This is not the best way to pose a question. In a future essentially without petroleum, and thus without gasoline, motor vehicles will be rapidly marginalized, and will then disappear altogether outside of a few regions. It is better to count on nothing but your muscular force or animals for transportation, working the fields, etc. Start reflecting now on what a world where one travels on foot, on horseback, by bicycle, by wagon, or on a donkey will mean for you and your SAB project.

We are not there yet, of course, but you should start to think about several alternatives to gas-guzzlers:

> **Bicycles** will be the best means of transport once you are in your SAB. They can be equipped with baby seats, carts, or luggage racks. The versatility of the bicycle, especially the mountain bicycle with its stability, allows you to travel quietly. Buy high quality and plan on purchasing enough tools to carry out repairs yourself, as well as basic replacement parts (air pumps, tires, chains, brakes, break-cables, speed cables, etc.)

> **Motorcycles, cross-country bikes, and mopeds** can be very useful. For getting from your dwelling to the SAB, a motorcycle presents the advantage of letting you laugh at the jammed high-ways, but with the corresponding disadvantage of not letting you transport very much baggage (ideal if all your supplies are already in your SAB), nor many passengers. Another advantage of the motorcycle is its relatively low consumption of gas. Remember the safety warnings: wear a helmet and dress adequately for avoiding needless injuries in a possible accident.

> **Automobiles** can also work. But don't think that buying the larg-est possible 4x4 or SUV will allow you to "own the road"! Besides the cost, you must take several factors into account, such as gas consumption, the availability of replacement parts, and the ease of carrying out repairs in a world without internet diagnostics. Do not choose the most modern model, crammed with electronic ac-cessories and impossible to repair. Choose a simple, robust vehicle with parts that are easy to make, like the old Mercedes 300D from the beginning of the 1980s, which are highly prized in Third World

countries for these reasons. A lot of American vehicles of the 1970s and early 80s had these qualities, too. Whatever model you choose, make sure it has a large trunk and a powerful motor, ideally capable of off-road driving and with good gas mileage. If you are able to have several vehicles, why not also have an electronic vehicle or golf cart that is rechargeable on an electrical outlet? Verify that the power of your electrical generator allows such use. As for propane, bio-ethanol, and other automobile fuel-types, they are a real possibility, and can be taken into account if the fuel in question is easy to make or distill locally. My own choice is to use my current vehicle, a diesel-fuel-powered Mercedes, until it dies, and then plan for a life without a car.

> As for **fuel reserves**, unless you live in an oil-producing country and have refineries that will continue to function, they will be hard to find. So you must stock up on fuel while there is still time. But be careful — fuels are highly flammable and toxic. Plan on installing tanks for stocking gasoline or diesel, and add stabilizers (Sta-bil©, Motorex©). Also remember to choose gasoline during winter, since the butane level is higher. The latter gives it a lower freezing temperature and makes the fuel last longer. I store and rotate about two hundred liters of diesel fuel, and I have stored a few twenty-liter jerrycans in some friends' garages (with their permission, of course), just in case. Furthermore, my SAB has an old central-heating system, which used to run on diesel, and I kept the three 1,000-liter storage cisterns full, so that I can use or trade that fuel if needed.

Now, let's get ready for our action plan!

Miguel thinks the whole thing sucks.

After the big panic last week, which saw the supermarkets literally plundered, he noticed that the people in his apartment building were getting increasingly active. While the water was cut off this morning, practically all the residents came to complain — "yell" might be a better word — and now, outside, looting is occurring. He says to himself that now is the time to be off for his SAB in Portugal.

He's glad his wife is there already. She left two weeks ago by plane. He calls his two sons and tells them they must set off right away. His problem is that his car does not have enough gas — half a tank. He'll barely get two hundred miles. Luckily, one of his sons has a car full of gas. He decides to take the car that gets the best mileage, transfer as many things to it as possible and siphon gas from the car they are leaving behind into cans, which they will use as necessary. They leave, avoiding the highways. They must take numerous little byways, because everything is blocked up. It seems like everybody is trying to get out of town, and there are endless lines in front of gas stations. After a certain time, they get on a little faster. In the small villages they pass through, the situation seems better. The people seem preoccupied with the news, but bakeries are still baking bread, and they were even able to buy ten liters of gas.

They arrive, close to empty, at the Spanish border, which the army has closed in the meantime. So they must cross the Pyrenees on foot. Fortunately, it is September, and this is possible. Moreover, the weather is mild — a pleasant side effect of this new weird dry weather. Once in Spain, where the situation is just as bad as elsewhere (but the population seems to have remained calm), Miguel and his sons get lucky: they can get on a train going to Valladolid, then Salamanca. From there it takes them four days to reach their SAB. Fortunately, having traveled these roads for years, they know practically all the shortcuts.

<<you buy furniture. you tell yourself, this is the last sofa I will ever need in my life. buy the sofa, then for a couple of years you're satisfied that no matter what else goes wrong, at least you've got your sofa issue handled. then the right set of dishes. then the perfect bed. the drapes. the rug. then you're trapped in your lovely nest, and the things you used to own, now they own you.

chuck palahniuk

_fight club

/1996/

An Action Plan

SURVIVAL IS NOT ABOUT THINGS one accumulates but about competences one acquires. If you have time and a little money put aside, you will quickly be able to acquire a lot of knowledge and capability that can help you when the economic collapse plunges the world into chaos.

Take out a notebook and a large sheet of paper.

On the large sheet of paper, write down an action plan. It's up to you to organize it. You might make a table with different columns for each type of action. You could also take the seven fundamental principles of an SAB as titles for the columns and add, say, a column for your physical or financial preparation and a column to list the necessary criteria for choosing a place for your SAB, etc.

In the notebook, you can use the same column headings, but this time use one per page. Note everything that comes to mind: the list of equipment to buy, the list of food to stock, the educational courses you wish to follow, etc. Try to note *everything*, but do it loosely; this is a brainstorm, and you will prioritize the items later. For each principle, note where you can find it, how much it costs, how long the training lasts, etc.

On the large sheet, draw a vertical axis defining the time you set for yourself, for example, two years, or five, or ten. Then, column by column, transcribe in chronological order (corresponding to the time scale you have chosen) the material, the training, etc., for which you have sought exact information. Be realistic: if you want to lose twenty pounds, do not plan on doing it in a month, but stretch it over six months to a year. If you wish to acquire a skill or know-how, give yourself a reasonable amount of time in which to do so. Go ahead and use colors and sketches, if you like, to represent the most appropriate way to reach your preparation goals.

This action plan will serve you as a measure of how far you have advanced, or how far you are behind, in your preparations. Do not despair if you get behind on everything; do your best, as your means permit. You will probably have to revise the plan a number of times, but it will let you check the pace of your progress at a glance. Believe me, if it is frustrating at first to see how many things there are to do and prepare — especially when the economic or international news makes you wonder if the collapse is about to begin — once you have carried out half of the plan and struck off a great part of your action items, you will feel a lot of satisfaction. It will motivate you and give you the energy to persevere.

Once your plan of action has been established, you must make lists for each category and sub-category. You will find examples of such lists in the appendix, but I encourage you not merely to copy them but improve and develop them according to your needs, your geographical location, and your idiosyncrasies. Remember that each SAB is different and that your set of needs is unique. So work intelligently when you establish these lists:

1 > First make a list of the courses available in schools, hospitals, universities, continuing-education centers, etc., for the domains that seem useful and interesting to you: first aid, metallurgy, mechanics, agriculture, electronics, woodworking, leatherworking, ceramics, pottery, cooking, gardening, soldering, making preserves, sewing, veterinary medicine, shooting, martial arts, amateur radio operation, etc.

2 > Then, list what you must buy: water filters, pumps, food, drinks, alcohol, surplus for barter, materials for first aid and minor surgery, disinfectants and medications, rechargeable batteries and

chargers, fuel, books, manuals, reference guides, fire protection, cold weapons, guns, ammunition, clothing, communication material, radios, etc.

3 > Finally, make a list of friends, professionals, and companies that have the ability to help you right away: specialists in solar panels, water heaters, renewable energy, electricians, woodworkers, masons, etc. If necessary, plan a budget for working with these people.

At the beginning, these lists may seem enormous and discouraging, but that does not matter: start small and divide certain tasks and purchases among your family members and the friends who will join you in your SAB. For example, you can train in the use of firearms and first aid; your wife can train in gardening and water purification; your children can learn how to care for animals; and your friends learn mechanics or solar-panel maintenance, etc.

Then distinguish between what you absolutely need and what you would like, but which is dispensable. Buy chocolate after you get in all your rice, the garden swing set for the children after the seeds and after the garden terracing is finished. If you do not make this effort, you will waste time and money; and even if you have unlimited wealth, you do not have unlimited time. Prioritize!

Do not spend your whole budget on purchases for your SAB before investing in a sufficient amount of quality training. You must balance knowledge and purchases. Read, learn, take courses, but above all, put what you have learned into practice. It is useless to try to become an expert on everything: a little education and a few tools in a useful domain is better than expert knowledge and a whole collection of tools in a domain that will not be useful to you.

This is why the preparation of an SAB is divided into seven essential principles. You must have at least some knowledge of each of these principles. And you already have that by virtue of reading this book. Now it is up to you to delve into each project, and, thanks to your action plan and lists, you will know exactly what you still have to do and learn.

<<do first things first, and second things not at all.

peter drucker

consultant & writer

/1909–2005/

<<he who is not busy being born is busy dying.

bob dylan

musician

/1965/

Exercises

TO GET YOU IN SHAPE, and help you prepare to survive, I propose ten exercises.

Media Detox

Unplug your TV and don't read any news — no newspapers, magazines, women's interest or celebrity rags, *nothing*. Go at least one month without exposing yourself to the media. At first, it will be hard. You will want to know what's happening and will deeply miss your favorite evening program or news website. But little by little, you will see that *not* knowing that some nasty fellow raped an old lady … that some college student has gone missing in South America … that some politician is sleeping with some prostitute … that some team won a championship … or that the stock market went this way or that has no real effect on you. After a month, begin to inform yourself on the internet, and for each piece of news, try to find different points of view. Then compare how the mainstream media treat the same information. Compare the facts and the arguments advanced.

When you have done this, you will have acquired the capacity to choose your sources of information and perhaps you will come to view the media differently.

Then sell or throw away your TV and never buy one again.

A Weekend without Electricity or Water

Coordinate with your partner if necessary and, one Friday evening, cut off the electricity to your house as well as the water, heating, and telephone. Do this in the autumn or at the end of the winter when the days are still short. Your exercise will be to stay at home without electricity, water, or heating until Monday morning, when you can restart everything to prepare to return to work or get the children ready for school. You will have to have enough to eat and drink at home for two full days. This exercise should not be too difficult, but you will see that many things you are used to do not work. No more water to wash yourself, or for boiling pasta or rice, no electricity or gas for cooking your food, no electricity for managing things at night. What will you do? Do you even have enough water for drinking? How will you wash? Will you eat your food cold? Do you have enough food? Is it sufficiently varied? How will you do your business if the toilet doesn't flush? Are you able to stand not going out?

If you have children, tell them it is a game. After all, it *is* a game! A game to prepare you mentally for the day when what you take for granted is no longer there.

The goal of this exercise is for you to take the measure of how important water and food are, but also to experience how it feels to be isolated. Note how you feel. Note what you miss the most. Note the evolution of your state of irritation. Did you succeed in holding out just forty-eight hours under the conditions that are considered normal by billions of people around the world? Over the course of this exercise, you may add many things to your preparation list.

A Week without Food

The third exercise is much more difficult. You may do it individually or as a group. Do not eat anything — that is, fast — for a week: no nourishment of any kind. You may, however, drink as much water as necessary. Only do this exercise if you are in good health: certainly not if you are sick, in pain, in medical care, or in a state of health that does not allow it (e.g. if you are pregnant). If you are in doubt, consult your doctor and use common sense. Before starting, drink a half liter of prune juice in order to clean out your intestines. Do this at home, when you're calm, and have three or four hours free time ahead of you.

For a week, you will experience hunger probably as never before. The first three days will be difficult. If you get a headache, you may take aspirin or mild painkillers, or, better still, let it pass naturally without chemicals. Note how you feel and your state of irritation: it may well be considerable, and this is why it is best to begin this exercise on a Thursday or Friday morning so that you will not be exhausted or on edge at work. Say you are not hungry if you must accompany someone at a meal — you will notice the extent to which eating is a social activity! After three days, if you succeed in not eating anything, note the changes in your mentality and physique. What sort of changes are these? Are you still as hungry as ever? Is your mind clearer and your capacity for concentration greater? Do you, paradoxically, have more energy than normal? Do you feel better and have less need of sleep? If so, this is normal and your body is reacting correctly to being deprived of food: it finds the necessary resources to improve your faculties temporarily, letting you seek food more efficiently. You are experiencing the original state of our species, that of the hunter-gatherer 15,000 years ago! If you succeed in holding out a week, do not then go and gorge yourself on steak, chips, and cake: this will be bad for your digestive tract. Instead, begin eating again gradually with vegetable soup, steamed vegetables, rice, and not too much protein, which you may start adding after one or two days.

A Week without Money

Another exercise with the object of getting you to reflect on our dependence on the modern system is to try to go a week without money and without making a payment of any kind, whether in cash or by check or by credit card. It's up to you to get along. Say you have forgotten your wallet, or that all your credit cards are lost or at their limit, and that it will take a week to work it out. Then confront, one day after another, your inability to pay. What will you do for your transportation, your food, your indispensable expenses? Will you ask someone else to pay for you? Will you try to barter? Note your impressions and what you dare do, or not do, with regards to the idiosyncratic relation we have with money.

One Day and Night in the City

Take advantage of a day of pleasant weather to walk about town with no particular aim. Block this day out in your schedule and do not agree to any meeting or any call, however important. Leave your phone and any other communication device at home and tell your colleagues and even friends and family that you will not be available for anything or anybody — not work, not household tasks, not children, not friends. Take public transportation. Be completely free. Walk in the town's parks, take a siesta on the grass, look at the clouds and the trees, breathe calmly and deeply. For the whole day, you will be alone with yourself with nothing to do. Do not read any newspaper or book. Do not go shopping or buy groceries. If hungry, eat some fresh fruit you took with you in the morning. Observe the town. Observe the people on public transportation and elsewhere: are they stressed? Smiling? Happy? Where do they come from? How do they look at each other? Are they satisfied? This exercise will allow you to spend one day radically different from the others and have time to do nothing. This doesn't happen often in life, and perhaps it has never happened to you at all. After a day like this, note your impressions and feelings. Were you bored? Did you feel panicked? Did you have a need for human contact? Did you have a need to talk? To spend money?

In the evening, dress in the most innocuous manner possible. Do not wear any ring or watch. Only take petty cash in small denominations for a few small purchases and the taxi ride home at daybreak, if necessary. Try walking around the town on a weekend, in neighborhoods where you do not often go. Are you afraid? Do you feel insecure or disturbed? Is this feeling normal and bearable for you? What do you observe? Note your impressions. On public transportation, observe people and imagine you are an aggressor. Ask yourself what person you would attack and rob. Why that person rather than another? You don't need to go to a bad neighborhood among cutthroats! Avoid all danger. If you do not feel safe or someone attacks you, give way, play for time and flee. Do not actually attack anyone verbally or physically, and don't play smart-ass. Don't go down blind alleys or where you don't see anyone else. Stay safe on a busy street and use common sense. The goal of this exercise, which should not be dangerous if you prepare correctly, is simply to let you observe the human fauna of the town, especially at night: probably a population you do not commonly see. What do you notice? Ask yourself how this population will act in a crisis or in the scenarios described in this book. What conclusions do you draw?

A Day as a Pickup Artist

This exercise may make you smile, but it is very difficult and could surprise you. The object is to get you out of your comfort zone, your possible introversion, and learn to approach someone about something. The idea is to approach someone of the opposite sex, chosen at random, but whom you find attractive; ask him/her for his/her telephone number so you can call him/her. That's all — nothing more. (If this exercise has consequences for you, that's your affair; I won't ask for your first born!) Avoid obvious pickup spots (nightclubs, the internet). Approach someone you do not know on the street and figure out how to ask him/her for his/her telephone number in order to see her/him again. You will see that it is not easy. (For a shy man like myself, this is the most difficult exercise of all.) Between getting up the courage to approach someone, finding the right words to strike up a conversation and not get rejected straight off, there is a whole art to be mastered. Then, try to convince him/her to give you his/her telephone number — the real one. (To check and make sure it is real, read it back to him/her with one deliberate mistake; if he/she doesn't correct you, the number is not real.) Never be insistent. The aim is not to get laid, nor to bother the person. What is your level of success? Zero? One percent? Ten percent? If you are over ten percent, you are quite talented!

Sell Something

This quick exercise consists in taking an object of small value from home and trying to sell it. How will you go about it? For what price will you sell it? Where will you go to make the attempt?

Negotiate Something

Go into a store and buy something you might need, but don't leave unless you have gotten a twenty percent discount. This is a little exercise to get you used to negotiating.

Learn to Say No

Say no to an innocent request that annoys you and learn to manage the consequences of your refusal. Try this exercise with your partner, your children, your colleagues, and your superiors. Use common sense: there's no need to lose your job or undergo a divorce for the sake of this exercise!

Preparation Exercise

Here is a six-day exercise that will give you some concrete experience preparing. You can do this exercise alone, as a family, or with friends.

> **First day** — Establish the scenarios that seem most probable to you (slow decline, civil war, revolution, etc.) and familiarize yourselves with their consequences. Make a list of dangers for each of these scenarios. As you reflect, note the basic materials you will need in each scenario. Once you have finished your reflection, prepare the important documents (property titles, identification documents, etc.) you will need to have with you if you must leave quickly.

> **Second day** — On the basis of the work you did the first day, you will begin to establish a list for a two-week food and water reserve. Start by taking the quantities of food indicated in the appendix, adapt it for a period of two weeks and multiply it by the number of persons in your family or on your team. Then you will know the

SURVIVE THE ECONOMIC COLLAPSE

amount of food required for two weeks. For example, the amount of flour for an adult corresponds to nine pounds per month, or about four and a half pounds for two weeks, multiplied by six (two adults in your family + two adults on your team + their two spouses), which makes 13.5 pounds for two weeks. After having established the list of foodstuffs to buy, do the same for water. Plan on an individual needing thirteen gallons of water per week for drinking, cooking, and bathing. This represents twenty-five two-liter bottles of mineral water. Multiply by six, and you have three hundred liters, or 79.3 gallons, which will be over 650 lbs! The usefulness of 20- and 200-liter (5- and 50-gallon) tanks soon becomes clear, doesn't it? End the day by making an inventory of articles for bodily hygiene and medicines available at home now. Is it enough for two weeks?

> **Third day** — This is shopping day. Buy the products on the list you have drawn up. Try to negotiate a bulk price in view of the quantities involved. Write the purchase date on the products with a permanent magic marker or pen. Stock these purchases in boxes or metal cans in a dry place. Congratulations! You now have a minimum stock for two weeks. Managing this stock will take a little discipline, for each item you take from the stock must be replaced. Always use the oldest item first. Finish your day by copying the documents you drew up the first day.

> **Fourth day** — This day is consecrated to energy. How do you keep warm or cook without electricity? How to you light up the house? For cooking, the simplest solution is a barbecue grill (which can also be used as an oven) and a camping stove. Plan on buying enough fuel (coal, propane tanks, etc.). For lighting, plan on choosing flashlights that work with a dynamo. The absence of heating will be more difficult to compensate for, but a good sleeping bag will let you keep warm. Plan on stocking newspaper and cardboard to insulate your windows in the winter. Energy is also the basis of long-distance communication. Buy a radio with a

dynamo. It will keep you from getting cut off from the rest of the world. Finally, if you have the means, buy a solar charger as well as accumulators for things that run on rechargeable batteries.

> **Fifth day** — Devote this day to securing your home, or secondary residence if you have one. Set up a plan. Which doors should you secure? What additional security (especially of windows) could be added? Always plan an emergency exit. Contact the police to find out if they offer a free advice service. Do not forget to buy curtains and a black tarpaulin. If you have light when no one else does, you will be a prime target! End your day by drawing up a plan of action concerning security measures. It should contain a schedule indicating where and when you will have any work done.

> **Sixth day** — Prepare your 72-hour survival kit/bug-out bag. It should contain all the elements you have familiarized yourself with over the preceding days and permit you to make the journey from your house to your SAB. Do not try to carry more than twenty kilograms / forty-five pounds per adult, otherwise you will not get far, unless you are in very good shape. Prefer foods with strong nutritive power that don't require much preparation. In the bag that contains your survival kit, put photocopies of your title deeds and identification papers.

Once you have carried out these ten exercises, you will already be much further advanced in your ability to survive than the vast majority of people around you. Good going! You have a long journey ahead, but you have already taken the crucial first steps.

<<the matrix is a system, neo. that system is our enemy. but when you're inside, you look around, what do you see? businessmen, teachers, lawyers, carpenters. the very minds of the people we are trying to save. but until we do, these people are still a part of that system, and that makes them our enemy. you have to understand, most of these people are not ready to be unplugged. and many of them are so inured, so hopelessly dependent on the system, that they will fight to protect it.

morpheus

_the matrix

/1999/

<<i'd like to share a revelation i've had during my time here. it came to me when i tried to classify your species. i realized that you're not actually mammals. every mammal on this planet instinctively develops a natural equilibrium with their surrounding environment, but you humans do not. you move to an area and you multiply … and multiply until every natural resource is consumed. the only way you can survive is to spread to another area. there is another organism on this planet that follows the same pattern. do you know what it is? a virus. human beings are a disease, a cancer of this planet. you are a plague, and we … are the cure.

agent smith

_the matrix

/1999/

Conclusion

APART FROM THE USUAL, but sincere, acknowledgments I must make to all those who helped me make this book a reality (they know who they are), I would like to conclude on a note of hope. In spite of what you have read in this book, I am not a pessimist. I am a realist ... with an imagination.

My aim is not to frighten you, but I believe the convergence of the immense problems facing humanity, combined with a decadent and failing culture and leadership, makes the catastrophe inevitable. If new information shows that I am wrong, I will be happy and revise my predictions. But I believe that all the big figures and tendencies show that it is too late.

It is too late.

The speed and form of the collapse could vary, but life as we know it is going to be shaken from top to bottom. There will be no *deus ex machina* — a god, politician, or magical new technology — to save us miraculously at the last minute.

I do not believe we are in the "End Times" as told in the Bible, but at the end of a cycle and the end of a world — that of progressivism, of the dominance of finance, of the bourgeoisie and the notion that its standard of living could be universal. A 400-year era is coming to a close.

I know that many readers will reflexively reject facts that do not correspond to the model of thought they have acquired, or because they cannot imagine the consequences. I can only encourage them to do their own research, verify the information on their own, and make up their own minds on the basis of these facts.

My describing an unpleasant world does not mean that I wish for its arrival, or that I rejoice at what is going to happen — far from it. It is my duty to maintain confidence in man's capacity to recover, to be resilient, to use his courage, his inventiveness, his sense of justice to pull through. But this attitude of mine is more an act of faith than an objective analysis (for I fear that modern man is in very bad shape).

My goal is neither to convince you nor to sell you anything. Although I offer a consulting service for installing SABs on my website www.Piero.com, my principle goal is to help raise people's awareness, to get you thinking about how you will survive and how to start taking action in order to do so. If enough people change their attitudes, if a sufficiently numerous group of people prepare, perhaps we will influence affairs and mitigate the effects of the collapse by our example. Take a good look at your children. Do you have confidence in the ability and moral fiber of your political and economic leaders? If the answer is yes, sleep easily, pal: your destiny and that of your family is in the hands of those I heartily hope regard you benevolently. But if the answer is no, you find yourself as a man or woman confronted with a choice — do nothing, or assume your responsibilities and act.

The choice is yours.

And it won't be easy. It's hard to change the world. Let us rather start by changing ourselves. Let us get rid of a lot of notions with which we have been conditioned and which we accepted without really questioning: infinite growth, happiness through consumption, freedom reduced to desire, wage labor, rush-hour traffic jams, the inversion of all values, and the manipulation of news and media.

We must learn to see the world differently, acquire new abilities, learn new trades, try new ways of working and thinking, rediscover the common good, and recreate strong social bonds. We can change a lot without it even showing and without "dropping out." Go on working at your job: use your salary and your wealth to prepare yourself.

Do it discreetly, for in our conformist society, attitudes or thoughts truly critical of the system — and not just expressions of the system's "right" and "left" — will increasingly become suspect; you could risk being consigned to the margins of society. Socially, many people simply won't understand you; friends and family will criticize you or make fun of you behind your back; your employers will find you to be a little too "fringe"; your career may slow down or even end with your firing. Over the long term, this is not a serious matter; in the short term, however, it could deprive you of resources useful for your preparation. So ignore the skeptics and focus on the preparation necessary to achieve your goal — *survival.*

Not everyone will make it. Most will not have the ability, discipline, or determination to survive. Others, conscious of what they should do, will not start to change until forced by events. Others still will remain in denial, and, like those who could not believe that the Titanic would sink since it was "unsinkable," they will be taken cruelly by surprise.

So take time to reflect carefully on what you have read in these few hundred pages. Make the time to do so. Take a vacation or decline that promotion and stay at a job where, thanks to your experience, you can get your work done quickly enough to have time for thinking, reading, verifying information, and beginning your preparation. Detachment and indifference can also be useful feelings: he who is depressed and feels himself a stranger in the world of today is perhaps ready for the one that's coming.

This is why I remain optimistic. Those who will change, who are able to prepare and transform themselves, who choose frugality and simplicity voluntarily, who want to rediscover the rectitude and dignity of man — *those who will survive* — will form the cultural and genetic foundation of a new world. And that world will be more beautiful and have more meaning than ours.

In any case, you have no excuse: you are a responsible person and, as my father used to say, a 100-percent shareholder of yourself! Your family is counting on you, so work hard, learn, train. Above all, I don't want to hear any whining! No moaning about it being too hard and that you will never get everything ready in time! If you do not achieve perfect results right away, do not be discouraged: persevere and start over, again and again!

Lastly, be able to take the time to stop, smell the flowers, contemplate the countryside, breathe, and profit from the little things in life. They are what is truly important.

Still there? Well then, get to work!

◆

2011–2021 What Has Changed?

THE BOOK YOU HAVE JUST READ was written in early 2011 but the ideas it contains sparked off after 9/11, after the invasion of Iraq of 2003 and after the financial crisis of 2008. Of course there were many other sources of ideas that converged into what I wrote: my experience traveling for work in over one hundred countries across Africa, the Middle East and Eastern Europe in the 1990s and 2000s; my sensibility about environmental issues; and my love of studying history, for what it teaches us about the rise and fall of civilizations. I remember that in 2004 I was drawing with my soon-to-be wife a few mind-maps on large pieces of paper about the threats and opportunities of the world, as well as my own personal likes, dislikes and skills.

As I started preparing for myself and my family for the possible futures that I envisioned, I had to structure my thoughts to develop a strategy. Instead of the usual "prepping" trends (buy this gun, buy that tool, get this mylar bag, try this fire-starter…), which I also indulge in, having a strategy enables a structure, a direction, and thus more efficiency and cost savings. It also provides a structure for meaning as you don't want to prepare because you fear an event, or hate a particular situation or group of people and their behavior, but you want to prepare because that's what responsible adults do. That's what anyone who does not want to bumble carelessly through (a way too comfortable nowadays) life without thinking about what could happen should reasonably do. Nothing may happen, but much could. And it's better to have a plan in such an event, rather than do nothing and hope to rely on someone else, usually the government, to come to your help. By the way, here's some info: the government is not there to help you.

I was fortunate that my first book was a commercial success with over 200,000 copies sold in its original French version, and was subsequently translated into English, Italian, Russian, Romanian, Arabic, Polish, Turkish and Spanish. This first book was followed by a second book about how to survive in the city should you not be able to move away from it soon enough. It was also a large publishing success. Much less successful was my third book[1] about women and the difficult odds they usually face in times of crisis — I really liked this book and thought it was important, but it seems the interest is not there — perhaps women think they can wait for whoever "wins" at surviving and join them? In 2016, I wrote a book on how to prepare for pandemics, industrial hazards and nuclear wars.[2] In light of the last two years, this one should have been read by all, if only to understand the difference between a pandemic and a plandemic and I think that it is an urgent read, considering the current drift towards war between atomic powers or civil wars in countries that have nuclear power plants...

To come back to the book you have just read or skimmed through, I wrote in it that I thought that the economic collapse I describe would happen by 2020 and, in several interviews since, I made my thoughts more clear by saying that collapse is a process, not an event (although events can trigger accelerations) and that I thought that the major acceleration of this process was highly probable between 2020 and 2022.

Predicting the future is hazardous at best. Sometimes people ask me, "When will the collapse happen?", to which I usually answer, "Tuesday, ten AM, get ready!" My work is neither to make predictions nor prophecies, but rather to imagine scenarios based on the facts I can gather, with some educated guesses and listening to my intuition.

---

1   *Women on the Verge of Societal Breakdown: Preserving Hard-Won Freedoms in Times of Uncertainty*, 2016

2   *CBRN: Surviving Chemical, Biological, Radiological and Nuclear Events*, Arktos, 2020

Not a scientific process, I humbly admit, but not a worse one than all the other "experts" out there.

I'll also admit that many people who announced a collapse in the last fifty years have been proven wrong. We still have oil; we have globalized and societies are more resilient and connected as ever, wars and violence have decreased everywhere if we believe statistics; there is still no hyperinflation nor any financial collapse; populations prefer their prison of cheap food and internet entertainment to revolting; and we seem to manage to feed 8 billion people. So far, so "good." But as I consider the events of the last months, I do think that we are nearing a major — perhaps global — collapse.

No one knows what that collapse will look like — we can only guess from what we saw in the fall of Yugoslavia, the USSR, the Weimar Republic, the Roman Empire... pick one. And as I wrote in my books, we have a vision of the collapse that is warped by movies and pop culture. It probably will not look like Mad Max, but it will not be a walk in the park either.

So what has happened, what has changed since 2011?

Let's look at this in more detail.

We are now 8 billion people living on our planet. And while the Caucasians of Europe and America and the North-Eastern Asian populations are decreasing, the populations of Africa, Latin America and India are still growing fast. If we look at these groups from a different, if more politically incorrect, angle, the high IQ people across all these populations seem to reproduce the least while the low IQ people seem to reproduce a lot — with the notable exception of religious people across all IQ levels, who do keep breeding prodigiously. Hey, no pain, no gain! So not only do we have more people in the world, each of them wanting to consume to the highest levels possible — thus requiring ever more resources — but the low IQ ones outbreed the others. Considering that the democratic process promotes politicians that promise free stuff to gullible people, and that automation in manufacturing and many other industries will not require a low-skilled workforce anymore, the gap between those who are economically productive and the others keeps increasing. This gap is mainly created by the huge wealth of the "elites," who control the deep state. Add to this the media which focus the resentment of the "have-nots" towards the hard-working population and you have a perfect storm for civil wars between angry mobs of moronic parasites and whoever still produces stuff and keeps the lights on.

As for resources, the trends remain the same towards depletion. The only notable change since 2011 has been the shale-oil bubble that, with heavy subsidies, managed to create a short-lived spike in oil production in the USA and Canada that postponed peak oil by a few years — perhaps by five or ten — to 2019 or 2020, but with the current Covid crisis and the subsequent drop in demand, we can't be totally sure if we did reach it. If we did, this raises the question if the current crisis hasn't been exaggerated, or manufactured, to hide the beginning of scarcity and the subsequent panic. Could 2020–2021 have been the start of a controlled demolition of the economies to avoid a sudden, unmanaged, collapse? We'll know for sure soon enough. It is interesting to note that the Club of Rome's calculations in the early 1970s stated that resource scarcity was set to hit the world's economies significantly starting in 2020. Again, we'll know for sure soon. But then, logically, it's just a question of time before the consumption needs of an increasing population hits the resource scarcity wall. Will innovation solve this? I doubt it, but it's a possibility. Will new, cheap, exploitable resources be found somewhere? The data I collected ten years ago remain valid: as fewer and fewer resources and sources of energy are exploitable and reserves are depleting, you can expect price spikes, scarcities or both. And I note that technologies like "cold fusion" or fantasies like "abiotic oil" have remained as much as they were ten or twenty years ago, nowhere that is; as for the vaunted renewables, they are high in oil consumption to manufacture and to install, and quite inefficient and expensive once in production.

As for agricultural output worldwide, food remains abundant. The world has never produced so much, thanks to more lands being available for farming (in Russia, in Brazil, etc.) and more efficiency in the supply chains reducing spoiling and waste, and it is doing so with fewer farmers than ever. This increased food production is not just of commodities but increasingly varied, personalized food options that respond to consumer demands. However, it remains fragile: fewer than 2 million farms feed America, and less than two percent of its population works in food and agricultural production. Brazil's agricultural juggernaut is driven by 4.4 million farms while the UK agriculture has a mere 140,000 farms, employing less than 0.8 percent of its population. Agriculture may be producing more than ever but as a percentage agriculture contributes less than it ever has to world Gross Domestic Product (GDP). As a result, an increasingly urban population is completely disconnected from the realities of how food is produced. Food is also cheap. For most people in the world, the price of food as a proportion of their income has never been lower. Americans spend less than an average of eight percent of their income on what they eat and a USDA report shows that 2018 was the first year that more US personal income was spent on food eaten away from home than on food at home. European citizens have seen the proportion they spend on food halve in the past twenty years, Brazilians spend less than twenty percent of their income on food, the Chinese twenty-two percent, Indians thirty percent. This is true even as consumers in developing countries trade up the protein chain, increasing their consumption of more expensive animal proteins (e.g. meat, eggs, milk, etc) and these have been growing at a steady two percent annually. The major exception is for African countries, where food prices remain high, at around sixty percent of consumer income, frequently over a dollar a day when their income is just over two dollars. All this, however, hides the trend that productivity is not increasing, except in local micro-farms that produce for the fast-growing demand for locally produced organic food. It could be that food production is not the problem I feared, as long as the supply chains keep functioning perfectly and as long as oil-fueled mechanization is possible. So I'll admit to have been overly pessimistic in this field.

I have also been pessimistic in my assessment of the environmental trends. While pollution and waste remain a problem, especially for the seas, rivers and lakes, the policies set up to preserve large swaths of lands and oceans from deforestation or overfishing have given good results. More trees are planted worldwide, thanks to modern land management techniques, than are cut and, generally, capitalistic interests start to value the conservation of the environment as its value is accounted for. We should rejoice over this and hope that government policies will not break these trends.

As for the anthropogenic global warming, now renamed "climate change," I admit to have been overly influenced by the media and the GIEC reports and I should have been more skeptical of an organization whose acronym stands for: Inter*governmental* Panel on Climate Change. It seems to me now that their reports have been based on faulty data collection processes, biased projection calculations and a general bias towards publishing conclusions that go for bigger legislations, heavier taxation and more government control, which happen to be the policies that those who bankroll them want. Add ideology to that and you get predictions which are consistently wrong. As Charlie Munger said, *"Show me the incentive and I'll show you the outcome."* So much for scientific integrity. That said, it could be possible that human activity does influence climate. Logically, it's certain. But by how much? Compared to what? And to what effect? Let's not dwell here on the details that made my conclusions evolve in the last decade, and let's assume that there is a significant change in weather patterns (more than usual), caused by human activity or not: the effects over the remainder of the century might not be as bad as feared. And even taking into account the relatively small increase of atmospheric CO_2, which contributes to faster plant growth, we can only notice that the rising sea levels are not happening, that the ice caps have not completely melted (as Al Gore predicted). And while I did notice in my lifetime a decrease in the size of the Alpine glaciers, I did also see more lands becoming available for agriculture in Russia and Canada and the equatorial rain patterns might well expand into the tropics, making much arid land available for farming. As for the feared melting of the permafrost, which would trigger an irreversible and catastrophic release of methane, the jury is still out. All in all, the extent of the panic seems exaggerated and, considering the rate of change, we have more urgent problems to tackle. So I don't worry much anymore about this topic and, dare I say, I'm happy to leave it to manipulated autistic teenagers...

One of the much more pressing problems is the insurmountable level of debt that the Western economies seem to accumulate. The debt to GDP ratio (total debt of country divided by total GDP of country, based on the reported data) is now, according to April 2021 data from the International Monetary Fund (IMF): 132.5 percent for the USA, 116.5 percent for Canada, 66.8 percent for China, 115.2 percent for France, 100 percent for the UK, 266 percent for Japan. To put these figures into perspective, the U.S.'s highest debt to GDP ratio was 106 percent at the end of World War II, in 1946. Debt levels gradually fell from their post-World War II peak, before plateauing between 31 percent and 40 percent in the 1970s — ultimately hitting a historic 23 percent low in 1974. And again, remember that these ratios are now calculated on severely minimized numbers.

You have to love the financial world and the magicians that rule it: since the first edition of my book, the levels of debts have increased by factors of four or five — in 2020 alone, the Fed has printed approximatively forty percent of all the money ever printed in the USA — and yet, the system has not collapsed; the dollar's value is not zero due to hyperinflation and no one seems to care that their great-grandchildren are now irremediably indebted.

Part of this is understandable: the dollar's worth is not just a factor of debt and expansion of M1 and M2 money[3] but also of its capacity to bomb into the Stone Age any nation not accepting the greenback as currency to buy oil, raw materials or manufactured goods. The negative interest rates — a novelty, but an economic absurdity — certainly helped to curb savings and add them to the massive injections from the central banks that keep raising the stock markets of the world. Through these, the wealth of the 0.01 percent of the richest has increased manifold. The working masses in the West, however, did not benefit much from the trickle-down effect and saw their wages stagnate at best, which can explain the relatively low inflation levels. And should you want to play the stock markets in the hope of riding up to wealth, beware that at some point they will crash, and you are not the one who decides when that will happen.

Just pause for a moment and consider these immense levels of spending. The 2022 U.S. extra spending package is now 6 trillion! Why not 60 trillion? Or 600? If printing money was a way to wealth, why hasn't it been tried before? Let's spend a trillion trillions so that we can all have condos on Saturn's moons and make every last poor African or Latin American a billionaire!

With no need to work to create money, why bother choosing between programs? You'll have social programs, mass immigration, large military budgets and subsidies for your friends and donors. Besides, you wouldn't want to upset those generous lobbyists, wouldn't you? So, everybody wins while politicians and their masters laugh their way

---

3   M1 is the money supply that is composed of physical currency and coin, demand deposits, travelers' checks, other checkable deposits, and negotiable order of withdrawal accounts. M1 includes the most liquid portions of the money supply because it contains currency and assets that either are or can be quickly converted to cash. M2 is a calculation of the money supply that includes all elements of M1 as well as "near money." M1 includes cash and checking deposits, while near money refers to savings deposits, money market securities, mutual funds, and other time deposits. These assets are less liquid than M1 and not as suitable as exchange mediums, but they can be quickly converted into cash or checking deposits. Debt creation tends to significantly increase M1 and M2.

to the bank. No matter the medium-term consequences, no matter the depleting resources, the disintegrating cohesion of the population, the dysgenic effect,[4] and the growing dependence of the population on the government.

While the super-rich re-invest their money (there are only so many mega-mansions, yachts or private jets you can buy) or spend it all over the world, the masses do spend all they get. And now, with the money injected directly into the economy due to the Covid-19 crisis, a decade later than I predicted, high inflation is appearing.

Contrary to any previous time, the central banks cannot use the well-tested method to raise the cost of money by increasing the levels of debt, as higher interest rates would make the payment of the debt extremely painful. So you will have even more printing of money, even more handouts to the economy and the cycle will keep increasing in speed, with continuous money printing, higher and higher inflation and low interest rates until it is out of control for good.

But what other options do these magicians have? If the money printing stops, the financial system crashes. If the interest rates rise above, say, two or three percent, the financial system crashes. The central banks are now cornered in a place where there is no alternative to collapse.

Or so I thought. And I still think so, but there are two other short-term options:

> Forcibly seize all assets, starting with money in bank accounts, put everything into a socialized (communist) system, like the "Davos people" seem to advise with their "Great Reset,"[5] and hope that people will be convinced, thanks to the efforts of the media and the

---

4 Subsidizing the least capable and the least intelligent into having many children, while taxing the smart, the creative and the hard-working pushes the latter to flee or into having fewer children, thus decreasing on the genetic level the average capacity of the nation to be efficient and productive.

5 See World Economic Forum's CEO Klaus Schwab's book *The Great Reset*, 2020.

GAFAM,[6] or else submit. We know how well this has worked out historically every single time it has been tried, whatever the latitude, the race and the average IQ level: death camps and economic ruin. Besides, forcing this onto an (American) population still mostly armed and with armed forces largely unsympathetic would probably fail even faster. In mostly unarmed Western Europe, this is more feasible, but as armed forces are not numerous, the chances of failure are also high. And even if it succeeds, why would people still work and be productive in such a system? Why would farmers feed the lazy, broke city dwellers? The starvation of large cities, like London, Los Angeles, New York, Chicago, Atlanta, Toronto, Paris, etc. would start almost immediately.

> Assume an authoritarian stance on monetary policy, replacing the devalued currency and imposing a new currency, like Germany did on June 20, 1948,[7] when it suddenly introduced the Deutsche Mark. Good luck with that in a world with cryptocurrencies and with people mostly working and living in urban centers. Again, why would farmers work to feed the rest in exchange for "monopoly" money?

There is another option, but difficult to imagine in a world with nuclear weapons:

> Go to war. That's what most bankrupt countries do, against a power they think they can beat, or against a fabricated enemy, foreign

---

6   The acronym for the internet-tech giants that are, at this moment, Google, Amazon, Facebook, Apple, Microsoft.

7   The introduction of the new Deutsche Mark was intended to protect West Germany from a second wave of hyperinflation and to stop the rampant barter and black market trade (where American cigarettes acted as currency) and was officially introduced on Sunday, June 20, 1948. The old Reichsmark was exchanged for the new currency at a rate of DM 1 = RM 1 for the essential currency, such as wages, payment of rents etc., and DM 1 = RM 10 for the remainder in private non-bank credit balances. In addition, each person received a per capita allowance of DM 60.

or domestic. And if there is money to be made (and there always is), so much the better. This is the reason I studied the topics and, together with a French anti-terrorist specialist, wrote my book CBRN[8] on how to prepare for chemical, biological and nuclear events (read: wars). Are we entering a world where we have to choose between *Doctor Strangelove* and *The Turner Diaries*? Here's a hint: you are not the one to choose! We might actually have both. But you can still choose to prepare accordingly.

And here is the moment I have to mention Donald Trump.

In the summer of 2015, as soon as he announced he would run for the presidency of the USA, I was one of the few who predicted publicly that he would win the elections in 2016 (I also predicted he would be re-elected in 2020) for the simple reason that all over the world, a tiny majority of people, mostly White and working class, are revolting against the current structure of power. The ubiquitous access to the internet and the day-to-day reality of lives for most Westerners, squeezed between the realities of their culturally enriched lives and the political correctness pushed by the corrupt media, interest groups and large corporations, makes any populist movement very palatable, especially as many figure out that in the USA, in Canada, and in Western Europe, demography and immigration will very soon make any democratic process meaningless and bring into power parties and politicians hostile to their interests. Brexit, the Yellow Vests, and Trump are but three of the visible effects of this trend.

During the presidency of Donald Trump, no significant imperial wars were started and the overextension of the U.S. military was reduced. Despite considerable and coordinated vicious media attacks on him, Trump managed — sadly not enough — to fight the deep state[9]

---

8   Piero San Giorgio and Cris Millennium, *CBRN, Surviving Chemical, Biological, Radiological & Nuclear Events*, Arktos, 2020.

9   The deep state (*Derin Devlet* in Turkish) is a concept created by Turkish prime minister Bülent Ecevit in the 1980s to describe the parallel hierarchies and networks that really govern a country. This concept was popularized in English by

and slow down, if not stop, whatever agenda it might have had. No wonder the globalist establishment was so furious. How could anyone challenge their plans for world domination!

However flawed Mr. Trump is, however his attempts proved futile, he probably won us four precious years to prepare and plan how to react to the inevitable acceleration — through the current administration, singularly helped by the Covid crisis — of actions to take control of whatever slipped away during the 2016–2020 period. Beware, for this process can be dangerous, as frantic actions lead to mistakes, and these can lead to unpredictable outcomes.

What has been tested and proven fragile in the last ten years are the supply chains, so essential to deliver our food, manufactured goods, spare parts, medical supplies, drugs, etc. The crisis started in 2008 and the 2020 pandemic tested the electric grid (which has since been improved in North America and in Europe, but will it be enough to avoid regular power cuts?), and the supply chains. The latter almost crashed in April 2020 and are still under a lot of stress. As anyone who wants to buy a bicycle or stock up on ammunition can attest, there are many products that are now in low supply or unable to be repaired. The disruption of the just-in-time production and distribution also has had effects on the price of commodities and raw materials like wood or petrol but, so far, they have withstood the crash. That's fortunate. And the COOs of major corporations are now probably scrambling to design more efficient and more resistant networks — hopefully with more inventory and redundant systems. Or not. Perhaps they will think that all is back to normal and, as every penny is saved for the

---

Peter Dale Scott and others. In reality, this is not new. Jefferson knew it would eventually happen; Eisenhower warned us about it; Kennedy was (among other reasons) killed for trying to curb it; Nixon tried to control it by appeasing it, and from Reagan onwards, most U.S. presidents went along with it. The financial-military-industrial-internet-Israeli-globalist-pedo-homo-complex (I made that one up, but it's realistic) now controls the USA and its empire (NATO members, Japan, Australia, New Zealand, etc.).

shareholder and for the management's bonus, the current profitability can still be pushed a little bit longer.

The 2020 crisis has had a significant effect on small businesses too. Many small companies, especially in the travel, food, catering, or event industries, have gone bust due to government decisions. As a result, large companies with deep pockets or with access to cheap credit are buying everything. The old joke about the opening of a Starbucks in the parking lot of a Starbucks is back! Will this consolidation be successful as energy becomes scarcer and people have less disposable income?

Where I have been disappointed in the last ten years is the attitude of the people around us. Of course, many have woken up to the realities of our world and about who really rules over us (Who are "they"? If you don't know, you need to do the research. If you know, you know.) and many have understood what really matters in their lives (and no, it's not that extra buck or dying at work). Thank you pre-censorship internet! But so many among us remain slaves. So many are happy about their enslavement as it brings them the illusion of safety and of predictability. The blue-pill/red-pill metaphor of *The Matrix* is quite valid. But it's not new. French philosopher Étienne de la Boétie[10] wrote in the 16th century that "[i]t is incredible how as soon as a people become subject, it promptly falls into such complete forgetfulness of its freedom that it can hardly be roused to the point of regaining it, obeying so easily and willingly that one is led to say that this people has not so much lost its liberty as won its enslavement."

Sadly, through the social engineering enabled by modern technology, the enslavement and the dumbing down of the masses has never been so potent. With "guaranteed" universal income and Netflix as the *panem et circenses* of today, the masses are becoming docile, numb and dumb. Nothing new, but I was naively hoping that more people would rise in their minds and spirits to become responsible adults and

---

10 For a great introduction about this fundamental thinker: https://mises.org/library/politics-etienne-de-la-boetie

not simple digestive tracts equipped with sexual organs, only interested in whatever knee-jerk response to their current feelings they have, with not much reasoning about why they are such perfect consumers. And I am not only describing the poor here; the middle class and part of the upper class are just the same, but with better looking cars and more spacious homes. These new slaves, who humorist George Carlin made fun of already in the late 1970s, are ripe for enabling the creation of a new religion, just as the slaves of the Romans did 2,000 years ago, enabling the rise of Christianity out of a small Jewish sect. "Things have to change for things to remain the same," wrote Italian writer di Lampedusa in his 1958 book *The Leopard*. Masses are thus manipulated by the promise of consumption and by using subjective and empty words like tolerance, democracy, social justice, inclusivity, etc. to enable the religion of *wokism*, with the iconoclast cancel culture, anti-White racism, nazifeminism and cultural Marxism as dogma and a new class of revolutionary priests coming out of the progressive universities and organizations like BLM. "War is peace; freedom is slavery; ignorance is strength." Orwell's dire warning in *1984* is almost a reality. Are the globalist owners of the system certain that this revolution will ultimately not eat its own, as revolutionary movements usually end up doing? I think they are in for a horrible surprise as the people who create wealth and productivity leave, secede or are sent to reeducation camps (I'm not joking). Morons led by the blind and the ideological. What could go wrong?

In the West, until very recently, institutions like traditional religions, the army, the police, which would normally stabilize and structure society, have been gutted, demoralized or have disappeared. Even the state apparatus seems to have transformed into, not just a corrupt parasite, but the enemy of the original populations of these countries. They are not able anymore to protect and defend but, on the contrary, participate in the violent oppression.

With the family restructured, human societies have no, or little, capacity to withstand collectively any crisis, they are psychologically as well as physically fragile, lacking love, lonely, isolated, lacking a vision of the future besides consumption, depending solely or mostly on the state for their lives, their security and their sense of belonging. Just like a slave on a plantation depends on his master for food, just like a drug addict depends on his dealer, society is at the mercy of the government and will defend it, no matter the incompetence, violence or suppression of freedoms.

Will this situation last? Can it last?

If we take the American situation — as this country leads the West — exorbitant debt, problems in the energy sector, unreformable political systems mired in corruption, and delusional elites in their feelings of omnipotence add up to the current culture of rising ethnic nationalism and separatism that mirrors (anti-)racism. Let's see what Russian President Vladimir Putin thinks about this, quoting him from his 2021 address at the World Economic Forum: "We are hearing threats coming out of US Congress and elsewhere. This is happening in the course of internal political processes within the USA. The people who make these threats are assuming, it would seem, that the power of the USA, its economic, military and political power, is such that this isn't serious, that they will survive this. That's what they think. But I'll tell you what the problem is, as a former citizen of the Soviet Union. The problem of empires is that they imagine themselves to be so powerful that they can allow themselves small miscalculations and errors. Some they'll bribe, some they'll scare, some they'll make a deal with, some they'll give glass beads to, some they'll frighten with warships — and this will fix problems. But the number of problems continues to grow. There comes a moment when they can no longer cope with them. The United States are making sure-footed strides directly along the path of the Soviet Union."

What about our great leaders? Having worked in Africa for many years, I can compare them to our current Western politicians and governments. Objectively, they are just as corrupt and crass. Who said we can't learn from the Third World? I'm only half joking, but this was inevitable. As the deep state grows, the front men and women have to be chosen among the most servile and easily bought to avoid any independent thought and action. Ergo, they are often chosen among the ones that have perversions or have committed criminal acts that, once on tape (something the Epstein pedo-island network enabled perfectly), make them very obedient. No wonder that all the echelons of the so-called "elites" are full of dodgy people you wouldn't want to trust with your wallet or have near your children. This happens at a time where the complexity of the world is at its highest ever and when we would need the most competent and open-minded people. The Covid crisis of 2020–2021 was a perfect example of how incompetence, stupidity, servility, butt-covering caused a drop of ten percent in the world's GDP and countless preventable deaths. As we used to say in the software industry: it's not a bug, it's a feature.

We now can expect that whatever will be the next major crisis — a *real* pandemic, an oil shock, a war, major social unrest, it will be managed with the worst result. Seriously, hope or pray for the best, but expect the worst from them.

Whether you are a New Age Buddhist or not, and as the Covid crisis perfectly showed, all is linked. Any event can create a crisis that can lead to more events or more crises and so on. Thus, the risk grows with time. I wrote in 2011 that the time of critical growth of risk of economic collapse will start in 2020. Here we are.

What now?

I have lived for almost fifty years in a country that is obsessively conservative and uber-prepared. Armed neutrality through both world wars and the Cold War instilled in the Swiss mind a sense of preparedness that is second to none: our army is a citizen militia, our mountains are full of deep bunkers (and airbases, barracks, hospitals, artillery emplacements, command centers, etc.), the population is (used to be at least) mostly armed and with mandatory stores of food and supplies for a minimum of two weeks, and a general love for physical health. This has obviously influenced my thoughts on how to prepare for economic collapse. And this is perhaps why this book is an international bestseller: it approaches preparedness, prepping, survivalism in a balanced way.

Water, food, health, energy, knowledge/skills, defense, social link — the seven pillars of survival that I describe in this and other books — what else is there in life?

To approach a conclusion, I would like to share with you what I have learned in the last ten years.

First, being a little bit prepared is better than not at all. So start now, slowly, according to your means and depending on whatever constraints you may have (family, work, geographical location, etc.). Step by step, like when one climbs a mountain. Focus on the next step. Know where you are going. Decide what is the best route. But do focus on that step. Don't slip; make it stable and sturdy. And keep an indomitable faith in the certainty that you will make it.

Another lesson is that you will never be prepared enough, and that after owning the basic tools, equipment and supplies, it's mostly a question of training, practice and work. Do the work. No complaining. Just do it.

Also, you cannot be prepared for EVERYTHING! You won't. Nuclear war. Racial war. Civil war. Tyrannical government. Communism. The zombie apocalypse. You can't. Your resources are limited. So go slow if you must, adapt to your personal or family situation. In the end, stuff is nothing without knowledge and training. Having a sound strategy with contingency plans is fundamental and, finally, having the mindset that will enable you to manage your emotions, and master and use your fear in stressful situations — and there will be plenty — will make the difference.

A fundamental lesson learned is that ninety percent of the troubles happen in the city, so move to the countryside. Sure, in South Africa for example, farms are targeted by racially motivated thugs. But as horrible and vicious as these commando operations are, the crimes committed in the cities are much more numerous and just as violent. Move to the countryside and be part of a local community.

So adopt the attitude of having "survival" as a lifestyle. Something that you have in the back of your mind all the time, but that is NOT the center of your life, that is not an obsession, the sole purpose of it. First, nothing may happen. And be grateful for not having to face that terrorist shooting, that criminal gang targeting your property, that angry mob or those alien invaders. Fundamentally, prepping, survivalism, however you want to call it, is all about getting back in control of your life.

And so, finally, enjoy life. Seek your dreams. But be prepared if something happens. You owe it to yourself, to your family and to your tribe.

Geneva, June 2021

APPENDICES

72-Hour Survival Kit

This list describes the contents of a 72-hour survival kit ("bug-out bag") for a family. Such a kit must be easy to access (so do not store it in the basement or the attic, etc.) and stored in a bag that is easy to transport (backpack or sporting bag). You can customize the contents — there are many videos on YouTube outlining different approaches — but, at the very least, it should include the following:

Food and Water (per Person)

> Water bottles — 1 gallon
> Dehydrated meals or MREs (Meals Ready to Eat) — 3
> Dark chocolate or cereal bars — 6 units
> Bouillon cubes

Clothing (per Person)

> Underwear — 1
> Thermal blanket and ordinary blanket — 1
> Shoes and socks — 1 pair each
> Trousers, wind-breaker, gloves and hat — 1
> T-shirts — 2

Medical Kit

> Roll of homeostatic bandages
> Scissors
> Headache tablets
> Anti-diarrhea tablets
> Compress bandage
> Disinfectant (chlorhexadine)
> Band-aids

Hygiene

> Toothbrush — 1 per person
> Toothpaste — 1
> Soap bar — 1
> Disposable razor — 1
> Tampons — 1
> Tissues — 1
> Water filter — 1
> Water purification pills — 1

Tools

> Pocket lamp with extra batteries
> Folding shovel
> Camp axe
> Multi-tool with tweezers and knife blade (e.g. Leatherman, Victorinox)

Other

> Plastic tarpaulin
> Paracord 550 — 10m / 33 feet
> Matches (wrapped or in a sealed container)
> Lighter
> Candles

> Aluminum cup
> Forks and spoons
> Aluminum plates — 1 per person
> Identity papers (e.g. Passport, etc.)
> Copies of property titles
> Vaccination history
> Outdoor survival manual
> Writing materials (paper, soft pencil, ballpoint pen, marker, chalk, etc.)
> Scotch© and duct tape
> Re-sealable bags (of the Ziplock© type)
> Garbage bags 40/60 liters (10/16 gallons) — 1-3
> Aluminum foil sheets
> Signaling mirror
> Luminescent stick
> Compass
> Charged battery or battery charger for your cell phone
> Road map
> Cash in small denominations
> Insect spray
> Sewing kit (needle and thread).

Auxiliary Items

These can be stored, but you should be ready to take them with you when you depart for your SAB.

> Camping material (sleeping bags, tent)
> Roll of aluminum foil
> Roll of plastic food wrap
> Bath towel
> Moist toilet wipes
> Small gas heater
> Shovel.

LIST 2

Foods to Stock

TYPE	UNIT	PER PERSON, PER MONTH	SHELF LIFE
Pasta	2.2 lbs.	10	30+ years
Canned fish	2.2 lbs.	2	10 years
Canned meat	2.2 lbs.	2	10 years
Canned vegetables	2.2 lbs.	15	10–15 years
Canned fruit	2.2 lbs.	5	10–15 years
Legumes	2.2 lbs.	4	30+ years
Flour	2.2 lbs.	8	3 years
Nuts (bagged)	1.1 lbs.	1	3–5 years
Oil	1 quart	1	3–5 years
Potatoes	2.2 lbs.	4	1–2 years
Rice	2.2 lbs.	3	30+ years
Salt	2.2 lbs.	1	30+ years
Sugar	2.2 lbs.	1	30+ years
Honey	2.2 lbs.	1	30+ years
Powdered milk	2.2 lbs.	1	3–5 years
Cheese	2.2 lbs.	1	1 year
Maize	2.2 lbs.	2	10 years
Dried fruit	2.2 lbs.	1	1 year

TYPE	UNIT	PER PERSON, PER MONTH	SHELF LIFE
Oats	2.2 lbs.	1	3–5 years
Dehydrated wheat	2.2 lbs.	1	30+ years
Dried vegetables	2.2 lbs.	1	3–5 years
MREs	according to need	1	30+ years
Bouillon cubes	5 oz.	1	30+ years
Condiments	2.2 lbs.	1	30+ years
Ovaltine©	2.2 lbs.	1	30+ years
Coffee beans	2.2 lbs.	1	10 years
Corn starch	5 oz.	1	30+ years
Powdered pudding	11 oz.	1	30+ years
Instant coffee	2.2 lbs.	1	30+ years
Mustard	1 lb 2 oz.	1	30+ years
Tea	2.2 lbs.	1	10 years
Yeast	1 lbs.	1	3–6 months (but can be "reproduced")
Multivitamins	3½ oz.	1	1 year
Vitamin C	3½ oz.	1	3 years at 20 °C and kept dry
UHT milk (=Ultra-High-Temperature processed milk)	1 quart	12	6 months
UHT fruit juice	1 quart	12	6 months
Dark chocolate	2.2 lbs.	8	30+ years
"Comfort food" (cookies, etc.)	2.2 lbs.	1	1–2 years
Vinegar	1 quart	1	30+ years
Wine	1 quart	8	30+ years
Liquor	1 quart	1	30+ years

TYPE	UNIT	PER PERSON, PER MONTH	SHELF LIFE
Jam	1.1 lbs.	4	30+ years
Sulfur (for drying fruit)	7 oz.	1	30+ years
Spices (to taste)	3½ oz.	1	30+ years
Baking soda	2.2 lbs.	1	30+ years
Food bags			
Aluminum foil	Store in large quantities for barter		
Bags for dried meat			
Jars and seals			

Gardening, Fishing, and Hunting Equipment

Hunting and Fishing

> Bow, crossbow and arrows
> Piano cords, metal boxes, copper, and aluminum wire, etc., for making traps
> Fishing rods, fishing nets, traps, etc.

Cooking

> Pans, pots, cast-iron pans, kettles, etc.
> Knives and kitchen tools
> Saw for bone and meat, chopper, metal buckets
> Kitchen gloves, aprons, etc.

Water

> Water filter with replacement filters
> Containers (5–10 gallons)
> Bleach — 5 gallons per person per year
> Water purification tablets in great number

Nutritional Supplements, Vitamins, and Minerals

> **Minerals:** calcium, magnesium, phosphorus, potassium, sodium, iodine, zinc, iron, etc.

> **Vitamins:** A, C (ascorbic acid), B<1, B<2, B<3, B<5, B<6, B<7, B<8, B<9, B<12, D, E, K, carotene, etc.

> **Hormonal, Oil, and Fat supplements:** Omega 3, DHEA, GnRH, etc.

> **Plant-Based Supplements** (according to need): fennel, meadow-sweet, mouse-ear hawkweed, ginseng, guarana, ginger, passion flower, hawthorn, linden, verbena, etc.

Hygienic and Cleaning Products

CATEGORY	PRODUCTS	PER PERSON, PER YEAR
WC	Sawdust for outhouse (22 lbs. sacks)	12
	Toilet paper rolls	120
DENTAL CARE	Toothbrush	12
	Floss (164 ft.)	4
	Toothpaste (7 oz.)	12
	Fluoride mouthwash (17 oz.)	2
BODILY HYGIENE	Bar of soap (200 g.)	12
FEMININE HYGIENE	Tampons (30)	6
	Sanitary napkins (30)	6
GENERAL HYGIENE	Cotton swabs (100)	2
	Moist napkins (100)	2
	Suntan lotion (10 oz.)	4
GARBAGE BAGS	Large (32 gal.)	12
	Medium (16 gal.)	12
	Small (8 gal.)	12
SHAVING	Disposable woman's razor	6
	Man's razor + brush	1
	Manual clipper	1

CATEGORY	PRODUCTS	PER PERSON, PER YEAR
COOKING	Dishwashing liquid (10 oz.)	12
	Sponges	12
	Dish detergent for plates, glasses (13 oz.)	12
	Detergent for pans (13 oz.)	12
	Rubber gloves	24
CLEANING	Stain remover	6
	Laundry soap (5 gal.)	7
	Soap for washing floors (1 qt.)	4
	Soap for washing wooden floors (1 qt.)	4
	Bleach (1 qt.)	10
	Brush	4
	Broom	4
	Mop heads	4
	Cleaning cloth	12
	Bucket and tub	2
	Baking soda (1 kg.)	2

Medicines and Medical Tools

Instruments

> Tweezers, surgical clips, sterile needles, and suture thread
> Forceps, retractors, haemostatic scissors and clamps
> Scalpel and disposable sterile scalpel blades
> Thermometers and stethoscope
> Suction tools, straws, boilers, wipes
> Markers
> Injection materials, syringes of various sizes, sterile needles, etc.
> Venom extractor
> Homeostatic tourniquet
> Preformed splints for ankle and fist, cervical collar (neck brace)

Bandages

> Dressings, plasters, band-aids, steri-strips, medical tape
> Gauze (rolls and 20 square-centimeter squares)
> Bandages in various sizes: rolls, triangles, scarf, etc.
> Sterile strips
> Cotton
> Safety pins

Medicines

> Disinfectant: chlorhexidine, tincture of benzoin
> Alcohol-based disinfectant for hands
> Antibiotic ointment (Neosporin©)
> Benadryl tablets (diphenhydramine — anti-allergen, cold-, flu- and nasal-congestion medications, and sleep aids)
> Ibuprofen tablets — for pain and fever
> Anti-diarrheal tablets
> Aspirin (325 milograms)
> Ophthalmic saline solution
> Painkiller: paracetamol, morphine
> Local anesthetic: lidocaine, procaine
> Antiseptic: chlorhexidine
> Antibiotic: co-amoxicillin
> Antacid tablets
> Iodine tablets
> Aloe-vera gel with lidocaine

Dental Material

> Periodontal curettes
> Dental picks (curved), mirror, pliers
> Clove oil
> Dental forceps

Other

> Baby soap
> Baking soda
> Gloves, mask, operating mask
> Plastic CPR mouth barrier

Tools

Systematically note the tools you use regularly and which ones you may need. Prefer manual to electrical tools.

Gardening Tools

> Mechanical-repair tools
> Animal-care tools
> Soldering tools
> Blacksmith tools
> Complete tool box (screwdriver, hammer, clamp, wrench, etc.)
> Woodcutting, carpentry, and cabinet-making tools
> Manual battery charger (crank-operated)

Other Tools

> Large pliers
> Crowbar
> Sledgehammer
> Axe
> Shovel
> Heavy-duty glue, paint, lacquer
> Iron wire
> Velcro strips
> Rubber bands

> Whetstone
> Metal saw
> Wheelbarrow

Protective Garments

> Protective gloves
> Protective shoes
> Kevlar protective strips
> Protective goggles
> Protective helmet
> Hearing protection

Other Material

> Replacement parts for all your materials
> Dark tarpaulin for covering windows
> Rolls of plastic insulation for sealing rooms and filling in broken windows, etc.
> Batteries of all kinds, especially rechargeable ones
> Candles, lamps, etc.
> Large receptacles for heating oil, gasoline, diesel
> Medium-sized receptacles for water (5–10 gal.), like jerrycans
> Cisterns (40 gal) for rainwater

Defense, Security, and Communication Materials

Weapons (among Many Choices)

> Primary Weapon — .223-caliber rifle
> + 5,000 rounds and 10 Chargers
> Secondary Weapon — 9 mm Pistol
> + 1,000 rounds + 4 chargers
> Hunting Weapon — 12-gauge shotgun
> + 2,000 rounds of different types
> Pocket knife (Swiss Army knife)
> Multipurpose tool (Leatherman, Victorinox)
> Combat knife or a bush knife
> Hatchet or kukri-type knife
> Emergency survival knife

Tactical Equipment

> Bandolier for long gun
> Holster for pistol
> Ear and eye protection
> Crotch protection
> Bullet-proof vest (Level IIIA)

> Kevlar helmet
> Belt, charging cradles
> Lashing, water bottle, backpack
> Gloves, cap, hat
> Gas mask and replacement filters
> Vacuum bags
> Rain gear, poncho, leggings
> Shoes and boots in sufficient quantity (at least three pairs)
> Flashlight and rechargeable batteries

Auxiliary Equipment

> Material for cleaning weapons (tools, lubricant, cleaner, grease, etc.)
> Geiger counter

Security Equipment

> Padlock
> Alarms
> Barbed wire
> Sandbags
> Chains and cords of various thickness and length

Communication Equipment

> Shortwave receiver
> Battery-driven radio, rechargeable batteries, battery charger
> Rugged laptop with Wi-Fi
> Field telephone
> Walkie-talkie, relays, and antennas
> CB radio

Bibliography and References

SECTION 1

Analysis

English

Bernays, Edward L., *Propaganda*, IG Publishing, 2004.

Blumenthal, Karen, *Six Days in October: The Stock Market Crash of 1929*, Atheneum, 2002.

Bruner, Robert F. and Carr, Sean D., *The Panic of 1907: Lessons Learned from the Market's Perfect Storm*, Wiley, 2007.

Davis, Mike, *Planet of Slums*, Verso, 2006.

Diamond, Jared, *Collapse: How Societies Choose to Fail or Survive*, Rev. Ed., Penguin, 2011.

Duncan, Richard J., *The Dollar Crisis: Causes, Consequences, Cures*, Wiley, 2005.

Ferguson, Niall, *The Ascent of Money: A Financial History of the World*, Penguin Books, 2009.

Galbraith, John K., *The Great Crash 1929*, Mariner Books, 1954.

Gardner, Dan, *Risk: The Science and Politics of Fear*, Virgin Books, 2009.

Heather, Peter, *The Fall of the Roman Empire: A New History of Rome and the Barbarians*, 2006.

Heinberg, Richard, *The Party's Over: Oil, War and the Fate of Industrial Societies*, Clairview, 2005.

____, *Peak Everything: Waking Up to the Century of Decline*, New Society Publishers, 2007.

Holmgren, David, *Future Scenarios: How Communities Can Adapt to Peak Oil and Climate Change*, Chelsea Green Publishing, 2009.

Huffington, Arianna, *Third World America: How Our Politicians Are Abandoning the Middle Class and Betraying the American Dream*, Crown Books, 2010.

Klare, Michael T., *Resource Wars: The New Landscape of Global Conflict*, Owl Books, 2002.

Lasch, Christopher, *The Revolt of the Elites and the Betrayal of Democracy*, W. W. Norton, 1995.

Luttwak, Edward, *Turbo-Capitalism: Winners and Losers in the Global Economy*, Harper Collins, 1999.

Lynas, Mark, *Six Degrees: Our Future on a Hotter Planet*, Fourth Estate, 2007.

Martenson, Chris, *The Crash Course: The Unsustainable Future of our Economy, Energy and Environment*, Wiley, 2011.

Monbiot, George, *Heat: How to Stop the Planet Burning*, Allen Lane, 2006.

Mullins, Eustace, *The Secrets of the Federal Reserve*, Bridger House Publishers, 2009.

Parker, Selwyn, *The Great Crash: How the Stock Market Crash of 1929 Plunged the World into Depression*, Piaktus, 2008.

Rothkopf, David, *Superclass: The Global Power Elite and the World They Are Making*, Little Brown, 2008.

Ruppert, Michael C., *Crossing the Rubicon: The Decline of the American Empire at the End of the Age of Oil*, New Society Publishers, 2004.

____, *A Presidential Energy Policy*, New World Publishing, 2009.

____, *Confronting Collapse: The Crisis of Energy and Money in a Post Peak Oil World*, Chelsea Green Publishing, 2009.

Schor, Juliet B., *Born to Buy: The Commercialized Child and the New Consumer Culture*, Scribner, 2004.

____, *The Overworked American: The Unexpected Decline of Leisure*, Basic Books, 1993.

____, *The Overspent American: Why We Want What We Don't Need*, Harper Perennial, 1999.

Taleb, Nassim Nicholas, *The Black Swan: The Impact of the Highly Improbable*, Random House, 2007.

Todd, Emmanuel, *After the Empire: The Breakdown of the American Order*, Columbia University Press, 2003.

Turk, James, *The Coming Collapse of the Dollar and How to Profit from it: Make a Fortune by Investing in Gold and Other Hard Assets*, Broadway Business, 2008.

Wolf, Naomi, *The End of America: Letter of Warning to a Young Patriot*, Chelsea Green Publishing, 2007.

French

Arnoult, Jacques and Blamont, Jacques, *Lève-toi et marche: propositions pour un futur de l'humanité*, 2009.

Attali, Jacques, *Une brève historie de l'avenir*, Le Livre de Poche, 2011.

Benoit, Alain de, *Demain, la décroissance! Penser l'écologie jusqu'au bout*, Éditions Edite, 2007.

Clouscard, Michel, *Néo-fascisme et idéologie du désir*, Le Castor Astral, 1973.

___, *Le capitalisme de la séduction*, Éditions ES, 1981.

___, *Critique du libéralisme libertaire — généalogie de la contre- révolution*, Éditions Delga, 2005.

Conte, Bernard, *La tiers-mondialisation de la planète*, Presses Universitaires de Bordeaux, 2009.

Drac, Michel, *Crise ou Coup d'État?*, Éditions Le Retour aux Sources, 2009.

___, *Crise économique ou crise de sens?*, Éditions Le Retour aux Sources, 2010.

Guénon, René, *Le règne de la quantité et les signes des temps*, Gallimard, 1945.

___, *La crise du monde moderne*, Gallimard, 2004

Holbecq, André-Jacques, *La dette publique, une affaire rentable : À qui profite le système?*, Éditions Yves Michel, 2008.

Jovanivic, Pierre, *777 : La chute du Vatican et de Wall Street selon Saint Jean*, Le Jardin des Livres, 2009.

___, *Blythe Masters : La banquière de la JP Morgan à l'origine de la crise mondiale*, Le Jardin des Livres, 2011.

Juvin, Hervé, *Le renversement du monde: politique de la crise*, Gallimard, 2010.

Latouche, Serge, *La déraison de la raison économique : du délire d'efficacité au principe de précaution*, Albin Michel, 2001.

Laurent, Éric, *La face cachée des banques: scandales et révélations sur les mileux financières*, Plon, 2009.

___, *Le scandale des délocalisations*, Plon, 2011.

Leconte, Pierre, *De la crise financière vers l'hyper-inflation : Comment vous protéger*, Éditions Jean-Cyrille Godefoy, 2009.

___, *La grande crise monétaire du XXIe siècle a déjà commencé!*, Éditions Jean-Cyrille Godefoy, 2007.

___, *Tragédie monétaire : quelle monnaie pour la mondialisation, le dollar ou l'or?*, Éditions François-Xavier de Guilbert, 2003.

___, *Les faux-monnayeurs: sortir du chaos monétaire mondiale pour éviter la ruine*, Éditions François-Xavier de Guilbert, 2008.

Lugan, Berard, *Pour en finir avec la colonisation*, Éditions du Rocher, 2006.

____, *Atlas historique de l'Afrique des origines à nos jours*, Éditions du Rocher, 2001.

Michéa, Jean-Claude, *L'enseignements de l'ignorance et ses conditions modernes*, Climats, 2006.

Sapir; Jacques, *Le nouveau XXe siècle: du siècle « américain » au retour des nations*, self-published.

Soral, Alain, *Comprendre l'empire: demain la gouvernance globale ou la révolte des nations?*, Éditions Blanche, 2011.

Todd, Emmanuel, *Après l'empire : essai sur la décomposition du système américain*, Gallimard, 2002.

Zaki, Myret, *La fin du dollar: comment le billet vert est devenu la plus grande bulle spéculative de l'histoire*, Éditions Favre, 2011.

Ziegler, Jean, *La haine de l'Occident*, Albin Michel, 2008.

Italian

Rubbio, Carlo and Criscenti, Nino, *Il dilemma nucleare*, Sperling & Kupfer, 1987.

Online Resources

(in English unless otherwise indicated)

www.ecologiste.org (French)

www.peakoil.net

www.energywatchgroup.org (German & English)

www.odac-info.org

www.ihs.com

www.energyinsights.net

www.worldenergyoutlook.org

www.cleanbreak.ca

www.grinningplanet.com

www.petroleum-economist.com

www.fao.org

www.dieoff.com

www.resilience.org

www.energybulletin.net

www.theoildrum.com

www.transitiontowns.org

www.postcarbon.org

www.urbandanger.com

www.wfad.org

www.forum-monetaire.com (French with some articles in English)

www.chrismortenson.com

www.lastoilshock.com

www.caseyresearch.com

www.asc-cybernetics.org

www.green-energy-news.com

www.foet.org

www.undp.org

www.worldbank.org us.fsc.org

www.oxfam.org

www.jovanovic.com/blog (French)

www.collapsenet.net

SECTION 2

Collapse Theory

English

Chamberlain, Shaun, *The Transition Timeline: For a Local, Resilient Future*, Chelsea Green Publishing, 2009.

Deffeyes, Kenneth S., *Beyond Oil: The View from Hubbert's Peak*, Hill and Wang, 2006.

Diamond, Jared, *Collapse: How Societies Choose to Fail or Succeed*, Viking, 2004.

Doucet, Clive, *Urban Meltdown: Cities, Climate Change and Politics as Usual*, New Society Publishers, 2007.

Greer, John Michael, *The Long Descent: A User's Guide to the End of the Industrial Age*, New Society Publishers, 2008.

Heinberg, Richard, *The Party's Over: Oil, War and the Fate of Industrial Societies*, New Society Publishers, 2005.

Hopkins, Rob, *The Transition Handbook: From Oil Dependency to Local Resilience*, Chelsea Green Publishing, 2008.

Kennedy, Paul, *The Rise and Fall of the Great Powers*, Vintage, 1989.

Klein, Naomi, *The Shock Doctrine: The Rise of Disaster Capitalism*, Picador, 2008.

Kunstler, James Howard, *The Long Emergency — Surviving the Converging Catastrophes of the 20th Century*, Grove Press, 2006.

Murphy, Pat, *Plan C: Community Survival Strategies for Peak Oil and Climate Change*, 2008.

Orlov, Dmitry, *Reinventing Collapse: The Soviet Experience and American Prospects*, Rev. Ed., New Society Publishers, 2011.

Ruppert, Michael C., *Crossing the Rubicon: The Decline of the American Empire at the End of the Age of Oil*, New Society Publishers, 2004.

Stein, Matthew, *When Technology Fails: A Manuel for Self-Relience, Sustainability and Surviving the Long Emergency*, 2nd ed., Chelsea Green Publishing, 2008.

Tainter, Joseph, *The Collapse of Complex Societies*, Cambridge University Press, 1990.

Taylor, Graeme, *Evolution's Edge: The Coming Collapse and Transformation of our World*, New Society Publishers, 2008.

Worth, Kenneth D., *Peak Oil and the Second Great Depression (2010- 2030): A Survival Guide for Investors and Savers After Peak Oil*, Outskirts Press, 2010.

French

Drac, Michel, *Eurocalypse*, Le Retour aux Sources, 2009.

Supplemental

Hermann Huppen, *Jeremiah* (comic book series), Glénat, 1979-2003. See: en.wikipedia.org/wiki/Jeremiah_(comics).

Jericho (television series), CBS Paramount, 2006-2008. See: en.wikipedia.org/wiki/Jericho_(TV_series).

Survivors (television series), British Broadcasting Corporation, 2008-2010. See: en.wikipedia.org/wiki/Survivors_(2008_TV_series).

SECTIONS 3 AND 4

Survivalism

English

Bridgewater, Alan and Bridgewater, Gill, *The Self-Sufficiency Handbook*, Skyhorse Publishing, 2007.

Department of Defense, *U.S. Army Survival Manual: FM 21-76*, CreateSpace, 2011.

Gonzales, Laurence, *Deep Survival: Who Lives, Who Dies, and Why*, Norton, 2005.

McNab, Chris, *How to Survive Anything, Anywhere: A Handbook of Survival Skills for Every Scenario and Environment*, McGraw & Hill, 2004.

____, *Special Forces Survival Guide: Wilderness Survival Skills from the World's Most Elite Military Units*, Ulysses Press, 2008.

Rawles, James Wesley, *How to Survive the End of the World as We Know It*, Plume, 2009.

Wiseman, James, *SAS Survival Handbook*, Collins, 2009.

French

Allègre, Jade, *Survivre en ville... quand tout s'arrête!*, 2nd ed., 2005.

Ayoub et al., *G5G: déclaration de guerre*, Éditions Le Retour aux Sources, 2010.

Bachman, Albert and Grosjean, Georges, *Défense civile*, Éditions Miles, Aarau, 1969.

Le Brun, Dominique, *Manuel de survie*, France Loisirs, 1988.

Maniquet, Xavier, *Survivre: comment vaincre en milieu hostile*, Albin Michel, 1988.

Provencher, Paul, *Vivre en forêt*, Les Éditions de l'Homme, 1973. Rabhi, Pierre, *Manifeste pour la terre et l'humanisme*, Actes Sud, 2008.

____, *Vers la sobriété heureuse*, Actes Sud, 2010.

Tyrode et al., *Manuel de survie face aux attentats et catastrophes naturelles ou industrielles*, Albin Michel, 2002.

German

Nehberg, Rüdiger, *Survival-Lexikon*, Piper, 2000.

Von Lichtenfels, Karl Leopold, *Lexikon des Überlebens: Handbuch für Krisenzeiten*, Anaconda, 2006.

Italian

Bertuccini, Ivan, *Sopravvivenza estrema : guida al piano B*, Macro Edizioni, 2010.

Maolucci et al., *Surviving : istruzioni de sopravvivenza individuale e di gruppo*, Hoepli, 2010.

Online Resources

www.survivalblog.com

www.terravivos.com

www.self-sufficiency.net

www.carninglipress.co.uk

Water, Water Filters, Etc.

Online Resources

www.survivalunlimited.com/waterfilter.htm

www.katadyn.com

www.bigberkey.com

www.steripen.com

www.crystalquest.com

www.seychelle.com

www.buglogical.com

Water, Plants, Agriculture, and Animal Husbandry

English

Ashworth, Suzanne, *Seed to Seed: Seed Saving and Growing Techniques for Vegetable Gardeners*, Chelsea Green Publishing, 2002.

Chioffi, Nancy and Mead, Gretchen, *Keeping the Harvest: Discover the Homegrown Goodness of Putting Up Your Own Fruits, Vegetables and Herbs*, Storey Publishing, 1976.

Emery, Carla, *The Encyclopedia of Country Living: The Original Manuel for Living Off the Land and Doing It Yourself*, Sasquatch Books, 1994.

Kindersley, Dorling, *The New Self-Sufficient Gardener*, Dorling Kindersley, 2008.

Klein, Carol, *Grow Your Own Garden*, BBC Books, 2010.

Layton, Peggy, *Emergency Food Storage & Survival Handbook*, Clarkson Potter, 2002.

Logsdon, Gene, *Small-Scale Grain Raising: An Organic Guide to Growing, Processing, and Using Nutritious Whole Grains, for Home Gardeners and Local Farmers*, 2nd ed. Chelsea Green Publishing, 2009.

Seymour, John, *The New Complete Book of Self-Sufficiency*, Dorling Kindersley, 2003.

Solomon, Steve, *Gardening When It Counts: Growing Food in Hard Times*, New Society Publishers, 2009.

Strawbridge, Dick, *Practical Self-Sufficiency*, Dorling Kindersley, 2010.

French

De Boivert, *Clotilde, La cuisine des plantes sauvage*, Dargaud, 1984.

Gerbault, Snezana, *Jardins et potagers de montagne*, Éditions du Rouergue, 2011.

LeConte, Yves, *Le traité rustica de l'apiculture*, Éditions Rustica, 2006. Renaud, Victor, *Le traité rustica du potager*, Éditions Rustica, 2007.

Thun, Maria, *Pratiquer la bio-dynamie au jardin: rythmes cosmiques et préparations bio-dynamiques*, Mouvement de Culture Bio- Dynamique, 2005.

English (Online)

permaculture.com

norseco.com (with French)

French

www.multiroir.com

www.multibac.com

www.ocongel.com

www.sobek-france.com

www.aideauxmontagnards.ch

www.eglisedejesuschrist.fr

www.eglisedejesuschrist.be

www.eglise-de-jesus-christ.ch

www.prospeciarara.ch (with German and Italian)

www.terre-humanisme.fr

www.bassins-et-jardins.com

www.afloredeau.fr

www.biogarten.ch (with German)

German

www.ettima.ch

www.hm-spoerri.ch

www.fsamasch.ch

www.discount.ch

Hygiene, Medicine, and Health

English

Craig, Glenn C., *U.S. Army Special Forces Medical Handbook*, Paladin Press, 1988.

Dickson, Murray, *Where There Is No Dentist*, Hesperian Foundation, 1983.

Doyle, Gerard, *Where There Is No Doctor: Preventive and Emergency Health Care in Challenging Times*, Process Media, 2010.

Werner, David, *Where There Is No Doctor: A Village Health Care Handbook*, Rev. ed. Hesperion Foundation, 1992.

United States Army, *68W Advanced Field Craft: Combat Medic Skills*, Jones and Bartlett Publishers, 2010.

United States Army, *NATO Manual on Emergency War Surgery*, Desert Publications, 1992.

French

Brunner et al., *Guide de soins infirmiers médicine et chirurgie*, Éditions de Boeck, 1998.

Druais, Pierre-Louis and Gay, Bernard, *Médecine générale*, Éditions Masson, 2009.

Energy

English

Degunther, Rik, *Solar Power Your Home for Dummies*, Wiley Publishing, 2008.

Thorne Amann et al., *Consumer Guide to Home Energy Savings*, 9th ed., New Society Publishing, 2007.

Woofenden, Ian, *Wind Power for Dummies*, Wiley Publishing, 2009.

French

Dubois-Pressof, Marie-Pierre, *Une maison écologique et économe*, Massin Éditions, 2009.

Fouin, Julien, *Construire sa maison écologique zéro énergie de A à Z*, Marabout Éditions, 2010.

Internet Links English

www.all-battery.com

www.mobilesolarpower.net

www.iland-solar.com

www.aceee.org

www.eceee.org

www.energystar.gov

www.p3international.com

www.wattsupmeters.com

www.brandelectronics.com

www.solarenergy.org

www.greenpowerscience.com

www.cleanenergy.com

French

www.websolaire.com

www.espaceampoules.fr

www.blueenergy.fr (with English)

German

www.magnet-motor.de (with English)

www.bsrsolar.de (with English)

Self-Defense, Tactics, and Combat

English

Grossman, Don Mann David, *The Modern Day Gunslinger: The Ultimate Handgun Training Manual*, Skyhorse Publishing, 2010.

Suarez, Gabriel, *The Tactical Shotgun: The Best Techniques and Tactics for Employing the Shotgun in Personal Combat*, Paladin Press, 1996.

DVDs from Magpul Dynamic

The Art of the Dynamic Shotgun

The Art of the Tactical Carbine, Vols. 1 & 2 The Art of the Dynamic Handgun

French

Baeriswyl, Alain and Perottie, Phillipe, *L'Instruction du tir*, NDS, 2006.

SURVIVE THE ECONOMIC COLLAPSE

Francard, Loup and Piroth, Christian, *Émeutes, terrorisme, guérilla...violence at contre-violence en zone urbaine*, Éditions Economica, 2010.

Habersetzer, Roland, *Tir d'action à l'arme de poing*, Éditions Amphora, 2009.

Malfatti, René, *Manuel de rechargement*, Éditions Crépin- Leblond, 2004.

Morel, Guillaume and Bouammache, Frédéric, *Protegor: guide pratique de scurit personelle, self-defense et survie urbaine*, Éditions Amphora, 2008.

Perotti, Philipe, *Tir de combat au fusil d'assault*, NDS, 2003.

____, *Le sniping de 4e génération*, NDS, 2008.

____, *Instruction de base au pistolet*, NDS, 2003.

____, *Tireur d'élite*, NDS, 2005.

Perotti et al., *Techniques d'action immédiate*, NDS, 2004. Perrin, Fred, *Combats à l'arme blanche*, NDS, 2005.

English (Online)

www.michiganknives.com

www.knifecenter.com

www.511tactical.com

www.arcteryx.com

www.blackhawk.com

www.bladecraft.com

www.bauer.com

www.steinbrucke.org/site/index.php?lang=en&page=training

www.chiefsupply.com

www.eagleindustries.com

www.galls.com

www.hatch-corp.com

www.newgraham.com

www.odlo.com

www.ortliebusa.com

www.orgear.com

www.petzl.com

www.surefire.com

www.szaboinc.com

www.usmkpro.com

www.uscav.com

French

www.lagardere.ch

www.armes-cornet.com

www.armurie-delattre.com

www.armurie-delmotte.be

www.armuriecarpentier.com

www.armurie-croixrousse.fr

www.armes-occasion.com

www.larquebusier.com

www.nantesarmes.fr

www.gatimel-armurier.com

www.expe.fr

www.unique-fmr.com

www.france-securite.com

www.generalarmystore.fr

www.gkprod.com (with English)

www.matiex-armurie.com

www.omega-ic.com (with English)

www.tir1000.com

www.protegor.net

www.feulibre.com

www.chassons.com

German

www.gunfactory.ch

www.kurse.ballenbergkurse.ch

www.armystore.ch

The Social Bond and Communal Life

Estill, Lyle, *Small is Possible: Life in a Local Economy,* New Society Publishers, 2008.

Lerch, Daniel, *Post-Carbon Cities: Planning for Energy and Climate Uncertainty,* Post Carbon Press, 2008.

Online Resources

www.maweb.ch (German)

PIERO SAN GIORGIO is a Swiss author and former businessman and software executive. For twenty years, he worked in international markets in Eastern Europe, the Middle East, and Africa. For the past decade, Giorgio has dedicated himself to studying the global economic system and its dependence on ever-expanding populations, debt, and resource exploitation. *Survivre à l'effondrement économique*, on the fundamental unsustainability of the system, was published in French to wide acclaim.

Index

Libya 73, 129, 149

M

Macronutrients 227–228

"Mad Cow" disease 101

See also diseases

Mad Max (film) 155, 413

Madoff, Bernie xxvi

mafia, the xxi, 38, 374

maize 47–53, 108, 231, 433

Malachy, Saint xxix

Malthus, Thomas 5–6, 32, 48

manufacturing 12, 31, 69, 138, 167, 181, 413

Mao, Zedong xx, 102

marine life 46

Martenson, Chris xxvii, 200

martial arts 318, 395

martial law 318–322, 395

See also social unrest

Marx, Karl 80

Maslow, Abraham 217, 309, 348–355

mathematics 304

Matrix, The (film) 155, 381, 406, 423

Mayan calendar xxix

meals ready-to-eat 232

meaning, existential or metaphysical 82–93, 107, 119–122, 163, 212, 323, 409–411

meat 43–45, 88, 150, 167, 228–253, 415, 433–436

media, mass 398–421

medicine and healthcare 245–277, 353–354

See also disinfection; hygiene

alternative medicine 277

bacterial infections 267–268

burns 264–265

children 272–273

chronic illnesses 271–272

classification 262

collapse of medical system 127, 163

death 274

dentistry and oral hygeine 256–257

eye and ear treatment 265–266

fungus and parasites 268–269

medical equipment 274–275

modern medicine 100, 245, 259

natural problems 272–277

psychology 92, 266–267

shock trauma 262–263

viruses 269–270

mental preparation 203–206, 315

Mercedes automobiles 390–391

metals 26–30, 110, 219–224

Michéa, Jean-Claude 80

microbes 51, 222, 248–251, 264

Micronutrients 227–229

middle class, the 59, 83–88, 165–185, 424

Midnight Oil (band) 194

militias 142–143, 156, 246

Milius, John 212

milk 139, 222–241, 337, 415, 433–434

milling 158

mining 168–176

Mises, Ludwig von 64–68, 423

mobs 246, 314, 414

See also civil unrest; violence

Mollison, Bill 110

money x–xxvi, 5, 57–97, 120–128, 151–174, 192–197, 294, 327, 350, 375–401, 417–421

See also inflation

money printing 66–67, 419

monoculture 46–50, 112, 139–141, 371

morality 80–86, 217, 346

Morgan, J. P. 59

Mormons (LDS) 230

vehicles 389–391

water 217–222, 403–404

Sahara desert 42, 345

salt 41–44, 159, 229–237, 258, 270, 433

sandbags 333, 445

sanitation 41, 127, 143, 221, 261, 363–374

See also hygiene

toilets 251, 254–255

SARS (Severe Acute Respitory Syndrome) 101, 269

Saudi Arabia 21, 42, 129, 178–187, 361

Scandal of Off-Shoring, The (Laurent) 58

scapegoating xi

scarcity 31, 85, 123, 139, 160–175, 296, 414

See also neoliberalism

Scarface (film) 326

Schmidt & Bender optics 325

sea levels 40–41, 388, 416

Seattle, Chief 36

secret societies

See elite, financial and political

seeds 40–49, 82, 159, 229–239, 396

self-defense 311–319, 334–339

See also defense

self-sufficiency 139, 177, 230, 362

Seneca 304

Shadow Government Statistics 70

shotguns 328, 342

Shute, Neville 155

silver 29, 62–64, 150–156, 332, 383–384

similarity, law of 203

Skull and Bones society 87

See also elite, financial and political

skyscrapers 162

slaughtering 242

"slow food" movement 111

slums 9, 101

See also Global South, the

poverty xxii, 66, 81–82, 85, 87, 112, 122, 136–137, 167, 351

Third World, the 33, 43, 73, 76, 81, 136, 169–170, 172, 175, 247, 369, 390, 425

smallpox 100, 269

soap 157, 249–258, 270–272, 357, 431–441

social bond, the 93, 142, 214, 339–355, 375

See also SAB

socialism 57, 82

social programs 63, 418

social unrest 75, 246, 340, 426

See also violence

French riots (2005) 136

Los Angles riots (1992) 136, 172, 176

sociopathic personalities 76, 84

Socrates 304

solar energy

See energy

Solomon, Steven 40

Soral, Alain xxvi, 96

Soviet Union, the 57, 121–125, 145–155, 237–238, 425

Spain 30, 42, 60, 74–83, 109, 135, 176–177, 291, 372, 392

Spanish-American War, the xxv

Spanish flu epidemic 101, 270

See also epidemics

Spetsnaz 315–318

spirituality 162

stagflation 67

Stalin, Joseph 102

Star Trek 93

Stiglitz, Joseph 59

Stone Age, the 104, 203, 418

storing food

See food

Strathan, David 36

Sudan 43

OTHER BOOKS PUBLISHED BY ARKTOS

OTHER BOOKS PUBLISHED BY ARKTOS

OTHER BOOKS PUBLISHED BY ARKTOS

	On Modern Manners
JAMES KIRKPATRICK	*Conservatism Inc.*
LUDWIG KLAGES	*The Biocentric Worldview*
	Cosmogonic Reflections
PIERRE KREBS	*Guillaume Faye: Truths & Tributes*
	Fighting for the Essence
JULIEN LANGELLA	*Catholic and Identitarian*
JOHN BRUCE LEONARD	*The New Prometheans*
STEPHEN PAX LEONARD	*The Ideology of Failure*
	Travels in Cultural Nihilism
WILLIAM S. LIND	*Retroculture*
PENTTI LINKOLA	*Can Life Prevail?*
H. P. LOVECRAFT	*The Conservative*
NORMAN LOWELL	*Imperium Europa*
JOHN MACLUGASH	*The Return of the Solar King*
CHARLES MAURRAS	*The Future of the Intelligentsia & For a French Awakening*
JOHN HARMON MCELROY	*Agitprop in America*
MICHAEL O'MEARA	*Guillaume Faye and the Battle of Europe*
	New Culture, New Right
MICHAEL MILLERMAN	*Beginning with Heidegger*
BRIAN ANSE PATRICK	*The NRA and the Media*
	Rise of the Anti-Media
	The Ten Commandments of Propaganda
	Zombology
TITO PERDUE	*The Bent Pyramid*
	Journey to a Location
	Lee
	Morning Crafts
	Philip
	The Sweet-Scented Manuscript
	William's House (vol. 1–4)
JOHN K. PRESS	*The True West vs the Zombie Apocalypse*
RAIDO	*A Handbook of Traditional Living* (vol. 1–2)
STEVEN J. ROSEN	*The Agni and the Ecstasy*
	The Jedi in the Lotus
RICHARD RUDGLEY	*Barbarians*
	Essential Substances
	Wildest Dreams

OTHER BOOKS PUBLISHED BY ARKTOS

Made in United States
North Haven, CT
21 March 2022

17354152R00307